The Community of Rights
The Rights of Community

The Community of Rights
The Rights of Community

DANIEL FISCHLIN

MARTHA NANDORFY

with a Foreword by

UPENDRA BAXI

OXFORD

OXFORD
UNIVERSITY PRESS

Oxford University Press is a department of the University of Oxford.
It furthers the University's objective of excellence in research, scholarship,
and education by publishing worldwide. Oxford is a registered trademark of
Oxford University Press in the UK and in certain other countries

Published in India by
Oxford University Press
YMCA Library Building, 1 Jai Singh Road, New Delhi 110001, India

First published by BLACK ROSE BOOKS, Montreal, Canada 2012
First published in India by Oxford University Press, New Delhi 2012

ISBN 13: 978-0-19-807662-9
ISBN 10: 0-19-807662-2

Printed in India by G.H. Prints Pvt. Ltd, New Delhi 110 020

Contents

Acknowledgements

In completing this third book in a trilogy devoted to alternative ways of thinking about rights we acknowledge the help of a number of research assistants. Michael Halliburton, our undergraduate research assistant (URA) at the University of Guelph, made significant contributions, providing stellar support with bibliographical and case study research. Christie Menzo and Jennifer Martino did important groundwork (as did, earlier on, Ben Authers), especially in helping establish parameters for the research on the social practice of community. Former students Ted Cousins and Don Moore stepped in at the last minute to help complete key aspects of the project with exemplary good will and generosity. Max Summerlee's passion for Aldo Leopold gave us much food for thought, and led us in new, unexpected directions.

The 2009 reading group of the Improvisation, Community and Social Practice Multi-disciplinary Collaborative Research Initiative hosted at the University of Guelph provided a fertile ground for discussion, as did multiple encounters with visiting scholars afforded by the project's outreach. We're also grateful to the School of English and Theatre Studies (SETS) at the University of Guelph, where we've both had rich opportunities to research and teach some of the materials that made it into this book. Many of our colleagues and students have, wittingly or not, influenced the outcome of this book. Both SETS and the College of Arts at the University of Guelph generously contributed funds to help with publication and research costs. We offer our sincere thanks to SETS' Director Mark Fortier and to the Dean of the College of Arts, Don Bruce.

We also wish to acknowledge American philosopher Alan Gewirth's 1996 book *The Community of Rights* (University of Chicago Press), which in sharing a portion of its title with ours provided an important starting point for our own ideas on rights and community. These ideas depart considerably from Gewirth's essentially conservative and statist views, which we address in greater detail in our introduction. And we thank Upendra Baxi, the inspirational legal scholar who has so influenced our work, for his provocative Foreword.

We are indebted to Oxford University Press and its editorial staff, not only for their foresight in coming to a unique arrangement with our North American publisher Black Rose Books, but also for their meticulous care while seeing this book into press.

Finally, to our own local community of friends and family, a heartfelt thank-you for unexpected kindnesses along the way: this book is for–and about–you.

In memory of Georges G. Y. Fischlin
and for our children, Damian, Hannah, Zoë, and Esmé

A thing is right when it tends to preserve the integrity, stability and beauty of the biotic community. It is wrong when it tends otherwise.
–Aldo Leopold, *A Sand County Almanac* (262)

A community is the mental and spiritual condition of knowing that the place is shared, and that the people who share the place define and limit the possibilities of each other's lives. It is the knowledge that people have of each other, their concern for each other, their trust in each other, the freedom with which they come and go among themselves.
–Wendell Berry, "The Loss of the Future"
in *The Long-Legged House* (61)

Foreword

Writing about human rights remains a formidable enterprise. If critical or funerary modes enhance and expose the barbarity of power, celebratory modes of writing may so increase the power of social illusions as to enfeeble our potential for resistance. This is overall the message of Daniel Fischlin's and Martha Nandorfy's insightful trilogy.

In continuing their voyage of discovery through the meaning(s) of human rights this third volume remains pervaded both by the spirit of the great Uruguayan writer Eduardo Galeano and a haunting sense of 'realism' about human rights based on a remarkable range of case studies. As before, this volume amplifies the virtue of communicative solidarity – not speaking *to* or *for* the rightless peoples but *with* them about what it means to say *being* and *remaining* human and *having* rights.

Deeply at work in this trilogy are anguished practices of 'resistance to theory.' Fischlin and Nandorfy take seriously Michel Foucault's invitation to confront 'totalitarian theories, or all-encompassing global theories' that need constantly to be 'ripped open, torn to shreds, turned inside out, displaced, caricatured, dramatized [and] theatricalized ...' They extol the Foucauldian virtue of 'the immense and proliferating criticizability of things, institutions, practices, and discourses,' contributing to 'a general feeling that the ground was crumbling beneath our feet especially where it seemed most solid, and closest [nearest] to us, to our bodies and everyday gestures.'[1]

In these contexts, this volume offers a sharp critique of the idea of 'community' and the ways in which it has been 'radically over-determined, corrupted, and co-opted by forms of discourse seeking to empty it of its meaning and potential power as a political force.' In a Nancean moment, our authors offer the 'testimony of the dissolution, the dislocation, or the conflagration of community.' This moment offers a marked contrast with Alan Gewirth's text *The Community of Rights*. Fischlin and Nandorfy recognize many a Gewirthean insight – the idea that human rights articulate social/community relations, not just juridico-political; not normative hierarchies/differentiations among human rights enunciations but their ethical interdependence across time and space remains crucial; and the discourse of human rights may not be separated, with any ethical intelligibility, from that of human *needs*. Yet, for Fischlin and Nandorfy the 'community' of human rights signifies the human rights of communities.

Their 'Eleventh Thesis' type task that seeks to restore the meaning of 'community,' and its 'potential power as a political force' presents a complex itinerary, certainly going beyond 'acts of discursive levitation.'[2] What makes us diversely 'human' are acts of choice and agency embedded in material relations that 'a community sustains with the land' and the 'ethical (or not) nature of this relationship is 'at the crux of all rights issues.' Land is 'the biotic, biological, environmental, and ecological ground from which everything grows.' Thus,

> Community emerges from the land, must maintain an on-going relationship to that land, and is defined by the values it enacts with regard to the land on which it depends. This idea is a vital starting point for any understanding of community as a material, enacted presence of biotic relations in which rights become thinkable.

The think-ability of human rights moves from this iteration in many richly productive directions. How far do the rights *of* communities reach out to the realization and enactment of rights-*in*-community? Granting the indictment of both acquisitive/predatory notions of rights over 'land' and of all anthropocentric narratives of human rights, how far may we re-personify sentient entities and other objects in ways of 'our' regard for duties owed to them that make a fuller sense of 'our' collective rights? And in turn how may 'we' proceed to de-personify aggregations of techno-scientific capital that claim a higher order of human rights than those born as human and that, in turn, also enjoy a near-complete immunity and impunity for crimes against humanity?

The rights of the communities are shaped by an 'ethics of encounter' in which our 'relational contingencies' (the 'community') stand mediated by values of civil rights and justice. Fischlin and Nandorfy present these values as arising from complex story-telling practices – 'complex' because stories are not just repositories of 'institutional narratives driven by commercial and imperial considerations' but also enactments of 'a critical form of rights ...' In this sense, then, 'community is always a latent context for storytelling: storytellers address, create, perform, and critique community in communicating with listeners who share in the narrative.'

In Fischlin's and Nandorfy's perspective, rights emerge pre-eminently as a set of narrative rights – the right to tell our stories as a means of achieving agency. And this means, in the first place, the 'destruction' of narrative monopolies, as Jean-François Lyotard would say – or at least of narrative oligarchies that silence the voices of human suffering, often in the name of human rights.[3] This is a task that Fischlin and Nandorfy perform eminently well in this book. The ways in which we tell 'stories' speak to us in various modes about the integrity of the narrative self; but that 'we'-ness, if partly given by one's location (or 'thrownness') in this world, also stands re-constructed in stories we choose to tell as well as *not* to tell.

This book, then, reconstructs the importance of storytelling, not just as exchanges of fairy tales or horror stories for amusement, but also as collective biographies of movement and resistance against contemporary forms of colonization. If that colonization occurs via soliloquies of power, resistance thrives on diverse dialogue and multi-logue. Those interwoven forms of speech and silence shape a complex code in which communities emerge, develop, disperse, and at times also disappear in the flux of narrative time and space.

Reading this text underscores how the labours of interpretive pluralism differ a great deal when the narrated communities comprise the *cognoscenti* rather than suffering peoples and the aggrieved communities in struggle. Bringing together different narrated communities, never an easy task, becomes even more complex and contradictory when the term 'human' is narrated as determining rights, rather than 'rights' as determining who may be named as 'human.' The difference is crucial, indeed, and Fischlin's and Nandorfy's text summons us to grasp the future of human rights via the difficult practices of communicative solidarity that emerge from diverse practices of community agency.

This trilogy contributes transcultural perspectives for understanding rights, not limited to social and legal theory, but also as local community-based telling and enacting of creative stories about rights that encompass multiple dimensions of being human. It excels in the art of asking questions while at the same moment reveals, to adapt a phrase of Hans-Georg Gadamer, 'the questionability of what is questioned.'[4]

UPENDRA BAXI
Professor Emeritus
University of Warwick and Delhi (April, 2011)

NOTES

1 Michel Foucault, *Society Must be Defended*, New York, Picador: 2003: 6.

2 Perry Anderson describes this syndrome vividly in relation to studies that suggest 'the France of the Ancien Régime lifted itself bodily into the thin air of revolution by suddenly discovering a new public language' (33) ('The Common and the Particular,' *International Labour and Working-Class History*: 31-36 [1989]).

3 See Upendra Baxi, 'Epilogue: Whom We may Speak For, With, and After,' in Gurminder K. Bhambhra and Robbie Shilliam (Eds.), *Silencing Human Rights: Critical Engagements with a Contested Project* (London, Palgrave McMillan: 2008).

4 Hans Georg Gadamer, *Truth and Method* (revised second edition), trans. J. Weinsheimer and D. G. Marshall, London, Sheed and Ward: 1989: 300.

The Community of Rights
The Rights of Community

Introduction

'Lorsqu'on pense savoir ce qui est juste, on devient inhumain. C'est la racine de toute forme de terrorisme, politique ou religieux'
[When we think we know what is just, we become inhuman. It is the root of all forms of terrorism, political or religious.]
–Michael Haneke

Community evokes belonging, self-sameness, unity via commonality and shared attributes, even if that extends to the negative community, those who identify as being without or beyond community. Community has temporal and spatial connotations: it must exist over time and is embodied in relation to specific locales and environments. At the same time a community is none of these things since the core notion of the term references a unity that is felt – a fellowship and sense of purpose that transcend its material aspects. Community is always potentially nomadic (because survival-oriented) in principle: it can be displaced – unjustly, forcibly – and somehow retain its identity even as that identity mutates in new circumstances. This was the case in the African diaspora that generated new communities throughout the Caribbean and the Americas or in the post-Holocaust diaspora of European Jews. A community can adhere to nomadic principles that define its relations with an environment that requires nomadism as a mode of survival.[1] Fixed notions of stability, in other words, are not always necessarily concomitant with successful (or ideal) community practices and identities.

Community also entails ideology – it is an expression of a system of thought and values: how does one ensure the community's survival and renewal? What beliefs does the community hold and how do these beliefs find expression through the community's collective agency? How does the community negotiate encounters with difference from outside and within? Does the community adhere to values that privilege self-sameness over difference? These, and a host of other questions circulate through discourses of community, as do fundamental concerns about the vacuity of the term 'community' having been so compromised by the ways in which it has been co-opted and deformed to purposes at odds with its ostensible meanings. When complex and surpassingly large entities associated with, for example, the so-called 'community of nations,' use that concept to obscure how large-scale actions taken in the name of that entity actually destroy traditional senses of community, as is often the case in justifications for military action, the political valences of the term need to be understood and vigorously critiqued.

As theatre historian Alan Filewod argues, 'Listen to it long enough and [community] loses all sense. *Community* has no meaning: it has become merely an index of power. Whoever invokes it, in government, in manifestos or in funding offices, draws strength from it but depletes its meaning. In consequence, the very word "community" has become as bankrupt as its rhetorical predecessor, "the people," had by the end of the 1930s' (1995 3). Interesting to note is how Filewod acknowledges an original meaning for the term that has been 'depleted.' There is, in other words, a deformation at work in the current usage of 'community' that is at odds with what the term has meant, or means elsewhere in other cultural contexts. Filewod's comments are consistent with French philosopher Jean-Luc Nancy's affirmation, at the beginning of *The Inoperative Community*, that 'The gravest and most painful testimony of the modern world, the one that possibly involves all other testimonies to which this epoch must answer ... is the testimony of the dissolution, the dislocation, or the conflagration of community' (1).

Genocide and egregious global military actions that have made the history of modernity also the history of total, excessive war and human cruelty, are the epochal testimony to the dissolution of community as a practice of living together within contexts that are renewable and sustainable. A consistent thread running through community theory is how community has been deformed, dissolved, and made meaningless. The implication is that there are specific, painful circumstances associated with the advent of the modern world that have created a crisis of theory and practice for community. In that light, this book aims to show the degree to which the term has been compromised and manipulated in the name of increasingly totalitarian and hegemonic state and corporate practices that represent a major threat to imagining global rights struggles (in all their diversity) as perhaps the most important manifestation of community practice(s). At the same time, we aim to recuperate that which has been depleted, in Filewod's sense, from the term 'community,' reinvigorating its potential meaningfulness to the practice of rights.

Just because community has been co-opted does not mean that we must abandon it to the vultures who feed on what is left of its meaning as the generative potential embedded in all relations. If the 'concept of community is dead' as sociologist D.B. Clarke puts it, 'it stubbornly refuses to lie down' and as 'fast as the attempt is made to thrust the concept ... into limbo, it as obstinately emerges again' (32). Clarke notes how sociologist G. A. Hillery's study of the term 'community' in the 50s yielded 'ninety-four different definitions,' the ambiguity around the term rendering it a so-called 'non-concept' (ibid.). But the plurality of meaning found in the term may also register the diverse notions of community that underpin its range of meanings: diversity and plurality, unsettled meaning, contestation may, in other words, just as convincingly reference the vitality of the term as an indicator of social practices too processual to reduce to a singular stable meaning.

We ask whether community is thinkable in other terms rather than as a reductive appeal to unity, what feminist scholar Iris Marion Young characterizes as a denial of difference 'by positing fusion rather than separation as the social ideal' (239). Both 'fusion' and 'separation' as markers of being 'in' and 'out' of community are highly questionable as absolute categories of one's social experience across a wide range of social practices. Young suggests that 'Community proponents conceive the social subject as a relation of unity composed by identification and symmetry among individuals within a totality' (ibid.). Is this not rescripting a tired model of collective alignment based on highly dubious notions of identification, symmetry, totality, and unity? Furthermore, these are the very notions co-opted by hegemonic political and economic structures to produce illusions of solidarity among docile state subjects stripped of their agency, both individual and collective. Might not community arise out of social practices that manifest disunity, the lack of totality and symmetry, the critique of reductive identification, the deep suspicion of unity that allows for the respect of difference, the frank understanding of how social relations are contingent? Might not these social relations in their most reduced form be governed by an ethics of encounter that allows for the reciprocal and sustainable dynamism (in which tension, disagreement, and alienation are just as much possibilities as are solidarity, unified purposefulness, and integration) that is the mark of generative, multiple real relationships among diverse entities?

Community theorist Peter Block argues, 'the challenge for every community ... is to discover and create the means for engaging citizens that brings a new possibility into being ... what gives power to communal possibility is the imagination and authorship of citizens led through a process of engagement' (114). This process of engagement, of necessity, requires a model of encounter with the other in which difference (and disengagement) are addressed. The nature of that mediation is a profound ethical problem at the heart of all notions of community in which the complex social practices of realizing possibility and becoming in relation to others are at stake. For better or for worse, then, community is the crucible term through which the ethics of becoming – of being in contingent (oftentimes problematic) relation to others – is understood.

This book avoids simplistic, utopian declarations about community. We struggle with language and the use of this term precisely because it has been appropriated by profoundly anti-communitarian discourses that fragment communities into *proliferating gated communities* – the business community, the arts community, the university community, the scientific community – when really communities are diverse, permeable, and have a place for everyone (including those who commit crimes and need community judgment and support to change their ways in order to live *in* community). Even as community carries with it overtones of utopian collective ideals of social consonance, the material realities of community can be based on contested and dissonant agencies.

Samuel Johnson's *bons mots* from *Taxation No Tyranny* (1775) remind us that 'There will always be a part, and always a very large part of every community, that have no care but for themselves, and whose care for themselves reaches little further than impatience of immediate pain, and eagerness for the nearest good' (427).[2] Disengagement, in other words, is one aspect of this non-utopian reality that is community. And Martin Luther King, Jr. reminds us that civil disobedience that puts the individual at odds with the community is often a necessary corrective to the injustice perpetrated by that community: 'I submit that an individual who breaks a law that conscience tells him is unjust, and who willingly accepts the penalty of imprisonment in order to arouse the conscience of the community over its injustice, is in reality expressing the highest respect for the law' (cited in Herman 132). And the reality of anarchic communities challenges notions of community-based order, as English playwright Alan Bennett wittily sums it up in Act One of his 1972 play *Getting On*: 'We started off trying to set up a small anarchist community, but people wouldn't obey the rules' (19).

Community, as these examples show, is neither necessarily positivistic nor a site of congruence and agreement. Opposition and tension within the community are as much attributes of what we mean by community as are conflict and disorder: the key is how the community negotiates these in relation to its sustainability and its ability to be responsive in a meaningful way to tension and conflict. So rather than trying to contain the term by affirming what it is or isn't, we have sought to understand community as a complex allegory for the relational identities, in their human, environmental, historical, and contextual fullness that arise as embodied, material presences in the here and now. This here and now is not the present of Western linear thinking about time, but is more akin to what Pueblo writer Leslie Marmon Silko comically refers to as 'tortilla time' ('Poetics and Politics' 20): a spatialized time where memories, stories, and prophecies are coeval and associated with the materiality of their relationship to locale.

Community is also a very loose, but unavoidable term for the necessary relations, what we call the *relational contingencies*, that link one to another – the crucible through which we mediate our relations with others, our needs and desires within a complex matrix of individual and collective being: hence, need and/or desire for food, for shelter, for interest, love and sex, for family, entertainment, governance, and for power. As such, community is inextricably affiliated with rights, ethics, and the values that give rise to action and agency, especially if one sees rights issues as wholly a question of how to deal with the *ethics of encounter*. Ethics of encounter is a term we use throughout the book to address this defining aspect of where rights come from. All rights are relational and aimed at mediating aspects of being in relation to someone or something else. Rights are the values encoded in how we negotiate encounter. Injustice occurs when this relational aspect of being produces inequity, suffering, alienation, and oppression.

A core starting point for us in this book and, indeed, in the entire trilogy, is (and has been) that the models of encounter currently in place that are the measure of how rights are enacted are largely dysfunctional and in serious need of rethinking. This book is the third we devote to oppositional thinking about rights discourses, the first two being, *Eduardo Galeano: Through the Looking Glass* and *The Concise Guide to Global Human Rights*.

The first book on Galeano examines the importance of emergent forms of literary and aesthetic discourses, alternative forms of storytelling, that evade simplistic and reductive ways of addressing social justice issues (not to mention exhausted forms of literary genre all-too-often driven by commercial expedients). In so doing we sought to displace the exceptional emphasis given to legal, juridical, and governmental discourses on social justice by addressing the importance of story as both a repository and an enactment of a critical form of rights at odds with institutional narratives driven by commercial and imperial considerations. Community is always a latent context for storytelling: storytellers address, create, perform, and critique community in communicating with listeners who share in the narrative, a topic we return to at length in this book.

In the second book of the trilogy, *The Concise Guide to Global Human Rights*, we focus on majoritarian world concepts of social justice, while critiquing the ways in which these concepts have been marginalized and minoritized. Coincident with this aim, the book gets at the radical disjunction evident in the Universal Declaration of Human Rights (1948) in terms of its assertions about human rights and its wholesale inattention to the environmental conditions that make humanity possible. Human being is an expression of collective being in difference, and also expresses relations of biotic co-dependence, topics we explore at greater length in this book.

This third book continues these vectors by shifting away from notions of 'human' rights, which privilege the individual but also are predicated on who has the power to define what it means to be human. By extension, we consider the ways in which community rights, that is, the rights of communities as a whole, have largely been marginalized in favour of individual rights. This sole focus on individualism adheres closely to the logic of neoliberal discourses of privatization and individual ownership through corporate entities (that are also given the status of the individual, though limited in their liability). This logic is a perversion of the very forms of being that have made 'being human' thinkable for multiple peoples and cultures from the majoritarian world. This book seeks to re-instate and reclaim community as a social practice that, in spite of its corruption by distorted notions of social justice, still has potential and political agency. Liberating the combinatory power of collective action reinforced by fused forms of agency and shaped by ethical encounter structures is the key challenge of post-1948 rights discourses.

Rights are a defining outcome and by-product of the social practice of encounter, the material agencies that produce functional or dysfunctional relations: and those relations must be in ethical balance with each other (however tense and problematic), both respective of difference but finding shared ground if the basic principle of equity is to have meaning. The ethics of encounter, then, is not only the foundation on which any conception of rights and justice must be built, but is also a way of articulating the mechanics of relations that describe community: different forms of community are not isolated entities. Rather, to be 'in' community is to be constantly calibrating both intra and inter-communitarian relations. The success of these relations is crucial to long-term community outcomes associated with renewability, sustainability, adaptation, and survival.

This book, then, advocates the importance of renewing rights discourses via providing alternative forms of thinking outside the traditional rights paradigms largely based on legal and self-interested institutional structures. We begin with the widespread critical discomfort over what the term 'community' has come to mean and how it has been deployed or marginalized. Rhoda Howard argues, in *Human Rights and the Search for Community* that 'different conceptions of social justice can be identified through the different values that societies place on equality, autonomy, and respect for the individual' (83). We would argue that yes, differential and diverse discourses of justice do indeed exist, but that the focus on the individual by 'societies' needs to be rethought. The artificial divide between the individual and the community or society is dysfunctional and has, since the Enlightenment, reigned a little too comfortably as a truism. Imagine reversing the terms of Howard's sentence so that it reads with the individual respecting the equality and autonomy of the community. Now imagine the same sentence doing away with both terms because they are so inter-connected and inter-dependent as to be virtually meaningless.

In this context, our book explores what it might mean to think about rights through a prism in which neither the individual nor the community has meaning the one without the other, and where neither term is privileged. It does so by also imagining the term 'rights' to have been equally compromised as a functional concept in need of rethinking and reclamation. What might it mean to replace all discourses of rights predicated on a tit-for-tat mentality that undermines social justice situations with discourses of peacemaking, integrity, sharing, discrepant engagement, and dialogic cooperation? The same might be said for notions of tolerance, which assume implicitly a relationship of inferior (the tolerated) to superior (the tolerator) in which the one merely 'puts up' with the other. But in order to re-conceive the discourse of rights along these lines we need to rethink what we mean by 'community' and the nature of the social relations that it embodies even as we rethink what it might mean to shift the ground of what 'rights' might meaningfully be said to represent not as a theory but as a social practice of the ethics of encounter.

French philosopher Maurice Blanchot, in trying to understand Georges Bataille's question, 'Why community?' turns to Bataille's notion that at the core of each being is a principle of incompletion, of insufficiency (Blanchot 15). In Blanchot's understanding of Bataille, it is not so much the need to find completion that is at the origin of community, but the fact that the knowledge of insufficiency can only come from the other. Thus community is a principle of becoming conscious of this fundamental incompletion and insufficiency:

> *L'être, insuffisant, ne cherche pas à s'associer à un autre pour former une substance d'integrité. La conscience de l'insuffisance vient de sa proper mise en question, laquelle a besoin de l'autre pour être effectuée* [The individual being, insufficient, doesn't seek to associate itself with an *other* to form an integrated substance. The awareness of the individual's insufficiency comes from its being put into question, which requires the other to be put into effect] (ibid. 15-16; our translation).

The ethics of retaining this knowledge of one's insufficiency even as one enters into relations with the other via community is at the root of why the term *community*, in this highly abstracted sense, is needed.

American philosopher Judith Butler, in a discussion of Michel Foucault's notions of responsibility, summarizes the core idea in the following way: 'I have a relation to myself, but I have it in the context of an address to an other' (*Giving An Account of Oneself* 131). When this recognition is in place, the co-generative aspects of self and otherness become indivisible and a source of action based on recognition of that mutuality and interdependence. This ecological relationship lies at the ethical crux of imagining re-invigorated discourses of community.

Community, in this ecological sense, requires the presence of the other by which the self comes to know its truly insufficient and incomplete nature – and in so doing moves away from static ways of being into dynamic and exploratory modes of addressing insufficiency. Moreover, the dynamic of this insufficient relation between self and other enables and triggers conscience, the simultaneous, empathic awareness of self and other. These all require critical awareness and self-evaluation that evolves and adapts to changing circumstances. Thereby, community is not an expression of fixed, moribund relations but rather of diverse, often unpredictable processes requiring self-critique and self-evaluation to reach more complex understandings of, and adaptations to, the nested relations within which we are imbricated.

The irony and theoretical trap implicit in thinking through relationships is that even the use of reductive language like 'self' and 'other' becomes extremely fraught. Neither truly exists autonomously except as a relational, co-dependent, and co-generative entity that is neither singular nor aggregate – a topic to which we return throughout this book. Master tropes like 'individual' or 'community' break down in this context because neither is wholly descriptive of the relational entity that is at once incomplete, insufficient, yet capable of agency and becoming, dynamism, and self- and other-awareness. Since we strive to compare different epistemologies and conceptualizations based on our conviction that fuller understandings emerge from transcultural thinking, this concept of insufficiency can be deconstructed as symptomatic of Western theorizing about desire in relation to absence and negation. From another perspective, community need not be predicated on negating anyone's sufficiency, but can focus instead on interdependency and interconnectedness as characteristic of all life on Earth. In this sense, community is a manifestation of relations of potential in which interdependence is a basic premise.

The rights implications of this dynamic are significant and somewhat captured in our chiastic title: the rights of community, the community of rights. What we propose with this title is a rethinking of rights via the prism of community, as opposed to the conventional default for thinking about rights via prioritizing the individual. Explicit in the title is the interlinked notion that not only is there a community of rights but that communities themselves have rights. The latter idea may seem self-evident but it is, in fact, not so clear-cut.

The term 'community' is found only three times in the Universal Declaration of Human Rights, the foundational instrument defining global notions of rights established in 1948:

> In Article 18: 'Everyone has the right to freedom of thought, conscience and religion; this right includes freedom to change his [sic] religion or belief, and freedom, *either alone or in community with others and in public or private*, to manifest his [sic] religion or belief in teaching, practice, worship and observance.'
>
> In Article 27, Section 1: 'Everyone has the right freely *to participate in the cultural life of the community*, to enjoy the arts and to share in scientific advancement and its benefits.'
>
> In Article 29, Section 1: '*Everyone has duties to the community in*

> *which alone the free and full development of his [sic] personality is possible.*' ('Universal Declaration'; our emphasis)

In all three instances, community, following on Filewod's analysis, is a given – an already received trope that could mean virtually anything, that anything usually being an evocation of orthodoxies and assumptions closely aligned with hegemonic self-interest. Article 18 opposes the public and private spheres as if these two are ever entirely separable. Article 27 pertains to vague aspects of the 'cultural life of the community' as if to suggest that culture is somehow distinct from community – and the same article tells a very interesting false story about how the arts are for enjoyment (thus entirely depoliticizing their valence) while the sciences are for benefit and advancement (as if to suggest that the sciences are only utilitarian and the arts only aesthetic). Such embedded master narratives are insidious in that they perpetuate assumptions about culture that are in themselves unexamined cultural constructs. This kind of reductive thinking tends toward monoculture, isolated despite being hegemonic, static despite its claim to progress. Monoculture, in this sense, is the negation of community because it works out of a principle that denies diversity and contradiction.

In addition to these remarkably narrow and vague claims, Article 29 names generalized duties of the individual to the community with the clear understanding that 'the free and full development of his [sic] personality' is being privileged conceptually. Now imagine changing the terms of Article 29 to suggest that all communities and individuals have specific reciprocal responsibilities to each other 'in which alone the free and full development' of both the individual and the community is possible. As slight a change as this to the wording of the Article produces a dramatic shift in the privileging of the individual that is one of the key problems with rights instruments generally. Thus, our title conveys imagining rights as a collective enterprise while at the same time positing a shift to thinking about communities as the object of rights practices.

Here, we part from Alan Gewirth's notion that community is given meaning and its rights are protected primarily as a function of constitutional government. This is the negative conception of rights in which they exist only insofar as you can enact them by legal, state-sanctioned means. We have critiqued at length the problem of how access to legal instruments is so often a question of resources that only a small elite can afford.[3] In his book *The Community of Rights*, Gewirth argues that 'a society whose government actively seeks to help fulfill the needs of its members, especially those who are most vulnerable, for the freedom and well-being that are the necessary goods of human agency' (5) is one in which the community of rights exists. Government is one aspect of thinking institutionally both about how rights may be protected – *but* also about how those same rights may be usurped.

Our conception of the community of rights is far more expansive, attributing ethical agency and protections to a wide array of participants in life dynamics, inclusive of the environment in all its biotic complexity. Gewirth himself somewhat recognizes this principle in the Preface to his book, when he states that it is 'the need for mutuality on the part of all members of society that constitutes the moral structure of the community of rights' (xiii). But mutuality in this sense is inter-human, not the function of a more expansive thinking about the conditions that make that humanity possible. Rights surrendered to institutional thinking are subject to the corruption and self-interest that are to be found in those forms of social organization – and they are radically exclusionary in their state composition, especially with regard to the environment and to marginalized, oppressed, and disadvantaged groups. Mutuality remains an abstract ideal without the environment and ecology that make such a relationship thinkable.

Rather than take this road, we argue for a community of rights that extends ethical thinking beyond the very institutions that delimit or bankrupt those rights. Social structures based on egregious militarization or infinitely consumable resources in which unrestricted growth is considered the telos – driving most of the developed nations on the planet – are in this light inimical with the community of rights, guided by an ethics fundamentally at odds with this telos. Little wonder, then, that one of the patterns we trace throughout this book reveals how community opposition to hegemonies of various sorts is under sustained attack by interests that claim to uphold community values while at the same time undermining them.

As a conservative who holds libertarian and progressive views, Gewirth's turn to government (constitutional) and economic democracy (market) rights as the safeguard is a remarkable contradiction in light of how the latter two have dismally failed to address problems relating to the poorest and most oppressed peoples on the planet. The baseline measure for success of rights instruments globally is the degree to which they protect the interests of the poorest, the most disadvantaged, the most fragile. Any discussion of access to power as a measure of how the rights of specific individuals or communities are prioritized must address the degree to which power shapes and deforms perceptions about rights from the perspective of different communities, especially those most marginalized by power relations.

As argued by Arthur J. Dyck in *Rethinking Rights and Responsibilities: The Moral Bonds of Community*, the 'uneven distribution of power within a community distorts the level of awareness to perceive clearly and correctly what is morally required' (225). Prioritizing one form of institutional organization as the basis of rights enactment rather than the general principles pertaining to the community of rights is simply another way of reinstating the very power structures that lead to compromised rights situations, especially when the latter are dynamic, diverse, and plural in their contingencies.

– Why has the individual largely superseded the community as the privileged focus of rights discourses?

– In an era of globalization and new networks of technological affiliation, is community a meaningful term?

– Is it possible to re-conceive rights discourses in ways that acknowledge the diverse communities from which they arise?

– How have contemporary notions of community betrayed the very origins of the term in the name of exploitative economic and political practices?

– Often idealized as a form of functional solidarity, has the notion of community been distorted and corrupted to the point where it is a catchall for practices that undermine the common good?

– Is the community itself a fragile life form intimately connected to the biosphere on which it depends?

The Community of Rights / The Rights of Community looks for transcultural responses to these questions and to rethinking the notion of community in relation to emergent rights discourses. Even as we seem bound to use the word 'rights' in this age of massive rights violations and hence their necessary defence, we also struggle against the hegemony of this Western notion of justice. Majority World people tend to defend human dignity instead, arguing that this concept is less predicated on the individual, and also includes social, economic, and cultural rights that Western rights discourse has tended to suppress in favour of political and civic rights. By extending this notion of dignity beyond the human, to encompass the full range of relations to being that make the human possible, reinvigorates thinking about rights. Howard notes how individualist self-interest, understood as an end in its own right (or as a right with its own end), has undermined a sense of shared obligation that is the basis of community: 'Just as the individual hand of the market economy symbolized private interest and removal from economic obligation, so the invisible spirit of bourgeois life has come to symbolize removal from social obligation. But if there is no social life, then there can be no public interest. In the eyes of its communitarian critics, modern bourgeois life has produced a society of automatons, unwilling to invest their energies in the promotion of the wider social good. Capitalist society ... preserves individual human rights at the expense of social solidarity' (36).

The problem so clearly identified by Howard's analysis is precisely the oppositional thinking that sustains the individual's interests and opposes them to the wider social good. This is a binary we seek to disrupt by arguing for the inherent indivisibility of the social good as a function of all forms of relatedness. And furthermore we argue that neither the individual nor the community is sufficient as a model to understand social relations encompassing more than just the dynamics of being human, as the ground on which both singular and collective models of human relations stand. Multiple forms of relatedness, in other words – to the land, to other forms of life, to inanimate being – inform social relations and agency. These must be addressed in order to come to terms with how definitions of community have been deformed in the service of simplistic oppositions that oppose it with individual self-interest.

Problems with Western definitions of community begin with how the term stresses commonality, sharing, and sameness at the expense of difference. Too often community, as a seemingly self-evident term, subsumes and reduces the vital differences that give it its unique qualities in the name of the self-same. Community, in this latter misnaming, is an outcome and not a process: a simplistic static entity rather than an evolving, complex set of relations with the broadest spectrum of contingencies that include non-quantitative components like feeling, intuition, empathy, or the lack thereof. Fundamentalist notions of community that base identity on a logic that is exclusionary and oppositional present a radical threat to imagining a rights scenario in which the common good, in the broadest sense of the term, is sustained. Doubt, skepticism, critical difference, ideological discomfort, and the like are crucial aspects of what makes the common good functional from a rights perspective: certainty and unshakeable conviction in one's worldview diminish the rich, co-creative potential out of which meaningful community grows.

American anthropologist Mark Goodale notes how research conducted by John Bowen on Islam, the law, and equality has 'demonstrated the social fact that in Indonesia value-pluralism is itself a value that is both the empirical and the normative basis for a sustainable political community' (8), a finding, as Goodale wryly observes, that overturns the last 300 years of Western political theory. Bowen discusses the notion of *adat*, an Indonesian word associated with localism, 'the rules or practices of social life ... feelings and a sense of propriety' that can (but not necessarily) be linked to tradition and customary practice. *Adat* references 'local ways of resolving disputes, rather than substantive rules ... and is counterposed to Islamic or state law' (13). As a practice of determining right action *adat* is multiple in how it is applied and irreducible except as a general principle that recognizes pluralist values. Bowen notes, 'the concept of "adat community" has provided a source of legitimacy for groups seeking to act in the name of society against the state' (60), a form of multiple community practices resistant to unilateral impositions from hegemonic monoliths. Value-pluralism, the capacity to enact and negotiate difference arising from multiple perspectives and practices, is a crucial aspect of sustainable communities that is wholly at odds with static models of community formation and belonging like the state. The recognition of the local as having standing against larger corporate entities is an important aspect of *adat*, and one to which we return repeatedly throughout this book. Equality arises out of the capacity to negotiate difference and plurality equitably, and not out of unnuanced conceptions based on singular ethical notions usually dictated by the powerful and arising out of self-interest. Too often these singular notions are directed against the weak and disempowered in the name of collective entities that abhor value-pluralist worldviews.

The stoning of women accused of adultery, for being victims of rape, or even for enjoying basic freedoms functions as a powerful parable across ancient and contemporary times: stoning constitutes 'community justice' according to the men in power and the women who defer to them, showing how highly compromised is the term 'community' in such a context. In the case of stoning, patriarchal, fundamentalist cultures are unwilling to admit value-pluralist notions of ethical comportment to their community practices based instead on static, corrupt ethical practices. This abhorrent practice cannot be attributed to any one culture or religion. While currently only fundamentalist Muslims have been charged, the precept advocating stoning people to death as a valid form of punishment for crimes may or may not appear in the Koran depending on who you consult, and *does* appear repeatedly in the Bible (in Joshua, Leviticus, Deuteronomy, Exodus, 1 Kings, and Numbers). Are such 'honour' killings, as they are called with no sense of irony, symptomatic of a totalitarian community or the individual's tyranny multiplied through power, coercion, terror to eradicate community completely? According to Amin Muhammad, a professor of psychiatry at Memorial University of Newfoundland who specializes in transcultural psychiatry, honour killings are not religiously motivated: 'Nothing in the Muslim religion would justify this. Nothing in any religion would justify this. It's based on personal agendas, personal egos, personal mindsets' (O'Toole 1). But while perpetrators claim to be recuperating their personal honour through murdering the perceived offender, such an understanding of honour is not purely personal. Community and religion are invoked to justify this kind of killing as belonging to a cultural tradition, not only by the critics but by the perpetrators themselves. Furthermore, as O'Toole points out 'numerous countries, including Iran, Syria, and Egypt, have legislation allowing for a partial or complete defence against criminal charges on the basis that it was an honour killing' (2). These kinds of contradictions reveal that community needs to be understood as the transcultural intersection or matrix of our social being, of our being social in a world in which transcultural negotiations and mediations are unavoidable.

Writing for the German magazine *Der Spiegel*, Jody Biehl interprets recent killings of Muslim women in Berlin as resulting from the clash between Western and Middle Eastern cultures. 'How can such a horrific and shockingly archaic practice be flourishing in the heart of Europe?' she asks. A small photograph illustrating the article shows Muslim women wearing headscarves walking by an advertisement showing a woman wearing nothing but a feather boa around her waist and black lace stockings held by a garter crossing her bare buttocks. The caption notes that the Muslim women's lives clash with the society that surrounds them. A more comparative and therefore less Eurocentric reading would consider how the images of women appearing to clash: naked/covered, can be traced to male dominance in *both* European and Middle Eastern cultures. The woman in the poster is meant to appeal to men who are afraid of women's minds, while the precept to cover women expresses men's fear of women's bodies, two sides of the same patriarchal coin. This sort of reading practice strives to acknowledge the pervasive deep patterns of cultural assumptions, and the profound implications they have within rights contexts that directly affect how different groups live their embattled lives.

In her bestseller *Reviving Ophelia*, psychotherapist Mary Pipher characterizes Western society as one that kills the souls of girls. What she says about teenage girls being pressured to conform to male desire can apply equally to Western, Eastern, and all other women: 'Authenticity is an "owning" of all experience, including emotions and thoughts that are not socially acceptable. Because self-esteem is based on the acceptance of all thoughts and feelings as one's own, girls lose confidence, as they "disown" themselves. They suffer enormous losses when they stop expressing certain thoughts and feelings' (38). This loss happens as girls become "female impersonators" who fit their whole selves into small, crowded spaces. Vibrant, confident girls become shy, doubting young women. Girls stop thinking, "Who am I? What do I want?" and start thinking, "What must I do to please others?"' (22). Leonard Sax, a family physician and founder of the National Association for Single Sex Public Education lists how in North America 'more than one in five girls is cutting herself/and or burning herself with matches. More than one in four high-school girls is binge drinking. Today, one in eight females in the U.S. takes anti-depressants. There's been an enormous escalation in anxiety and depression among girls and young women' (Fillion). Where is this sense of despair and anxiety coming from? Considered in the larger social context, the damages experienced by adolescent girls are a significant loss for the community at large, even as it is the community or the lack thereof that is at the heart of the problem: 'Margaret Mead believed that the ideal culture is one in which there is a place for every human gift. By her standards, our Western culture is far from ideal for women. So many gifts are unused and unappreciated. So many voices are stilled. Stendhal wrote: "All geniuses born women are lost to the public good"' (Pipher 22).

Angela Henderson, researcher on violence against women, takes a comparative view, noting that 'eleven percent of women can expect to experience some form of violence from somebody they know in their lifetime ... it's about power and control, a way of enforcing what a man thinks a woman should be doing' (O'Toole 2). Aysan Sev'er, professor of sociology, asserts, 'there's nothing in Islam that sanctions the practice [of honour killing through lapidation]. Some perpetrators use religion as a "cloak" but honour killing is about patriarchy, not religion' (Proudfoot 2). In this book, we question whether such clear distinctions can be made, and attempt also to examine how notions of community dominated by a particular political ideology like patriarchy contradict notions of community where everyone has an equitable place emerging from fundamental respect for the dignity of all being. Community is also about how the commons, which includes both physical and intellectual resources, gets shaped, and frequently, deformed – a topic we explore at considerable length in this book.

From an institutional or bureaucratic perspective community is understood reductively as an outcome of resource allocation, with little attention paid to the underlying structures that shape how choices get made about resources. Notions of common good and public trust are made subordinate to already determined dispositions of wealth accumulation that pervert the public trust and undermine the common good. In such a context, what does it mean to have public sphere rights in which the use-value of community is more often than not window dressing for vested, dominant interests? Community security has become a touchstone for appropriated discourses of the common good that have corrupted public discourse and created a vast network of surveillance whose efficaciousness is doubtful and whose cost is astronomical:

> Since the Sept. 11 attacks, top-secret intelligence gathering by the government has grown so unwieldy and expensive that no one really knows what it costs and how many people are involved, *The Washington Post* reported Monday [July 19, 2010]. A two-year investigation by the newspaper uncovered what it termed a 'Top Secret America' that's mostly hidden from public view and largely lacking in oversight. In its first installment of a series of reports, the *Post* said there are now more than 1,200 government organizations and more than 1,900 private companies working on counterterrorism, homeland security and intelligence in about 10,000 locations across the U.S. Around 854,000 people – or nearly 1.5 times the number of people who live in Washington – have top-secret security clearance, the paper said. ('U.S. Intelligence')

Such a vast expenditure of resources results in the impoverishment of community, not only through the waste and redundancy engendered by the sheer volume of useless information generated (and the environmental and ideological consequences of that waste), but also through the reinforcing of degraded notions of community as a function of state surveillance, a pre-emptive version of Orwellian Big Brother totalitarianism.

Yet a further problem is the way in which notions of community confuse majority with mainstream and dominant hegemony, and minority with marginal and disempowered. Often the empowered are in the minority (as in corporate oligarchies and managed democracies), while the majority is disenfranchised and marginalized. And it gets more complicated when culturally repressive states divest minoritized groups of their rights, while in liberal states, human rights tribunals empower individuals and groups who put forward narrow political agendas against the larger interests of the diverse community. Paradoxically, in both instances fundamentalist and anti-libertarian forces seem to benefit from how rights have been theorized and legislated. In Canada, for instance, this situation is further aggravated by the fact that the Human Rights Commission's laws – for instance Section 13, which allows charging someone with communicating hate or contempt – conflict with the Charter of Rights and Freedoms. People who are unfairly accused of discrimination can end up spending thousands of dollars on legal defence, and are not reimbursed by the Human Rights Commission. In the province of Alberta, some parents have tried to bring in a bill that would require teachers to forewarn parents of any discussion about sex or sexual orientation, so that parents can make a decision to pull their children from the offending class. Critics point out that this would severely restrict teachers' ability and responsibility to deal with issues as they come up, such as homophobic bullying. In any dynamic classroom where real learning is happening, students ask questions that teachers cannot foresee. The proposed legislation would encourage teachers to stick to a scripted lecture and to avoid improvising and responding to questions and situations that might land them before a human rights tribunal.

This book examines how rights might be based on the principle of *equality in difference* as articulated in discrepant engagements. That principle is enacted in alternatives to traditional Western thinking about rights that are narrowly predicated on the (hu)man individual, posited as citizen of the nation-state. The corporatist agenda further reduces identity to that of customer or client. This move largely excludes all those who lack purchasing power, and therefore identity or existence, viewed through this distorting lens of the citizen as consumer. Individual-based rights both subordinate alternative formations to which rights need apply, while also reinforcing normative conceptions about what might constitute an 'individual.' The corporation, for instance, has been conceived of as a legal entity, an 'individual' person, with attendant rights that limit its liabilities and responsibilities. Expansive rights that exceed individual and even collective rights accrue to these complex, deeply authoritarian entities in the name of the individual. These legalistic rights emanate from and reinforce cynical rationalizations to support economic disparity and social injustice. In our view, the individual exists as a function of a community of relations that extend beyond mere humanity and not, as is so often assumed, the reverse.

Henry David Thoreau writes in *Civil Disobedience* that 'It is truly enough said that a corporation has no conscience; but a corporation of conscientious men [sic] is a corporation with a conscience. Law never made men a whit more just; and, by means of their respect for it, even the well-disposed are daily made the agents of injustice' (9-10). Thoreau's insight hints at two directions we explore throughout this book: the first posits the power of collective action in the service of conscience, what Thoreau calls 'the right,' a collective expression of values rooted in a critical engagement with what it means to undertake conscientious civil behaviours. The second direction addresses how injustice arises out of collective misapprehensions exemplified in the law vitiated by state or corporate self-interest, the corporation without conscience, the collective state undertakings that so often reduce in Thoreau's reading to unjustified wars that co-opt the 'well-disposed' to unjust pursuits. In both directions, community is a key trope for human potential and agency – and for structures of injustice in which 'the right' is subsumed by collective structures of disengagement that enable unethical behaviours. A direct recognition of this duality is needed as we develop this book's project of rethinking community in relation to rights discourses.

These discourses are embedded in a long philosophical tradition that is at once anthropocentric and patriarchal, and, moreover, in an oppressive relationship to all things not Man: nature, land, women, animals, othered forms of being, and communities that are not aligned with hegemonic self-interest. What can 'community' mean in such a worldview? The fundamental mainsprings of this epistemology – supremacy and domination – are based on excluding those who do not belong, or exploiting that which only exists for its use-value. This is what transforms humanitarianism into *he*-manitarianism. What is the community of interests that exists outside the sphere of use-value as a function of profit, infinite progress, and the commercialization of all social spaces, and how can community intervene to change this destructive scenario?

Symptomatic of hyper-capitalist logic, the resources being managed by communities become the main focus of debate, thereby ignoring how collective decisions should be made equitably and in environmentally sustainable ways. Reactions to the massive oil catastrophe in the Gulf of Mexico in May 2010 reveal a seemingly irreconcilable clash between those who see it as the worst ecological disaster in U.S. history, in dire need of collective effort and response, and those who only compute profit losses. The BP Deepwater Horizon Gulf offshore well released huge quantities of crude oil during the summer of 2010, contaminating water, land, and air.[4] Yet no one knows the toll on wildlife because BP banned photographers, journalists, and scientists from the beaches where dead animals were washing up.[5] For reasons inexplicable to most Americans who assume that the First Amendment cannot be revoked by a corporation, the Coast Guard, federal wildlife officials, Louisiana and Florida sheriff's deputies and air traffic controllers were all complicit in the visual news blackout, according to a growing number of frustrated and outraged journalists (Evans, McClelland, Philips, Young). Dr. Leo Drollas, chief economist and deputy director of the Center for Global Energy Studies predicts that BP will be spared massive fines in order to protect America's own financial interests and continued deep-sea oil exploration in the Gulf (and later, very ominously, in the Arctic, whose waters are thought to contain as much as 27 billion barrels of oil). Differing radically from how most people view this disaster, Drollas (ridiculously) enthuses that the massive gush of crude indicates a 'huge success, in terms of exploration, for the American people' ('NYT: BP's Oil Spill Fines' 2).

In August 2010 Scientists from the respected Woods Hole Oceanographic Institute (WHOI) reported in *Science* that, in addition to the massive surface spread of the oil from the disaster, they had found 'a plume of hydrocarbons that is at least 22 miles long and more than 3,000 feet below the surface of the Gulf of Mexico, a residue of the BP Deepwater Horizon oil spill ... Moreover, they reported that deep-sea microbes were degrading the plume relatively slowly, and that it was possible that the 1.2-mile-wide, 650-foot-high plume had and will persist for some time' ('News Release'). The chemical constituents of the plume include benzene, the dissolvent toluene, ethylbenzene, and xylene. Oceanographers from the University of Georgia estimated that 80% of the oil from the disaster was still in the ocean as of August 2010 (Santini). Reporter Jeff Goodell affirmed that the BP Deepwater Horizon debacle was the 'biggest environmental disaster in American history' noting that

> crude oil contains hundreds, perhaps thousands of chemical compounds, many of which are lethal in high concentrations. As soon as oil began erupting out of BP's well and into the water, the compounds in the oil began to separate, some drifting up to the surface, others remaining near the bottom, where they will inevitably spread a toxic brew into the cellular structure of virtually every plant and

> animal in the Gulf, from microscopic plankton all the way up to sperm whales. Even worse, BP has responded to the disaster by pumping nearly 2 million gallons of toxic chemicals into the Gulf in an effort to break up the oil into smaller, camera-friendly slicks. The cleanup operation, in effect, has turned the Gulf into a vast science experiment, one whose consequences – untested and unforeseeable – are likely to haunt the planet for decades to come.[6] (60)

The disaster occurred on a scale hitherto unthinkable (and in a remarkably rich and productive ecosystem). The amount of crude being released into the water was roughly equivalent to one *Exxon Valdez* (1989) *every* four days (ibid.). This means that local communities will be affected for years to come by the fall-out via damaged ecosystems, sustained pressure to clean up the mess, depressed real estate values and other economic impacts, and long-term health concerns related to physical and mental well-being. Health concerns alone, based on previous experiences related to the Exxon Valdez, are significant. According to scientist Gina Solomon 'the oil spill can cause miscarriages, nausea, vomiting, headaches and difficulty breathing ... For a sign of what could lie ahead, take a look at what happened to communities after the 1989 Exxon Valdez disaster. According to this report, it left a legacy of depression, domestic violence and alcoholism. The number of divorces and bankruptcies increased too' ('BP's Oil Spill'). The chain of consequences for communities directly confronting the long-term effects of a disaster of this magnitude is significant.

To further complicate the social dynamics already perverted by the corporate control of government officials in the Deepwater Horizon disaster, BP hired prison labourers instead of local community residents to try to clean up the oil-covered beaches. Most of these prison laborers were African-Americans from Louisiana 'known to some as the "inmate state,"' having 'the highest rate of incarceration of any other state in the country' (Young). Here again we see how government comes to the corporation's aid by supplying BP with cheap labour through the Welfare to Work legislation created by the former Bush administration. As if this weren't enough of a grab for BP, 'businesses earn a tax credit of $2,400 for every work release inmate they hire. On top of that, they can earn back up to 40 percent of the wages they pay annually to "target group workers,"' thereby completing the circle of government taking a huge chunk of the hit for what should be entirely BP's clean-up costs. Local community residents, whose livelihoods as fisherfolk and charter boat captains are destroyed by the contamination, find themselves with few options besides ferrying BP officials around in their boats while denying the same services to journalists, due to threats from the corporation of losing their new, precarious, and temporary jobs with BP (Philips 3).

The prison labour clean-up crews, many of whom would ironically have been previous victims of Hurricane Katrina, are once again subjected to environmental racism as they rake and bag the highly toxic crude: 'Although the dangers of mixed oil and dispersant exposure are largely unknown, the chemicals in crude oil can damage every system in the body, as well as cell structures and DNA' (Young 2). Further typical of environmental racism, the prisoners are coerced into remaining on the job, which can average 72 hours per week, since refusing the job would look bad on their prison records and could translate into having to stay in prison longer (ibid. 2).

Anna Keller, who works with Gulf Recovery LLC to help develop community-based responses to the oil disaster, thinks that 'the use of inmate labor takes recovery one step further away from those people who are most intimate with the ecology, culture and landscape of the area. In her view, they should be hired first, and not just for the grunt jobs. "Community members should be hired in the planning stages, and paid for their expertise. The local people are the experts here"' (Young 5). Instead of such reasonable collaboration, BP controls the operation to the point that all journalists are automatically directed to BP's 'Command' and 'Information' Centres, even by state officials (Philips 2; McClelland 1-2). Hence, while coastal communities in Louisiana, Mississippi, and Alabama all face long-term challenges to their health and well-being, they have little power to influence the lax corporate and state policies that led to the disaster or to how the response to the disaster was implemented. Such a situation points to a key argument we sustain throughout this book, the pressing need to establish the rights of community as a substantial aspect of how to address abuses and violations that impact collectivities.

Connected to this kind of story of how local communities have largely been excluded from having a say in crucial decisions that can alter their lives dramatically, and how this underscores the current all-out war on democratic principles, is the corporate battle to do away with class action suits, a collective way for aggrieved individuals and communities to sue for damages, often caused by corporations or state entities. Under the George W. Bush administration, the legal system became increasingly privatized. Corporate lobbies convinced the government and the Supreme Court that mandatory arbitration (primarily run by credit card companies) is cost-effective, and it certainly is for corporations. The National Arbitration Forum is dominated by MBNA/Bank of America, JPMorgan Chase, and Citigroup, and not surprisingly, appointed arbitrators rule in favour of the company against the plaintiff in 95% of cases (Martens 3-4). Basic civil rights are suddenly erased by what is called liberal federal policy: 'Under any rational interpretation of contract law, contracts must be a meeting of minds, freely entered into, between parties of equal bargaining power. But just as profits have been privatized on Wall Street and losses socialized, the right to a jury trial in a court system paid for by individual taxpayers is now increasingly reserved for corporations, not people' (Martens 2).

From the perspective of community, tax paying is not only about how individual resources are collectively re-allocated, often to provide disproportionate support to state and corporate self-interest (as in the awarding of massive military contracts or the allocation of state resources to fight unjust wars) – but also about how taxation when fairly implemented is a means to sustaining and renewing community. Unfair and corrupt taxation laws and courts of justice are enabled by a society in which individuals are alienated from each other, and cast their solitary votes for representatives who, disguised behind their public relations masks, are playing a whole other game behind the campaign scenes. In a democratic society, communities – made up of individuals in open discussion with each other – would share their ideas about how they want their taxes to fund the public good, as well as decide how to make the legal system accessible and fair for common people who cannot bribe or lobby top officials and courts as corporations do. This corporate fascism, as many call it, or social fascism as sociologist Boaventura de Sousa Santos calls the pervasive climate that now characterizes so-called liberal (read: *false* or *managed*) democracies, is the context in which we write this book. It is also the context in which we try to imagine a different but possible reality rooted in communities and community values that have existed and already exist and do have the power to spread.

We propose a notion of rights as a complex expression of inter-relatedness with *all* aspects of being, including the environment and the biosphere, including the exceptions that challenge what it means to 'be,' to exist. To this end, community can be imagined as belonging to, and being a pluralist, diverse manifestation of a vast ecological interweaving of different life forms and environments interacting locally and globally. Such a view of the world challenges us to listen to a diversity of stories, and to try to understand other ways of knowing and being. De Sousa Santos speaks of an ecology of knowledges in the plural, a concept we discuss at length, and predicts that the most productive interventions will come from people he identifies as the cosmopolitan indigenous, cosmopolitan in that 'indigenous people were the paradigmatic inhabitants of the other side of the [abyssal] line, that ideal-typical playground for appropriation and violence' (24). Cosmopolitan, too, in that the oppressed knows the oppressor, as assassinated liberation theologian Ignacio Ellacuría said, and not the other way round. Indigenous peoples are also cosmopolitan due to having been displaced and forced to migrate great distances and to come into contact with many cultures while retaining their respect for the land. De Sousa Santos also foresees the coming preeminence of the epistemology of the South, or what we call the Majority or Majoritarian World to include marginalized and deterritorialized peoples in any region. The challenge he poses is structured around three clusters of questions that 'relate to the identification of knowledges, to the procedures for relating them to each other, and to the nature and assessment of real-world interventions made possible by them' (42).

Accepting this challenge involves diversifying the sources of our stories and interpretations. Coming at this subject, as we have, from an Arts and Humanities background, we have never thought about human, community, or environmental rights, or even civil rights as being limited to sociological and legal discourses, or to Western modes of thinking and writing. Hence, a key methodology we have deployed throughout this trilogy has been to engage with so-called alternative sources of information. Indigenous storytelling, for instance, accessible as aural narrative, published literature, or film testimony, has helped us understand Western forms of ignorance – and has helped re-think human rights and dignity from land-based perspectives that are ecological in the most comprehensive sense. Indigenous stories also offer a revisionary framework for examining how dominant Western discourses on rights are rooted in capitalism and colonialism, as well as offering more equitable alternative practices rooted in the collective idea of *conscience*, whose etymological meaning is 'knowing together.'

Transcultural thinking is adaptive thinking to an increasingly hybridized and interdependent world. We have sought to work with a methodology that takes account of critics, scholars, and thinkers whose work reflects this transcultural scope. Surprising connections and synergies emerge between ancient European and contemporary indigenous struggles once we realize that some histories are foregrounded and others silenced. As Marmon Silko explores in her novel *Gardens in the Dunes*, and as independent Scottish scholar and author Alistair McIntosh does in his auto-history of the Scottish Hebrides *Soil and Soul*, European commoners were brutally colonized and subjected by the elites. Their land-based, shamanistic, animistic, and feminine principled beliefs were persecuted by institutionalized religion. Therefore, when we say 'Eurocentric' we must be conscious of meaning the dominant/dominating European world-view, and to remember that the majority of Europeans – peasants and later workers – have other stories that still need to be remembered and restored to the community of story. In their drive to dominate others and to accumulate wealth, elites reduce all aspects of reality to monoculture. The current tendencies of monoculture are best served by Frankenstein science: biotechnology that reduces diversity through cloning, creating terminator seeds, and robbing the vast storehouse of communitarian knowledge through patenting. Scientific discourse dominates, together with the ubiquitous advertising that colonizes cultural space, pushing other kinds of stories to the margins, often beyond the boundaries of our technological world.

In recent years, global conflicts, mass migration, and increased transcultural communication have greatly confounded and expanded how people conceive of community and collective rights. We are guided by an ethical principle of transcultural research: to examine how communities define themselves – how they tell their stories – and thereby envision their significance and enact themselves within specific locales as well as trans-communally. While the desire for justice depends on recognizing specific rights that must be upheld across different regimes of truth and governance, we wish to put pressure on any notion of rights as a master narrative that hides concrete realities. We want to ask how rights might escape the paternalistic logic inscribed in their allocation, and to question the arbitrary nature of their existence as material practices in law, ethics, and tradition. Ultimately, we explore how institutionalized notions of human rights preclude a more holistic notion of rights, ecologies, and collective synergies.

While such critiques of current problems are important, this book also strives to move beyond pondering failures through a tragic worldview, to explore life-affirming interventions, and community connections that do not get nearly enough coverage by Western media. From people who struggle to develop their potential while living marginalized in poverty, to artists who improvise across national, ethnic, and generic borders, to border crossers of all kinds – whether driven by their own economic necessity and/or the desire to better the lives of others – the stories of communities in this book tell of enacting collective will that offers the potential to take us beyond just hope, survival, and resistance. These terms, heavily over-determined as they are, tell only one side of what it means to live collectively, and are reliant on a master narrative dominated by the very terms these words contradict: despair, death, and compliance. What might it mean to think outside this paradigm?

The Community of Rights / The Rights of Community is divided into three sections that encompass a range of different emphases that shift dominant paradigms for thinking rights in relation to community. Section one is an overview of our sense of how theoretical ideas linking community to rights discourses can be understood via practical examples. Section two gets at the crucial relationships among environment, community, and human agency, arguing for the connectedness of all forms of being as produced by relational contingencies and the ethics of encounter. Section three takes on notions of globalism, globalization, and different versions of that much-overused term the 'global community.' In our last section we return to storytelling and community as we summarize some of the key arguments this book makes in relation to imagining the rights of community within a larger community of rights.

A final note: as the epigraph of this introduction suggests, we have written the book with Austrian filmmaker Michael Haneke's comments about moral certainties in mind. These comments were made in relation to the remarkable 2009 film *The White Ribbon*, which details a series of disturbing events involving children in a pre-World War I northern German community and subtly links its ethical dysfunction with the rise of fascism. Settled assumptions about rights and justice, including whether the terms even remain viable, can produce the very reductive mindset Haneke attacks that allows for injustice. Complex realities, emerging from a combination of collective and personal histories and multiple contingencies, many of which are obscured or misrepresented, require nuanced critical tools if the discourse and thinking about justice and rights is to evolve. We hope this book contributes to providing the means to achieving this end. Our own sense that settled assumptions about rights need challenging and rethinking, and that these too will require remaking, has led to the writing of this book. We encourage readers to take its ideas forward in discrepant engagement with the dynamic agencies that make achieved civil communities and ethical action thinkable – and attainable.

NOTES

1 Nomadic, and semi-nomadic communities where this principle is in effect continue to exist worldwide, with there currently being an estimated 30 to 40 million nomads globally. In Mongolia, approximately 30% of its population of 3 million are nomadic or semi-nomadic; peripatetic minorities like the Gitans, Tsigani, Roma, Romanichals, and the Manouche live throughout Europe in various states of nomadism; the Berbers of North Africa and the desert Bedouin of Africa have extended histories of nomadism and semi-nomadism and have come under pressure from industrialization and government policies that impose sedentarization. Nomadism is a key aspect of cultural interchange, testing community capacity to address difference, and bringing with it traveling forms of expression and knowledge: 'Avant le transistor, bien avant la télévision, ce sont les nomades qui dans les villages de France apportaient avec eux la nouveauté' [Before the transistor, well before the television, it was the nomads who in the villages of France brought with them innovation' (our translation)] (musician Thierry 'Titi' Robin cited by Kaval 74).

2 Johnson's pamphlet, ironically enough, addressed the Declaration of Rights of the First Continental Congress of America in 1774, which argued against taxation without representation and led to a boycott of British goods, a series of events that culminated in the outbreak of the American Revolutionary War in 1775.

3 See *The Concise Guide to Global Human Rights*, Chapter 1; 43-49; 216-217.

4 The most recent report at the time this book was going to press, and based on research by Columbia University scientists, suggested that the total approximate spill figure is '185 million US gallons, or just over 700,000 cubic metres' (Amos).

5 In a similar move to legislate the banning of photographs whose purpose would be to keep communities informed, Florida and Iowa have put forward bills that would make it illegal to take pictures of farms, and perhaps also of 'county fairs, rodeos and other situations involving livestock' (Dunning). Stephanie Brown, director of the Canadian Coalition for Farm Animals, interprets this form of censorship as 'a move to cover up the horrible realities of factory farming,' a simple-minded attempt to thwart journalists and activists from disseminating information about our food sources and animal welfare: 'What you don't see, you don't know' (Dunning).

6 The BP Deepwater Horizon disaster is only one among many oil-related extraction situations where serious pollution occurs. An August 2010 report authored by Erin Kelly and David Schindler, Killam Memorial Professor of

Ecology, at the University of Alberta on the Syncrude Alberta oil sands project determined that 'High levels of toxic pollutants in Alberta's Athabasca River system are linked to oilsands mining ... The findings counter the reports by a joint industry-government panel that the pollutant levels are due to natural sources rather than human development. Mercury, thallium [a highly toxic element] and other pollutants accumulated in higher concentrations in snowpacks and waterways near and downstream from oilsands development than in more remote areas, said a study to be published ... in the Proceedings of the National Academy of Sciences. Upstream and undeveloped sites exposed directly to the McMurray Geologic Formation, the natural source of the oilsands, did not show high levels of pollutants. The study ... also found that levels of the pollutants cadmium, copper, lead, mercury, nickel, silver and zinc exceeded federal and provincial guidelines for the protection of aquatic life in melted snow or water collected near or downstream from oilsands mining' ('Oilsands mining linked to Athabaska River toxins'). Work by Schindler on growing, significant numbers of fish deformities in Lake Athabaska downstream from the oilsands is part of a wider spectrum of research investigating the links between oilsands by-products and severely degraded environments: 'In 2007, Environment Canada completed work showing high levels of deformities in fish embryos exposed to oilsands. In 2008, Schindler himself did research that led to two published studies showing that levels of hydrocarbons – some carcinogenic – and toxic heavy metals, including mercury and lead, are both growing and linked to industry' (Weber). Local communities including First Nations communities receive the immediate and long-term effects of such pollutants: as Robert Grandjambe, a representative of the Mikisew Cree First Nations, states about his own community: 'Fort Chipewyan is not healthy. A lifestyle is being stolen away' (ibid.).

SECTION I

'All life being one life'

The 'Common' Good, Rights, and the Meaning of Community

PREAMBLE

The Parable of the Flute

All notions of community are based on belonging to a social group in which members share interests and concerns: from basic needs like clean water, food, shelter, and a clean environment to needs that include association, creativity, spirit, intellect, and the like. 'Belonging' and 'sharing' in this context are fluid concepts ranging from full-on engagement at multiple levels of agency (material or abstracted) to passive disengagement or even alienation. There is nothing in the concept of community as it relates to the impossibly wide spectrum of practices associated with it that exempts disengagement and alienation as potential aspects of relating to group concerns and interests. And such alienation can indicate stagnation or dysfunction within a community prior to its demise, or its rebirth in new form. This is to say that from a rights perspective, there are more and less ethical ways of being in a community – and notions of community solely predicated on individual and group behaviours, like similar notions of so-called 'human rights,' are severely impoverished in how they abstract 'human being' from vital connections to the biosphere, local environments, and other forms of sentience (whether plant or animal).

What we propose is to dislocate community from current contexts in which the term has been radically over-determined, corrupted, and co-opted by forms of discourse seeking to empty it of its meaning and potential power as a political force. A number of theses are crucial to this project. One involves the degree to which thinking about rights has for far too long been individual-centered with little consideration for the implications of this on the multiple forms of community to which the individual contributes, and by which the individual is defined and given meaning. For us this is a false binary that is in need of radical re-examination.

A second connected thesis, in which we try to overturn assumptions that have been overlaid on rights discourses, is the idea that perhaps the most radical way forward in rights theory is to address the basic preconditions that make human life and diversity possible: the biotic, biological, environmental, and ecological ground from which everything grows. For this reason, we spend a significant portion of this book addressing the issue of land (earth) and community relations to land as the basis for any form of rights practice that truly addresses the relational dependencies that exist between physical locales and living beings. These dependencies are largely ignored in rights discourses and instruments, yet without them life in a community (or otherwise) is unthinkable.

Communitarian discourses – however co-opted and corrupted by neoliberal notions of the 'gated community' in which the public commons has been privatized and sold off to the highest or most connected bidder; or the online community, in which virtuality falsely becomes an avatar of embodied agency; or the global community, in which hegemonic and imperial cultures seek to enforce an exploitative system on the majoritarian world – must deal head on with the specific localized and complex web of related environments in which a given community is embodied. Rights emerge from that relationship between life form and environment as surely as they emerge from the ethics of encounter enacted among different social groupings. Lamentably, these sorts of recognitions are largely marginal to current rights institutional formations and instruments, though there is increasing pressure to revitalize and renew rights discourses relating them to environmental discourses.

The 'gate,' like the fence and the barrier, are powerful metaphors that denote community relations and their relative health. In China gated villages 'have for years been symbols of affluence; places where the rich can live in villa-style homes, surrounded by private schools and swimming pools, with fences to keep out those who don't belong. Now China is gating off low-income villages, where migrant labourers from the countryside (the people who built those expansive villas) live in near squalor. The newly erected fences and nighttime curfews are designed to hold in the residents, and the criminality that supposedly emanates from these communities. "Enhance the idea of safety and reduce illegal crimes," reads a red banner hanging over the main road to one such village south of Beijing, home to some 7,000 migrants' (MacKinnon). These paradoxical communities – gated for the security of the rich and gated to imprison the poor – can be found around the world. Both as containment and as protection (or even as concealment of social inequity), the gated community is a metaphor throughout this book for community dysfunction.

A third crucial thesis to this book is the degree to which storytelling writ large, that is modes of narrative that address multiple aspects of being in relation to others (including sentient beings, environments, and forms of knowledge), is a crucial component in re-figuring rights discourses holistically. Rights, in this view, are a form of open-ended story in which ethics, pedagogy, precedent practice, multiple knowledge formations, allegory, spirit, embodiment, and agency all come together. In *Storied Communities*, Martha Nandorfy argues that understanding 'community identities as evolving out of storytelling ... breaks down a number of dualisms that had for centuries divided the world into people who made and wrote history, and those who had history imposed upon them, thereby marginalizing or silencing their stories' (333). Awareness of the power dynamics that shape community as a function of access to story-making is a crucial component in any progressive rights context. Embodied rights practices not only depend on a full understanding of one's relationship to the land, but also on the storytelling that sustains that relationship as a dynamic, processual, and sometimes ambiguous or conflicted way of being in the world, of accessing the agency that is such a vital component of the survival of community.

Finally, a fourth thesis that we address in our section on globalization and community undermines trite commonplaces about the 'global community,' a phrase so thoroughly compromised by evidence to the contrary that it is hard to imagine how it has gained such widespread use. Global community discourse is predicated on modernist and post-modern notions that privilege the newness of global trade, access to global media like the worldwide web ('worldwide' only if you have access to the technology and the bandwidth; 'web' only if you have the imagination to use the technology in ways outside the norms established by Google's search engines driven as they are by corporate profit and advertising imperatives), and the inter-penetration and triumph of capital culture globally. This form of global community is illusory and predicated on all sorts of myths. Global trade routes pre-exist Europe, as the work of Enrique Dussel, Immanuel Wallerstein, Walter Mignolo and others has shown so effectively. Hybridization and shared cultural formations have also been around long before the term global community came into existence, as have imperial power vectors that have sought to dominate increasingly large sectors of the globe. The inherent problem with the term is how it naturalizes only one form of global community, one largely determined by hegemonic, capitalized forces.

As argued in *The Concise Guide to Global Human Rights*, rights and social justice issues must be read through the filter of resource allocation: a country that spends infinitely more money on its military than on its rights initiatives is severely compromised when it comes to talking and enacting rights. Global community in such a context is a political sleight of hand and a sham. Which is not to say that there do not exist alternative models of thinking planetary interconnectedness that operate outside the discourses of state power and self-interest. It is to these that we turn in trying to re-imagine what it might mean to discuss community meaningfully within the context of globalization discourses.

In this book we disavow idealized and utopian notions of community, which have for far too long been used to disable the practical effectiveness of directed group action by reducing complex and often conflicted forms of local culture to the convenience of a trope. And we do so fully acknowledging the degree to which community has become such an over-determined and co-opted term that it has virtually no meaning or valence – while at the same time acknowledging that regardless of this circumstance, the term itself is part of a vocabulary that is unavoidable and in need of reclamation.

To show how compromised are the discourses of community, we cite from the January issue of the French magazine *Le Point*, in which the 1998 Nobel Prize winner in Economics, Amartya Sen, relates the parable of the flute. Sen's story addresses the impossibility of achieving global justice via the example of three children fighting over possession of a flute. Clara has made the flute; Anne is the only one who knows how to play it; and Bob is a child who has no toy at all with which to play. The dilemma for Sen is *who* gets the flute. Sen states that '*Dans cette petite parabole, selon que l'on privilégie l'une or l'autre dimension de la justice, chacun des trios enfants peut avoir la flute*' [In this little parable, depending on which version of justice we privilege, each of the three children can have the flute]. Hence, Anne can have the flute if one subscribes to utilitarian notions of justice; egalitarians give the flute to Bob, and libertarians to Clara. And for Sen, '*il faut non seulement prendre en compte les circonstances particulières, mais aussi faire intervenir des preferences morales et politiques*' (Lévy) [One must not only take into account particular circumstances but also intervene with moral and political preferences].

The problem with this parable is how it frames the question. Unthinkable in this equation, and wholly unmentioned in Sen's analysis, is why anyone *should* own the flute – or why single-ownership models are the only thinkable ways of addressing the problem. Moreover, concepts of reciprocity, mutuality, sharing, group resolutions in which the needs of each of the children are met equitably are wholly absent from the story and its framework. In short, the very means of addressing the problem in a non-particulated way that renders some form of justice and addresses the rights dimensions of this parable, namely community, is not present in Sen's telling. A public commons that balances the three dimensions represented by the three children (making, playing, poverty) sidesteps the issue of ownership as unnecessary to resolving the needs of each child. Does the maker of the flute necessarily want to play it? Does the player of the flute want to keep it only for herself? Why is Bob poor? Where did the wood used to make the flute come from? Can Clara make more flutes?

None of these contextual issues, issues that a community-based solution to this problem would have to address, is remotely thinkable in the framework of the story as told by Sen, which then justifies in the abstract global injustices and the radical inequalities that undergird them. We cite this example as a shorthand way of exposing the degree to which communitarian thinking has been undermined by the privileging of narratives of ownership, in which single individuals are abstracted by their ownership from the very communities that make that ownership possible. We also cite this story as a useful way of thinking about how the terms of the debates over social justice get too often set by stagnant forms of institutional thought fundamentally inimical to real forms of communitarian ethics and embodied practice. These latter might argue that *all* the children in the story have rights to the flute in different ways, dependent on their need, interest, volition, and how these intersect with the ethical health of the community and its conceptions of social justice. In that regard, the rights of the community to enact strategies that guarantee its health and happiness are in balance with the community of rights that address social justice issues.

The parable of the flute parallels that of the Prisoner's Dilemma, a product of game theory that imagines a situation in which non-cooperation occurs in spite of it being in the best interests of the prisoners to cooperate. Nobel prize winning (2009) economist, Elinor Ostrom, has elegantly critiqued the framework of the dilemma in her book *Governing the Commons: The Evolution of Institutions for Collective Action*, which suggests that

> People are trapped by the Prisoner's Dilemma only if they treat themselves as prisoners by passively accepting the suboptimum strategy the dilemma locks them into, but if they try to work out a contract with the other players, or find the ones most likely to cooperate, or agree on rules for punishing cheaters, or artificially

> change the incentive ratios – they can create an institution for collective action that benefits them all. This resonates with Peter Kollock's taxonomy of strategies for dealing with social dilemmas – one strategy is to change the rules of the game. ('Governing the Commons')

Sociologist Kollock's work on online communities, *Communities in Cyberspace* (1999), argues that cooperation in online communities places into relief the problem that 'Many of the favors and benefits provided in online communities are public goods, i.e. a good from which all may benefit, regardless of whether one has helped create the good. In such a situation there is a temptation to free-ride on the efforts of others, but if all do so, everyone is worse off' (18).

The problem, like that framed in Sen's parable, is how to negotiate the dilemma of creating and managing public goods responsibly and in a way that does not rely on premises or institutional orthodoxies that prohibit creative solutions. Communities that resolve these issues with respect to diverse ecologies of knowledge, or environmental challenges that require rapid responses to crisis situations, often arise from moribund communities in which institutional imperatives have displaced and overridden larger community outcomes having to do with renewability and survival.

Ostrom's ideas about public commons dilemmas and collective action responses to these dilemmas provide a useful alternative to Sen's parable, which ostensibly does not allow for alternative premises or solutions to be deployed. A useful summary of Ostrom's work avers that

> Changing the rules of the game to turn zero-sum games into non-zero-sum games may be one way to describe the arc of civilization for the past 8000 years: using symbolic media and social inventions, people have created institutions for collective action since the emergence of agriculture spurred the invention of writing. But for the most part, we've overcome obstacles and built these institutions blindly, without any systematic knowledge about how the game works. Ostrom takes an empirical approach: By examining legal records and other public documents, is it possible to determine whether every population over-consumes and under-provisions all common pool resources? She found that in many different cultures all over the world, some groups would find ways to overcome the obstacles that defeated others – by creating contracts, agreements,

> incentives, constitutions, signals, media to enable cooperation for mutual benefit. ('Governing the Commons')

Though a self-proclaimed 'institutionalist' (Ostrom 25), and thus limited by that framework, which cannot account for how alternative forms of community with remarkably distant or loose notions of institution can nonetheless be effective, Ostrom gets at a crucial problem: 'What is missing from the policy analyst's tool kit – and from the set of accepted, well-developed theories of human organization – is an adequately specified theory of collective action whereby a group of principals can organize themselves voluntarily to retain the residuals of their own efforts' (24-25).

Retention of outcome and effort is surely one desirable possibility in imagining collective responses to the commons. But, in our view, it is not the only outcome associated with collective action if only because it too rests on latent notions of property and ownership, which are not always, in themselves, the precondition or outcome driving collective action. Responsibility, empathy, altruism, unconditional responses to crisis, and giving (where the needs of the other preempt what one gets in return) – all need to be figured into the space of thinking about collective ethics. The need for residuals suggests a game paradigm that may not always be applicable (and thus is productive of a paradox in Ostrom's own thinking, which allows for changing the terms of the so-called game but then imposes terms based on retention of the residuals of effort).

Ostrom's theories are based on two key notions: the commons and common-pool resources (CPRs):

> The commons is a general term for shared resources in which each stakeholder has an equal interest. Studies on the commons include the information commons with issues about public knowledge, the public domain, open science, and the free exchange of ideas – all issues at the core of a direct democracy.
>
> Common-pool resources (CPRs) are natural or human-made resources where one person's use subtracts from another's use and where it is often necessary, but difficult and costly, to exclude other users outside the group from using the resource. The majority of the CPR research to date has been in the areas of fisheries, forests, grazing systems, wildlife, water resources, irrigation systems, agriculture, land tenure and use, social organization, theory (social

> dilemmas, game theory, experimental economics, etc.), and global commons (climate change, air pollution, trans-boundary disputes, etc.), but CPR's can also include the broadcast spectrum. ('Governing the Commons')

Both concepts entail significant implications for rights and social justice discourses. In the case of the commons, measuring the equal interest of stakeholders is more than a little problematic if only because it reverts conceptualizing about rights generally to individual stakeholders in a market of similar stakeholders. Ironically, the very term 'commons,' in this perverse sense, comes to stand for a relation privileging individuals as opposed to balancing those individual components of the commons in relation to collective needs and rights. The framework, then, for imagining the commons in these terms is already compromised ethically. A simple example might suffice to show how this might work: an individual whose self-interest trumps others' self-interest might decide to obstruct passage to a source of water that has traditionally been used by the community thus depriving the community of potable water. Or the same individual may decide to use the water source for non-renewable purposes (sanitation, industrial applications, and the like). In both cases, self-interest is at odds with community interest because private property and individual ownership of a common-pool resource trump collective rights to a basic resource. This concept, adapted to corporations that have accrued individual legal rights, has in many ways become the dominant paradigm for thinking rights issues, and it is deeply at odds with the rights of community as we describe them.

Corporate Personhood and the Attack on the Commons

Shared resources of the commons are at odds with stakeholder self-interest defined by property accumulation, yet as is usual in rights discourses, self-interest, so long as it is legal but not necessarily just, trumps collective interests. This kind of reasoning is often used to justify exceptional abuses of the commons by corporations understood, legally, to be individuals in spite of their being corporate entities. The creation of corporate entities that lay claim to aspects of community entitlement to the commons, while also being granted individual rights (without necessarily individual or even corporate liability), superseding the rights of communities has been a remarkable legal sleight of hand used to pervert and confuse the rights and social justice landscape. A summary of the perversity of the situation in the U.S., whose policies affect global structures of corporate governance, notes that

> The structure of federal and state law – both statutory and constitutional – empowers corporations to override local democratic decision-making. Since the early 1800s, corporations have gained rights and protections under the United States Constitution. While we never find the word 'corporation' in the Constitution, corporations are able to invoke constitutional 'rights' and protections under the Commerce Clause and Contracts Clause, as well as under the First, Fourth, Fifth, Sixth, and Fourteenth Amendments.
>
> Corporations use these 'rights' to challenge state and local laws, and to chill efforts at the local level to fight corporate siting plans. Thanks to the U.S. Supreme Court's ruling in the *Dartmouth* case in 1819 [discussed below], 'private' business corporations first gained constitutional protection from government interference in internal governance, ostensibly under the Contract Clause of the Constitution. Curiously, the court found no reason to similarly protect municipal corporations, such as towns, boroughs, cities and counties from state interference with self-government. ('The Aristocracy of Our Monied Corporations')

Constitutional principles of collective priority in the U.S. have been tied closely to corporate economic self-interest, while at the same time overriding or ignoring other forms of collective undertaking. Economy-based forms of collective organization are but one aspect of a much broader spectrum of practices any community must envision, put into practice, and modify in relation to other forms of collective organization. This is especially so for public commons spaces in which economic self-interest is very much secondary to collective undertakings that may fall entirely outside of corporately thinkable economic models driven by profit and competition. Yet, examples abound of the corporate model of collective self-interest supplanting local governance. One such example involved

> the Waste Management Corporation [which] was able to successfully sue the State of Virginia under the Commerce Clause to overturn a state law which prohibited the importation of out-of-state waste, arguing that the law interfered with the flow of commerce.

> With the First Amendment, we see corporations participating in the writing of our laws and the election of candidates at all levels of government. Citing the Fifth Amendment 'Takings Clause,' the U.S. Supreme Court ruled in *Pennsylvania Coal Co. v. Mahon* (1922), that coal corporations must be compensated for property value lost due to laws protecting homes from mining subsidence. Under the Fourteenth Amendment, corporations are able to claim equal protection and due process rights.
>
> Charters of incorporation seem to grant special privileges for private wealth, including limited liability protections from legal responsibility by individuals benefiting by dint of this corporate shield, along with the 'rights' of personhood bestowed by the courts. And yet charters do not actually grant rights, but rather they deny rights held by all by identifying corporations as a specially protected class under the law. ('The Aristocracy of Our Monied Corporations')

The seminal *Dartmouth College v. Woodward* case, as described by American historian Jon C. Teaford, occurred in 1819 when

> the U.S. Supreme Court introduced a distinction between the rights of a public corporation and a private one. The U.S. Constitution's contract clause did not protect the political powers granted in the charter of a public corporation such as a municipality. State legislatures could, therefore, unilaterally amend or revoke municipal charters and strip a city of authority without the municipality's consent. But the charter of a private corporation, such as a business enterprise or a privately endowed college, was an inviolate grant of property rights guaranteed by the nation's Constitution. (Teaford quoted in 'The Aristocracy of Our Monied Corporations')

The basics of the *Trustees of Dartmouth College v. Woodward*, 17 U.S. (4 Wheat.) 518 (1819) landmark ruling are as follows:

> the United States Supreme Court case [dealt] with the application of the Contract Clause of the United States Constitution to private corporations. The case arose when the president of Dartmouth College was deposed by its trustees, leading to the New Hampshire legislature attempting to force the College to become a public institution and thereby place the ability to appoint trustees in the hands

> of the governor. The Supreme Court upheld the sanctity of the original charter of the College, which pre-dated the creation of the State. The decision settled the nature of public versus private charters and resulted in the rise of the American business corporation. ('*Dartmouth College v. Woodward*')

Interestingly the principle of the autonomy of the university is at the root of the establishment of corporate autonomy and, indeed, personhood. As outlined on the Reclaim Democracy website ('Corporate Personhood'), *Dartmouth College v. Woodward* was only the first in a series of decisions over the next almost two hundred years to reinforce this principle of corporate personhood: these included the 1893 *Noble v. Union River Logging Company*, which was the first instance of a corporation's claim of Bill of Rights protections under the 5th Amendment; the 1933 *Liggett v. Lee* decision in which chain store taxes were prohibited as a violation of corporations' due process rights; and *Ross v. Bernhard*, which in 1976 gave 7th Amendment rights of jury trial to corporations. Thus collective entities defined by for-profit motivation with only the fiduciary interests of its shareholders to motivate it (and with little or no regard for larger issues related to local community management of commons resources) slowly attained the rights of personhood with few of the responsibilities and liabilities.

According to Noam Chomsky corporations are 'private tyrannies' or 'totalitarian' institutions and he backs up this characterization by looking at their inner workings :

> These shocking terms [tyranny and totalitarian] accurately describe the constitutional structure of private corporations: power moves from the top to the bottom. Those who work at the lower levels of the corporation have no representation at the highest levels. Legally, they have no more access to these institutions' decision-making than the local community, the state, or the populace in general ... in the absence of protests by shareholders or the Board of Directors, the CEO effectively holds legislative, executive, and adjudicatory powers, a concentration of power that James Madison once called 'the very definition of tyranny.'[1] (Wilson 252)

These sorts of concentrations of power within extraordinarily deformed notions of personhood combined with the total neglect of community-oriented legal (constitutional) definitions of rights (what we call throughout this book *the rights of community*) have led, in a very short time, to remarkable deformations of natural community rights.

Totalitarian structures of empowerment contradict community self-interest and not, as French sociologist Alain Touraine argues, the other way around: 'A communitarian society is suffocating and can be transformed into a theocratic or nationalist despotism' ... and something like a 'cultural totalitarianism' is emerging today with community being resurrected by 'authoritarian forms of religion' (Delanty 117). Vital here is the question of what constitutes community? Touraine's comments suggest that community is as much defined by how it generates the self-critical, adaptive capacity for dissent as by how it produces non-vertical power structures that allow for dissonance and mediation in coming to conflicted decisions. Theocratic fundamentalist communities, like corporate communities, operate out of principles of self-interest that exclude equitable understandings of rights principles because these are at odds with their priorities. The reductive notions of community and communitarianism that are based on tropes of totalitarian consensus is at odds with how many real communities define themselves more as a function of balances and imbalances that are co-generative and co-creative. Community rights entail addressing difference and dissidence. The capacity of community to generate and mediate that dissidence is a defining aspect of an effective cultural commons. This is not a static process and involves constant iterations of self-critical thought as well as decisions about that thought that are based on fundamental principles of equity.

Local community engages with a full set of contingencies comprising environmental concerns, concerns over the equitable sharing of the commons, and equitable processes of decision-making over the allocation of resources and community priorities. Such community is wholly at odds with the corporate collectivity that vitiates these basic terms of relational engagement, while ascribing to itself debased notions of personhood. Personhood always exists as a relational entity within multiform, diverse community structures in which intimacy, responsibility, dissidence, and negotiation are crucial values. Corporate entities sidestep these terms of engagement, while appropriating the terms of collective self-interest (they too claim to be community-oriented, concerned, and the like) and personhood, as a means to prioritizing their rights over all other forms of being.

Comparing debacles like the BP Deepwater Horizon oil spill and the Bhopal chemical leak show the largely ineffectual power (let alone willingness) of the state to intervene to address corporate liability. The Union

Carbide (now Dow Chemical) Bhopal disaster of 3 December 1984 released 47 tons of methyl isocyanate, killing over 10,000 people and 'imposing various degrees of suffering and disability on nearly a quarter of a million human beings and creating extensive environmental damage' (Baxi 23). Ultimately in both the BP and the Bhopal disasters local natural communities are the most impacted through loss of livelihood, health, environmental degradation, and responsibility for dealing with the aftermath. The corporations responsible for such devastation monetize the cost of what they call an 'accident' in terms that maintain shareholder value for the corporation as the result of perverse cost-benefit analyses. Thus the corporation profits from the situation by avoiding the real full costs of the disaster, while local communities pick up that cost in addressing their immediate and shared need to resolve the issues of the clean-up. Local community resilience, in other words, becomes the unpaid solution to large-scale corporate abuses.

In Bhopal, some 26 years later, 390 tons of toxic chemicals continue to leach into the land and groundwater from the abandoned plant, and seven ex-employees were convicted to a paltry two years in jail each and given a fine of $2000 (in June 2010). The glacial pace of the judgments not to mention the limitation of these to Indian citizens but not to their American counterparts coupled with the ineffectual cleanup symbolize the degree to which corporate culture trumps local natural community culture. Indian human rights and legal scholar Upendra Baxi, who has written extensively about the Bhopal crisis, calls the anemic and belated legal and state responses to Bhopal a second form of catastrophe, anticipating a third, which is a re-victimization of the victims. Baxi notes that 'adjudicatory biopower/biopolitics ... creates and circulates "politicized bodies" of collective subjects of mass industrial disasters' (39-40). The process reinscribes local communities' and individuals' sufferings into the collective logic of statist self-interest. This re-inscription follows a precise political logic in which state impunity and the compensatory rhetoric used to quantify appropriate levels of state remuneration are deployed, usually at the expense of any serious approximation of the specificity and full magnitude of the unthinkable suffering they ostensibly address. Baxi points to how the state and corporate response to the Bhopal-violateds' many ongoing sufferings produces profound moral, legal, and rights challenges to the ways in which corporate legal liability and moral responsibility have systematically been perverted via 'the way of merger and amalgamation and of divestiture of assets to successors-in-interest' (42). In Baxi's reading of the disaster,

> the continuing movement of the Bhopal-violated beckons a new jurisprudence of human solidarity in a runaway globalizing world. Their movement more fully revitalizes India's original intent in devising *the principle of absolute multinational enterprise liability for ultrahazardous industry*, process and application when seeking compensation ... via this *jurisprudence of solidarity* ... The message of Bhopal, in the main, thus constructs some new alternate futures beyond the new paradigm of trade-related, market friendly, and environmentally hostile human rights. (44; our emphasis)

Such a vision of a jurisprudence of solidarity is a crucial reason behind our argument for establishing vigorous and progressive means for enacting the rights of community in instances of abuses or violations by corporations, and subsequent reinscriptions of those communities into corporate / statist political models of rights governed by hegemonic self-interest.

In Canada, one of the remarkable battles over charter rights has been to determine whether people whose charter rights have been breached even have recourse to damages. The fact that this is a problem in a so-called advanced democracy is remarkable. This situation is part and parcel of a systemic choking off of adequate material resources to achieve rights outcomes that would restore some degree of equitable balance to a system too often skewed to suit hegemonic powers. Often the cost of accessing rights is so prohibitive as to make them inaccessible – and no equitable means for allowing David-and-Goliath type cases to move forward exists (especially when pitting an individual's meager resources against corporate or institutional resources). Only very recently, in a unanimous July 2010 Supreme Court of Canada ruling was the principle of damages for charter breaches upheld. Lawyer Alan Cameron Ward, who was strip-searched and imprisoned after falsely having been suspected of plotting to throw a pie at then Prime Minister Jean Chrétien in 2002, won a protracted legal struggle to assert this principle: 'The ruling marks the first time the high court looked at monetary damages for violations of rights. It means that people whose rights have been infringed can seek damages even if they suffered no actual loss and even if the authorities acted in good faith' (Alphonso). When 'good faith' arguments are made by corporatized entities like the state, any individual or community entity that challenges these in a rights context will be severely compromised by access to the legal means and financial resources to exercise those legal means in equitable proportion to the state's (or corporation's) relatively unlimited resources.

Aside from considerations of how corporations disguise and protect themselves as both persons and collective entities whose artificial community rights override natural community rights, the rights of so-called interest groups have from the inception of the Universal Declaration of Human Rights (UDHR) in 1948 been a challenge theoretically and pragmatically. Author and research fellow Raj Patel tells the story of how major signatories to the UDHR, like the U.K., Russia, and the U.S. were 'worried about what "rights" would mean to groups deprived of them within their own borders' (116). Patel goes on to show how crucial was a petition drafted and presented to the United Nations in 1947 by octogenarian author and activist W.E.B. Du Bois in the name of the National Association for the Advancement of Colored People (NAACP): *An Appeal to the World: A Statement on the Denial of Human Rights to Minorities in the Case of Citizens of Negro Descent in the United States of America and an Appeal to the United Nations for Redress*. This extended appeal, involving documentation and five papers by prominent scholars, had been long-simmering in Du Bois's mind–the 1947 Appeal being exactly the same in title as was a 1900 Appeal drafted by Du Bois for the first Pan-African conference in London. The 1947 Appeal came out of Du Bois's 'initiative in assembling representatives from twenty organizations involved in civil rights to meet at the Schomburg Collection building of the New York Public Library in Harlem on 5 October 1946. Du Bois presided and the substance of the 18 September petition to the United Nations was presented, debated, and adopted' (Aptheker 166).

Patel outlines how one of the outcomes of this sort of appeal for the redress of aggrieved groups' rights, entailed a backlash that ended with a watered-down compromise: 'while the language of individual rights was strident, the enforcement mechanisms would be left to individual countries to decide' (Patel 116). Notably excluded from this agreement were environmental rights and the rights of community. Moreover, as Patel's analysis shows,

> governments have encouraged their citizens to wait for rights to be delivered [largely the view of rights as a negative state], while the government addresses the concerns of each citizen in turn ... asking for patience ... [This] is a way of demobilizing popular demands, and of letting governments wriggle out of providing any-

> thing at all ... In other words, rights can be understood as a bedtime story, in which the future ends happily ever after, if only we allow the profit-driven markets to continue their reign undisturbed, and agree that the most fundamental right of all is that of individuals to private property. As W.E.B. Du Bois and the civil rights movement have shown, however, the way to make governments deliver rights is not to wait, but to demand ... From women's movements to the demands of indigenous people, it is a mark of the success of rights talk that there are millions of people promoting democratic social change in the name of rights, despite calls from their governments for patience until they can find the political will to enact change. (ibid. 117)

Patel's analysis hints at the effectiveness of group struggles for rights while sidestepping the problem of the lack of specific rights ascribed to community. Negative access to rights, state intransigency, and structures of thinking rights predicated on corporate self-interest and private property notions of the commons, all present challenges to meaningful enactment.

Important precedents have been established over two centuries of litigation that include the modern development of rights instruments in the first half of the twentieth century. As we have seen, the *Dartmouth College v. Woodward* and subsequent related rulings favoured corporations with the legal rights of personhood. These rulings may be understood as part of the same pattern that devolved the universal rights of the UDHR to state structures as principles that were not necessarily enforced or enforceable. Hence, both corporate personhood and state autonomy have become obstacles to imagining the enforceable rights of community from within the larger perspectives of a globally enacted community of rights. In the U.S., especially, both corporate personhood and state exceptionalism have firmly rooted themselves. Remarkably, this state of affairs was made possible even though the concept of 'corporation' is wholly absent from the American Constitution and even though state exceptionalism has been clearly understood (and used) as a way of abdicating universal rights in favour of state self-interest.

The ironies and paradoxes are especially present in assessing the challenges facing the rights of community within the community of rights. One measure of the extent to which state interests actively work against community assertions of rights is detailed in the 'Postscript' to African-American scholar Clyde Woods's provocative book *Development Arrested:*

The Blues and Plantation Power in the Mississippi Delta. Woods describes two instances, among many, of how African American communities were attacked or deprived of benefits through state intervention:

> On Tuesday, March 18, 1998, the United States Circuit of Appeals ordered the release of 124,000 pages from the files of the Mississippi Sovereignty Commission. The documents contained the names of more than 87,000 activists who had been spied upon, harassed, smeared, falsely jailed, beaten, or murdered between 1956 and 1977 as part of the campaign to destroy the 'Mississippi Freedom Movement.' (291)

A year earlier, more than two years after President Bill Clinton

> awarded the Delta Council control of the Mid-Delta Empowerment Zone (MDEZA), not a dime of the $40 million in direct federal grants available had been spent. Led by the Delta Council, the plantation bloc and Governor [Kirk] Fordice's [the 61st Governor of Mississippi] Mississippi Department of Human Services, the state organization charged with monitoring the expenditure of funds had blocked the release of any monies that might remotely contribute to development of the African American community. (ibid.)

In both these cases state and corporate interests were arrayed against community interests along racial lines, blocking access to resources and machinating against an extraordinary number of people in order to impede progress on the rights of African Americans in Mississippi.

Woods's more recent analyses of post-Hurricane Katrina New Orleans have been equally trenchant about how regressive state notions of rights are at dramatic odds with community aspirations and health:

> Katrina revealed the present and future human costs of a fragmented, de-linked, privatized and devolved state; no one is in charge ... the practices of residential segregation ... kept the black community of New Orleans in a floodplain surrounded by a faulty levee system further devastated by recent Bush administration budget cuts. Black Louisianans have also been systematically subjected to some of the worst instances of environmental racism in the world. In 1990, Louisiana legislator Avery Alexander described an environment that had been turned against the African American community ...

"among African American women, near Saint James ... vaginal cancers are 36 times the national average ... here in Louisiana ... we have found the job promises empty and the risk of poisoning inevitable."' (Woods 'Do You Know' 510-11)

Corporate and state rights, when seen in this light, override historically constituted community entities with, in many cases, a much longer history of precedent social and environmental practice. They thus negate and undermine local forms of community organization, precisely the very forms of relationship and governance that have the most contact with and meaning to local community life.

Farmer and cultural critic Wendell Berry's writings on community remind us (following on Thomas Jefferson's ideas[2]) that while the health of a free public depends on mistrust, the 'health of a community depends absolutely on trust' (1992 161). Corporate structures, whose only responsibilities are fiduciary to their shareholders and not balanced (or checked) by principles of localized collective good (what we call the rights of community) or even by state imperatives, override and threaten in the most fundamental of ways community structures. The problem is that structures that warrant a fundamental relationship of distrust with regard to their capacity to negotiate their own self-interest in relation to others, have gained the upper hand in determining how completely different collective structures, based on very different relations of trust, operate.

Berry's notion of localized trust is a precondition of community health founded on the intimacy of face-to-face embodied contact:

> A community knows itself and knows its place in a way that is impossible for a public (a nation, say, or a state). A community does not come together by a covenant, by a conscientious granting of trust. It exists by proximity, by neighborhood; it knows face to face, and it trusts as it knows. It learns, in the course of time and experience, what and who can be trusted. It knows that some of its members are untrustworthy, and it can be tolerant, because to know in this matter is to be safe.' (ibid.)

Localized embodiment, in other words, is what permits community diversity, and constitutes what may be called 'natural community.' Local knowledges allow for difference within the collective and for adaptations and accommodations. Like arbitrary notions of personhood, which presume a distinction between natural persons (the individual) and artificial persons (the corporation), which is to say a wholly false notion of personhood that serves hegemonic economic interests, communities have undergone a similar semantic attack, with again large public corporate entities (like the nation-state, the community of nations, the online community, the corporation, and the like) defined as artificial communities usurping to themselves the perceived rights that accrue to natural communities, the kind that Berry is addressing in the comments we quote above. When these artificial collectivities define themselves by class or ethnic self-interest, and these interests are aligned with specific mechanisms of power (police, military, corporate economic and legal power) that largely determine the framework of social relations, then access to the political or resource commons in equitable and just terms is sure to be compromised, especially in the localized circumstances that are most relevant to natural communities.

Distracted Community: Facebook and the Real of the Illusion

Online community is perhaps the most over-used and uncritically charged term to have crept into the global vocabulary of triumphal technologies associated with post-industrial capital. A recent Google search (summer of 2010) for the terms *Facebook* and *community* yielded over 2.3 billion returns. Another Google search for the terms *online* and *community* produces just over 2 billion hits. The results of these searches mark not only the degree to which the terms are conjoined but the degree to which Facebook has implanted itself as one of the key conduits for producing so-called online community. Trumpeting that it connects you 'to everything you care about' ('Connecting to Everything') and that it has built itself on a community of hundreds of millions of users (some 500 million at last count), community is at the core of Facebook's messaging about what makes it cool, socially worthy, and endlessly viable as a platform for building community but also as a platform for realizing Facebook's corporate profitability.

Forget that the Internet community is more often a euphemism for nested market groups of consumers to be targeted by sophisticated online ad campaigns, or that commercial advertising on the net has given birth to the putatively most powerful brand in existence (Google) associated with one of the most sophisticated and successful advertising strategies ever devised (99% of Google's revenue comes from advertising). Forget that the virtual world depends on the real components and resources that give it agency: the Internet is no more virtual than a garbage dump, in the sense that it takes material objects relayed globally to produce; it takes human beings' ingenuity and time to make it operate; and it takes enormous amounts of material resources to run it on a continuous basis.

Spam alone accounts for a staggering amount of energy consumption: a study 'commissioned by anti-virus software maker, McAfee, and produced by the consulting firm ICF International, found that spam emails worldwide wasted 33 billion kilowatt-hours of electricity in 2008, an amount equivalent to the electricity used in 2.4 million American homes. At the individual level, a single spam email emits only 0.3 grams of carbon dioxide into the atmosphere, but with an estimated 62 trillion spam emails sent worldwide in 2008, the cumulative emissions of spam are approximately 17 million metric tons of CO2 – a number equivalent to the emissions from approximately 1.5 million American homes' (Hurst). These numbers apply to the global spam traffic generated in 2008 – they are higher today. The real of the illusion is that online virtuality (the illusion of physical absence) actually masks significant allocations of resources, human and otherwise. Facebook reports that each month 'more than 30 billion pieces of content (web links, news stories, blog posts, notes, photo albums, etc.) [are] shared' on the site and its members spend roughly 700 billion minutes per month on the site ('Statistics'). As of 2009 Facebook was managing 'more than 25 terabytes of data per day in logging data ... the equivalent of about 1,000 times the volume of mail delivered daily by the U.S. Postal Service' on some 30,000 servers' (Miller). The implications of this amount of data circulating in this particular interface are staggering insofar as this distracted spectatorship produces a disembodied, virtual form of community (dis)engagement.

With 500 million members (roughly 1 in every 14 people on the planet) the online social networking firm is also a potent platform for selling advertising and for creating huge fields of data that can be mined for business purposes. The firm uses dubious techniques for producing friendship groups that are driven by marketing, whether it be vodka groups for teens who drink, or fashion groups that place significant pressure on those who become part of the network to buy certain categories of commercial product. The extraordinarily limited and juvenile ways of self-defining profiles on Facebook also produces a reductive, homogenizing effect where difference is all-too-often the cause for Facebook bullying and ridicule. The number of young girls who disturbingly self-identify using (unbeknownst to themselves) soft-porn visual techniques is astonishing, as is the degree to which clever design principles manage to infiltrate every Facebook page with an overwhelming amount of advertising targeting user groups (so-called communities) because algorithms have noted buying preferences or demographic spreads that are ideal for marketing specific products. Tellingly, a U.S. customer satisfaction study conducted in 2010 reveals that Facebook users rank it near the bottom:

> Facebook landed with notoriously despised airlines and cable television companies in the bottom 5 per cent of private companies ranked in a 2010 American Customer Satisfaction Index E-Business Report produced in partnership with ForeSee Results. 'Our research shows that privacy concerns, frequent changes to the website, and commercialization and advertising adversely affect the consumer experience,' ForeSee chief executive Larry Freed said in a release.' (AFP. 'Facebook membership')

Facebook's site-name riffs on a key component of enacted community agency, which we argue following on Wendell Berry, requires face-to-face material proximity and an embodied relationship to one's immediate physical environment. Facebook evokes face-to-faceness and community, many teens actively engaging in building up enormous quantities of 'friends' whose only presence in their life is as a digital file occasionally accessed and often in the most banal of terms. Digital intimacy is as much about distraction and absence as it is about revealing (often unknowingly because Facebook's privacy protocols are so opaque) personal details to people you have never met face-to-face. The real of the illusion here is that of a substantial distracted community of real people spending enormous quantities of time and effort creating virtual profiles as a mode of self-promotion often based on celebrity culture (as opposed to creating embodied communities with outcomes that do not play into this narcissistic logic). Like so many virtual technologies the interface becomes a strategic tactic for evading embodiment, where virtual presence is down- or uploaded as a deceptive simulacrum of material, physical presence. This latter form of necessary community embodiment remains the highest form of interactivity available to humans sadly too often distorted by virtual prosthetics.

Jaron Lanier the 'father' of virtual reality technologies and author of *You Are Not A Gadget: A Manifesto* opines, 'You have to be somebody before you can share yourself' (ix), a cutting dig at the vacuity of much of what passes as online digital community activity. Sharing requires something substantial to share for meaningful community to exist. Embodied community is predicated on being known by your community as an agent capable of determined, meaningful action: whether planting a tree in the local park, teaching school kids about science, serving as a crosswalk guard, or responding to a differently-abled neighbour's need. Embodied relational action that feeds the needs of the community is a precondition for community existing at all. Virtual community requires embodied action – a person at the keyboard sitting in front of equipment connected to a vast network of global servers that require power, maintenance, and human and mineral resources in order to exist. The problem is that the agency is disembodied but given tropes of active, illusory presence: surfing, trolling, creeping, rickrolling (an Internet meme in which a duplicitous hyperlink ostensibly points users to a relevant link but instead takes them to a Rick Astley video 'Never Gonna Give You Up'), hits, pokes, chats, crashes, hacks. It both *is* and *is not* real and an illusion simultaneously. In such a community the distraction lies in how the illusion of presence is manipulated: presence does indeed occur but heavily mediated by the material technologies of virtual agency, which disembodies and abstracts the agent from facing the community as a 'somebody' with 'something' to share. Facebook is neither a 'face' nor a 'book': but as a conveyor of advertising ideologies it makes effective use of its pretenses to being both a simulacral 'face" and a 'book' to humanize its agenda.

The range of criticisms levied at Facebook is worth noting not only because they invoke specific rights issues related to privacy and the purpose of online community:

> Facebook's growth as an Internet social networking site has met [with] criticism on a range of issues, especially the privacy of their users, child safety, the use of advertising scripts, data mining, and the inability to terminate accounts without first manually deleting all the content. Many companies removed their adverts from the site in 2008 because they were being displayed on the pages of controversial individuals and groups. The actual content of users' pages, groups and forums has been criticised for promoting controversial topics such as pro-anorexia and holocaust denial. There have been several issues with censorship, both on and off the site. The changes made by Facebook have been criticised, in particular the new format launched in 2008 and the changes in Facebook's

> Terms of Use, which removed the clause detailing automatic expiry of deleted content. Facebook has also been successfully sued several times for violation of intellectual property rights. ('Criticism of Facebook')

And more recently Facebook has been sued by holders of U.S. Patent 6,519, 629, who invented a 'system for creating a community for users with common interests to interact in' (Masnick). Patenting community is a remarkable extension of neoliberal logic and transformation of citizens into users who interact within a system. Yet this is precisely what Facebook has done, creating a massive platform that serves its commercial self-interest. Remarkable in all this is the exploitation of public commons resources, including the people spending billions of minutes on Facebook interactions and the actual physical resources required to sustain an upload rate of 30 billion items per month. Such a staggering amount of information is perhaps only meaningful to the data miners who capitalize on it, largely unbeknownst to the users providing the information. What might it mean for the users of Facebook to focus the 1797 years of effort spent on the site per month collectively on pressing issues related to social justice, to education, to the environment, to over-militarization? Imagine what other forms of human endeavour could be developed over 1797 years if it were guided by meaningful creativity.

Transparency on the ways in which the Palo Alto, California based privately-held company (founded in 2004) deploys advertising strategies and data mining techniques is a problem, in spite of the fact that in 2009 it generated revenues of approximately 800 million dollars: '"We can provide really good, relevant advertising to people because they tell us exactly what they are interested in, and who they know, and those people tell us what they're interested in," Facebook Chief Executive [Mark] Zuckerberg said at the All Things Digital conference [June 2010]' (Oreskovic). In other words, the ostensible purpose of community in Facebook terms is to provide the company with the information it needs to feed advertisers in order to optimize their selling strategies. Moreover 2010 reports from the Electronic Frontier Foundation (EFF) following on reporting done by the Wall Street Journal reveal that 'Despite Facebook's various polices and promises about users' privacy when using apps, apps have been feeding Facebook users' information to advertisers and Internet tracking companies regardless of the individual user's Facebook privacy settings' (Esguerra). Earlier in the year EFF had reported that 'Facebook was caught leaking the exact same data to advertisers. At the time, Facebook promised to fix the problem, but it's clear that their so-called fixes failed to apply to the more than half a million apps available on the site' (ibid.). Even more ominously, a 12 October 2010 report from EFF released a report based on a Freedom of Information lawsuit on social networking it had filed with the help of the University of California Berkeley's Samuelson Clinic. The documents reveal government surveillance of individuals using social networking sites 'to investigate citizenship petitions and the Department of Homeland Security's use of a "Social Networking Monitoring Center" to collect and analyze online public communication during President Obama's inauguration' (Lynch). A disclosed May 2008 memo from the Office of Fraud Detection and National Security (FDNS) revealed a cynical read on the surveillance potential of social networks like Facebook as a source of intelligence information for the government. A key passage from the memo states:

> Narcissistic tendencies in many people fuels a need to have a large group of 'friends' link to their pages and many of these people accept cyber-friends that they don't even know. *This provides an excellent vantage point for FDNS to observe the daily life of beneficiaries and petitioners who are suspected of fraudulent activities.*
>
> This social networking gives FDNS an opportunity to reveal fraud by browsing these sites to see if petitioners and beneficiaries are in a valid relationship or are attempting to deceive [United States Citizen and Immigration Services or USCIS] about their relationship. *Once a user posts online, they create a public record and timeline of their activities. In essence, using MySpace and other like sites is akin to doing an unannounced cyber 'site-visit' on a [sic] petitioners and beneficiaries.* (ibid.; emphasis added by EFF)

EFF's report notes that the memo suggests 'USCIS is specifically instructing its agents to attempt to "friend" citizenship petitioners and their beneficiaries on social networks in the hope that these users will (perhaps inadvertently) allow agents to monitor their activities for evidence of suspected fraud, including evidence that their relationships might not live up to the USCIS' standard of a legitimate marriage' (ibid.). The permeability of social networks to intrusive monitoring, surveillance, data mining, and other forms of exploitation of which the end-user is unaware marks these spaces in their underlying community reality as remarkably productive for state and corporate interests related to intelligence gathering and profit.

Facebook's capacity to 'capture' profiles is perhaps only matched by its reluctance to delete them – that is, to give end-users the power over their own data. The facility with which one can join is in inverse proportion to the difficulty in completely removing your file and its data traces. Community under these conditions is a laughable term, but nonetheless highly commodifiable because it is used as a platform to sell a perceived ethics of encounter that generates the membership that in turn generates the data fields that make Facebook its profit. The Facebook Blog states, disingenuously,

> Facebook has always been about helping people make connections. We started with helping people connect with their friends, and over time we expanded this model to mirror more of the connections you make in your life – including organizations and interests that may not be people. We developed Pages, for example, so you could connect to your favorite celebrities, musicians and businesses on Facebook. All of these say something about who you are and the things you care about. ('Connecting to Everything')

In this context, connecting to celebrity and business and musicians means digital contact of the most managed and trivial kind: parasitic marketing that feeds off of people's inadequacies and need for validation via such illusory contact. Why people need help connecting with their friends if they are really friends is something wholly set aside by this fatuous pitch. Nonetheless, real people are expending real resources in the pursuit of such connections: again, the real of the illusion.

More importantly, the real of the illusion is that by contributing to an ostensible online community, distracted end-users think they are satisfying their own needs for connection when in reality those needs are providing Facebook with the very means to make itself profitable. The addition of so-called 'Community Pages' to the Facebook site in April 2010 is predicated on a putatively 'new' form of page 'dedicated to a topic or experience that is owned collectively by the community connected to it. Just like official Pages for businesses, organizations and public figures, Community Pages let you connect with others who share similar interests and experiences' ('Connecting to Everything'). Community here is a function of a virtual ownership that is meaningless, since the real purpose of creating online communities in this context, is to provide the company with the information it uses to generate advertising revenue. What does it mean to own a community after all? The language in this sort of company blurb is insidious for how it imposes corporate terms on a commons where ownership is at the very least a highly contested term. Community in this sense is a fatuous excuse for business that creates an artificial commons whose purposes are obscured to participants in the commons (users of the system). 2010 estimates suggested that 40% of Facebook users were under the age of 25, an especially important demographic for advertisers trolling to create lifelong customers (Smith). Commonspace in this context is dominated by notions of property, of profit, and of end-users (as opposed to citizens with agency), and the aim of commonspace is to distract its users from the illusion of their non-community in commonspace so as to satisfy its own appetite for the very real data that enhances a corporatized community vision.

In July 1945, George Orwell published a short essay in *Leader Magazine* entitled 'Personal notes on Scientifiction.' By scientifiction, Orwell meant 'steel robots, invisible men, prehistoric monsters, death rays, invasions from Mars' (Orwell 884) – the stuff of cartoons associated with *Marvel Comics* and *Famous Funnies*. Orwell read these fantasies as 'disquieting,' claiming that they 'stimulate fantasies of power, and in the last resort their subject matter boils down to magic and sadism ... The whole thing is just a riot of nonsensical sensationalism with [no] genuine scientific interest ... Who reads these papers is uncertain. Evidently they are intended primarily for children, but the advertisements and the ever-present sex-appeal suggest that they are read by adults as well' (884-85). The real of the illusion here involves manipulating reality in such a way as to give the illusion of empowerment and magic while undercurrents of sadism and sex are framed by advertising – that is, the larger economic context that the medium serves.

The parable implicit in Orwell's reading is applicable to Facebook and other illusory models of online community, where 'magic' technologies putatively connect and empower people, while at the same time serving larger economic imperatives that have no real interest in community except as a mode of generating self-interested profit. The magic and the sex distract, and yet are sustained by the ethical status of their reflecting the so-called community, while the dirty business of profiting from that distraction marches inexorably forward. Illusory community here generates real profit. What might it mean in this context to posit community as outside the corporate logic of ownership and the corresponding fantasies of power Orwell discerned to be at work in popular culture? What 'face' might a commons have that is outside the logic of exploitation, animated by the embodied, attentive agency driven by imperatives other than economic gain?

Particulated Community vs. Interconnected Communities: The Challenges of Viral Resistance

Orwell's penchant for laying bare uncomfortable realities was not limited to his cynical take on comic-book fantasies. In his discussion of pacifist and anarchist communities published in the *Manchester Evening News* in February 1946, he argues that

> The pacifist and anarchist ideal can only be realised piecemeal, if at all. Hence the idea, which has haunted anarchist thought for 100 years past, of self-contained agricultural communities, within which the classless, non-violent society can exist, as it were, in small patches. At different times such communities have actually existed in various parts of the world – in nineteenth-century Russia and America, in France and Germany during the between-war years, and in Spain for a brief period during the Civil War ... The trouble with such communities is that they are never genuinely independent of the outside world, and that they can only exist so long as the State, which they regard as their enemy, chooses to tolerate them. In a wider sense the same criticism applies to the pacifist movement as a whole. (1014-15)

Orwell's sensible assessment of communities at odds with power structures on whose whim they depend amounts to a monumental challenge: how to change the terms of engagement between state practices of oligarchic resource and power allocations, and diverse communities within that framework that embody differential values or seek to change the terms of the relationship. Further, Orwell's reading excludes analysis of so-called successful (perversely so) models of non-State entities, like corporations, that have undermined or gotten around the preeminence of both the state and the local, natural community as the ultimate arbiter of relations to the commons.

The problem in these sorts of Orwellian nihilistic analyses is that envisioning social justice requires diverse frameworks for enacting communities in difference as an embodied aspect of being human. Recognized rights that place communities in clear, equitable relation to the commons – the rights of community, in other words – are a crucial way of understanding basic social relationships and practices of encounter across multiple levels of social organization. Communities that enact differential values, like anarchist and pacifist communities, or like communities that do not define themselves by such terms but adhere to values associated with pacifism and/or anarchism, do not exist in necessary isolation from each other. Interconnected, diverse forms of networked communities that learn to share values and to organize resistance to impositions that threaten their way of life or long-term survival *do* represent a potentially powerful political force.

Viral contagion of ideas spread within such a community can have extraordinary resilience and staying power: thus even though it may be reductive to invoke a notion of the African American community because to do so is to homogenize complex and real differences under that rubric, the civil rights movement that sought to end segregation and racism targeting that group, nonetheless was able to mobilize significant portions of the social justice community to produce change. Similar types of viral resistance to inequity and injustice have produced other forms of change-provoking resistance, including the Via Campesina movement,[3] the organics movement located in the Navdanya network associated with Vandana Shiva's activism in India (currently found in 16 states across India including 54 community seed banks and an educational program that has trained some 500,000 farmers ('*Navdanya*'), and even the rights movement itself with its varied strategies for addressing abuses and violations in multiple, complex circumstances (inclusive of the aboriginal rights movement, feminist and gay rights movements, the farm animal rights movement, the digital rights movement, the disability rights movement, and the immigrant rights movement, to mention only a few).

Stand-alone communities of the sort envisaged by Orwell are doomed to failure and Orwell had yet to witness the massive changes in networking and politically-effective organization that were to come in the 60s and later. But, by contrast, interlocked structures of diverse communities that establish community of rights objectives have proven to be a powerful structure for resisting inequitable distributions of power that privilege state oligarchies and corporate (shareholder) self-interest. Furthermore, there are emergent forms of governance related to states like the United Nations and the European Union that imagine macro-relations among states and the nested communities those states represent.

Xavier Groussot, in his study *General Principles of Community Law*, notes that, 'whenever a European citizen is lawfully present in the territory of another Member State and exercising Community rights, he [sic] will be entitled to protection of his fundamental rights as defined by Community law. The European Convention on Human Rights (ECHR) represents an essential element of the fundamental rights protection. The ECHR may go further than the protection afforded at the national level. Accordingly, the EC [European Community] national can invoke such a potential higher standard so as to object to any human rights violation' (292). Though case law in this area is still highly contentious, the challenge such a community-oriented structure presents is a supra-State standard of rights behaviours that is enforceable because agreed upon by all members of the community. In such a situation the community standard, in other words, potentially trumps individual state interests, especially so when it is a community of communities that agrees to an overarching standard.

In a 2010 interview German social philosopher Jürgen Habermas argues that, 'Time and again, a sufficient equilibrium between the market and politics was achieved to ensure that the network of social relations between citizens of a political community was not damaged beyond repair. According to this rhythm, the current phase of financial market-driven globalisation should also be followed by a strengthening of the international community' (Jefferies).

The International Criminal court (ICC), as one example of this potential strengthening of international community, is the first permanent international judicial body with the right to try individuals for genocide, crimes against humanity, war crimes, and the crime of aggression. Even though the ICC presumes international standards, it is important to remember, as the 2010 Amnesty International Report points out, that 81 countries have not signed on to the ICC including seven G20 countries. The 111 countries to have joined the Court as of March 2010 including almost all of Europe and South America, only account for a minority of the global population. Additionally, Israel, Sudan, and the United States have unsigned the Rome Statute that created the ICC, effectively releasing them from any legal obligations arising from their original signature of the statute. This points to a significant failure by the so-called international community to address global issues of injustice. The ICC is but one aspect of a complex web of global abnegations of rights responsibilities, and one of the reasons why talk of a global community is so risible: impunity for torturers exists in at least 61 countries; freedom of expression is restricted in at least 96 countries; there are prisoners of conscience in at least 48 countries and unfair trials in at least 55 countries ('Facts and Figures').

According to Geoffrey Bindman, one of the biggest challenges facing rights from within a community of rights context is acceptance of the principle that rights are universal and 'should be recognized as binding on all nation-states. The international community and other states should be able to enforce these rights even against the will of states that have failed to act against human rights violators in their own territories. That is what we mean by universal jurisdiction over human rights' (160). The plodding movement toward these sorts of supra-state global community constitutional rights structures – like the International Criminal Court (ICC), which presumes international standards of rights comportment – shows the degree to which community-based structures for imagining rights have yet to be implemented or to be made thinkable and enforceable. Our book advocates both movement in this direction at the global (or global-regional) level and more localized initiatives that instate community-based modes of thinking about equity, diversity, and sustainability in relation to all aspects of the commons. Such a movement will require both realistic thinking outside state structures and alternative thinking from within those same structures to establish a meaningful notion of the rights of community within a global community of rights.

A crucial issue in going forward on these initiatives arises from how community meaning is tied to ideologically restrictive legal definitions (or the wholesale absence thereof except in very particular application of statutes that frequently entail the notion of property). Remarkably, legal definitions of community can mean, variously: the body of the people, the right of all people to use all things according to the laws of nature, corporations and the body politic, and, especially in French civil law, the partnership formed in marriage that entails distribution and ownership of property ('Legal Definition of Community'). Over and above these general definitions are notions of community law arising from the European Union, seen as a community of states – the constitutional and charter rights arising from European states participating in the legal, economic, and cultural interchanges made possible by this social organization. These legal understandings are all problematic or potentially compromised by their reductive association of community with property; with the body politic, as if that cultural formation is the only form of community relation; with corporations as an expression of community, itself a highly vitiated notion especially when, as we show throughout this book, community interests and corporate interests are so often in conflict; and with the vague right of use that derives from natural laws, themselves always subject to mediation and interpretation by self-interested legal, political, or class[ed] communities.

In all these instances, community is undermined by the very framework in which its potential is constrained and in the ways in which it is made to fit to notions of property, economies of individual self-interest (class), state-driven conceptions of allowable forms of community, and the like. Our view argues towards developing a notion of the rights of community that shifts the terms of the game, as in Ostrom's salutary analysis, by a radical rethinking of the way in which key terms like the commons have been defined in relation to how they are accessed and how negotiations to regulate equitable access to them are configured. As Ostrom stated in a 1986 lecture:

> Scholars and government officials presume that all participants in situations with the structure of a PD [Prisoners Dilemma] game are necessarily trapped in the structure of the situation; as prisoners are trapped in their cells, participants are themselves trapped in their own mental apparatus. I shall argue that the structure is conceptually and methodologically necessary for analysis, but not an empirical necessity. The inability of participants to change the structure may be an empirical reality in some situations. It is not an empirical reality in many situations, however. ('Governing the Commons')

As discussed earlier, Ostrom's notion of common-pool resources is predicated on the individual user as a subtractive force in relation to other individual users, all subtracting from the common pool. Subtractive individualism is very much a problem for all common-pool resources, especially in the terms we have outlined above where the notion of the individual has been co-opted by corporate entities or where individual self-interest (whether manifested by an aggregate entity or a solitary person) trumps collective rights seen as a balance between desirable common good outcomes and individual liberties.

When collective rights have virtually no standing or meaning juridically, except in the vaguest and most diluted ways, how possible is it to move toward a vision of rights that addresses the realities of collective rights not privileging the individual? This opposition is, in our view, largely dysfunctional for excluding the additive potential implicit in diverse collective social formations, where individual and collective agencies are seen as co-generatively responsible for the sustainability of both forms of being in relation to the world.

The Ends of Community: Rethinking the Commons

Ostrom's insights into collective action, as one summary puts it, understand that 'all efforts to organize collective action, whether by an external ruler, an entrepreneur, or a set of principals who wish to gain collective benefits, must address a common set of problems.' These problems are 'coping with free-riding, solving commitment problems, arranging for the supply of new institutions, and monitoring individual compliance with sets of rules' ('Governing the Commons'). Ostrom's research suggests that groups able to organize and govern their behavior successfully are marked by the following design principles:

1 Group boundaries are clearly defined.
2 Rules governing the use of collective goods are well matched to local needs and conditions.
3 Most individuals affected by these rules can participate in modifying the rules.
4 The right of community members to devise their own rules is respected by external authorities.
5 A system for monitoring members' behavior exists; the community members themselves undertake this monitoring.
6 A graduated system of sanctions is used.
7 Community members have access to low-cost conflict resolution mechanisms.
8 For CPRs [common-pool resources] that are parts of larger systems: appropriation, provision, monitoring, enforcement, conflict resolution, and governance activities are organized in multiple layers of nested enterprises. (ibid.)

This set of conditions for organization and governance overlooks one major problem: that organization and governance are *not* the ends in and of themselves of collective action, and that undue focus on these aspects of community distract from sustainability, adaptation, and long-term renewal – the cultural survival of the community as it adapts to changing circumstances over extended periods of time.

Community is not always a cost-benefit analysis governed by dispositions of property, access to the commons, and the institutional structures of governance. Organization and governance are necessary conditions of some communities, but not necessarily their *raison d'être*. Survival and the flourishing of community in all its dimensions requires the capacity for renewal and for response to changing contingencies: often institutional structures that stand in for communities oppose this sort of change out of self-interest, blindness, or the incapacity to respond quickly to circumstances, itself one of the signs of atrophied collectivities. This is not to say that organizations and institutions are not, and cannot be, elements of community relations that exist and do matter, but undue emphasis in discourses of community on these elements has made community a metonymy for economic and hegemonic self-interest, while relegating other defining aspects of community to the sidelines.

The underlying principle that individual and collective rights are indivisibly connected to the environment from which individuals and communities spring, and on which they depend for their long-term survival, is something that has largely been excluded from rights instruments associated with community. The Preamble to the April 2010 Cochabamba, Bolivia Universal Declaration of the Rights of Mother Earth, states that 'we are all part of Mother Earth, an indivisible, living community of interrelated and interdependent beings with a common destiny' and that 'in an interdependent living community it is not possible to recognize the rights of only human beings without causing an imbalance within Mother Earth.' The declaration also affirms that to 'guarantee human rights it is necessary to recognize and defend the rights of Mother Earth and all beings in her and that there are existing cultures, practices and laws that do so' ('Draft: Universal Declaration of the Rights of Mother Nature'). Some 62 years after the Universal Declaration of Human rights, in other words, there is momentum gaining to understand rights of all sorts as fundamentally tied to environmental and ecological imperatives, a topic we discuss at length in the next section.

The codification into law of seemingly commons-oriented practices has been ineffectual or disastrous, heavily slanted toward non-community oriented outcomes. The Pennsylvania-based Community Environmental Legal Defense Fund (CELDF), for instance, in its discussion of the 'rights of nature' recognizes that

> environmental protection cannot be attained under a structure of law that treats natural communities and ecosystems as property. By

> most every measure, the environment today is in worse shape than when the major U.S. environmental laws were adopted over thirty years ago. Since then, countries around the world have sought to replicate these laws. Yet, species decline worldwide is increasing exponentially, global warming is far more accelerated than previously believed, deforestation continues unabated around the world, and over-fishing by corporate trawlers in the world's oceans is pushing many fisheries to collapse. These laws – including the Clean Air Act, the Clean Water Act, and similar state laws – legalize environmental harms by regulating how much pollution or destruction of nature can occur under law. Rather than preventing pollution and environmental destruction, these laws instead codify it. In addition, under commonly understood terms of preemption, once these activities are legalized by federal or state governments, local governments are prohibited from banning them. ('Rights of Nature')

Important to recognize here is how alternative forms of community-building from within the legal system are challenging superstructures that normalize the abuse of equitable rights accruing to natural communities. Again, the lack of specific instruments that have teeth and are associated generally with the rights of communities (within the larger community of rights) presents a significant challenge to groups like the CELDF.

Property-based, corporate conceptions of the commons, codification of weak laws that permit environmental abuses, superstructures that override local community capacity to make laws that suit their local circumstances, all present a picture of a highly corrupt and severely disabled state system that is incapable of responding properly to the most significant challenge facing the community of communities that is this planet. The CELDF site details how

> For decades, people across the U.S. have formed neighborhood groups and organized themselves to block corporate assaults against their communities. Those citizens have confronted incinerator corporations, power corporations, factory farm corporations, sludge corporations, big-box retail corporations, water bottling corporations, waste-hauling corporations, 'development' corporations and others.
>
> While those efforts have led to some increased regulation of the ad-

> verse environmental impacts caused by those corporations, their efforts have failed to fundamentally challenge the legal authority that has been reserved for corporations – and their directors – that enables them to override community decision making with their own. Thus, while we see community after community fight to stop a new factory farm, a Wal-Mart, or mining, under our system of law communities don't have the power to simply say 'No.'
>
> Communities always ask us 'Why?' Why can't they – and not Smithfield Foods – decide what agriculture is going to look like in their community? Why can't they decide that Wal-Mart is too destructive to the local environment and economy and therefore doesn't have a proper place in their town? Why can't they pass a local law to prohibit longwall coal mining, which destroys rivers, streams, and other natural systems? ('Community Organizing')

The disempowering of local (natural) community needs by artificial collective structures of state, judiciary, and corporate intent have meant a radical degradation of the commons while at the same time producing monstrous inequities: exploitation of local community resources in the developing world almost always result in those communities not seeing equitable benefits. In the collectively written book titled *The High Cost of Cheap Oil* published by the World Rainforest Movement, the authors note that

> The prevailing development model is to a large extent based on oil, which has been imposed as one of the main energy sources for most human activities (industry, transportation, heating, cooking, etc.). However destructive its extraction and use may be, the main reason for its success is its cheapness. Because it is cheap, its continued use is enhanced and because its use increases, so does its extraction. In theory, oil companies should be extracting less oil to achieve a higher price and hence more profits. However – as happened during the past oil crises – a more expensive oil opens up opportunities for other sources of energy (e.g. solar, wind, biomass) to become economically competitive. And this is something oil companies fear very much.

This would explain why Occidental Petroleum, for instance, insists on trying to drill oil out of the U'wa indigenous peoples' territory

> in Colombia, in spite of their opposition and the ensuing damaging publicity this is entailing for the company. It would also explain why Shell and other multinationals continue to be active in the Ogoni territory in Nigeria in spite of the international outcry following the legal murder of Ken Saro Wiwa and the blatant human rights abuses linked to oil in that country. For oil to be cheap, the extraction rate must never diminish and new oil wells need to be identified and explored ... ('The High Cost of Cheap Oil')

Like the earlier cited example of the case involving the Waste Management Corporation and the state of Virginia, global economic imperatives trump local community interests while rights abuses proliferate. Even so-called 'glocal' solutions that involve consensus-building across global and local constituencies are mitigated by the degree to which economic structures based on profit and exploitation underpin the ways in which priorities are assigned. And the lack of sustained, properly resourced alternatives to this model only serves to reinforce the kinds of abusive rights situations that the U'wa or the Ogoni peoples are forced to endure:

> The major cost is of course human. In the tropics, oil extraction is carried out in areas inhabited by people. The rights of those peoples are disregarded and their territories are taken over and given in concession by the government to the oil companies. In many cases this leads to struggles against the companies and to official and unofficial repression and human rights abuses. All the resources, which since time immemorial had served to meet the needs of local indigenous peoples are degraded. Drinking water is poisoned. The air becomes polluted. Wildlife becomes scarce. Forests disappear. All this impacts on the health and livelihoods of local people.
>
> Oil extraction at the same time affects the health of the forest ecosystem. Firstly, oil exploration and extraction are direct causes of the deforestation of large areas of tropical forests and of the degradation of the forest as a whole through its impacts on water, air, wildlife and plants. Secondly, the oil activity constitutes an underlying cause of deforestation and forest degradation because it opens up the forest and thus creates the possibility for logging and forest conversion to agriculture and cattle-raising. ('The High Cost of Cheap Oil')

The oil industry's consistently rapacious practices that disrupt community commons worldwide are one example among many evident in the developing world: similar analyses can be made with regard to military industries, farming monocultures (especially those based on genetically modified organisms), forestry, and of course mining companies (coal, gold, diamonds, uranium).

An April 2010 report from Camberwell, Australia describes how the village commons, which had been in use since the 1890s 'as a place [for villagers] to keep their horses and dairy cows, and to let their children fish, swim and ride horses,' had been handed over, with state complicity, to a mining corporation:

> A pair of officers from the Department of Lands arrived, called together members of the [Camberwell] Common Trust, and told them the Crown land would be immediately ... turned over to the Ashton [coal] mine that looms over the Upper Hunter village in the form of a hollowed-out hill on the other side of the creek. This action is apparently part of a pattern, in which the [Australian] government uses its authority to seize common lands for mines. The secretary of the Camberwell Common Trust told the reporter, 'When we go to community meetings with the mines they are always talking about what they will do "when" they get approval. They never say "if" they get approval.' Both mining companies and government do fairly well for themselves by enclosing the commons. The mining companies get access to the minerals, and the [Australian] government earns about $1.5 billion in royalties and fees from the region's mines each year. (Bollier)

This pattern of identifying freely held commons and public spaces and commodifying them for profit invariably leads to exploitation and the degradation of local communities. In the case of Camberwell, nearly two-thirds of the village population has given up the attempt to preserve the commons from the mining industry and has migrated elsewhere. At the same time a report by Alan Kennedy from the magazine *Mining Industry* noted how the coal-mine at Camberwell was constructed in a very short time, 'reflecting the new streamlined approval process for coal leases' (Kennedy, A.). There is no measurement for the sustained consequences of this sort of attack on the commons. But one study indicates that this sort of betrayal of the commons, when egregious enough, leads to significant political shifts. In her book *A Paradise Built In Hell: The Extraor-*

dinary Communities That Arise In Disaster, American author and activist Rebecca Solnit's analysis of the Chernobyl nuclear disaster is largely based on Mikhail Gorbachev's reading of one of the consequences of the disaster being the fall of the Soviet Union. Solnit points to how 'Part of the catastrophe was due to the secrecy that was by then habitual to Soviet bureaucrats, which endangered millions, and to the overall sense of unaccountable, incompetent, and callous government' (159). Calamitous mismanagement, in this case, helped cement the collapse of a major state power.

The cumulative effect of these sorts of attack on the commons is a major contributor to erosion of the public trust, a key element in the constitution of sustainable community relations. The failure to think through long-term consequences of attacks of all sorts on communities and community commons is a failure to understand the connections between all social beings, and the potential inherent in such failures to produce a radical reworking of the terms of social relations that have become inequitable. In all these examples, some of which we address at greater length further on in the book, the underlying pattern is one in which artificial collective entities usurp, deny, or abuse local, natural communities with the full support of legal structures and state-imposed practices of governance that are at odds with the interests of local community practice.

The global aggregate of local communities forms a commons that represents diverse irreplaceable practices of survival, sharing of multiple forms of knowledge and of spaces of encounter in co-generative ways that have stood the test of time. Sustained attacks on this global commons of communities not only degrades the material environment tied to those specific locales but also degrades the diversity of healthy natural communities that has traditionally been the source of human sustainability and renewal. These biodiverse aspects of the social or human commons are the result of extraordinary, long-term processes of adaptation that have been successful and that have utility insofar as they have allowed for the flourishing of life, a state of affairs that is now moving in the opposite direction with scientists estimating that the current number of species will be halved by 2100 ('Extinction').

Charles Darwin's *The Origin of Species*, refers multiple times to 'communities of descent,' part of a process by which species survival is articulated as a function of natural selection. For Darwin 'every production of nature' is one 'which has had a long history' and every 'complex structure and instinct' is the 'summing up of many contrivances, each useful to the possessor, in the same way as any great mechanical invention is the summing up of the labour, the experience, the reason, and even the blunders of numerous workmen' (361). Darwin's analogy is heavily tainted by the inescapable reference to industrial revolution tropes, which inflect his observation with a utilitarian telos. Unfortunately this presumptive analogy has been deformed to support industrialization and worker-bee arguments about essential aspects of humans' relations to the natural world, with the former privileged over the latter. Physical morphologies and natural selective processes though, and especially in the case of complex human behaviours, cannot be separated from ideological and epistemological formations that effect survival and species renewal. Practices of thinking that lead to the destruction of the very natural habitat that has made those practices possible, are ultimately untenable and contrary to the community self-interest of long-term survival. This state of affairs is one of the reasons why we argue for a rapid shift forward in theorizing and practicing rights via implementing policies that empower the rights of community within the larger framework of the community of rights.

Communities and what define them do not reside solely in technocratic definitions associated with 'nested enterprises,' 'sanction,' 'rules,' 'monitoring,' 'conflict of interest,' and the like, as Ostrom indicates in identifying her earlier cited criteria for success in community organization. Some of these same identifiers, successfully embodied, could be said to apply to extraordinary deformations of community, think fascist National State Socialism that led to the Nazis and the Holocaust. Ostrom's first category of success – 'Group boundaries are clearly defined' – in that case led to historic rights abuses and genocide based precisely on pathological notions of group identity that destroyed a pluralist, differential approach to the ethics of encounter. That category of success in conjunction with her fourth category, which articulates how the right of community members to devise their own rules is respected by external authorities, can produce perfect storms of ideological extremism that allow for radical attacks on communities in the form of genocide. The examples of the Holocaust and, more recently, of Rwanda (1994), where in both cases so called external authorities stood by (Chamberlain-ian appeasement or Clinton-ian non-intervention) until it was too late thus allowing for unthinkable atrocities to occur. In the case of Rwanda, as reported in *The Guardian* in 2004 by Rory Carroll,

> President Bill Clinton's administration knew Rwanda was being engulfed by genocide in April 1994 but buried the information to

> justify its inaction, according to classified documents made available for the first time. Senior officials privately used the word genocide within 16 days of the start of the killings, but chose not to do so publicly because the president had already decided not to intervene. Intelligence reports obtained using the US Freedom of Information Act show the cabinet and almost certainly the president had been told of a planned "final solution to eliminate all Tutsis" before the slaughter reached its peak. It took Hutu death squads three months from April 6 to murder an estimated 800,000 Tutsis and moderate Hutus and at each stage accurate, detailed reports were reaching Washington's top policymakers.' (Carroll)

We must also consider communities where observing sanctions and rules in Ostrom's terms meant perpetuating historic injustices, as was the case with African American diasporic community struggles that culminated in the Civil Rights movement of the 60s.

It is important to recognize that in this disputed terrain, *who* has the power to authorize a community or even to accept a community, as such, very often has a significant say in *how* that group of social relations gets defined. Interpretation of what the community means, who belongs to it, what its underlying framework is, how it allocates its resources, what it values, and what its purpose is – all matter and these key premises are often not critically examined and are produced arbitrarily or in the service of special interests that reside where power is to be found within a community. What to do when your imagined community is deemed to lie outside of such authorizations, is not seen as valid by external authorities, and where the '[r]ules governing the use of collective goods are well matched to local needs and conditions' ('Governing the Commons') only because a dominant group's self-interest says as much? In many instances the rules governing the use of collective goods are established and maintained by local needs and conditions that are a matter of interpretations arising from those who hold power.

Patriarchy and militarized responses to conflict are prime examples of gendered ways in which collective goods and the rules governing them are deformed to suit self-serving interpretations of local needs and conditions. The so-called war on terror waged by U.S. and other developed state (read: G8) interests is as much about the imperatives of creating local security state apparatuses as it is about feeding the pathological economies of the military-industrial complex. These no doubt serve, and are in neoliberal interpretations, well-suited policies to local needs and conditions. But from another vantage they are morally bankrupt (because they play the game of defending democracy by attacking its core principles) and indefensible in addition to being a colossal and criminal waste of precious resources, human and otherwise.

Creative communities, improvised communities, spiritual communities, anarchic communities, dissident communities, communities based on affection, family affiliation, and other forms of being in solidarity or co-creative relation to others, beloved communities[4] – even communities of solitude, that propose a spiritual, exemplary function to other forms of community, all are alternatives to thinking of community solely through the filter of institutional organization. Solnit, in her work on communities that arise from disaster and crisis, identifies how everyday life can become a social disaster when community relations prioritize the individual:

> Most traditional societies have deeply entrenched commitments and connections [among] individuals, families, and groups. The very concept of society rests on the idea of networks of affinity and affection, and the freestanding individual exists largely as an outcast and as an exile. Mobile and individualistic modern societies shed some of these old ties and vacillate about taking on others, especially those expressed through economic arrangements – including provisions for the aged and vulnerable, the mitigation of poverty and desperation – the keeping of one's brothers and sisters. The argument against such keeping is often framed as an argument about human nature: we are essentially selfish, and because you will not care for me, I cannot care for you ... Better yet, I will take your wealth and add it to mine – if I believe that my well-being is independent of yours or pitted against yours – and justify my conduct as natural law. If I am not my brother's keeper, then we have been expelled from paradise, a paradise of unbroken solidarities. Thus does everyday life become a social disaster. (3)

Community values can be as much about attacking essentialist discourses about human nature as they can be about overturning those assumptions and providing alternatives. In the case of essentialist discourses that argue for the underlying selfishness of humans, as described above by Solnit, or other arguments about the essential evil in human nature, our predisposition to war, it is important to recognize the self-serving ways in which these stereotypes self-propagate. The stories we tell about community and the values it embraces or struggles to achieve belong to an important, if largely ignored, repertoire both oral and written. Often, as in the case of greed- or death-based narratives that justify free-market or militaristic corporate structures, these narratives determine and justify egregious state or corporate abuses of community rights. Do these narratives mark the end of community or do they bring into perspective the real ends of community and collective action?

Community and Total War

American psychologist, Dacher Keltner, in one of many examples from his book *Born To Be Good* that overturn notions that humans are essentially evil, cites the work of American army lieutenant colonel S.L.A. 'Slam' Marshall. In 1947 Marshall published a study of soldiers under fire on the Pacific and European fronts called *Men Against Fire: The Problem of Battle Command*. The 'problem' identified by Marshall, resulting from hundreds of interviews with veterans of WWII, was that soldiers reluctantly fire on the enemy: only 15% of WWII riflemen 'had fired on the enemy during combat. Often soldiers refused to fire at the enemy with superior officers barking commands nearby and bullets zipping past their heads' (Keltner 52). As Keltner goes on to describe, 'In the wake of this revelatory finding, the army radically changed how it prepared soldiers to kill. Infantry training exercises played down the notion that shooting kills humans. Soldiers were taught to shoot at nonhuman targets ... The effects were dramatic. According to army estimates, 90 percent of soldiers in the Vietnam War fired at their enemies' (ibid.). Keltner goes on to cite Darwin's idea that individual habit shapes conduct: 'the social instinct, together with sympathy, is, like any other instinct, greatly strengthened by habit, and so consequently would be obedience to the wishes and judgment of community' (cited in Keltner 54). Crucial in Keltner's analysis, then, is the degree to which instincts that prohibit killing for instance are deformed by 'habit' that accustoms soldiers to killing, even if there are consequences like post-traumatic disorders. Here, a change in community practices with regard to how war is waged is also a change in narratives about the meaning of community and the values that govern it.

But the story is not quite so simple.

There is a widespread understanding that the use of psychotropic drugs by American combat personnel is a growing, significant problem:

ephedrine-based psychotropic medications can alleviate pain and stress reactions, while producing side effects that include sudden onset anger and sadism. In the so-called Tarnak Farm incident, two American F-16 pilots bombed a column of Canadian soldiers, 'accidentally' killing four and injuring eight on April 18 2002 in Afghanistan (near Kandahar). The two pilots were found to have been under the influence of amphetamine stimulants ('go-pills') and sedatives ('no-go pills') that they had taken prior to the bombing ('Tarnak Farm Incident'). The legal defense of the two American pilots involved, Major Harry Schmidt and Major William Umbach, was largely based on the two pilots having been told by superiors to use 'go pills' prior to their missions and the use of 'no-go pills' after their missions to calm down. The implications are simple: even the U.S. military's most highly trained fighters (at an approximate cost of training per pilot of $2.6 million [Hoffman]) have significant difficulty executing their tasks.

A June 2010 report stated that,

> The Defense Department's Military Health System cannot track the use of prescription medications, especially psychotropic drugs such as antidepressants, and antipsychotic drugs used by troops engaged in combat operations in Afghanistan and Iraq, according to a report released by the Senate Armed Services Committee on Monday. At a hearing in March, members of the Military Personnel Subcommittee of the Senate Armed Services Committee described widespread use of prescription drugs throughout the services and by deployed troops. Sen. Jim Webb, D-Va., estimated that one out of six service members is taking some form of psychiatric drug. Sen. Benjamin Cardin, D-Md., said internal Army studies showed that 12 percent of its troops in Iraq and 17 percent in Afghanistan have been prescribed either antidepressants or sleeping pills. Army statistics indicate 'we have an alarming use in the increase of antidepressants,' Cardin said. 'In 2005, there were a little over 4,000 combat troops using antidepressants. That's about 1 percent. By 2007, it grew to over 19,000, or 5 percent, of our troops on antidepressants. That's a huge increase in the use of antidepressants. And that number remained pretty constant for 2008.' (Brewin)

Similarly, a 2008 *Time Magazine* report noted that

> The increase in the use of medication among U.S. troops suggests

> the heavy mental and psychological price being paid by soldiers fighting in Iraq and Afghanistan ... Such ailments ... begin with mild anxiety and irritability, difficulty sleeping, and growing feelings of apathy and pessimism. As the condition worsens, the feelings last longer and can come to include panic, rage, uncontrolled shaking and temporary paralysis. The symptoms often continue back home, playing a key role in broken marriages, suicides and psychiatric breakdowns. (Thompson)

These reports only address prescribed drugs and do not deal with non-prescription recreational drug and alcohol abuse among the military. Even as state imperatives driven by 'might is right' thinking try to change the instincts of civil human beings not to kill each other via powerful techniques of indoctrination, these instincts are shown to be virtually impossible to eradicate either through behavioural training or psychiatric drugs. Killing others is, after all, a profoundly anti-social behaviour, at odds with community standards globally, except in the most egregious situations where civil community is under exceptional attack. And the percentage of human beings actively engaged in militarized killings is remarkably small in proportion to the total population of the planet, though this fact is masked by the fog-of-war rhetoric that invokes nations going to war against each other. Only the U.S., India, China, and Russia have troop complements of over a million soldiers (many of them not in active combat roles). Bolivia and Canada have roughly equivalent forces (56,500 and 66,949 respectively) – a statistically insignificant number of people in the context of the total global population of 6.6 billion ('List of Countries'). Nonetheless, these military forces use up a significant portion of resources and cause disproportionate misery and suffering.

Killing others may not be as instinctual and natural as some would make it out to be. Dehumanizing humans who for millennia have had to rely on adaptation skills involving co-operation and negotiation and a taboo on killing other humans (non-violence) is not so easy. The deep local community roots of such a predisposition to *not* kill have as much to do with the local intimate circumstances of kinship and trust that permit communities to remain stable and to survive over the long-term, except when their immediate circumstances are challenged by either internal or external aberrations. In the case of the Afghanistan and Iraq wars, a situation in which neither country has launched a direct attack on North American civilians and their local spaces (and moreover a situation in which the regimes in Afghanistan and Iraq being attacked by North

American military forces were either put in place or sustained by those very same forces) it may be exceedingly difficult to overcome instinctual urges that prohibit gratuitous attacks on communities that have not attacked you directly.

The Times of India reported in 2001 that a leading American expert on South Asia, Selig Harrison from the Woodrow Wilson International Centre for Scholars, had told a conference on terrorism and regional security that 'The CIA made a historic mistake in encouraging Islamic groups from all over the world to come to Afghanistan.' The U.S. provided $3 billion for building up these Islamic groups, and it accepted Pakistan's demand that they should decide how this money should be spent, Harrison said. Harrison ... told the gathering of security experts that he had meetings with CIA leaders at the time when Islamic forces were being strengthened in Afghanistan. 'They told me these people were fanatical, and the more fierce they were the more fiercely they would fight the Soviets,' he said. 'I warned them that we were creating a monster' ('CIA worked in tandem...').

If the Taliban emerged out of short-sighted U.S. foreign policy so too did Saddam Hussein's reign in Iraq, which received 28 years of U.S. support, beginning with the CIA underpinning in 1963 of the Ba'athist Party overthrow of General Abdel-Karim Kassem, who was assassinated with other leaders from a list supplied by the CIA. Hussein, one of the conspirators in the assassinations, came to power in 1979 and was supported in his war against Iran by American foreign policy. As American writer-activist Paul Rockwell states, in a summary of the ways in which U.S. foreign policy was closely interlinked with Hussein's war crimes:

> The victims of Saddam and his accomplices, Iranians as well as Iraqis, have a right to know: Who armed Iraq? Who built Saddam's arsenal of terror in the '80s? They also have a right to interrogate Rumsfeld, other U.S. officials, CIA agents, and U.S. arms merchants as suspects or witnesses. The executives of Alcoliac International of Maryland, that transported mustard gas precursors to Saddam; the Tennessee manufacturers that provided sarin-based [an organophosphorus compound used as a chemical weapon] chemicals; the heads of Dow Chemical who sold toxins that cause death by asphyxiation; the heads of Bechtel that produced chemicals for Saddam in their Iraqi plant; the CIA agents that made covert arms deals and transported heinous cluster bombs to a known war criminal – all the participants in Iraq's machine of death should come before

> an international court and answer a single question: What did you know, and when did you know it? It is not just the buyers, it is [the] suppliers of death who are accountable under the Nuremberg Conventions.' (Rockwell)

Rockwell's observations point to the structural imperatives that link business interest with military outcomes, part of the structure that demands soldiers and other operatives to make use of the materials of war that generate profit, political and economic, even if that usage goes against the very community values and prohibitions against killing that make civil society desirable.

When state imperatives to produce soldiers that will kill unthinkingly trump local community imperatives that associate community health with a prohibition on killing (except in truly exceptional circumstances), the stakes are high. Naturalizing unnatural, inhuman, and destructive (both self- and other-) behaviours produces a deformation of community, itself based on the dignity and respect for life (however tense or conflicted and imperfect that life-in-community may be). Respect for the dignity of life in difference is a fundamental interconnecting aspect of being that lays the groundwork for the reciprocal understandings, which in turn allow for diversity to co-exist and survive over extended periods. Communities in which localized values are disrupted in the name of state or corporate imperatives must retain the ability to critique and resist these disruptions. This ability for any community to self-critique and to propose alternatives to its (and others') dominant orthodoxies is a fundamental aspect of the ability to adapt. Failure to nurture this community asset predicts the almost certain death of that form of the community in the face of radical changes in circumstance, crisis, and the like.

Ostrom, in her co-edited book with Charlotte Hess, *Understanding Knowledge As A Commons: From Theory to Practice*, identifies adaptation as a key quality to institutional success. Again, we have significant issues with reductively troping community and collective action solely as a function of institutional undertakings. Community-responsive actions that challenge a community to adapt to inequitable circumstances, as was the case throughout the history of the American Civil Rights movement, was not solely a function of institutional behaviours, *pace*, Rosa Parks, the Little Rock Nine (who were the first black teenagers to attend the all-white Central High School in Little Rock, Arkansas in 1957), and any number of individuals and small groupings of people who took action in support of changing racist, segregated America. Ostrom's analysis argues that,

> Institutions must be designed to allow for adaptation because some current understanding is likely to be wrong, the required scale of organization can shift, and biophysical and social systems change. Fixed rules are likely to fail because they place too much confidence in the current state of knowledge, while systems that guard against the low-probability, high-consequence possibilities and allow for change may be suboptimal in the short run but prove wiser in the long run. (Hess and Ostrom 68)

What Ostrom's argument does not address is what happens when change is required but stagnant institutions with entrenched self-interests refuse to act. Whether in the case of the wasteful allocation of resources to militarized expenditures that benefit small elites, or in the case of climate change where global communities are certain to be radically affected if no action is taken (or if diluted action is taken too late), it becomes the duty of the emergent community to place itself in opposition to the vested interests that refuse to adapt. Thus the notion of oppositional community formation is one of the key principles for restoring meaning to the term as it has come to stand for entrenched hegemonic interests.

A July 2010 *Globe and Mail* report out of Baghdad stated that 'The U.S. Defense Department is unable to properly account for over 95 per cent of $9.1-billion in Iraqi oil money tapped by the U.S. for rebuilding the war ravaged nation, according to an audit released Tuesday. The report by the U.S. Special Investigator for Iraq Reconstruction offers a compelling look at continued laxness in how such funds are being spent in a country where people complain basic services like electricity and clean water are sharply lacking seven years after the U.S.-led invasion that toppled Saddam Hussein ... The funds are separate from the $53-billion allocated by Congress for rebuilding Iraq' (El-Tablawy). Money earmarked for restoring basic necessities to the Iraqi people, in other words, and money derived from their considerable oil holdings, has been mismanaged by the U.S. Defense Department. This pattern of resource-concentration in military undertakings without real accountability is a major problem for re-appropriating to the commons resources it needs for its own survival.

As of 2010, the global situation is extremely bleak. Global Issues editor Anup Shah reports the following using the Stockholm International Peace Research Institute's (SIPRI) findings (2010):

- World military expenditure in 2009 is estimated to have reached \$1.531 trillion in current dollars;
- This represents a 6 per cent increase in real terms since 2008 and a 49 per cent increase since 2000;
- This corresponds to 2.7 per cent of world gross domestic product (GDP), or approximately \$225 for each person in the world;
- The USA with its massive spending budget, is the principal determinant of the current world trend, and its military expenditure now accounts for just under half of the world total, at 46.5% of the world total;

SIPRI has commented in the past on the increasing concentration of military expenditure, i.e. that a small number of countries spend the largest sums. This trend carries on into 2009 spending. For example,

> The 15 countries with the highest spending account for over 82% of the total;
> The USA is responsible for 46.5 per cent of the world total, distantly followed by China (6.6% of world share), France (4.2%), UK (3.8%), and Russia (3.5%). (Shah)

In light of these remarkable indicators of excessive, imprudent resource allocation to military expenditures what might an oppositional community practice that overturns this failed model of community mismanagement look like?

One form of oppositional practice entails communities of practice that respond to crisis and disasters where the state shows itself to be unprepared, incompetent, or unwilling. Solnit's book, which we reference earlier, is a remarkable reading of multiple case studies – from the Halifax explosion in 1917 that killed some 2000 people and injured some 9000, to the post-Hurricane Katrina debacle in 2005, which killed close to 2000 people and displaced thousands more – in which disaster produces unique instances of spontaneous, improvised community where altruism, solidarity, selfless giving, and the like are firmly in evidence as components of the intangible social capital that give community meaning. Multiple other instances of this are to be found wherever crisis and community collide.

Community discourse that focuses on the rules of social engagement as a matter of institutional imperatives fails to recognize the degree to which the intangible qualities that comprise a community's social capital – its capacity to engender volunteer extra-institutional agencies in the face of challenge – are determinative of community meaning. Such meaning differs significantly from disconnected state narratives of cultural hegemony or imperial imperatives, and restricted and highly codified structures of conflict management.

Total war of the kind we are now witnessing is unthinkable in such a context, though it is allegedly conducted in response to security threats caused by terrorism. This is so because it threatens all those who wish to survive and one of its predicates is the breakdown of the essential difference between civilians and non-civilians in ways that lead to heightened abuses and violations of basic rights both of the individual and of the community in which the individual lives. Former Canadian Prime Minister Lester Pearson (1963–68) articulated a vision of international community-building based on his own experiences of war, both as a soldier (stretcher-bearer for the Canadian Army Medical Corps) in WWI and as a civilian during WWII and the Cold War. In his acceptance speech for the 1957 Nobel Peace Prize, Pearson stated: 'The stark and inescapable fact is that today we cannot defend our society by war since total war is total destruction, and if war is used as an instrument of policy, *eventually we will have total war*. Therefore, the best defense of peace is not power, but the removal of the causes of war, and international agreements, which will put peace on a stronger foundation than the terror of destruction' (Pearson; our emphasis). Pearson could not have anticipated the way in which the concept of total war was to insinuate itself into state thinking post 9/11, a way of addressing issues of security profoundly at odds with the peacemaking through international agreement he advocated. Nor could he have imagined the degree to which state structures of agreement would be undermined by special interests that included the military-industrial complex.

Though exact figures are difficult to achieve in civilian casualties, Matthew White's website estimates the number of twentieth-century civilian dead as the result of hemoclysm, 'that string of interconnected barbarities which have made the Twentieth Century so fascinating for historians and so miserable for real people.' White's estimates are roughly parceled out between the two World Wars and the state sanctioned sponsoring of civilian killings by Communist China and the Soviet Union, 'which together account for maybe 3/4 of all deaths by atrocity in the 20th Century,' to be in the order of 141.5 million deaths (White,

M.) – figures for injuries (*not* deaths) and the suffering caused by those injuries in the hemoclysm do not exist but they would be exponentially larger. Such monstrous numbers are so because they elide the specific suffering and consequences of each and every one of those deaths while also reducing the irreducible whole of rights violations and atrocities to a number that is intrinsically unfathomable. As if imagining that the 6 million dead figure associated with the Holocaust is anything but a number that cannot ever address the specificity of the unthinkable sufferings associated with that number.

The number of civilian deaths far outstrips the number of military deaths by war and is a major indicator of the utter failure of states that choose (total) war as a method of conflict resolution. The U.S.-Iraq war launched by George W. Bush to topple Saddam Hussein saw remarkable disproportion between civilian and military deaths. As of July 2010, approximately 4414 American soldiers and 1487 contracted paramilitaries were dead as opposed to somewhere between 97,000 and 106,000 Iraqi civilians dead since 2003 and the war's inception. These numbers tell only part of the story of people wounded by the war, with some 31,897 American soldiers wounded (1135 amputees among them) and an unconfirmed number of Iraqi civilians wounded (in 2007 alone a reported 34,500 Iraqi civilians died) (Fisk). As a result of an October 2010 release of classified documents by WikiLeaks, 'Iraq Body Count, a private British-based group that has tracked the number of Iraqi civilians killed since the war began, said it had ... found 15,000 previously unreported deaths, which would raise its total from as many as 107,369 civilians to more than 122,000 civilians killed since the 2003 invasion ... Al Jazeera, one of several news organizations provided advance access to the WikiLeaks trove, reported the documents show 285,000 recorded casualties, including at least 109,000 deaths. Of those who died 66,000, nearly two-thirds of the total, were civilians' (Gearan and Burns). The numbers are skewed by undercounting, by challenges on the ground in getting accurate reporting on civilian casualties, and by methodologies influenced by different political factors – and by the politics of what these numbers mean in terms of the justifications used to sell the invasion.

In addition to these substantial casualty figures, as of November 4, 2006, 'the United Nations High Commissioner for Refugees estimated that 1.8 million Iraqis had been displaced to neighboring countries, and 1.6 million were displaced internally, with nearly 100,000 Iraqis fleeing to Syria and Jordan each month' ('Casualties'). All of this occurs within the contexts of over 700 billion dollars reportedly spent by the U.S. on the war with a long-term cost estimated at 3 trillion dollars for the 7-year war, a massive amount of resources that has facilitated the carnage (Lévesque).[5] The implications of these staggering numbers of casualties, refugees, and of resources allocated to the war are of profound consequence to multiple communities in which the localized dimensions of these numbers are given reality.

The Rome Statute that established the International Criminal Court in 1998 affirms that 'intentionally directing attacks against the civilian population' is illegal, but remarkably the Statute only came into effect on July 1, 2002 and has not been ratified globally (with Israel and the United States being major non-signatories). A 2005 *Human Rights Watch Report* noted that in the case of Israel,

> The Israeli military has fostered a climate of impunity in its ranks by failing to thoroughly investigate whether soldiers have killed and injured Palestinian civilians unlawfully or failed to protect them from harm ... Since the current Palestinian uprising began in 2000, Israeli forces have killed or seriously injured thousands of Palestinians who were not taking part in the hostilities. However, the Israeli authorities have investigated fewer than five percent of the fatal incidents to determine whether soldiers were responsible for using force unlawfully. The investigations they did conduct fell far short of international standards for independent and impartial inquiries. ('Israel: Failure to Probe Civilian Casualties')

Similarly, the recent release by WikiLeaks of more than 90,000 pages of detailed intelligence reports in the Afghan War Diaries, 2004–2010 tells the story of 'unreported incidents of Afghan civilian killings' (Dozier). Founder and editor of WikiLeaks, Julian Assange, in comments about the release of this intelligence noted that,

> we can see a broad range of suspicious events. 181 people killed with no proper description of why. On one day, only one person wounded, no captives and only one US soldier killed. Many of these events have a disparity and they need to be investigated. We also see hundreds, and there's probably thousands of, 'a child killed here, a girl killed there,' people taken to hospital, lots of corruption by the NDS – the Afghan Intelligence agency and of course Taliban abuses, IEDs and blowing up hotels and so on. (Jepson)

Assange holds up WikiLeaks as the 'vanguard of a particular ideal that justice comes about because of the disclosure of abuse' (Sachs) and the site's release of the Afghanistan material, while prompting a storm of international discussion, also pointed to the ways in which media all over the world are utterly failing to do the job of critically reporting on pressing issues related to military operations undertaken in the name of democracy. This is especially significant considering that the archive released by WikiLeaks 'shows the vast range of small tragedies that are almost never reported by the press but which account for *the overwhelming majority of deaths and injuries*' ('Kabul War Diary'; emphasis in original). Cover-ups of civilian casualties are also cover-ups of attacks on community, as in the operations of Task Force 373, 'a secret US Special Forces assassination unit ... exposed in the Diary' and responsible for, among others, 'a raid that lead to the death of seven children' (ibid.).

David Leigh reports in *The Guardian*'s analysis of the WikiLeaks War Diaries that

> Behind the military jargon, the war logs are littered with accounts of civilian tragedies. The 144 entries in the logs recording some of these so-called 'blue on white' events cover a wide spectrum of day-by-day assaults on Afghans, with hundreds of casualties. They range from the shootings of individual innocents to the often massive loss of life from air strikes, which eventually led President Hamid Karzai to protest publicly that the US was treating Afghan lives as 'cheap.' When civilian family members are actually killed in Afghanistan, their relatives do, in fairness, get greater *solatia* [compensation] payments than cans of beans and Hershey bars. The logs refer to sums paid of 100,000 Afghani per corpse, equivalent to about £1,500. US and allied commanders frequently deny allegations of mass civilian casualties, claiming they are Taliban propaganda or ploys to get compensation, which are contradicted by facts known to the military. But the logs demonstrate how much of the contemporaneous US internal reporting of air strikes is simply false. (Leigh)

Such investigative reports clearly show how state security is the justification for falsehoods that obscure the effects of war: these effects represent a sustained attack on community rights with long-term consequences for the communities that have to deal with the legacy of the violence they suffer. State security in this context must be understood as protecting the governments responsible for such actions from its own citizens' repugnance at the violence committed in their name. And they perpetrate a perverse logic of compensatory payments for lives lost, a cost-benefit approach to death that is violently at odds with the lived reality that the death of a member of a community actually represents. How many dollars, how many cans of beans or Hershey bars are the measure of human loss? The question itself is absurd and insulting and amounts to a corporate-state delusional vision of how to treat the victims of violence, a compensation technology severely at odds with community-based means of grieving and redressing the gratuitous and violent loss of life.

The language of collateral damage, friendly fire, compensatory payment, and severity metrics, in concert with the lack of attention paid to civilian casualties by military and state reporting all whitewash the degree to which war generally has mutated into an attack on civilian communities across the globe. A 2008 report by the Carnegie Council for ethics in international affairs noted that, 'The Pentagon has ... released optimistic figures about violence in Iraq. What they neglect to say is that while overall violence has declined there in the last few months, civilian deaths at U.S. hands increased approximately 70 percent in 2007 over the prior year. Non-combatant death at U.S. hands grew in Afghanistan by a similar percentage' (Crawford). The casual, barbarous disregard for civilian life in the name of state self-interest (and the disinformation relating to so-called non-combatants/civilians) marks another aspect of total war on the specific communities and living commons, where these deaths are suffered by their children, women, and elderly.

Even soldiers who revert to being civilians are subject to this systematic pattern of attacks on civilian populations that include abuses and violations of their rights. These attacks have profound localized effects for the families and communities that must directly face the overwhelming consequences of civilian injustices wrought by the systematic practice of total war. In the U.S. a 2010 report reveals that

> Suicides among United States military veterans ballooned by 26 percent from 2005 to 2007, according to new statistics released by the Veterans Affairs (VA) department. 'Of the more than 30,000 suicides in this country each year, fully 20 percent of them are acts by veterans,' said VA Secretary Eric Shinseki at a VA-sponsored suicide prevention conference on Monday. '*That means on average 18 veterans commit suicide each day*. Five of those veterans are under our care at VA.' The spike in the suicide rate can most clearly be attrib-

uted to the ongoing wars in Iraq and Afghanistan and the high number of veterans returning to the U.S. with post-traumatic stress disorder (PTSD). 'We have now nearly two million vets of Iraq and Afghanistan and we still haven't seen the type of mobilisation of resources necessary to handle an epidemic of veteran suicides,' Aaron Glantz, an editor at New America Media editor and author of "The War Comes Home," told IPS. (Clifton; our emphasis)

While astronomical amounts are spent on fighting wars (and producing inordinate numbers of civilian casualties), dealing with their aftermaths both in rebuilding war-ravaged civilian zones and in addressing the health needs of veterans gets barely a drop in the bucket. Too many examples exist of this systematic undermining of local civilian needs by the logic of total war. A 2009 *Washington Post* article reported that

Steven Napper and Robert Ranghelli blew the whistle on the unethical and unsanitary conditions at the National Funeral Home. Napper and Ranghelli reported that bodies destined for burial at Arlington National Cemetery were left, sometimes for months, on unrefrigerated racks because coolers were full and the company did not want to spend money on additional coolers. They stated that the facility stored as many as 200 bodies in unrefrigerated areas, including the garage, and that the bodies, sometimes fully exposed, leaked fluids on the floor. (Williams 2009)

Add to this lugubrious scenario the shocking statistics around homelessness and veterans in the U.S. where 'Only eight percent of the general population can claim veteran status, but nearly one-fifth of the homeless population are veterans' ('National Coalition'). Moreover,

the nation's homeless veterans are predominantly male, with roughly five percent being female. The majority of them are single; come from urban areas; and suffer from mental illness, alcohol and/or substance abuse, or co-occurring disorders. About one-third of the adult homeless population are veterans. America's homeless veterans have served in World War II, the Korean War, Cold War, Vietnam War, Grenada, Panama, Lebanon, Afghanistan and Iraq (OEF/OIF), and the military's anti-drug cultivation efforts in South America. Nearly half of homeless veterans served during the Vietnam era. Two-thirds served [the U.S.] for at least three years, and one-third

> were stationed in a war zone. Roughly 56 percent of all homeless veterans are African American or Hispanic, despite only accounting for 12.8 percent and 15.4 percent of the U.S. population respectively. About 1.5 million other veterans, meanwhile, are considered at risk of homelessness due to poverty, lack of support networks, and dismal living conditions in overcrowded or substandard housing. (ibid.)

Homelessness materially embodies a state of alienation from community. Hence, returning soldiers are doubly compromised by not only their participation in the destruction of communities elsewhere, but also by the ways in which their actions lead to disorders that undermine their relations to their home communities. The racialization of the vast suffering that the above statistics barely hint at is also significant as an indicator of ethical community comportment as is the perceived threat of homelessness to such a vast number of at-risk people (some 1.5 million veterans). Incalculable damage is wrought upon communities by this sort of suffering produced by various injustices that begin with militarized responses to complex geopolitical realities, and then extend into the ways in which service to one's country becomes a convenient jingoist trope to justify war, while at the same time obscuring how the country's service to the individuals it employs in exercising its self-interest is shamefully inadequate.

In Canada, according to a report from Sean Bruyea, himself a veteran,

> When Canadian Forces members are injured on duty, they receive pain and suffering payments from Veterans Affairs while keeping their full salary. If soldiers are so disabled as to be unemployable, those soldiers are kicked out of the military and paid 75 per cent of their salary through a long-term disability plan held by the Canadian Forces. Then, in some seeming petty act of revenge, the Canadian Forces insurance plan deducts amounts for pain and suffering paid by Veterans Affairs. No other long-term disability income plan in Canada is allowed to deduct Veterans Affairs payments for pain and suffering. This is why Dennis Manuge has brought his case to the Supreme Court of Canada as his case represents more than 4,000 disabled soldiers similarly affected ... The National Defence Ombudsman has called the deductions 'profoundly unfair' and said 'the inequity might very well be serious enough to attract the protection of human rights legislation' including the Canadian Charter

> of Rights and Freedoms, 'which identify physical and mental disabilities as prohibited grounds of discrimination.' (Bruyea)

Ironically, Pat Stogran, the Canadian Veterans Affairs ombudsman who has proactively sought to rectify the situation (via a veterans Charter/Bill of Rights) was told his appointment would not be renewed in August 2010. As is so often the case with rights instruments that largely serve to window-dress injustices, the gap between the stated goals of the veterans charter and the implementation of meaningful rights outcomes is enormous and the subject of considerable outrage.[6] These brief examples highlight the degree to which total war makes rights victims of even the soldiers who fight on its behalf when they return to being civilians. State self-interest and corporate cost-benefit analyses responses to the complex problems of re-integration trump the real-life problems of severely traumatized soldiers who have done the State's bidding (usually in highly dubious and remarkably under-debated military undertakings like the wars in Iraq and Afghanistan). Hence, community fractures on both sides of the total war equation, underlining the vulnerability of civilian and community formations that need collective and meaningful rights protections.

Total war's reductive logic of complicity in abuses and violations of the basic predicates of human and biotic interconnectedness is one deeply inimical to achieved civil communities all over the globe. From within the contexts of the community of rights in which communities are also thought to have rights (the rights *of* community), then, it is important to recognize how narratives of right and wrong are constructed in light of state and corporate imperatives that, as we have shown throughout this section, instate their own self-interest at the expense of local community ecologies and autonomous, interlinked structures of knowledge and conflict resolution.

John Cheney's 2004 study on 'Land Conflict Resolution within an Autonomous Space,' examines community and land relations in eastern Nicaragua with respect to the 'culturally significant and vital aspect of land to indigenous and ethnic groups inhabiting this region [that] has made for conflicts ... over the process of demarcation of community lands [among] the communities themselves, the state, and *terceros* – or third-party peasants entering into indigenous or ethnic communal property' (4). His conclusions suggest that community autonomy and localized shared cultures to be found in community are key aspects of successful conflict-resolution – more so than state intervention:

> The common mode of communication, be it language, sense of history, or sense of culture, all play into the success of the resolution of conflicts without obstacles, problems, or the continuation of unresolved struggles – be they violent or not. The importance of autonomy in this aspect is quite obvious, as the acceptance of local languages and customs to be taught and practiced in communities not only preserves what is culturally significant to indigenous and ethnic people, but it continues the common outlook and history of groups that aids conflict resolution between two culturally similar groups. The influence and intervention of the central government, for example, ruins such a common balance. (Cheney 33)

Central governments lack the embodied, sustained presence that makes possible diverse and nuanced responses to complex problems – and are driven by their own overriding self-interest in ways that undermine other forms of community priority- and decision-making. Like any monoculture that seeks to reduce to singular purposefulness a host of bio-diverse practices, contingencies, and knowledges, governance in this form is deeply antithetical to the very communities from which this diversity arises. What might it mean to think of the rights of community from within a system of governance predicated on the community of rights that emerge from such diversity of practice?

Community and Meaning: The Problem of Relational Contingencies

The word-use and concepts associated with community vary widely. There is no adequate definition that can possibly contain the multiple forms of practice, emergent and embedded, associated with the specificity and diversity of communities the world over. It can be argued that community per se does not exist: it is always emergent, a function of practices that change, that often are oppositional or differential, and not given to static definition. As a metaphor for relational contingencies, community becomes an event-horizon of the possible: an always-to-be-achieved potentiality that emerges from the web of histories, material realities, traditions, and adaptive, improvised contexts that occur when people are in proximity to each other for the purposes of affiliation, creation, renewal, sustainability, and survival.

We articulate a specific notion of community as a relationship largely defined by material proximity and common(s) interests shaped by the most basic practices that guarantee sustainable life: food, water, shelter, an ecosystem that is renewable, and cultural values, that however differential, are largely understood as a product of the mutual respect for difference that enables survival. Communities understood in this sense are not isolated, impenetrable entities but rather, living complex organisms with multiple shifting characteristics that are as much a function of internal relations within the community as they are of external relations with contingencies beyond the immediate community. Notions of community dominated by the master narrative that identifies them as fixed vessels that 'contain' individuals whose interests are the only reason for communities to exist are empty, failed notions of community. And yet, notions like this have come to be the dominant discourse when articulating the rights of the individual in relation to the community.

By contrast, if one posits an alternative narrative that neither ignores the individual nor places the community as subordinate to the individual's volitions, but rather sees both as two aspects of the same set of relational contingencies, the conception of rights then must shift. By this we mean that individual-driven rights outcomes are not ends in themselves if they ignore the consequences for community rights, for the rights of community commons to exist and be protected. In this context it becomes thinkable to argue for a more expansive notion of rights deriving from the interconnected realities that govern relational contingencies. Necessarily, then, the rights of community need to be addressed in equal part as a key element in thinking through these relational contingencies.

This is not to say that uncritical uses of the term community exist, especially as it has been co-opted by multiple forms of power that actively seek to disempower its potential meaning within a rights context. Community meaning derives from embodied social practices more so than it does from rhetorical forms that have emptied it of meaning. Theatre historian Alan Filewod, whose work we have referred to earlier, in a discussion of community mobilization through theatrical practice, begins by noting,

> *community* is arguably the most misused word in contemporary political discourse. As a rhetorical instrument, it is an empty signifier that demands allegiance and marks value without specificity. *Community* implies a system of shared interest, but the word is often deployed as a strategy of ideological mapping that centers the subject in a field that masks individual interest ... The sentimental

> quest to rediscover a sense of community, allegedly lost in the alienated world of postindustrial transnational capital, has framed much of the political theater work of the past two decades, particularly in North America, where *community* frequently erases *class* in popular discourse. (Filewod 'Coalitions of Resistance' 89)

Filewod's salutary reading of community marks the way in which the term has been appropriated, deformed and sentimentalized even as its political import has been reshaped in the name of individual and hegemonic self-interest.

What better way to enforce ideology than through communities that think of themselves as such even as their political agency has been undermined to the point of a disabling inertia? Democratic voting patterns along party lines are an example of this: how can it be meaningful to surrender one's community engagement by proxy through a vote made once every several years that symbolically transfers one's individual agency (itself an expression of a form of community engagement) to another who in turn represents a multitude of similar gestures that alienate the voter from the actual agencies in which real power is enacted? Community in its oppositional sense to Filewod's reading never means easy coalitions or the absence of discord or even necessarily facile agreement; nor does it mean disembodied alienation. Instead, it invokes embodied agency that must address the specific environmental and cultural ecologies out of which it arises.

Polish sociologist Zygmunt Baumann's *Community: Seeking Safety in an Insecure World*, argues that community 'stands for the kind of world which is not, regrettably, available to us – but which we would dearly wish to inhabit and which we hope to repossess ... it is always in the future. "Community" is nowadays another name for paradise lost – but one to which we dearly hope to return, and so we feverishly seek the roads that may bring us there' (3). This abstracted, sentimentalized view of community is to be contrasted with the view that community is not an ideal but a practice embodied in specific agencies to be found in the here and now. Jean Vanier, Canadian founder of L'Arche (1964), the international organization that creates communities based on bringing together people with developmental disabilities and those who assist them, sums this idea up neatly in his observation that 'The community is neither heaven nor hell, but planted firmly on earth' (79). So, while community, per se, may always be in the future as an event-horizon of the possible it is, by virtue of its embodiment of the ongoing processual dynamics of relational contingencies (governed by the necessity of encounter), also a way of speaking about the permanent project of making relations and the conditions that sustain and contradict those relations.

In this sense, community is no sentimental paradise, but an unavoidable material reality that is made and remade on a continuous basis. This multiform remaking occurs in the contexts of alienation, uncertainty, and dissidence, just as surely as it does in affiliation, solidarity, mediation, and negotiation. When alienation is mediated in community it must be embodied and present. Agreement, discord, engagement, and alienation are all negotiated in community. The process of this negotiation gives community its meaning as differential, processual, embodied, unsettled. A key aspect of the meaning of community is *embodied agency*, a concept very much at odds with how vitiated meanings of political community, especially in Anglo North America, have evolved. And there are other ways of understanding community that are equally at odds with the corporatized, state-driven models Filewod so ably critiques.

For instance, we note Vanier's spiritual understanding of community as based on a general principle of 'life-giving and of liberation' (88) that has multiple manifestations:

> The communities started by St Benedict in the sixth century were centred on prayer. Communities founded by Mother Teresa of Calcutta are centred on the lonely, the broken and the dying. The Covenant House community in New York City cares for street kids while the Catholic Worker and Simon Communities are centred on men and women who are down and out. The [ecumenical] Taizé Community [in France] is centred on prayer and a life dedicated to the unity of all Christian churches. The community of Lanzo del Vasto (also called l'Arche) is centred on a way of life close to nature and on the principles of non-violence. The basic communities in Latin America are centred on the poor, restoring to them their basic dignity and rights, and their voice and place ... (ibid.)

Vanier's radical notion of community is that it is based on departure, a nomadic regrouping that generates new possibilities of interaction: 'When I use the word "community" ... I am talking essentially of groupings of people who have left their own milieu to live with others under the same roof, and work from a new vision of human beings and their relationships with each other ...' (10). Departure entails risk-taking, adaptation, improvisation, and encounter with difference. The ability to negotiate these challenges, then, is fundamental to community formation.

A further key notion in Vanier's community philosophy is that 'Belonging is for becoming' (22) – that affiliation enables self-actualization seen not just as a determining aspect of individual growth but also as an aspect of community wellbeing. Though largely a Christian-based view strongly influenced by liberation theology, Vanier's practical experiences in founding communities devoted to enhancing the lives of those with developmental disabilities have a remarkably wide application beyond spiritual-based communities. If anything, Vanier's notions of community address the underlying spiritual component that is closely connected to the ethics of encounter and the relational community of rights.

To Vanier's spiritual notions of community we may add Louis Massignon (1883–1962), the renowned French Islamist scholar

> who in his youth had daringly converted to Catholicism in the land of Islam [and] founded a community called Badaliya [1947], a name deriving from the Arabic term for "substitution." The members took a vow to live *substituting themselves* for someone else, that is, to be Christians *in the place of others* ... According to Massignon ... substituting oneself for another does not mean compensating for what the other lacks, nor correcting his or her errors, but *exiling oneself to the other as he or she is* ... This substitution no longer knows a place of its own, but the taking-place of every single being is always already common – an empty space offered to the one, irrevocable hospitality. (Agamben 23)

Massignon's ideas, which align with Gandhi's notions of non-violence as a form of ethical action and with Martin Luther King Jr.'s earlier cited notion of 'beloved community,' sought peaceful coexistence especially for Arabs living in Palestine after the creation of the state of Israel in 1948. Community in Massignon's sense is defined by substitution of oneself for another, a form of permanent exile from self-centred notions of identity that is based on a persistent offering to the other *of oneself as other* in the mode of *irrevocable hospitality*. Ethical communities undertake this encounter with otherness as an underlying aspect of their participation in a wider community of rights that recognizes otherness, difference, and the need to enact irrevocable hospitality as a way of negotiating differential identities both within and across communities.

American literary scholar Michael Hardt and Italian political philosopher Antonio Negri articulate another model of community in their co-written book *Commonwealth* (2009). In their read, community becomes a 'multitude-form' that poses 'a real political problem' in that it is the site of resistance to supranational and corporate entities that have imposed the rule of capital – a concept that in their reading (both in *Commonwealth* and *Empire* [2000]) subsumes everything into its inexorable logic. The multitude-form is an 'open set of social singularities that are autonomous and equal, capable together, by articulating their actions on parallel paths in a horizontal network, of transforming society. Multitude is thus a concept of applied parallelism, able to grasp the specificity of altermodern struggles, which are characterized by relations of autonomy, equality, and interdependence among vast multiplicities of singularities' (2009 111). In this conception of altermodern community Hardt and Negri identify the common, public resources like water, gas, soil, and the like, that 'will not be privatized ... The multitude of altermodernity ... runs counter to the republic of property' (ibid.). The common is, in this sense, not just shared material resources but also 'a social product, and this common is an inexhaustible source of innovation and creativity' (111-12). Finally, the notion of the singularity as a stable entity is undermined by the idea that 'every singularity is a social becoming' characterized by 'constant metamorphosis, its mixture and movement' (112).

These observations at once maintain the co-related, co-creative aspects of shifting and transformational identities and agencies that ultimately blur the singularity into the multitude, the multitude into the singularity. Such a model acknowledges the unstable mixing of formative, historical specificities with the transformative dynamic of always-becoming characteristic of the relational contingencies in which both the singular and the collective agency of social relations are shaped. This agency is enabled by relational contingencies and bound by both the ethics of encounter and the necessity of sustaining the commons as the generative space of all social relations – including those that determine the shared values that become rights.

It is impossible to detach the agency associated with the commons from ethical considerations related to how that commons enacts itself in multiple, diverse, shifting horizontal structures of inter-connectedness and affiliation.[7] This is at the core of what community means. We say this knowing full well how slippery terms like community can be, especially as one moves laterally in and between cultures that offer alternative epistemologies and words for the English term community.

Traditional, land-based forms of identification with shared cultural and historical heritage might, as in the case of Anishinaubae, link a root word like *odae* (heart) to related words signifying family relationships, totemic family, clan, expanding outward to words denoting village, town, city, and nation. Many First Nations languages simply do not have a word for community because it needlessly abstracts a much wider holistic entity having to do with the 'people' or 'peoples' in their specific relations with other life forms and the earth (a concept we explore at length in the next section of the book).

In Western usage, the word 'community' tends in the opposite direction to shrink meaning by identifying a singular activity as basis for membership in occupational, professional, activist, and artistic groupings of people who share concerns and interests: the business community, the artistic community, the military community, the academic community, and so forth. In part, this shrinkage is part of a discernible trend to engineer social realities by manipulating language recognized as the very basis of people's perception and interpretation of reality.

Orwell identified this aspect of totalitarian control in his prophetic story *1984*, especially in ironic observations on how propaganda parades as information and knowledge. The managerial class, deeply informed by advertising strategies, has since become hyper-aware of language's power to distort and obscure. As we have alluded to earlier, the darker sides of communications and military technologies are distorted by calling software 'user-friendly,' anthropomorphizing bombs as 'smart,' munitions fire on allies as 'friendly' – killing in different contexts is called harvesting, culling, or collateral damage, shifting the focus away from the most primordial reality of taking life to evoke purely utilitarian or benignly agricultural associations. While language is a living, growing, and continually shifting system, writers have often reminded themselves that at times it is necessary to return to the ancient and etymological sense of words, to dust off the layers of accumulated connotations settling on things within competing contexts and power struggles.

Writing from the context of the technologically over-developed and wisdom lacking First World, we must acknowledge that the word 'community' has a nostalgic ring to it, evocative of an attempt to recuperate land-based roots and direct social relations. In this context, all such words are fraught with multiple meanings that cannot be linearly imagined according to any obsolete historical model of progress. Any idea of going back to an older way of life is double-edged, yielding both insight into why certain practices were in fact more viable than current ones, while also being overshadowed by a self-conscious criticism of fabricating a past that is inevitably romanticized and therefore impossible to pick up and continue. As in art, imagining realities that are completely original can produce solipsistic abstractions that are difficult to share and to act upon collectively. The worst option though is to accept the dominant powers' version of a reality dominated by consumption, productivity, capital, and use-value, as the only possible world. What we argue for in this book is a material practice of community based on diverse agencies and identities in the service of a sustainable and renewable commons – a vision radically at odds with reductive visions of community modeled on exploitative capital and driven by individual self-interest.

'Community,' as we understand it, is nonetheless replete with all these tensions. As we contemplate what it has meant in the past, what we now will it to mean, how it is appropriated by power and how that power has failed to eradicate commons-based human agency, we must also keep in mind how culturally and economically specific and limited are our reflections, circumscribed by historical developments, philosophical traditions, and all manner of unconscious baggage that are the product of each of our specific formations, our specific historicity. Some of these function as constraints, blind spots that inhibit the imagination, while others throw open windows that enable fruitful interventions.

According to Uruguayan writer Eduardo Galeano the communitarian sense of life is the truest expression of 'common' sense. Galeano tends to foreground the community as the very basis of the individual and often uses corporeal imagery to evoke the integrity that a person can only claim in relation to others. He re-tells an indigenous story that likens the individual to a tooth, which if fallen from one's mouth, is useless outside of the context of the other teeth. Galeano characterizes authentic culture as growing from the feet up, another corporeal image that he borrows from the singer-storyteller Alfredo Zitarrosa. By authentic, he does not refer to any kind of racial/racist purity, but to the notion that true culture evolves collectively and communally, as opposed to the mass culture engineered, managed, manipulated by the powerful with access to technology, or the elite that Noam Chomsky refers to as cultural managers.

Galeano's view of history is similar in that he denies that politicians and armies produce it. He affirms that history is created by those who do not realize it and are simply living their lives, that history too evolves from the feet up, and that the only thing that is made from the top down are holes. Community, like story, is literally and figuratively rooted in the land, an idea that we return to at length in the next section of this book. Community, in this sense, is an allegorical term that tells of how humanity came to be through collective relations that include the land without which life would not be possible – an idea to which we devote the entire next section.

Story, as a key aspect of community identity, also comes from the land, and is rooted in it. In this view, then, life is contingent upon a collective relation to the ecosphere and the stories that the ecosphere gives up through its embodied offspring, human and otherwise. In *A Sand County Almanac*, by the great American conservationist Aldo Leopold, Leopold takes this web of relations even further suggesting the following: 'All ethics so far evolved rest upon a single premise: that the individual is a member of a community of interdependent parts ... The land ethic simply enlarges the boundaries of community to include soils, waters, plants, and animals, or collectively, the land' (239). This book was written in 1948; the same year in which the Universal Declaration of Human Rights was to enunciate a view of ethics that had little to say about the rights connections among community, land, and the individual: except, lamentably as a function of ownership. In the Forward to this book he states uncategorically: 'That land is a community is the basic concept of ecology, but that land is to be loved and respected is an extension of ethics. That land yields a cultural harvest is a fact long known, but latterly often forgotten' (xix). By book's end Leopold advances a collective land ethic predicated on an ecological conscience that is itself a function of individual and collective responsibility. Like community, the health of the land is measurable by its capacity for ongoing renewal and sustainability (258-59), and the contingent relationship between land and human community is what defines an ethics, which is to say a notion of rights and justice writ large, beyond the ethical narcissism of the terms 'human rights' and 'social justice' – as if rights and justice are only social, only a function of being human.

Galeano's allegory of the tree (being rooted and growing upwards) and Leopold's views on the integratedness of community, land, and ethics are a far cry from notions of community that associate it with ownership. In the OED the first definition of community references 'The quality of appertaining to or being held by all in common; joint or common ownership, tenure, liability, etc.; as in *community of goods*' (OED). In its derivation from the Latin word *communis*, 'meaning "fellowship, community of relations or feelings"' (OED) by the time the word had filtered into English it had already transformed into a concept associated with ownership, liability, tenure, and 'goods.'[8] Moreover, an early usage of the word in English, dating back to 1561 (from Thomas Norton's translation of *Calvin's Institutes of the Christian Religion*) explicitly associates community with power, the phrase in question stating, 'By community of power, he is the author of them' (OED). This tidy phrase encapsulates the logic of power invested in singularities via the collective and neatly captures the twisted way in which collective power is usurped in the name of the individual who, in turn, is said to authorize the collectivity. The phrase resonates as much in Christian theology as it does in early modern monarchic self-investiture, the two being not unrelated, and was to set a dysfunctional frame for imagining the contingent relations of the individual to the collective, one that saw the individual as somehow superceding the collective as opposed to being a contingent expression thereof.

This profoundly anti-egalitarian discourse that divests unity from the sense of community while at the same time perpetuating notions of joint ownership (later to morph into stock holdings and corporations) as the foundation of community is where at least a portion of current-day neoliberal discourse can be traced. Other OED versions of the meaning of community locate it variously in the 'Right of common,' in 'commonness, agreement, identity' as in '*community of interest*,' in 'social intercourse,' 'life in association with others,' and importantly, the 'body of those having common or equal rights or rank, as distinguished from the privileged classes.'[9] From the start, in other words, dating as far back as 1375, the 'common' in community was a highly classed term meaning vulgar, or equal, but only by virtue of *not* being privileged. Early meanings of *community* (dating to the fourteenth century) in English also associate it with 'A body of people organized into a political, municipal, or social unity' meaning a state or commonwealth. Again, commonwealth in these terms identifies collective ownership but invested in the few who actually control that ownership, a fact that from early on compromised any utopian notion of community as anything other than a social structure for masking the true disposition of power in the hands of the few via the illusion of common wealth.

Early seventeenth-century meanings of the word associate community with locale (as in a neighbourhood community) and by the eighteenth century had evolved to mean the general public. By the mid-twentieth century the term is used to describe the construct of 'A body of nations acknowledging unity of purpose or common interests' a sense that precedes the evolution of the term to reference community care, community feeling, community theatre, community centre, community homes, community colleges, and the community chest, a term applied to 'a fund made up of individual donations to meet the needs for charity and social welfare work in a community.' Along the way, the term community was also applied to socialistic or communistic societies as well as to ecological groupings (of plants or animals) 'growing or living together in natural conditions or inhabiting a specified area'.

Welsh critic and academic Raymond Williams argues in *Keywords* that the 'complexity' of the term community derives from 'on the one hand the sense of direct common concern' and

> on the other hand the materialization of various forms of common organization, which may or may not adequately express this. *Community* can be the warmly persuasive word to describe an existing set of relationships, or the warmly persuasive word to describe an alternative set of relationships. What is most important, perhaps, is that unlike all other terms of social organization (state, nation, society, etc.) it seems never to be used unfavourably, and never to be given any positive opposing or distinguishing term.' (76)

It is precisely this sentimentalizing of the term 'community' that occludes its ideological uses as a way of co-opting people to the index of power that community has come to represent. A community of interest defined by its subversion of rights (as was the case in apartheid South Africa) is, despite its ethical failure, still a community. Or is it? Our argument here is direct: the rights it embodies define community. Failure to enact those rights equitably is symptomatic of the failure of community, the failure to reproduce the ties of affiliation that bind relational contingencies in a sustainable matrix of being. The collapse of white South Africa because of its ethically bankrupt segregationist policies – and its replacement by the emergent hybridized, 'rainbow' nation only confirms the degree to which the ethical commons is at stake in long-term community survival.

This very brief history of the evolution of the meaning of the English term *community* teaches a few lessons. Not only is the term explicitly classed and used to describe power relations, it is also associated with ownership and 'goods' said to belong to the collective. That the collective surrenders its 'community of power' to the singularity, which then authorizes the community, is a key point to hold in mind as we advance the arguments of this book – especially those that attack compromised notions of community in need of functional alternatives with constructive rights implications. We point out the extent to which these definitions and understandings are alien to those we describe earlier on by way of the examples from Galeano and Leopold. What might it mean to re-think community by way of an ethics that dispenses with homo- or androcentric and goods-driven forms of individualist ownership discourses? What might it mean to critique community meaning from the point of view of an ecology of relations necessary to all forms of being in order for biotic renewal and sustainability to be enacted?

Community meaning, in this latter sense, is 'so called because it holds all things in common' (Dussel 1988 11) by virtue of the proximate, often intimate relations that enable survival. The more abstracted these relations become the less vital the community, the more compromised by interests that supersede those of the community, the less capable of survival. In liberation theologian Enrique Dussel's terms, community is the 'real, concrete agent and mover of history. In the community we are "at home," in safety and security, in common' (11). The breakdown of this space 'in common' is ethical because, as we have argued elsewhere, ethics is a key component of being civil, of sustaining relations to the other. Community, in these terms, is a metaphor for this ethical relationship to the other and to otherness: the ethical commons embodied in our title – the rights of community, the community of rights – implies a correspondence between imagining ethics in community terms and imagining a wider community of shared ethical agencies that empower communities as agents of history. The problem is that this vision of community meaning is at odds with the ways in which rights discourses have evolved.

The German cultural critic Walter Benjamin in his fragmentary historiographic work *The Arcades Project* identified the dilemma in exceptionally clear terms via his citation of Marx's critique of the rights of 'man' as distinct from the rights of the 'citizen':

> None of the so-called rights of man goes beyond egoistic man ... Far from the rights of man [sic] conceiving of man as a species-being, species-life itself, society, appears as a framework exterior to individuals ... The only bond that holds them together [in this view] is natural necessity, need and private interest, the conservation of their property and egoistic person. It is ... paradoxical ...

> that citizenship, the political community, is degraded by the political emancipators to a mere means for the preservation of these so-called rights of man; that the citizen is declared to be the servant of egoistic man; that the sphere in which man behaves as a communal being is degraded below the sphere in which man behaves as a partial being; finally that it is not man as a citizen but man as a bourgeois who is called the real and true man. (Marx as cited by Benjamin; 668-69)

Marx's trenchant analysis of how rights discourses had been aligned with specific notions of bourgeois commodity culture defined by egoism and property ('private need') is a salutary reminder of what is at stake in the critical discourses surrounding how we define rights in relation to both the 'political community' and the citizen within that community. Benjamin well understands how assigning the property of rights to 'man,' defined by Marx in anti-social terms as an egoistic being, produces a fetishization of that property and a self-image that Benjamin calls a form of 'phantasmagoria.'

The key, then, in getting at the meaning of as over-determined and commodified a term as community, is to lay bare the stakes in struggles over its meaning and to recognize how *community* (like the term *rights)* can be deformed in ways that suit the strategies of hegemonic mass culture. The fetishization of deformed understandings of rights and community, based on an egoism that corrupts civic discourse, in other words, reflects on a process by which the very terms themselves are commodified and made to serve, paradoxically as Marx points out, the very interests they are supposed to oppose.

Early modern French essayist Michel de Montaigne's essay 'On Habit' launches a similar attack on individualism that compromises community:

> it seems to me that there is a great deal of self-love and arrogance in judging so highly of your opinions that you are obliged to disturb the public peace in order to establish them, thereby introducing those many unavoidable evils and that horrifying moral corruption ... into your own country ... Is there any kind of vice more wicked than those which trouble the naturally recognized sense of community? (De Montaigne 135)

These comments point to the fundamental conflict in community discourses that oppose individual self-interest and the 'public peace.' Montaigne's observations, though, avoid the problem of how the 'public peace' and 'naturally recognized' are tropes that can be used to sustain dysfunctional community practices.

This dynamic of self-renewal via self-critique is a vital aspect of community practice from a rights-based perspective. The tension between salutary traditionalism and salutary attacks on embedded practices that over the long-term make a community unrenewable or unsustainable is at the crux of debates over community meaning and practice. The alienation of the individual from both him- or herself and from his or her community was, as Habermas argues, supposed to have been healed by the *contrat social* [the social contract]: 'everyone submitted to the community his [sic] person and property along with all rights so as to have from then on a share in the rights and duties of all through the mediation of the general will' (Habermas 97). But problems arise when the 'general will' is deformed and usurped by communities defined by both their self-interest and their empowerment to achieve those interests at the expense of the political commons – as is the case in most forms of government where oligopolies implant and maintain themselves in the name of profit or in the name of nationalism. The ethics of encounter with the other is here a crucial aspect of the dynamic that associates community with values from which emerge embodied practices and vice-versa.

It is important to understand Habermas's 'critique of communitarism' as having been shaped by his understanding, from within the post-WWII German context, of how 'Community has been one of the major legitimations of nationalism and in the extreme case has provided a justification for fascism. As a moral totality, community is a dangerous sentiment since it reduces society to a non-social principle and it binds modernity to a premodern conception of society' (Delanty 116). Habermas's social theories, while critical of communitarian thought that leads to the monologic of state self-interest given its most extreme form in fascist Germany, nonetheless argues for the 'idea of a "communication community" [meaning] that social relations in modern society are organized around communication rather than by other media such as authority, status or ritual' (ibid. 115).

Our own view is one that avoids essentializing about either premodern or postmodern manifestations of social relations by reducing them to stereotype. Any reduction of social relations to communication cannot avoid addressing status (*who* has privileged access to various modes of communication?) and authority (*who* has the right to produce communications and how are they disseminated?). Communication is predicated on structures of encounter heavily mediated by the values subsumed in how encounter is embodied, how it is negotiated, and what its outcomes are for equitable participation in the commons. No communication is devoid of the contingencies that feed into discrepant engagement with the other or the mediations (of history, of circumstance, of volition, of education, of class, of gender, and so forth) that influence relations. When these structures of encounter are deformed by self-interest associated with authoritarian hegemonies, community is at risk.

In all colonized countries, the disastrous effects of unethical encounter with the other – including apartheid, reservations, townships, residential schools, and segregation – are seen in politically utilitarian terms, and not as catastrophic for the marginalized indigenous or for the country as a whole, or even as a profound threat to the ecosystem of communities within the larger state. Often, these disastrous effects are treated as localized political scandals to be contained by minimal efforts to resolve the problem, or to defer a solution that gets at the very root of the problem, as has been the case with First Nations land treaty claims for centuries – or as has been the case with impoverished communities who have suffered the effects of environmental catastrophes. Often the motivation to address these deep-rooted problems issues from the threat of retaliation bolstered by human rights instruments and international scrutiny based on the global reach of NGO and UN reports and recommendations.

In most of these situations, the concept of state implementation of rights resolutions is passive and non-proactive: 'clamour loud enough for a fix and get enough media attention and *maybe* we'll respond.' Instead of addressing the global claims of indigenous peoples, for instance, governments pretend to right previous wrongs through long-term legal wrangling and deferral or through an outdated call to assimilate; even in countries like Canada, whose policy of multiculturalism is supposed to respect and even encourage (multi)cultural difference.

Insisting that the lives of First Nations people will be improved by being assimilated into cities and urban employment is just the prolongation of the colonialist project to deny their land- and community-based ethics, and to impose instead the individualistic worldview based on private property and private need. It is obvious that indigenous people everywhere are struggling to protect the land from further degradation caused by mining, forestry, hydroelectric dams and other encroachments on their local communities' relations to the land. The government's best corporate interests are served by removing people from their land and disenfranchising them from their natural communities by encouraging them to integrate into 'mainstream' society. If that assimilationist strategy fails, it can buy off communities that wish to maintain their autonomy through corporate deals that on the surface resolve some of the issues of poverty and disempowerment endemic to First Nations communities.

Yet, indigenous communities – and by extension all communities that see themselves bound by shared interests via the responsible and sustainable treatment of land – pose a direct risk to exploitation and corporate profitability, founded on a very different set of values and desired outcomes. How do communities redress imbalances between their localized practices, and rights to those practices, and the systemic undermining of these by state and corporate imperatives? Community meaning is as much to be found in opposition to these interests as it is in the modes of resistance enacted to sustain these localized rights.

The legal context of group interests defended through class action suits is one of the few expressions of non-indigenous claims to community justice. As a result, the George W. Bush administration in 2005 proposed to ban various forms of class action suits and to further fragment people by limiting them to the legal actions of the isolated individual. This produced a David-versus-Goliath situation, with a predictably opposite outcome from this myth of the underdog hero triumphing over a seemingly undefeatable adversary. A 2005 report on various initiatives by the Bush administration to ban litigation that directly targets corporate responsibility in a wide range of areas including the arms industry, food-related businesses, and the medical industry shows the extent to which state- and corporate-interests are protected:

> The latest bill banning lawsuits against gun makers and sellers has been approved by the US Congress and is now being sent to President Bush where he is expected to eagerly sign it. The President long called for the ban on lawsuits against gun manufacturers and retailers, saying that the lawsuits impeded business and commercial enterprise in the country. The bill's proponents include the National Rifle Association and the majority of the Republican-held Congress. Opponents and gun control groups say they will fight the bill on constitutional grounds.
>
> The bill was long sought after by gun manufacturers who say that a series of gun reform laws instituted in the late 1990s were meant

> to put gun companies out of business. During that era, expensive lawsuits were filed putting the blame on gun manufacturers and sellers for any gun-related criminal activity. The companies could not have paid the suits that followed and they were expected to go out of business or enter bankruptcy.
>
> Opponents say that the bill is a political move to guarantee gun rights through the banning of litigation, rather than making new laws governing the use and sale of guns. The new bill follows an end to a decade long ban on assault weapons that Congress allowed to expire late last year. President Bush has passed or attempted to pass several key lawsuit related measures with nationwide implications. The House on Wednesday passed a measure that seeks to stop lawsuits against food-related businesses for obesity or health related problems. Bush also signed a bill earlier this year that limits class-action lawsuits and is seeking another bill from Congress that would put caps on medical malpractice awards. ('Gun Control Lawsuit News')

In short an agenda curtailing the legal means to redress corporate responsibility and implication in a range of areas with profound impact on community life throughout the U.S. was put into place: a clear example of state pro-activism congruent with the denial of legal rights of communities and individuals to hold corporations accountable for what they produce. With regard to handgun violence alone, 'The Centers for Disease Control and Prevention (CDC) estimated 52,447 deliberate and 23,237 accidental non-fatal gunshot injuries in the United States during 2000' ('Gun violence in the United States'). When the corporate profitability of gun manufacturers is at odds with the impact of the products they make across a wide ecology of communities in the U.S. (with the U.S. leading the world's richest nations in gun deaths and injuries by handgun ['Gun Deaths – United States Tops The List']), banning those communities' rights to hold the gun manufacturers accountable is a significant attack on the rights of community (especially when class action suits are a limited and hugely expensive undertaking).

In contrast to the example of the U.S. chill on litigation representing group interests (and we note how these class action litigations are primarily rooted in consumer rights as opposed to a much wider range of rights applications), Noam Chomsky, relying on work done by Ching

Kwan Lee on Chinese labor, describes the situation in China where astonishing numbers of workers in the so-called rustbelt (industrial area) of the Northeast are disaffected and organizing.

> According to official statistics, there were 58,000 'mass incidents' of protest in 2003 in just one province of the rustbelt, with three million people participating. Some 30 to 40 million workers who were dropped from work units – quoting Lee – 'are plagued by a profound sense of insecurity,' arousing 'rage and desperation' around the country ... in the rustbelt, there's nothing like civil society support that exists, to some extent, here. Both Lee and the studies of the US rustbelt make it clear that we should not underestimate the depth of moral indignation that lies behind the bitterness about what is perceived to be the treachery of government and business power acting exactly as we should expect them to, unfortunately. (Chomsky interviewed by Amy Goodman)

When 58,000 protest incidents occur involving three million people, and when these protests coincide with the loss of basic community rights – to work, to land, to equitable treatment, to a functioning, equitable civil society with a healthy commons – it is clear that this form of state-corporate organization cannot sustain itself. Both these contexts, then, with the restriction of legal means to seek redress in the U.S. and the significant increase in worker protests aimed at exploitative conditions in China represent two sides of the same coin, in grasping the meaning of community as a cultural practice under sustained attack. On the one hand, community has been compromised as the basis for encompassing ethical action. On the other, community is the event-horizon of a potential alternative discourse in which, by virtue of the very contestation it unleashes, new social practices emerge.

Assumed Communities and Unavowable Communities

Individual-centered rights discourses prioritize the singular against the plural rather than addressing the imbalances that keep the two in a constant state of fluid relation to each other. If 'community' has become at once a convenient term for forms of political subterfuge that appropriate its positivist meanings to other ends, while at the same time remaining a fraught term that remakes the sense of community in the image of the individual and individualist priorities, then of what use is the term at all?

In the former case, where macro-notions of relational human energies are at stake – think the state, government, the nation, the city, the army, the corporation, and the like – the assumption is that these communities represent the appropriate default against which lesser, micro-communities subsumed within the larger entity are to be measured, the larger general entity standing in for the smaller particularity. This relationship is what we call the 'assumed' community, assumed in the sense that the relations between large and small are usually elided over in the name of majoritarian self-interest. It is assumed, for instance, that the judiciary represents adequately the particularities and interests of smaller groupings within the larger entity. It is assumed that military undertakings are effected as a function of global interests embodied in the silent relations governing the large-scale community that stands in for the particularities by which it is constituted. And yet, multiple instances of conflict exist between what the state represents as in its own interests and what smaller differential communities' interests are within the state's military, legal, and institutional frameworks. Such conflicts reinforce very precisely the way in which divergent interests are as much definitive of assumed communities as are conjoined interests. In this sense, assumed community points to the impossible, illusory conjunction of interests expressive of the tension that frames community as an instrumental term in debates over how to wield power.

Assumed communities are thus entirely different from those in which community is taken on – assumed in the French sense of 'assumer' – as a direct expression of the relation between the individual and the larger group ('prendre sur soi' or to 'take on oneself'). The notion of 'assuming' community in this latter sense conjures up a host of ethical and relational energies implicit within this 'taking on.' How does one choose what one takes on ethically? How does one ethically address shifts in relational energies that are contrary to the initial compact that binds the individual to a community? How to adhere to the twin formula of 'I am, therefore you are; you are, therefore I am' that is the beginning of an ethics of engagement between an individual and a community? How to understand the matter of 'taking on' as an ongoing processual energy of critical engagement with otherness and difference in the name of collocated energies that overlap and diverge in the name of community being and becoming?

These energies are closer to the root of how rights discourses that privilege individual self-interest need to shift to address how that self-interest must be exercised in relation to the 'taking on oneself' of community. We note for the record that community is neither a singular nor a plural term: it is both at once. Relational humanity cannot be reduced to any singular vision of adherence and belonging, in the same way that the ethical dimensions of being human invoked by rights discourses cannot be separated from the ways in which that 'being human' is a function of the full skein of relations, between any living thing and the multiple environments that enable its life. The biosphere and ecosphere co-exist as an expression of different forms of energy that is the true ground out of which community is made possible, but the fullness of that rich relation has yet to find its way into the highly circumscribed institutional languages that have evolved around the notion of '*human* rights.' We deliberately avoid this term because it prioritizes normative and politically delimited notions of the human, that are in opposition to the anarchic realities that can only approximate the fullness of all forms of being and becoming human.

Moreover, the term 'human rights' has been appropriated to ends that suit legal and juridical interests (some of them no doubt laudable) that all-too-narrowly circumscribe what it means to be human: so, the right to play and improvise, the right to non-violence, the right to a sustainable environment, the right to art, the right to information and multiple forms of knowledge and pedagogy, the right to take on an ethical engagement with one's community, what many might argue as being closer to the forms of rights that define the purposefulness of what it means to be human, these are barely visible in key instruments associated with legal mechanisms for enacting rights. If such is the case, and the divide between lived human realties and enacted institutional notions of rights is so highly fraught – distorted by oligarchic discourses that serve interests and values driven primarily by commerce, profit-taking, and the exercise of strategic power relations – then how to give voice to the majoritarian world minoritized by the ways in which it has been disenfranchised from the communitarian values described above, in the name of deformed locutions about human rights?

This is no easy question. At its heart lies the crucial problem we try to get at in this book: how to rewrite discourses that link the rights of community with the community of rights? How to account for the individual as a function of community and the community as a function of the individual? How to think the fullness of relations that link the human with all other forms of being in ways that provide a clear map for articulating a renewed form of rights discourse, a new ethical disposition toward both global and particular relational energies?

To begin to piece together some answers we argue the need to distinguish between 'assumed' communities and 'assuming' community. The distinction is central to what we argue, insofar as it marks the range of unthought assumptions that shape community as an object from which the individual is distanced, via the deferrals and displacements that reduce that individual's agency as a community member. Thus, in managed democracies the assumptions that govern what might be said to constitute community depend on the ways in which the individual surrenders agency via multiple state and institutional entities that supposedly act in the individual's name. The crucial assumption is that belonging via some abstract form of citizenship is sufficient to guarantee one's ethical disposition vis-à-vis the larger commune, a hugely problematic assumption in large-scale entities that purport to represent complex populations. The passive citizen who assumes the community is functional is too much of a reductive stereotype to be entirely credible. However the disempowerment, political or otherwise, that comes with disengagement propped up by assumptions that community is a given, is all too real in how state and nation function as agglomerative entities.

An assumed community depends on the passive political subject to maintain its self-interest, which is largely congruent with the assumptions that underlie communitarian discourse founded on the eradication or fear of difference. Thus, the not-so-anodine bromides associated with bumper slogans like 'We support our troops' that appeared throughout Canada during its engagement in the war against Afghanistan. Such slogans assume a shared community that might agree with this statement. But at the same time the declaration arises out of anxiety that there is an unspoken counter-proclamation in need of a response as in: 'We don't support our troops.' Or, as we have briefly shown in our discussion of the neglect of veterans upon their return home from war, there is embedded in the slogan a bitter irony in saying 'we' support when in fact that support is inadequate. Who the 'we' is and who the 'our' represents in this common trope is as much an assumed community as is the group against which the trope is targeted. Embedded within the phrase is an ancient idea that incarnates the foundation of community in the sacrifice of a community member for the community as a whole, a sacrifice that any and all members of that community must be capable of in order for that community to exist. The soldier's death emblematizes this sacrifice. The bumper sticker slogan resonates with this sacrificial martyr model of community while also marking the enormous gap that exists between the slogan and the reality. The metonymy between this 'we' and the nation-state is yet another assumption implicit in the phrase: as if to suggest that the 'we' includes all forms of citizenship, even as the anxiety that this 'we' is largely illusory lies behind the declaration.

The bumper-sticker phrase nicely encapsulates some of the myths that are embedded in commonplace usages of the word community: that the 'common' in community defines community (as opposed to the uncommon or differential aspects that are equally definitive of what might be said to constitute a community); that the community is a function of possession as in 'our troops,' 'my country,' 'our common values' when in fact all these terms are at once extraordinarily reductive and for that reason useful in the empty rhetoric and demagoguery associated with political discourse. Elided in all this are the ways in which 'support' is enacted via the distance that separates a common citizen driving a car to the mall and a soldier in battle. The distance is enormous but the slogan collapses diverse realities in the name of an assumed community that is highly fraught and riddled with contradictions.

A more virulent bumper sticker soon appeared, as if to underscore that the first appeal to support was too optional and pacific: 'If you don't stand behind our troops ... feel free to stand in front of them.' This later slogan communicates a blatant threat against those who dare to doubt or disagree. The message here extends militaristic aggression beyond the war zone, to wage war against those branded as dissidents, unpatriotic, cowards, peaceniks, and so forth. Rhetoric like this re-engages the extremist language and actions practiced by totalitarian regimes of terror. It is reminiscent, for example, of the fascist regime in Argentina where the political rhetoric and actual disappearance of people quickly escalated from attacking the enemies of the regime to promoting the extermination of all those who did not wholeheartedly identify with its agenda. In these specific contexts, but also more generally in the relational-differential practice we propose, 'If you're not with us, you're against us' becomes a dangerously reductive preemptive strike against difference – and, by extension, an attack on community under the very auspices of promoting a community of support. Such are the consequences of unthinking jingoist sentiment.

The direct consequences of 'support' for violent resolution to complex geopolitical problems are assumed. This is so only because the community in this case is at (more than) several removes from the realities it produces. This removal is one of the fundamental problems facing any discussion of community in a context in which the hypertrophy of personal agency has been accelerated through the very means – technological, political, and economic – that appear to give the individual more autonomy than ever, while at the same time producing a virtual relationship to the material consequences of state agency (which has been hyper-accelerated by the hypertrophy of individual agency).

Autonomous disengagement and community are far from synonymous, especially in how they mark one's agency and ethical contingency in relation to what we are calling 'assuming' community. Never before has as much autonomy existed and perhaps never before has that autonomy been as correspondent with a decline in agency where the so-called autonomous individual has been supplanted and displaced by the very tools that supposedly ensure that autonomy. Fractured, isolated in a sea of increasingly particulated communications (think Twitter, blogging, texting, Facebook, and the billions of Internet sites, personal communication devices, and irrelevant media that produce the distracted anomic spectator), and dependent on networks whose job is to subject the individual according to implacable economies of extraction and subjection (all in the name of personal freedom) there is a clear and present danger in assumptions about community that do not confront these new realities.

'Assuming' community, by contrast, implies ethical relations of direct agency and reciprocal contingency that are not solely driven by profit-oriented economies. Anarchic in a hyper-mediatized economy in which the illusion of community is created via various electronic prostheses (as in Donna Haraway's notion of the human cyborg), community entails, as discussed throughout this book, a 'taking on' of consequences via direct action and direct interpellation into the skein of material relations that allow community to exist. This is not to say that aspects of virtuality cannot be present in community dispositions. Only to say that the ethical agency of community participants shifts dramatically when one 'assumes' community via embodied face-to-face presence, thereby questioning all 'assumptions' about community as a static entity whose predominant feature would be commonality.

What if the defining feature of community were *not* the common ties that are said, proverbially, to bind but instead the very differences that make community in its most achieved state an unsettled, self-critical, processual coming-into-being based on constantly shifting relational contingencies and embodiments of encounter? What if the ties that bind are in fact the differences that disrupt and the ways in which these differences are negotiated in a manner that creatively allows differential forms of potential to be enacted in an ethical and contingent manner? Is community more a function of alterity than commonality? Is the rupture between the self-same and difference the very thing that gives community meaning? Assuming community presumes addressing that which cannot be avowed about community, precisely its dependence on difference. Self-sameness produces static and inflexible structures, a guarantee of atrophy and self-limitation. The rhetoric of community is riddled with this sort of discourse: the discourse of the amorphous 'we' that subsumes and reduces. But community must begin with frank recognition of the realities that make all communities contingent on any number of factors – environmental, relational, creative, economic, political, and so forth. Is the unavowable community, to borrow French philosopher Maurice Blanchot's term, defined by the illusory nature of the common in the face of the overwhelming disruptive presence and creative potential of difference?

Rights discourses are predicated on two fundamental, overweening realities. One is relational, marked by how the individual assumes agency in relation to a full range of contacts with forms of otherness, human, environmental, and the like. The other is differential and determined by how that agency is negotiated in ways that must address difference, the constant potential that the nature of the other will somehow challenge our own assumptions governing our integral sense of who we are and where our agency begins and ends. Twelfth century poet Sa'adi sums up just this sense of complementarity of the individual's belonging to humanity on the very basis of responding to the other:

Tous les êtres humains sont membres d'un même corps,
Si le sort s'archarne contre l'un d'eux,
Alors, les autres ne peuvent rester en paix.
Celui que reste indifférent a la souffrance d'autruie,
Ne mérite pas d'être appelé 'humain.'

[All human beings are members of the same body,
If fate persecutes one of them,
Then, the others cannot remain at peace.
Whoever stays indifferent to the suffering of others,
Does not merit being called 'human.'] (our translation)

Empathy is a fundamental component of human relations, a precondition of meaningful community. It arises from the recognition that self and other must be mediated for community to exist. Both these realities – the relational and the differential – work out from another unavoidable context for thinking about rights, one that blurs the reductive and binaristic assumption that the social field (the socius) is constituted by the individual and the community. As we argue throughout this book, this distinction has had sway for far too long as a model for thinking about these issues, especially in a context that requires more sophisticated modeling to produce useful outcomes from thinking about rights in relation to community.

No individual lives in a vacuum or emerges from nothingness into his or her full human potential. No community exists solely as a conglomerate of self-same identities sharing communal interests. What this means is that the individual and the community per se are illusory aspects of a co-creative, shared reality that at once allows for individual agency within a common context, and allows for common agency that over-rides or is congruent with the individual's agency. Both terms represent event-horizons or opposed places on a continuum of shared and co-creative (or destructive) agencies that define human relational energies as aspects of *both* singular and collective experience. The arbitrary designation of these overlapped realities as separable and as thinkable in terms that exclude each other has been one of the significant theoretical deformations to inform discourses of the community of rights and the rights of community.

Neither the individual nor the community, in the alternative discourse we hope to provoke via this book, has meaning without the other and the two as co-implicated in the contextual fullness that makes human 'becoming' thinkable. This may seem a tad obvious to state in these terms. But we emphasize that our critique of rights discourses that emerged from early modern and later, post-Enlightenment political philosophies that trumpeted the individual as the epicenter of human experience, recognizes that coincident with this understanding emerged those collective institutions created to serve the individual (the state, the judiciary, the university, the military). These institutions were defined, paradoxically, by their corporate nature, their corporate self-interest. This praxis of self-interest is one of the profound anomalies that rights discourses must address if they are to have any sense of critical mindfulness. Moreover rights discourses have followed this same trajectory, with the individual assumed as the focus of rights even as the institutional aspects of rights instruments have aligned with corporate interests that do not always necessarily support the protection of individual rights and freedoms. The enunciation of the individual as the focus of the very institutions that override the individual has elided a third fundamental reality: namely, that neither the individual nor the collective is thinkable without the other.

Aspects of the community of rights discourse we describe in this book address individual realities as much as the rights of community address how corporate entities must comport themselves within a fully-elaborated, ethically justifiable rights context defined by community contingencies. The language in key rights instruments has a great deal to say about the individual as the focus of rights but little to say about the communities in which the individual is an agent. This imbalance is problematic for one very simple reason: all too often it is the corporate identity that trumps the individual in the actual exercise of rights and all too often it is the corporate identity that falls outside of the domain of rights instruments' ability to exact material consequences for rights abuses. Conversely, where communities fall outside of the institutional norms that set the terms for rights – think the San Bush people of South Africa, the Yanomano of the Amazonian rainforest, or any other nomadic group that tries to survive apart from legal and institutional norms that have become paradigmatic and normative – the right to remain outside those norms is barely even thinkable *as it should be*. The ethical bottom line in these cases remains driven by different communities' capacity to recognize and honour each others' differences within a rights context that allows alternate forms of community, allows the right to not be assimilated to dominant norms. This is the ethical event-horizon for any discussion of community. For community is the crucible in which rights are delineated, given shape, re-articulated, enacted as material reality, and made subject to a constant critical process by individuals with *both* reciprocal and differential needs.

Community diversity as part of a complex ecosystem of relational being that is quite literally 'human being,' needs to be understood as a key aspect in determining universal and site-specific notions of rights. Differential notions of what is a right, rather than posing a negative challenge to the fundamental ethical questions invoked by rights, posit the dialogic as the beginning of any form of ethical engagement. Differential ways of forming and exercising community as a lived social practice require not only a pedagogy of understanding and reciprocity but also a frank recognition of where the collision of difference occurs and how it can lead to meaningful, potentially hybridized social formations.

'All life being one life:' The Ethics of Encounter and 'Being-with'

At stake in relating community meaning to rights discourses is what we have called an ethics of encounter, in which the narratives we tell each other about how to enact encounter – what to learn from it, how to reshape our own being as a function of that process, how to do so with respect for common-good principles – are a key aspect of being-in-community. The ethics of encounter is the fundamental question that each community as a whole must solve (and of which each community is an enacted expression) in relation to larger issues of cultural survival. Inadequate or ill-conceived notions of how to encounter otherness produce dysfunctional communities. This applies not only to encounters with difference outside the community in which one lives, but also to encounters with fellow community members.

Relational contingencies inform the ethics of encounter: the more fully understood are the complex forms of relational interconnectedness, the more capacity for understanding the integrity and dignity of the other. How a community (in)forms its members to undertake encounter and the examples it sets for acceptable and unacceptable practices of encounter play, what we argue is, *the* key role in enacting rights agencies across all forms of social practice. Ethical engagement with otherness is at the root of all forms of rights discourse, a reflection of the interconnectedness of all life: the first article of what may well be one of the earliest non-European charters of rights, the Kouroukan Fouga or Kurukan Fuga the so-called constitution of the Mali Empire (1235–1645), begins by articulating the principle that *'Les enfants de Sanènè et Kòntròn déclarent: toute vie étant une vie, tout tort causé à une vie exige réparation'* [The children of Sanènè and Kòntròn declare: all life being one life, all wrongs caused against a life demand reparation] (Cissé n.p.).[10] From this simple articulation flow any number of ethical and rights corollaries in which the reciprocity and interconnectedness of all life must be acknowledged in order for the consensual agreement that allows for community to exist. And where wrong is done reparations for that wrong need to be enacted out of respect for the affiliations that bind all living things together.

Embedded narratives that propagate dysfunctional modes of encounter have played an extraordinary role in shaping the current global geo-political realities in which elite minority interests exercise egregious power over the majoritarian world. The next two sections of this book unpack some of these narratives, ranging from the largely dysfunctional colonial encounter narrative based on false notions of cultural superiority, domination, and oppression through to oppositional narratives told by aggrieved communities about their struggle to assure their cultural survival. In this context, dissident communities, what one might call *commutinies* (in the sense of mutinous, resistant communities) have a great deal to teach about the living potential of community enactment and engagement as opposed to the all-too-often co-opted notion of passive communities (or managed communities) in which agency is restricted to limited and periodic (as opposed to sustained) forms of political expression and engagement.

French philosopher Jean-Luc Nancy, whose influential work on theorizing community encompasses several books, articulates in *Being Singular Plural* a vision of justice bound by engagement, reparation, and interconnection, three of the key components of thinking relationally outside the framework of the tired binary individual/community:

> 'Justice' designates what needs to be rendered ... What needs to be restored, repaired, given in return to each existing singular, what needs to be attributed to it again, is the giving which it is itself. And this also entails that one not know exactly ... what or who is an 'existing singular,' neither where it begins nor where it ends. Because of the incessant giving and sharing of the world, one does not know where the sharing of a stone starts or finishes, or where the sharing of a person starts or finishes ... Each existence [*existant*] appears in more ensembles, masses, tissues, or complexes than one perceives at first, and each one is also infinitely more detached from such, and detached from itself. Each opens onto and closes off more worlds, those within itself [and those outside itself] bringing the outside inside, and the other way around. (186)

Nancy's vision of undefined yet incorporate interconnections that become the ethical ground for justice is a powerful idea that is to be found in other sophisticated non-Western philosophies. Justice in this sense is predicated on 'returning to each existence what returns to it according to its unique, singular creation in its coexistence with all other creations' (ibid. 187). Such an idea of justice entails a recognition that shared being depends on the impossibility of knowing where the singular being begins and ends. Justice is a giving of that which is also the recipient: rather than an imposition of a judgment it is a rendering from both within and without the singular being, a recognition of the interconnection that grounds all relational coexistence.

Elsewhere, in *The Inoperative Community* (1991), Nancy argues that 'The community that becomes *a single thing* (body, mind, Fatherland, Leader ...) necessarily loses the *in* of being-*in*-common. Or, it loses the *with* or the *together* that defines it. It yields its being-together to a being *of* togetherness. The truth of community, on the contrary, resides in the retreat of such a being. Community is made of what retreats from it: the hypostasis of the "common," and its work. The retreat opens, and continues to keep open, this strange being-the-one-with-the-other to which we are exposed' (xxxviii). Here, too, Nancy attempts to get at the plurality of the singular: to be '*in* common' is to retreat from the singular into the relational that then makes justice thinkable. In such a situation neither the individual nor the community are identifiable as such: neither has substance except in their relational contingencies. These translate, in their most achieved understanding, into an ethics of encounter based on interconnection and coexistence. Might such an ethics ground a rethinking of the rights of community in ways that recognize the community of rights as a crucial aspect of being-in-common?

A later short reflection by Nancy on community in *La Communauté affrontée* (2001) reveals the stakes of thinking in this way, something we explore throughout this book:

> *En face des monstruosités de pensée (ou d'«idéologie») qui s'affrontent pour de non moins monstrueux enjeux de pouvoir et de profit, il y a une tâche, qui est d'oser de penser l'impensable, l'inassignable, l'intraitable de l'être-avec sans le soumettre à aucune hypostase. Ce n'est pas une tâche politique ni économique, c'est plus grave encore et cela commande, à terme, et le politique et l'économique. Nous ne sommes pas dans une «guerre de civilisations», nous sommes dans une déchirure interne de la civilization unique qui civilise et barbarize le monde du même mouvement, car elle a déjà touché à l'extrémité de sa proper logique: elle a remis le monde entièrement à lui-même, elle a remis la communauté humaine entièrement à elle-même ... C'est avec cela qu'il faut travailler: avec la communauté affrontée à elle-même, avec nous affrontés à nous l'avec affrontant l'avec. (50-51)*

> [Faced with the monstrosities of thought (or of 'ideology') that clash with each other for no less monstrous stakes of power and

> profit, there is a task, which is to think the unthinkable, the unassignable, the intractability of the 'being-with' without submitting it to any hypostasis (singular underlying reality). This is not a political or economic task and is much more serious and dominates, in the long term, both the political and the economic. We are not in a 'war of civilizations.' We are in an internal rupture of a unique civilization that civilizes and barbarizes the world in the same movement, because it has already reached the extremities of its own logic: it has given the world entirely to itself; it has given the human community entirely to itself ... It's with this that we have to work: with the community confronted with itself, with us confronted with ourselves, 'being-with' confronted with 'being-with.' [our translation]

'Being-with' ('être-avec') is the only response to deformations of power and profit that are the result of the internal ruptures of a world driven by capital. A world that gives unlimitedly to itself is a world that has appropriated everything to itself. This monstrous logic of total possession, which necessarily leads to total poverty and privation, departs from the philosophy of community that sees the commons as a shared, equitable space beyond mere profit and power – a space that is literally and figuratively unpossessable. The co-generative, co-creative power of the commons lies not in taking everything unto itself but feeding into the commons via renewable coexistent practices of living. The anomaly for Nancy is that it is the community that has generated this rupture with itself and the challenge now is how to confront that rupture. How to see ourselves as we are? How to confront the 'being-with' we have become with the 'being-with' we remain to become? These are the questions that confront any community in which rights struggles occur. Rights are the response to how we engage with ourselves and others – and they are also the ground that shapes what it means to encounter *the other that we are to ourselves* and the other that we are to others.

The Unpossessed Community: Coyote's Story

While in this first section we tackle the discussion of community rights from theoretical perspectives read against concrete, historical examples of how encounters play out in specific locales, especially between corporate-state bodies and communities, we are deeply committed to the idea that this kind of theoretical discourse and political analysis is only one of many ways to tell stories about community and encounter. The density of theoretical discourse is more at home perhaps in the realm of legalistic and academic discussion of rights than in the transcultural stories whose significance evades any simplistic summing up of a 'moral of the story.' If we are to imagine ways in which communities can empower themselves to reinvent rights discourses related to the biotic connectedness of all things, theory is but a first step to understand the processes involved in the creation of such entities as corporations, and how these determine their sphere of action and modes of encounter with individuals, communities, and the land for which they have such obvious disregard, further troubled by how governments have been hijacked by corporate interests.

One of the striking features of a corporation is that it is created, owned, managed, served, and traded by individuals, yet is almost completely devoid of any component relating to what we have called earlier natural community. The injustice perpetrated by a corporation cannot always and easily be attributed to one or even more individuals, though there is a movement, as we discuss earlier with regard to the Bhopal incident, to hold CEOs and top management accountable for obvious negligence and wrongdoing. The system is self-perpetuating and takes on a way of being of its own, which then influences, affects, even coerces all those involved into thinking there are no alternatives save for 'unrealistic' utopian scenarios. It is a radical over-simplification to represent corporations as immutable beings in a Hollywood scenario of good versus evil, just as it is a radical over-simplification to deride alternatives to current social practices of rights predicated on the individual as the be-all and end-all of thinking rights outcomes.

Indigenous stories provide rich counterpoints to such simplistic representations given their complex expressions of the ambiguity of intentions, conflicts, and contingencies that any community gives rise to. We note above that theoretical discourse tends to be dense and demands layers of prior disciplinary knowledge for understanding. But in teaching indigenous stories, we have discovered in the classroom that non-indigenous students struggle to understand the complexity of indigenous stories, whose combination of ancient, contemporary, and hybrid elements have much to teach about transcultural thinking. Theory, like story, takes many guises and shapes. We open this section with the limitations of Sen's 'parable of the flute' and now contrast that story (whose limitations tell us so much about reductive economic understandings of community relations) with a hybrid-Native story by way of a brief consideration of how indigenous stories represent or enact conflict and encounter. In that context we turn to 'The One about Coyote Going West,' a short story by Canadian *mestizo* author Thomas King included in his 1995 collection *One Good Story, That One*, in which the narrative voice imitates storytelling strategies used by Native elders.

Any discussion of the paradoxical and ambiguous character of the coyote, or any trickster figure for that matter, merits a long discussion of its own, as does this one short story. Here, we limit our reading of the tale to those aspects that relate to our previous discussion of the concept of 'being-with,' the monstrous logic of total possession, and the struggle to sustain community and the commons as thinkable spaces of ethical encounter in radical opposition to thinking community only as a function of possession. This reading of community as defined by the ties of unpossession is a radical challenge to state notions predicated on conforming to a singular state-defined identity. Italian philosopher Giorgio Agamben argues, in some remarkable insights into the 1989 Tianamen uprising in *The Coming Community*, that

> What the State cannot tolerate ... is that the singularities form a community without affirming an identity, that humans co-belong without any representable condition of belonging ... The State ... is not founded on a social bond, of which it would be the expression, but rather on the dissolution, the unbinding it prohibits ... A being radically devoid of any representable identity would be absolutely irrelevant to the State. This is what, in our culture, the hypocritical dogma of the sacredness of human life and the vacuous declarations of human rights are meant to hide.' (85)

Passports and Social Insurance numbers do not define co-belonging except as an aspect of state self-interest. Co-belonging without possession is the state of story: the teller is only one instance of a telling that can change as the teller changes or that changes from one teller to the next. Neither the teller nor the listener owns the story, though they co-belong to its shifting reality as an embodiment of unpossessed (unpossessive) community.

Other stories exist about bonds that bring us together in a mutual recognition of multiplicity and ambiguity while also affirming the complex, irreducible relations that cannot be inscribed in singular notions of possession and identity. Coyote (like humans) is both a fecund creator and a haphazard destroyer who often messes things up precisely in the process of trying to fix them. Destruction is the flip side of creation and often an important precursor to unexpected creative shifts in both theory and practice – a mark of the unstable structures that need to be swept away in order for new forms of creation to arise. King's story is co-told in a dialogic way with Coyote and another narrator who shifts gender and is sometimes referred to as 'Grandmother' and at other times as 'Grandfather.' From the start, then, multiple narrators engender a story within a story making it unclear where the story begins and ends, and giving the impression that stories are picked up wherever the tellers and listeners decide together.

The narrative ambiguity reflects the open-ended way in which community creates identity for itself as an aspect of ambiguous co-generative activity. The narrators interweave known cultural and historical elements with new ones improvised in the telling itself as an act of co-creation, in which the participants respond to each other's spontaneous interventions. This plurality of voice embedded in the very form of the telling addresses encounter and negotiation between self and others as an insistent possibility that is inherently ambiguous, mobile, and subject to contradictions.

In the story one cannot help but notice that the human narrator is suspicious of Coyote, especially when told of her intentions to 'Tell those stories. Fix this world. Straighten it up' (69). Coyote offers to tell stories about encounter and conquest by misnamed but historically recognizable figures like Eric The Lucky and the Vikings, Christopher Cartier, and Jacques Columbus. This misnaming draws attention to the interplay of history and the fallibility of memory. And it is also suggestive of a humoristic disavowal of the Western obsession with accuracy when it comes to factual detail that is unconnected to an underlying ethical dimension – the obsession with Truth (with a capital 'T') as opposed to *truthfulness*. When the human narrator rejects Coyote's repertoire saying 'Everyone knows those stories ... Whiteman stories. Baby stories you got in your mouth' (70), they agree on the narrator telling the story of who discovered Indians.

The story begins with Coyote going west in a world where there are still only coyotes, nothing else. The story goes on to tell how the creator aspect of this mythical being starts to make things and fix the world. Contrasting in striking ways with the omnipotent and perfect God of Western culture, 'the first thing Coyote makes, I tell Coyote, is a *mistake* ... Big one, too, I says. Coyote is going west thinking of things to make. That one is trying to think of everything to make at once. So she don't see that hole. So she falls in that hole. Then those thoughts bump around. They run into each other. Those ones fall out of Coyote's ears. In that hole' (72; our emphasis). The deceptively simple language tells of Coyote's good intentions, frailty, distraction, inattentiveness to the very ground she treads on, and how the mistake she makes takes on a life of its own, in that hole with her where the mistake (thought turned physical presence) falls out of her ear. The mistake actually has its own identity and agency, even addressing Coyote and engaging her in conversation as they encounter each other from time to time in their journey westward.

The 'mistake' has sly parodic resonances with the Biblical Satan (in the Book of Job, Satan is an angel submitted to God) but the very fact that the representation is humorous creates a very different being (mistaken but not intrinsically evil): 'I don't want to tell you what that mistake looks like. First mistake in the world. Pretty scary. Boy, I can't look, I got to close my eyes. You better close your eyes, too, I tell Coyote' (72). The mistake separates itself from Coyote: 'Then that one leaps out of the hole, wanders around looking for things to do' (73). Other voices enter the story asking questions and complaining about Coyote's singing through her butt hole and stinking up the place. These voices belong to ducks that have gotten tired of waiting for Coyote to create them, so they go ahead and create themselves. The storyteller suggests that self-creation is always possible and dependent on initiative. Autonomy arises out of initiative. The ducks' self-creation is the first hint in the story of what might be termed, and will later become, a human community when some of these ducks transform into Indians. Far from being any form of evolution or improvement (as Western philosophy represents human superiority to all other life forms), these duck-Indians lament their human form: 'This is pretty disgusting, they says. All this ugly skin. All these bumpy bones. All this awful black hair' (81). The story thereby weaves a different hybrid worldview, epistemology, and ethics, and at the same time, addresses contemporary capitalist consumer culture obliquely attributing it to the mistake's doing. Coyote goes 'looking for that one who is messing up the world' (77). She finds nothing in any of the cardinal directions but then, 'she goes to the west, and there is a pile of snow tires. And there is some televisions. And there is some vacuum cleaners. And there is a bunch of pastel sheets. And there is an air humidifier. And there is a big mistake sitting on a portable gas barbecue reading a book. Big book. Department store catalog' (77).

When Coyote asks the mistake if it has seen any Indians (remember this is supposed to be what the story is about), it offers her everything from toaster ovens to a computer with a color monitor. Despite the fact that this mistake was cooked up in Coyote's own head and fell out of her ear, they now dispute what the world, and they, and the Indians need and don't need: 'We don't need that stuff, says Coyote. You got to stop making all those things. You're going to fill up this world' – to which the mistake calculatingly replies: 'We need these things to make up the world. Indians are going to need this stuff' (78). The only humans in this story are Indians, so over- or mal-development, consumerism, unsustainable production, garbage, and lack of community development are not blamed on white people, though the fact that piles of stuff reigned over by the mistake are found in the West, is suggestive of a source related to Western culture.

The beauty and complexity of this story told in broken English is how it interweaves so many factors, tendencies, and relational contingencies. Instead of blaming anyone specifically in the adversarial (and reductive) mode of blame heaped on an 'other,' it invites us to examine our own mistakes: part of us yet also different and separate from us. The outcome of this particular journey of Coyote's is to realize that the mistake she creates innocently, while being inattentive and unmindful (as we all are a lot of the time), has far reaching repercussions for the world. At the end of the story, the angry 'duck-Indians come over and stomp all over Coyote until she is flat' (82). But the fact that the mistake is paradoxically its own entity (even though created by Coyote) also means that Coyote has the distance to evaluate and respond to it. After the duck-Indians leave, 'That big mistake leave, too. And that Coyote, she starts to think about a healing song' (82).

If as King claims, stories are all we are, and our actions are the direct outcomes of the stories we tell each other and thus live by, then these kinds of healing stories have profound implications for how we think and enact ethical encounter and 'being-with.' Stories are the very predicates of sustainable, co-creative relations that require improvisation, adaptation, and unexpected turns in how the story gets told in response to the diverse, contingent aspects of the community that no one telling will suffice to express. Bearing that thought in mind, we now turn to key related questions of community ethics in relation to the most important underlying aspect of 'being-with' – the relations to the land and the environment that constitute the commons as a co-generative space for the unpossessed 'being-with' that is community in its most promising, achieved form.

NOTES

1 James Madison was the fourth president of the U.S. (1809–17). Before taking office, he played a leading part in drawing up the U.S. Constitution (1787) and proposed the Bill of Rights (1791).

2 Jefferson, in a letter to George Logan, dated November 12, 1816, had also anticipated the problem of corporate oligarchies usurping constitutional structures: 'I hope we shall crush in its birth the aristocracy of our monied corporations which dare already to challenge our government to a trial by strength, and bid defiance to the laws of our country' (Jefferson 68).

3 The Via Campesina is an 'international movement of peasants, small- and medium-sized producers, landless, rural women, indigenous people, rural youth and agricultural workers. We defend the values and the basic interests of our members. We are an autonomous, pluralist and multicultural movement, independent of any political, economic, or other type of affiliation. Our 148 members are from 69 countries from Asia, Africa, Europe, and the Americas' ('What is La Via Campesina').

4 Beloved community was Martin Luther King Jr.'s term for an 'ideal of fellowship, justice, and peace' (Solnit 285), one associated with the civil rights nonviolent movement against racism and the oppressions of aggrieved communities associated with the African diaspora. Kenneth L. Smith and Ira G. Zepp, describe King's theory of community in the following way:

> In 1957, writing in the newsletter of the newly formed Southern Christian Leadership Conference, he described the purpose and goal of that organization as follows: 'The ultimate aim of SCLC is to foster and create the "beloved community" in America where brotherhood is a reality ... SCLC works for integration. Our ultimate goal is genuine intergroup and interpersonal living – integration.' And in his last book he declared: 'Our loyalties must transcend our race, our tribe, our class, and our nation ...'
>
> King's was a vision of a completely integrated society, a community of love and justice wherein brotherhood would be an actuality in all of social life. In his mind, such a community would be the ideal corporate expression of the Christian faith ...
>
> Behind King's conception of the Beloved Community lay his assumption that human existence is social in nature. 'The solidarity of the human family' is a phrase he frequently used to express this idea. 'We are tied together in the single garment of destiny, caught in an inescapable network of mutuality,' he said in one of his addresses. This was a way of affirming that reality is made up of structures that form an interrelated whole; in other words, that human beings are dependent upon each other. Whatever a person is or possesses he

owes to others who have preceded him. As King wrote: 'Whether we realize it or not, each of us lives eternally "in the red."' Recognition of one's indebtedness to past generations should inhibit the sense of self-sufficiency and promote awareness that personal growth cannot take place apart from meaningful relationships with other persons, that the 'I' cannot attain fulfillment without the 'Thou.'

King saw the participants in the civil rights movement as representing the Beloved Community in microcosm. The people who attended the movement's mass meetings and rallies, joined in its demonstrations, and supported its aims in many other ways came from every section of American society. The educated and the illiterate, the affluent and the welfare recipient, white and black – men and women who heretofore had been separated by rigid social and legal codes were brought together in a common cause (Smith, K.).

For an extended discussion of the concept of 'beloved community' in relation to issues of social justice see Charles Marsh's book, *The Beloved Community: How Faith Shapes Social Justice, From the Civil Rights Movement To Today* (2005).

5 Journalist Robert Fisk opines on the results of the Iraq invasion that 'the millions of American soldiers who have passed through Iraq have brought the Iraqis a plague. From Afghanistan – in which they showed as much interest after 2001 as they will show when they start "leaving" that country next year – they brought the infection of al-Qa'ida. They brought the disease of civil war. They injected Iraq with corruption on a grand scale. They stamped the seal of torture on Abu Ghraib – a worthy successor to the same prison under Saddam's vile rule – after stamping the seal of torture on Bagram and the black prisons of Afghanistan. They sectarianised a country that, for all its Saddamite brutality and corruption, had hitherto held its Sunnis and Shias together. And because the Shias would invariably rule in this new "democracy," the American soldiers gave Iran the victory it had sought so vainly in the terrible 1980–88 war against Saddam.'

6 According to a CBC report, 'On coming to office, the [Prime Minister Stephen] Harper government also enacted a new "Veterans Charter," which was designed to change how veterans' benefits and services work. The charter was meant to be a "living" document that could be adapted as unforeseen issues developed. But many veterans now argue that the charter is rife with problems that are not being addressed. For instance, injured vets no longer receive a monthly disability pension for life. Instead, they are granted a lump sum payment up to a maximum of about $276,000, based on the level of disability. The issue is that, even if invested properly, the amount

equals hundreds of thousands of dollars less than what someone would have received under the previous system over the course of a normal lifetime. And that's if it's invested. Many also question the wisdom of giving a young, injured serviceman, who is perhaps also suffering from PTSD [posttraumatic stress disorder], a large sum of cash up front' (Roman).

7 Defining community in this way is hardly a radical gesture. A report written by Brenda L. Murphy and Richard G. Kuhn for the Canadian Nuclear Waste Management Organisation (NWMO), which attempts to address issues arising from the disposal of waste in places where communities will be affected, comes to the following conclusions: 'Given the socially constructed nature of communities, their fluid boundaries, power relations and embeddedness within the broader social matrix, it can be suggested that the conceptualisation of either place-based or interest-based communities as discrete entities with firm boundaries is both deceiving and inaccurate. Instead, as Day (1998) suggests, we should conceptualise communities as networks of relationships to which people have multiple affinities and connections. Davies (2002), in aligning the concept of community with sustainable development, defines networks as the inter-relationships among individuals, organisations and *the non-human world* through which flow "resources, arguments and knowledge." Understanding these networks and the flows that occur allows for the evaluation of the power dynamics within the particular process or project under consideration. She concludes that initial conditions wherein power imbalances exist among various communities often means that elite actors tend to control the undertaking. Further asserted is that top-down attempts "to generate bottom-up actions for sustainable communities" are seriously flawed, partly because localities are usually not considered within the context of wider relationships at different scales. Conceptualising communities as networks means that the form, boundary, power relationships, and so on of the community are fluid and dynamic and only exist as far as the people involved recognize and maintain the network identity and connections. This conceptualisation also suggests that if communities are not concrete and static, there is potential for their meanings and relationships to be renegotiated; potentially this leaves space to include excluded "others" and to redefine moral values and perspectives' (Murphy 6).

8 'The Latin term "communitatus" from which the English word "community" comes, is comprised of three elements, "Com-" – a Latin prefix meaning with or together, "Munis" – that means "the link" and "-tatus" a Latin suffix suggesting diminutive, small, intimate or local. German sociologist Ferdinand Tonnies, defined that "community" is perceived to be a tighter and more cohesive social entity within the context of the larger society, due to

the presence of a "unity of will." He added that family and kinship were the perfect expressions of community but that other shared characteristics, such as place or belief, could also result in a community. Perhaps, the key is "unity of will." Communities can be truly empowering and could provide a tremendous support system to all of us. The Indian term "satsang," that talks of a group of like-minded souls is the seeker's solace, support and mainstay' ('Community').

9 Some of these meanings remain active in the French system of governance in which the smallest administrative unit is called the *commune*, a word that appeared in the twelfth century from the medieval Latin word *communia* meaning 'a small gathering of people sharing a common life ... from Latin *communis*, things held in common' ('Communes of France'). French communes, akin to municipalities elsewhere retain a responsibility to local populations that is at once historic, cultural, and functional. And they also partcipate in a larger form of organization known as intercommunality, a system for fostering cooperation among different communes. France has close to 37,000 communes and is only equaled by Switzerland in the density of these forms of social organization. Significant pressure exists to reduce this density as a function of neoliberal and state interests severely at odds with the ways in which communes benefit from state resources to achieve relative political empowerment and autonomy.

10 In the Mandinka culture of West Africa Sanènè and Kòntròn are the personages without race or country who embody idealized figures of human virtue.

SECTION 2

'None can survive unless all survive'

Community, Story, Land – Making the Connection

Indigeneity and Sacred Geographies Versus Imperialist Monoculture

Communities are created through shared cultural practices, yet are inherently diverse. Communities emerge from a specific set of embodied circumstances only made possible by their capacity for renewal and self-sustenance, a precondition for existence that unerringly links a community's being with the land and the environment that makes any given community possible. We use 'land' in its broadest sense: neither as property, nor as an object of ownership, nor solely as the environment that surrounds human beings, an object of detached exploitation or scientific inquiry. Land grounds everything, all embodied relations between all things animate and inanimate: from the smallest pebble to the ant hidden beneath that pebble to the human who picks the pebble up and throws it, to the feelings and objective realities that the pebble potentially stands in for. Land produces diversity, and as surely as diverse life forms emerge from the land, so do diverse cultures, feelings, spirit, stories, and the values associated with those stories (what we might call rights in an intensely conflict-ridden world).

This crucial relationship to the land has been distorted and obscured by the onset of intersecting interests – military, industrial, commercial, economic – which have had significant negative impact on rights discourses and the intent underlying the legal instruments associated with those discourses. The iPhone or Blackberry user immersed in the seductive virtual world of the shimmering screen is largely unaware that the technology is only made possible as a result of coltan, a dull-black metallic ore which provides the elements niobium (formerly columbium) and tantalum used in making parts (primarily capacitators) found in consumer electronics, including cell phones, DVD and video game players, digital cameras, inkjet printers, pacemakers, computers, and even rockets and jet engines. Raj Patel notes, these earth-extracted elements come primarily from 'bloody conflict' in the Congo, where 'In patrolling access to these resources, military units in the Congo have raped, tortured, enslaved and killed. Women struggling to bring up children in the Congo have a life expectancy of forty-seven years, continue to suffer through the world's worst rape epidemic and earn just over half of what men do – $191 per year' (54). Moreover, 'Export of coltan from the eastern Democratic Republic of the Congo to European and American markets has been cited by experts as helping to finance the present-day conflict in the Congo, with the DanChurchAid agency asserting that "much of the finance sustaining the civil wars in Africa, especially in the Democratic Republic of the Congo, is directly connected to coltan profits"' ('Coltan').

A recent report on tech firms like Apple identifies outsourcing and resourcing as two areas in which such firms are implicated in abuses: Apple outsources 'to a Chinese factory, Foxconn, where stressed-out workers have been committing suicide. And on sourcing the "blood metals" tantalum, tin and tungsten essential to wired devices from places like Congo, where a civil war over ore deposits is killing about 45,000 people a month' (Olive). Foxconn, the Taiwan-based largest manufacturer of electronics and computer components worldwide was making in 2008 as many as 800,000 iPhones per week (Grothaus). A *Financial Post* report states that 'Global Witness, the international conflict observer, reports that rebels, militias, and army units have hijacked the trade in mineral ores from the eastern Congo. And it also says large international companies are complicit in the trade by buying the minerals, usually after they have been sent through smelters in Malaysia and Rwanda' (Mason). Steve Jobs, chief executive of Apple Inc. was quoted as saying, in response to concerns over sourcing of these gadget minerals, that 'We require all of our suppliers to certify in writing that they use *conflict few materials*' (ibid.; our emphasis). Remarkable here is the ambiguity of Jobs's language: what precisely might 'conflict few materials' mean, especially in rights contexts that show a significant proportion of the minerals used in electronics to be anything but 'conflict few'?

Global disconnects between products sold in 'free' markets and their sourcing in markets that are ethically and rights-compromised point to the hypocrisies that underlie terms like global community. In such a context, the abstracted actions of the teenager listening to iTunes via an iPhone interface may seem overtly disconnected from any land- or earth-based realities – but the connections run deep and they have profound rights implications involving multiple, globally dispersed forms of community (oppressed women, underpaid workers, military units, gadget buffs, scientists and engineers, and so on).

Plans for carving up the earth to create enormous mines have now spread to Afghanistan where approximately $1 trillion in untapped mineral deposits have been found by Pentagon officials and American geologists. One might wonder why the Pentagon is involved in mineral exploration. Interestingly, the Americans first caught wind of the vast resources, hidden beneath what previously looked to them like a wasteland, from documents left behind by the previous invading army, the Soviets. *New York Times* reporter James Risen tells a confusing story of great promise for Afghanistan due to the heavy foreign investment these mines will attract together with the 'possibility of jobs' for the locals (1). The story is confusing because so many of the details should set off alarm bells but go uninvestigated. We are informed that 'Afghanistan has a national mining law, written with the help of advisers from the World Bank' (2), which for those who know anything about the WB's track record from a Majority World perspective, would indicate that laws are already being drafted to favour the wealthiest countries and corporations. The ubiquitous word 'help' is associated with the Pentagon, which according to the report 'has already started trying to help the Afghans set up a system to deal with mineral development ... The Pentagon is helping Afghan officials arrange to start seeking bids on mineral rights ...' (3). Fortunately for the bidders (but that is not how Risen expresses it), Afghanistan 'has little or no history of environmental protection' (3).

Deputy Undersecretary of Defense for Business (a revealing name that would seem to have a wider sphere of application than just Afghanistan) and leader of the Pentagon team, Paul A. Brinkley, wonders 'can this be developed in a responsible way, in a way that is environmentally and socially responsible?' and concludes 'No one knows how this will work' (3). We could go to many other places in the world where mining 'developers' don't worry about responsibilities beyond liabilities to see exactly how it will work. A comparative perspective on stories usually brings up critical questions as well as suggesting compelling answers. American officials are said to worry about the Taliban launching into even more fierce fighting to gain control of the country (now predicted to become the Saudi Arabia of Lithium), with the added problem that 'the corruption ... already rampant in the Karzai government could also be amplified by the new wealth, particularly if a handful of well-connected oligarchs, some with personal ties to the president, gain control of the resources' (2). Again, a comparative, transcultural reading immediately begs the question: how is this any different from how business is done in the U.S. and other 'liberal democracies'? How does a community's relationship to the land differ radically from the so-called 'development' promoted by this system of corporate and state exploitation?

Community emerges from the land, must maintain an ongoing relationship to that land, and is defined by the values it enacts with regard to the land on which it depends. This idea is a vital starting point for any understanding of community as a material, enacted presence of biotic relations in which rights become thinkable. It is vital because it does not, as we have earlier argued, privilege human 'being' over other forms of being, recognizing that multiple forms of being *all* contribute to what ultimately makes community. If rights represent the site in which community values emerge and are contested, then unavoidably, any discussion of rights and community must begin with the very ground (quite literally) from which those rights, those communities emerge. Abstracted notions of community that divorce it from this basic understanding, and that also detach rights considerations from this fundamental premise, are extremely suspect. Community is in this view impossible, inconceivable, without the material relations it sustains with the land. The ethical (or not) nature of this relationship is at the crux of all rights issues.

In this section we consider how communities with a shared past, and spiritual values rooted in the land, struggle to decolonize themselves and, by extension, to decolonize the nation-state whose boundaries and governance were imposed on them through colonization. Alternative understandings of how connection to the land is primary, spiritual, and outside legal frameworks based on singular, exploitative ownership (an understanding at odds with contemporary capital culture) are to be found in indigenous communities. These communities, however compromised they have been by the pressures of industrial and postindustrial capital culture, are an important locus of thinking that anchors land-based rights and communitarian narratives. In contemporary Western usage, the term 'indigenous' is automatically associated with people of colour because the history of British and European imperialism since the Renaissance is one of white colonizers dominating racialized others around the globe. Colonialism, however, starts at home, and the history of the unification of the British Isles provides the prototype of colonization centuries before English imperial expansion to other parts of the world. Historian John Gillingham situates the emergence of a set of cultural images by which the Anglo Saxons forcibly anglicized Ireland, Scotland, and Wales in the twelfth century. Scottish writer Alastair McIntosh tells of his community in the Hebrides as being the story of the indigenous Celts who were viewed as barbarians by the English. The reality of the 'civilizing' mission of the English was imperial takeover and the subjection of diverse indigenous Celtic communities to the monoculture of English rule via control of the land: 'Indeed, in England the process of enclosure had started to deprive the common people of their lands in earnest under Henry VIII as far back as 1530, and by 1780, it had virtually all been stitched up by the powers that be' (McIntosh 54).

Any discussion of differences between culturally belonging to an indigenous community and belonging to the nation-state as a citizen must involve a comparative study of law, and not take for granted that only the state's legal system constitutes law. The law from indigenous perspectives connects humans to the land and has a sacred or spiritual dimension that is fundamentally different from the conceptions and practices of either secular governments or institutionalized religions. Indigenous Australian writer Alexis Wright's novel *Carpentaria* continually compares Australian Aboriginal conceptions of law with the legal system of the state imposed by English colonizers. Aboriginal law is shown to have emerged from time immemorial, from creation, the land, animals and ancestors all inter-related in what anthropologists call *sacred geography*: 'The inside knowledge about this river and coastal region is the Aboriginal Law handed down through the ages since time began ... It takes a particular kind of knowledge to go with the river, whatever its mood' (Wright 3). 'If you are someone who visits old cemeteries, wait awhile if you visit the water people. The old Gulf country men and women who took our besieged memories to the grave might just climb out of the mud and tell you the real story of what happened here' (11). Wright's words remind us of the particular knowledges, the memories under siege that are preserved in the land: out of the river mud emerges the 'real story' and presumably that story reveals uncomfortable truths about injustice and oppression.

Since we glean our insights from transcultural stories, it is not always useful to impose Western distinctions between fiction and non-fiction or history, and segregated disciplinary theories. McIntosh makes the same case for the inclusion of poetic sources in his epic storied account of how a small community decolonized the Isle of Eigg in the late 1990s, taking it back from a laird, or landlord: 'As David Corkery said of the Irish bards' perspective, "the downfall of the Gaelic [culture and] the downfall of the woods – these two went together in their verses." To ignore such poetic evidence would be unscholarly, uncultured and unacceptable' (90). Recognizing poetry's connection with shamanism creates bridges among cultures, and shifts the false and simplistic divisions of race to meaningful distinctions between diversity and monocultures, loving life and serving death:

> Cultural healing entails coming alive to community with one another, with the place where we live, and with the soul. This interconnection is, at its deepest level, poetic. Such poetics can be deeply political, which is why, in many parts of the world, the bard has been the king's closest advisor. It is also why the poetic function has been seen as dangerous from Plato onwards. If we are to restore meaning and heal our broken cultures, if we are to be concerned with the blossoming of human potential, then we must learn again to use such techniques that in some cultures would be called 'shamanistic.' These ... can be highly effective tools for community empowerment. (4)

The poetics of community are an important aspect of its empowerment, its enabling potential. Dissolution of, and disregard for, this poetics lead to breakdown and alienation.

Native writers emphasize *how* a story is told – the same event or set of circumstances can be configured as a story that can heal or harm. In the case of Wright's *Carpentaria,* the reference to the dead possibly telling the real story is not meant to be read as the stuff of Western ghost stories, but as a wholly plausible form of communication. As in other indigenous philosophies, time is spatialized and therefore the past is not behind us, over and done with and lost in time, but can be actualized (made present) through ritualized practices, altered states of consciousness, and awareness of the sacred geographies that carry memory as a vital aspect of communitarian knowledge. The law emanates from the land and is premised on the concept that the earth is perfect, that we live in paradise, and that there is nothing to change, fight, fix, or escape from. This belief does not diminish human creativity and responsibility but instead directs human activity to maintaining the earth's complex biotic balance through regular spiritual practices, without which it is believed that the earth would end.

The epic Inuit story *Kiviuq,* to which we return later in this book, tells of a similar belief. Kiviuq, a shaman-hero figure, undertakes a spiritual journey through the land of the North, mating with other beings from the animal world and fathering hybrid creatures, before turning South and becoming half-human, half-earth. In the Inuit telling of the story, his existence as a hybrid entity is crucial to the survival of all things: 'Those who saw him most recently (in the 1940s, according to Samson Quinangnaq,) say that his face was getting covered with lichens and that he had a very hard time moving around, especially in winter. When he dies there will be no more air to breathe and life on earth will end' ('Goose Wife'). The story gets at the importance of the land to human survival, and the necessity of adaptation and hybridization to realizing fully one's contingent being.

Like the autochthonous Australians, the Inuit sang travel songs as a way of mapping their complex relations with the land on which they traveled. In the Australian Aboriginals' cosmology these particular practices include the walkabout: re-tracing the dream tracks inscribed on the earth as sacred scripture read and re-created by the bodies of the pilgrims through walking, singing, dancing, storytelling, re-visiting sacred sites and belonging places.

Anthropologist Wade Davis's 2009 Massey Lectures title, *The Wayfinders: Why Ancient Wisdom Matters in the Modern World,* clearly sets out the book's relevance to contemporary knowledge and practice. However, by representing indigenous practices as based exclusively on ancient beliefs, Davis sets up a problematic dichotomy between Australian Aboriginals' knowledge represented as bound and finite, and Western epistemology's supposed freedom to generate new ideas continuously. While Davis's thesis is that ancient wisdom is needed to save the planet from imminent disaster, he falls into a constant of anthropological error: he represents this ancient, indigenous vision of the world as locked in time, even as he states that these people have no word for time and therefore no such concept:

> But, critically, the Dreaming is not a myth or a memory. It is what happened at the time of creation, but also what happens now, and what will happen for all eternity. In the Aboriginal universe there is no past, present, or future. In not one of the hundreds of dialects spoken at the moment of contact was there a word for time. There is no notion of linear progression, no goal of improvement, no idealization of the possibility of change. To the contrary, the entire logos of the Dreaming is stasis, constancy, balance, and consistency. (158)

Citing Australian anthropologist W.E.H. Stanner, Davis slides from the problematic use of the present tense in the above quote to the past (of Stanner's findings?): 'But the overriding mood of the civilization, as W.E.H. Stanner described, was one of acceptance of belief. There was little place for skepticism, inquiry, or dissent' (158). To describe a worldview as a 'mood' again signals the impossibility of clearly differentiating stasis from change, yet Davis pushes this representation to contrast starkly with the Western tradition in which 'existence is something to be contemplated. Our thinkers and philosophers step outside of life to discern abstract ideas that we define as insights. The Dreaming makes such reflection both meaningless and impossible' (159). To delineate and contrast worldviews clearly, Davis also separates the world into them and we – 'our thinkers and philosophers' – and ends his intriguing chapter on sacred geography by implicitly and perhaps inadvertently suggesting that the Aboriginals' Dreaming is a trap and a mental prison:

> It envelops the individual in a web of belief and conviction from which there is no exit, for one cannot think that one's thoughts are wrong. To violate a law of the Dreaming is a transgression not limited to the moment, but rather one that reverberates through all dimensions, through the eternal past and the limitless future. The Aborigines, as Stanner understood, were not a people without a history. They were, he wrote, a civilization that in a sense had defeated history. (159)

This observation also contradicts Davis's account of violent conflict: rather than looking at the history/stories of inter-tribal warfare that would necessarily imply politics, struggle for power, disagreement, displacement, and consequent social change, he supports his observation on violent conflict with a reference to an initiation ritual among the Warlpiri that 'involved the cutting and transformation of the male sexual organ, a vertical incision that ultimately left the penis fully splayed' (158). This telling of an enigmatic (and barbaric?) ritual shifts focus from the many possible stories about community and inter-community conflict and resolutions to something the Western reader would see as incomprehensible and perhaps even inhuman – a bizarre ritual in a static cosmology with little bearing on social interaction.

Stanner's interpretation of the Aborigines' defeat of history resonates with the same static view that characterizes American political economist Francis Fukuyama's totalitarian dream of capitalism's ultimate perfection culminating in the end of history. We would argue that this defeat of history originates in Western thinkers' drive to secure their colonizing and globalizing supremacy, rather than describing the 'mood' of any indigenous community. In political terms, what Stanner is really telling about is history's defeat of the Aboriginals, a dead-end story, a story that harms and must be deconstructed to understand the ideological underpinnings and motivations for claiming the end of history, especially the history of indigenous peoples.

The Law of the Land

In Wright's epic story *Carpentaria*, Aboriginals are neither static nor idealized much like they are in Thomas King's story discussed at the end of the last section. While the earth is essentially perfect and eternal, the environment is being degraded and destroyed. Wright represents inter-tribal conflict, violence, and the inevitable degradation of human life in a colonized and exploited land. She makes the point that the inter-tribal conflict far antedated the arrival of the Europeans, who only exacerbated it by forcing enemy tribes to co-exist in close proximity against their better judgment to avoid each other. The term 'community' has deeply negative connotations in this story given that it is a euphemism used by white administrators to name the ghettos where Aboriginals are forced to relocate. A humorous element of regional language captured by Wright is the racialization of people as 'blackfellas' and 'whitefellas' and to call groupings of people mobs – 'mob' being the most apt term for the highly suspect and co-opted notion of 'community.'

As is customary in indigenous storytelling, a creation story opens this epic since it is essential to establish how the earth came to be, the relationship of earth and sky, and the people's connection to the earth, before their stories can be told. In this case, the original being is the ancestral serpent, 'a creature larger than storm clouds, came down from the stars, laden with its own creative enormity' (1). The reader is addressed as being potentially like an animal, further strengthening the bonds of cosmic interconnection: 'It moved graciously – if you had been watching with the eyes of a bird hovering in the sky far above the ground' (1). The story tells how this huge serpent scoured out the valleys and riverbeds by crawling on its heavy belly and how it 'continues to live deep down under the ground in a vast network of limestone aquifers. They say its being is porous; it permeates everything. It is all around in the atmosphere and is attached to the lives of the river people like skin' (2). This telling implies that people who live by such a story, who feel the creator as they do their very skins, view the land and water as sacred, and consequently cannot conceive of depleting aquifers for any reason since they are the home of the creator. Whether one takes this figuratively or literally, both interpretations work: without clean water community is impossible.

Such a sense of land-bound community contrasts markedly with a globalized Christian, Muslim, Jewish or any other institutionalized religious 'community' tenuously connected by a master text: the Bible, Torah, or Koran, and a set of often arbitrary decrees and governing bodies that are profoundly removed from the wisdom in Wright's telling of the Aboriginals' creation story. While the great creator serpent has cosmic dimensions, its tangible making of and living in the land eschews any abstraction and dissemination of belief through language, further abstracted through the written word in a book that is disconnected from concrete earthly space. In this sense, while the novel *Carpentaria* takes the form of a published book, the narrator insists on the primacy of oral storytelling that connects these specific communities to specific sites. Oral storytelling marks the embodied presence of the storyteller before the community, and necessarily entails a responsibility and an exchange, what we call throughout this book, an ethics of encounter. The storyteller, in this sense, is a living embodiment of the community both in action and in memory, and a reminder that true community cannot exist without this form of embodiment that is always itself a reminder of the abiding connection to the land.

The characters of *Carpentaria* are multidimensional and rife with contradictions: the elders are at times wise seers, and at others mean-spirited rivals. The walkabout incorporates modern technology and morphs into what would more accurately be called a drive-about in old jalopies, despite the seeming contradiction that oil extraction is represented as one of the prime causes of the land's devastation. The participants are represented as both holy men and as a motley mob of derelicts. While their use of cars attests to their having adopted Western ways, the cars are barely held together by the jerry-rigging genius of bricoleurs whose *modus operandi* is improvisation. This ability to adapt to invader culture contradicts Davis and other anthropologists' simplistic binaries relegating Aboriginals to static constancy. These Aboriginal improvisers build and maintain their vehicles and precarious but adaptive way of life by scavenging elements at hand, or recycling them from the dump.

> The men in this moving mirage of battered vehicles felt they had well and truly followed the Dreaming. Travel had become *same, same* and mandatory, as the convoy moved in reptile silence over

> the tracks of the travelling mighty ancestor whom they worshipped through singing the story that had continued for years. The crossing of the continent to bring the ceremony north-east to the Gulf, to finish it up, was a rigorous Law, laid down piece by piece in a book of another kind covering thousands of kilometres. 'Start em up again!' the Fishman's voice would ring out each morning. The men would rise from the face of the world where they slept like lizards, dreaming the essence of a spiritual renewal rotating around the earth, perhaps in clouds of stars like the Milky Way, or fog hugging the ground as it moved across every watercourse in the continent before sunrise. The convoy journeys were a slower orbit of petrol-driven vehicles travelling those thousands of kilometres. The pilgrims drove the roads knowing they had one aim in life. They were totally responsible for keeping the one Law strong by performing this one ceremony for the guardians of Gondwanaland. (124)

The law in such a philosophy originates in the land, which is intimately connected to humans through the ancestors who are also connected to animals and other life forms, in a web of inter-related being that Western science is only beginning to comprehend. These ancestral spirits are ever-present and can manifest themselves as natural elements like wind, storms, rain, and so forth.

A similar Eastern concept of the law is the Tao (or Dao) meaning 'the way' associated with the fundamental or true nature of the world. Yet Asian philosophies also tend toward the universal, and away from the land, the earth. Both Eastern and Western dominant traditions headed by priests and monks (as opposed to shamans) view the material world as illusory: materiality is disarticulated through opposites that forever cancel each other out in Asian philosophy, and in Western philosophy opposites are conceptualized as hierarchies premised on binary oppositions like superior/inferior, positive/negative. Since the Tao abides in non-action and the certainty that nothing is left undone, Eastern philosophy sees wisdom in quiet contemplation. While such practices also inform Western monastic faith, the separation of secular and sacred thinking and practice in the Western world tends toward knowledge as an active quest that separates humans – as observers, experimenters, interpreters – from the world they study, discover, conquer, and subject to their will. The law in both Eastern and Western traditions has a transcendental origin and does not value the land as the sacred origin and seat of the law. Community-based, indigenous people worldwide differ significantly from both Western and Eastern dominant traditions in that they actively locate the sacred in the land, thereby premising their ethics on their interaction with it and all life forms.

Contrary to Davis's representation of the Australian Aboriginal worldview as static thereby implying that Aboriginals would be unable to respond to new problems in practical ways, the main political dimension of *Carpentaria* is the struggle against a mining company. Though the elders do have a harder time of dealing with fighting for the land, Mozzie Fishman, the leader of the drive-about, derives his guiding principles from the Law, yet launches political critiques and advocates for action:

> Now, even we, any old uneducated buggers, are talking globally. We got to help United Kingdom money. Netherlands lead air problems. Asia shipping. United States industry, and we don't even know German people. 'I says,' he says like he is singing, 'we mobs got to start acting locally. Show whose got the Dreaming. The Laaaw.' He liked to empathise 'The Laaaw' whenever he was heating up around the ears on the subject of globalisation. (405)

The protagonists of the future in *Carpentaria* are the youth, suggestively named Hope and Will, the archetypal Romeo and Juliet of historically feuding mobs. While Will is true to and embodies the ancient wisdom, he sabotages the pipelines and finally blows up the mine in a scene of apocalytic proportions. An act some might call eco-terrorism is represented as being in full accord with the Law:

> The finale was majestical. Dearo, dearie, the explosion was holy in its glory. All of it was gone. The whole mine, pride of the banana state, ended up looking like a big panorama of chop suey. Wonderment was the ear of the ground listening to the great murmuring ancestor, and the earth shook the bodies of those ones lying flat on the ground in the hills. Then, it was dark with smoke and dust and everything turned silent for a long time. 'You think they heard it in Desperance?' some young lad whispered carefully through the settling dust, because he did not want to frighten anyone by making the first sound of this new beginning. (408)

Here, a renegade individual acts on his convictions to secure the land from the cancerous development, or mal-development, driven by profits and the corporations that make and enforce their own laws without relation to community, and in direct opposition to the common good.

Community in indigenous writing can be tenuous and divided, frankly depicting the tensions and internal dissonances that comprise community practices, but nevertheless rooted in the land and stories that bind all together *in spite* of their differences. Those of European descent often lack stories about interconnectedness and the land as foundational. Authors like Tucson-based Charles Bowden might distrust language's ability to convey anything meaningful about such things, together with a deep distrust of his own kind cutting him off from any human community: 'Here the land makes promises of aching beauty and the people always fail the land' (1988 1). Land in Bowden's writing eludes language and the dominant stories of his destructive Euroamerican compatriots. His own storytelling breaks with logic and rational language to convey poetically the insights he gains by walking the desert, much like the Australian Aboriginal walkabout but without traditional stories or songs to connect these experiences:

> I went walking – walking mountains, walking bajadas, walking deserts, walking with scientists, walking with Indians, and most often walking alone. I learned with my feet what the books, reports, symposiums, commission conclusions, and studies skirted: that resources are limited and that technology, invention, and industrial voodoo cannot increase the amount of a resource but simply accelerate the destruction of a resource through consumption. (136)

Bowden's own culture does not afford him any meaningful stories because it promotes harmful lies about progress and supremacy. But the desert tells Bowden stories of extinct tribal peoples and of recent deaths: 'Our bodies whisper: Yes, the stories are here' (172). What one might call poetic insight here has profound implications for ethical human conduct even if Bowden refuses to weave such reflections into his story due to his deep distrust of certainty, of knowing what is right. His stories nevertheless insist on the ways in which the land, story, community, and right action are bound together.

Another reason for not drawing out ethical imperatives may relate to the indigenous influence on Bowden's poetics. He often observes how his Native friends shrug their shoulders when telling of horrendous defeats and tragedies. While in white culture that gesture might suggest not caring, being resigned, or even being fatalistic, there is evidence in indigenous stories that complaining about hardship, and criticizing others for bad behaviour is useless. Frustrated defence attorneys have even discovered that their clients do not bother speaking up in their own defence for cultural reasons; not because they are intimidated or abjected by legal process, but because they accept the wisdom that promoting oneself and blaming others or circumstances achieves nothing.

In his prophetic and intimate stories about facing death – the death of his parents, his own eventual death, and the death of the world as we know it – Bowden explores his connection, beyond reason and language, to other bloods, other tribes, other nations. In his retelling of the beliefs of others, he reveals transcultural influences that come to shape his own worldview. Being a white, Anglo-American does not cage him into Western epistemology, which he constantly questions through other perspectives. Referring to an unidentified Native man ('He's standing out in front of the tribal gambling hall at seven A.M. smoking' [2009 54]), Bowden observes: 'In his language, the word *ni'* has two meanings: Mind. And land' (ibid. 55), and that 'his people once believed the trees and shrubs were hair, the rock and mountains bone, the streams blood, and the wind the earth breathing. Some of the old people still do' (ibid. 56). The consistency with which this worldview is to be found in indigenous communities is worth noting: sacred geographies occur because the land and the mind are unthinkable the one without the other. Spirit and story inhabit both. There is no romanticizing or appropriation of indigenous beliefs in Bowden's highly personal and isolated discourse, yet he strives towards other forms of knowledge, other stories and suggests, as does Wade Davis, that they are our only chance at saving ourselves and the earth.

In the chapter titled simply 'Serpent' in *Some of the Dead Are Still Breathing*, Bowden states his position in characteristically explicit yet paradoxical terms. Each sentence opens with the first person pronoun, sign of identity and individuation, both a place of possibility and a prison from which to escape:

> I have never believed in a hierarchy of being, with complex organisms up in the tower room and less complex organisms toiling in the fields.
> I have never trusted the word *I*.
> I have never felt comfortable with the word *nature*.
> That is why I have come to snakes.
> I want in. (ibid. 46)

Bowden's insights have implications for how to think about community, even when his own American brand of individualistic anarchism, or depleted faith in his culture does not lead him there. The individuated 'I' is untrustworthy as is the hierarchy that assigns complexity a greater value than simplicity. False binaries like 'I and we,' 'simple and complex,' 'superior and inferior,' move people away from integrated relational thinking that posits the simultaneity of contradictory terms as the precondition for meaningful discourse. Yet communities, in their most achieved forms, are an expression of such relational, holistic understandings of reality. After retelling two Yaqui stories about prophetic, end-of-this-world encounters with a gigantic snake, Bowden warns of the consequences of ignoring Native stories:

> They are fable, of course, things that have no standing in our world. But they are on the menu. And if you order them and swallow them, you will tear through the veil that hangs like a shroud and blows you from them.
> Eventually we must enter the gigantic snake. Or we will learn no music and our spirits will grow lean and blow away like ash from a cold fire. (ibid. 89)

The giant serpent appears in prophetic stories in Africa, the Americas, Australia, and other regions of the world. The difference between these stories and the master texts of institutionalized religions is that the giant serpent stories spring from concrete telluric sites of ancient communities, and do not spread to other regions through proselytizing universal doctrines. Bowden is perhaps influenced by Arizona-based stories of the Pueblos who prophesize the return of *Ma ah shra tue ee*, the giant serpent and 'sacred messenger spirit from the Fourth World below' (Silko 1997 127) of which a mysterious rendering in stone suddenly appeared next to the open-pit Jackpile uranium mine in the spring of 1980. The prophecies of the Pueblos (prophecy being a vital form of storytelling in indigenous communities) offer an intriguing view of how community is forged by the land as it interacts with its inhabitants. This idea radically inverts the European and anthropocentric paradigm of man's power over and ownership of the land. The Pueblo understanding is that the land does not belong to people but that the people belong to the land.

It is prophesied that all things European will disappear, meaning European ways and customs, but that the people will develop a rooted relationship to the land that will eventually claim them: 'The gravity of the continent under their feet begins this connection, which grows slowly in each generation. The process requires not hundreds, but thousands of years' (Bowden 2009 124-25). This non-static view of the land-based evolution of communal identity is nevertheless also dependent on stories bringing it into being. Bowden's imperative in the above quote echoes Silko's description of how 'Pueblo communal systems value cooperation and nonaggression above all else,' which she speculatively attributes to the harsh climatic reality that demands cooperation and conciliation for growing precarious crops. 'Moreover, this system of cooperation extends to all living things, even plants and insects, which Laguna Pueblo elders refer to as sisters and brothers, *because none can survive unless all survive*' (ibid. 130; our emphasis).

Community, then, is rooted in the land and interwoven into this web of life that calls out story, prophecy, interpretation, and dialogue. The worrisome aspect of the Pueblo prophecy about invader or migrant cultures slowly becoming rooted in the land is that we know that we do not have thousands or even hundreds of years to develop this wisdom for survival. Hence the urgent tone of Bowden's prophetic and life-affirming warning in the face of imminent Western-driven apocalypse. Within the limited time frame of human comprehension, the battle of competing stories evinced by Bowden is happening now. This battle will determine whether we can radically shift paradigms to reclaim the world from the destroyers, as Silko calls those whose actions and thinking are in the service of cancerous monoculture and ultimately, death-driven consumption.

Community Conflicts With the State

> 'No place is more sacred, and no peoples more worthy of honour, than those that have made beauty blossom anew out of desecration.' –(McIntosh 93)

Taiaiake Alfred, a member of the Mohawk Nation, draws much of his inspiration for the struggle to decolonize the Americas from Mohandas K. Gandhi.[1] After the first stage of agitation professed by Gandhi within the context of British imperial rule in India, civil disobedience is identified by Kanien'kehaka (Mohawk) author Alfred as 'a mass surge of indigenous power against the divisive and controlling state structures' (204):

> These forms of resurgence took on life when people gave up allegiances to the state and began to withdraw from the colonial bu-

> reaucracies and local colonial offices that were used to control the indigenous population. They started to boycott government structures and developed alternative structures of government in their communities. Following civil disobedience, the functions of the imperial government were usurped by parallel indigenous governments in order to challenge the authority of the empire. (204)

It is somewhat problematic that Alfred fails to distinguish 'indigenous' from 'Indian' in his discussion of India's decolonization, but his intention is to differentiate collective rights from the laws of an unlawful colonial government. Colonialism in this sense references imperial practices that homogenize and destroy communities in the name of the nation-state – a monocultural encounter model based on assimilation rather than on diversity. This blurring of indigenous and united anti-imperialists also avoids distinctions where they would be unnecessarily divisive, and suggests that all people who are committed to decolonizing a shared territory can work together toward that common goal. In this sense, his use of the term 'indigenous' is not racially or even culturally exclusive.[2]

While it is misleading to generalize about cultures, let alone such an extensive concept as indigeneity referring to peoples found on every continent, there is nonetheless a commonality among such diverse groups that is acknowledged by many indigenous people. In an interview with Isabel Altamirano, a Zapoteca from Oaxaca, Mexico, Alfred asks her if she has found anything that is common, or shared, culturally, among indigenous peoples. Altamirano's response acknowledges cultural diversity among indigenous people and denies that there is a unique, universal indigenous identity, and yet she also gives an affirmative answer:

> indigenous peoples have a strong relationship with their land and territories; they see them as the social space where they recreate themselves, so land and territory are not only commodities. To indigenous peoples, religion and culture are linked to their natural contexts. It is not rare to find animal representations being linked to human beings, as with the raven in cultures from the Pacific or the deer in Northern Mexico. The role of elder is something shared among indigenous peoples too. Elders are seen as those who have accumulated knowledge, who have answers, or who know how to do things according to tradition. *In many communities, the idea of keeping balance or equilibrium among the different elements within a community is expressed in the way those who transgress the*

> *rules are punished.* In non-indigenous people's justice, those who do something wrong must go to jail. For many indigenous communities, punishment has to be implemented more as a way to restore the equilibrium and heal communities than as punishment. These are some of the things I see indigenous peoples here and anywhere share. (ibid. 142; our emphasis)

Such an ethics of balance and equilibrium has profound social and environmental implications and is therefore persecuted by non-indigenous state law, which is inseparable from either state or private capitalism based solely on exploiting land for profit. According to sociologist Duane Champagne, 'Native rights will not prosper within an international system of nation-states, whether strong or weak ... Relatively strong nation-states, like Canada and United States, have moved in limited ways to recognize indigenous rights, as long as those rights do not challenge the fundamental or constitutional laws of the nation-state' (Champagne 18).

Cecil Foster, a Black Canadian of Barbadian (Bajan) descent, credits Haiti and its Revolution (1791–1804), which created the first republic ruled by people of African descent, and Haiti's ongoing struggle to uphold the ideals of racial equality, with giving humanity a radical alternative narrative to that of colonial domination. Canada's official policy of multiculturalism is heralded by Foster as a set of ideals, regardless of the hard realities of culture clash and marginalization on the ground: 'In the nation-state, we may not be a single nation, but at least we can act *as if* we are one – and as if all members have equal status' (Foster 59; our emphasis). Here, Foster's use of the hypothetical 'as if' suggests that *if* we act according to this new narrative, a new reality will eventually take hold. Contrary to Foster's optimism about an overarching narrative uniting different racialized groups, Patricia McCormack, a professor of Native Studies at the University of Alberta, argues that

> The major barriers preventing indigenous and non-indigenous peoples from building effective partnerships in specific endeavors and as citizens of Canada are, first, the profound differences that persist in their respective narratives about themselves as peoples within Canada, and, second, the difficulties they have experienced in building third spaces, which are contingent upon building bridges between those narratives. (110)

The 'third space' of hybridity and relational thinking is the space of achieved community. Despite identifying Modernity as a period 'associated in world history with the assertion of the identity and culture of the individual, or self, as a unified whole and with what is called development and progress,' Foster's view of modernity rests on the paradigm of progress, implied by his celebration of 'the *new spirit* of modernity' serving as the sub-title of his book (2; our emphasis). The underlying concept here relates to a Hegelian understanding of spirit as pertaining to the historian or author's times, to strictly human affairs, and to rationally guided progress toward self-awareness and freedom.

Scottish writer Alistair McIntosh's definition of the essence of spirit as 'truth and beauty and love' (60) instead connects human spirit with the spirit of all life, and takes us out of linear time to regenerate the present through the past, and toward a rooted future:

> The great disease of our times is meaninglessness. If fresh wellsprings of hope are to be found, we must first cut through the collective hallucination that 'there is no alternative' to nihilism. We must dig where we stand. We must get beneath the grassroots of popular culture and down to the eternal taproot. Here new life can grow from ancient stock ... Maybe a new song will emerge when ancient ways inform our times. (2010 2)

We would clarify here that 'nihilism' masks itself as the 'new spirit' of progress in both corporate and governmental discourse. McIntosh's comparative view situates all times as potentially present via the taproot that is always present, but such an insight overflows the limits of rationalism and modernity:

> The function of the shaman or bard ... is to step outside of consensus trance reality, observe the psychodynamics of individual or social disease, and then step back in to protest for change. 'Protest' – now there's another uncomfortable word! It comes from the Latin *protestari*, meaning 'to testify for something.' As such, work of social and ecological witness is necessarily about protest. Theologically speaking, this makes it prophetic. (121)

It is misleading, then, to de-racialize the concept of modernity as Foster does by simply attributing it to world history, without examining how it continues to be used to uphold white supremacy, and to devalue people of colour as primitive and in need of modernization. It seems partial to praise Canadian Prime Minister Trudeau (1968–79; 1980–84) for his vision of multiculturalism and to ignore that his government devised what Thomas King calls a termination plan for Aboriginals – the 1969 White Paper. Foster's insights into the paradigm shift implied by the Haitian understanding of fraternity based on the nuances of the mind instead of on skin colour demands a deeper understanding of other aspects of Afro-Haitian stories, such as humans' relation to the land and other life forms. Foster's privileging of European political and social philosophy, however, creates a potential blindness toward radical and non-European thinking that could not possibly be contained by any nationalist discourse, any discourse of state-sanctioned multiculturalism. Conversely, a radical politics of place would imagine richer connections among us all in relation to the land, through the sharing of intercultural stories and the creation of a meaningful third space in which the relational contingencies among, story, land, and community identity are activated.

Portuguese sociologist and cultural critic Boaventura de Sousa Santos traces the splitting of the world along the 'abyssal line' drawn and constantly re-drawn by the elites of the North. This concept of the abyssal line, together with his assertion that we are globally governed by pluralistic fascism – social fascism coexisting with liberal political (managed) democracy – clarifies why one nation's multicultural policy cannot exempt it from the global power politics traversing all nations. Santos explains how democracy is trivialized to such a degree that it is no longer necessary, or even convenient, to sacrifice democracy to promote capitalism. Instead, we have expanding states of exception, and a new totalitarian state form: 'the state of exception, which contrary to the old forms of state of siege or state of emergency, restricts democratic rights under the guise of safeguarding or even expanding them' (16). This is the logical outcome of Western modernity, which 'can only spread globally to the extent that it violates all the principles upon which it has historically grounded the legitimacy of the regulation/emancipation paradigm on this side of the line (north; privileged). Human rights are thus violated in order to be defended, democracy is destroyed to safeguard democracy, life is eliminated to preserve life' (16). This damning critique of Western modernity begins the process of finding a way out instead of celebrating falsehoods.

This perspective also diverges from Foster's idealism and faith in a new modernity in that Champagne calls for a multinational, rather than a multicultural state. He believes that such a model would reap more pragmatic benefits for actual communities, instead of the seemingly empty multicultural discourse of an imaginary unified national community:

> An advantage of a multinational state model is that it can recognize a variety of institutional, cultural, political, land, lifestyle, and national arrangements and try to develop a consensual basis for social and political participation in a multinational community and multinational state. A multinational state structure would more effectively recognize the social, political, territorial, cultural, and lifestyle powers of its constituent national community than do the unified or multiethnic state models. (19)

This proposal means to counteract the multicultural model that promotes historical amnesia while celebrating superficial and non-threatening forms of diversity. One can pay lip service to multiculturalism as a unifying force while ignoring treaties, or even considering them detrimental to unity by characterizing them as having special (meaning 'unfair') legal status. McCormack identifies pragmatic differences relating to the land between indigenous and settler cultures that no amount of multicultural celebration can bridge: 'The indigenous point of view mandates respect for individual choices but resistance to imposed policies and especially to any attempt to interfere with their access to and control over their homeland and its resources' (114). Multicultural policy does not necessarily recognize this understanding of 'homeland' but a multinational state would have to.

Looking to Bolivia as the expression of a new paradigm in national politics with the indigenous majority gaining power, Uruguayan writer Eduardo Galeano focuses on an aspect of indigenous law that breaks with European paradigms:

> The entire world, stunned as it is, is wandering about like a blind man in the middle of a crossfire, having to listen to those voices. They teach us that we, tiny beings called humans, are part of nature, relatives to all those who have legs, paws, wings, or roots. The European conquest condemned the indigenous, who lived in that communion with nature, for idolatry, and for believing in that communion they were flogged, their throats were slit, or they were burned alive. (2)

While Bolivia will remain multicultural, the difficult shift from neocolonial and Eurocentric domination over the majority, to that majority's decolonizing itself gives voice to a worldview that has been silenced and forced underground for centuries. The greatest expression of multiculturalism on a global scale is the process of decolonization that allows previously suppressed stories to be heard and to inspire people of all backgrounds to shift from an ethically and economically bankrupted paradigm to one based on equality for all and respect for the diversity of human community within the larger context of that community's contingency on the earth and other forms of life. Particular stories about humans' equality to other life forms also radically alter the understanding of community. Rights are no longer reserved for individuals or even for humans. As Galeano asserts, 'the rights of human beings and the rights of nature are two names of the same dignity' (ibid. 2).

Georges Erasmus, former national chief of the Assembly of First Nations in Canada, and president and chairman of the Aboriginal Healing Foundation, talks about misunderstandings across languages and worldviews. He tells of how Aboriginal people have been forced to negotiate using alien terms to launch claims to lands that according to elders 'have supported our peoples since time immemorial' (102). Furthermore, the elders also teach that people belong to the land and not the other way around, therefore land should not be claimed by anyone because it supports us all. Here a profound epistemic and philosophical split occurs between the Western notion of claims and rights, and the old Native notion of values embedded in the land. While the old Native notion would not require litigation, new colonial realities force Native peoples to lay claim to land as a right.

The government is willing to engage in legalistic dialogue but the very language co-opts Native speakers. In *The Truth About Stories*, Thomas King credits Canada with taking the lead in legislating Indians out of existence with the 1876 Indian Act. While he shows legislation up for what it is: a kinder, gentler, and sneakier form of cultural genocide, he humorously turns the tables on cultural stereotypes, characterizing the government's logic as magic – but the kind we associate with hokey advertising for such products as laundry detergent:

> It would be too torturous a journey to try to explicate the Indian Act at one sitting, for *it is a magical piece of legislation* that twists and slides through time, transforming itself and the lives of Native

> people at every turn. And sprinkled throughout the Act, which, among other things, paternalistically defines who is an Indian and who is not, are amendments that can make Indians disappear in a twinkle.
>
> An 1880 amendment allowed for the automatic enfranchisement of any Indian who obtained a university degree.
>
> Get a degree and, poof, you're no longer an Indian.
>
> Serve in the military, and abracadabra, you're no longer an Indian.
>
> Become a clergyman or a lawyer and presto, no more Indian. *Legislative magic.* (132 2003; our emphasis)

King's satiric words get at the arbitrariness and self-serving idiocy of state-imposed definitions of community belonging. Of note, in the examples he cites, is the fact that if an Indian participates in colonial structures of just about any sort (education, military, religion, the judiciary), this immediately disqualifies that person, in the state's legal understanding, of their *ur*-identity. The examples show how assimilative and community-breaking colonial state practices are profoundly cynical, immoral, and vacuous in their grasp of the ethics of encounter.

Getting at the root of the problem, namely the lack of communication and equality among speakers, Erasmus says: 'we need to talk "people to people" as well as "nation to nation." I propose to try shifting the terms of discourse along three lines: from Aboriginal rights to relationship[s] between peoples; from crying needs to vigorous capacity; from individual citizenship to nations within the nation state' (103). This shift from individual to nation is also a shift to community – communities bound together consensually and with the openness of spirit required for listening to each other with genuine shared interest. Erasmus, who also co-chaired the Royal Commission on Aboriginal Peoples, remembers the insight gained by a non-Native member of the Commission about his own relationship to the land: 'These are my treaties too. They legitimize my place in this land' (106). It is precisely this sort of shift in colonial discourse that is needed, where the colonizer assumes responsibility for the telluric commons, and in so doing opens into the third space of hybridized communitarian understanding.

Revolutionary Community: The Strange Case of Gerrard Winstanley and the Diggers

Community is a constant source of contradiction and paradox. Out of these emerge its capacity to rethink itself and to produce creative alternatives in the face of orthodoxies that seek to limit ambivalence. The deeper a community's understanding of itself as an expression of relational contingencies guided by an ethics of encounter, the more achieved a community is in generating the co-creative forces that contribute to its long-term sustainability and its capacity to adapt in the face of crisis or necessary change.

Gerrard Winstanley (1609–1676) was an English freeman of the Merchant Tailors Company, who had been bankrupted in 1643 as a result of the effects of the English Civil War on his business that turned him into a cowherd in Cobham, Surrey. Winstanley, in addition to his eventual association with the Quakers (via Edward Burrough, an early Quaker leader), was a member of one of the revolutionary communities that came into being at this time, which included the Levellers, agitating for the reform of government along egalitarian lines and led by John Lilburne, and the True Levellers or Diggers (also known as the Christian communists), who shared deep-rooted, Biblically-founded beliefs in egalitarianism extending back, at the very least, to the Peasants' Revolt in 1381. What distinguished the Levellers from the True Levellers was that the latter took direct action by literally digging and planting land thought to be part of the public commons (hence their moniker, The Diggers). On April 1, 1649, Winstanley's True Levellers began to plant common, public lands in Buckinghamshire, Kent, (George-Hill) Surrey, and Northamptonshire. Worse, in planting and raising crops on these lands they also *freely* distributed their produce to followers and members of their community.

Reaction was swift from threatened landowners, who sent thugs to beat community members and destroy their plantations on the commons. A remarkable pamphlet describing what happened to the Diggers, *A Bill of Account of the Most Remarkable Sufferings that the Diggers have met with from the great red Dragons power since April 1, 1649*, lists the extent to which the thuggery against the Diggers was a combination of local and state apparatuses:

> *The first time, divers of the Diggers were carried Prisoners into* Walton *Church, where some of them were struck in the Church by the bitter Professors and rude Multitude ... The Dragonly enemy pulled*

> *down a House which the Diggers had built upon* George-Hill, *and cut their Spades and Howes to pieces ... Divers of the Diggers were beaten upon the* Hill *by* William Star *and* John Taylor, *and by men in womens apparel, and so sore wounded, that some of them were fetched home in a Cart ... And indeed at divers times besides we had all our Corn spoyled; for the Enemy was so mad, that they tumbled the Earth up and down, and would suffer no Corn to grow.* (Hopton 96)

The pamphlet lists numerous beatings, razing of houses and of fields, breaking of tools, attacks on animals and children, random imprisonments, mob attacks, many of these involving the local sheriff, soldiers, gentlemen, and the Lords of local manors. A key factor in these attacks was that the Diggers' numbers were seen to be growing steadily in April of 1649 with no end in sight and that they had started to fire the heath, burning at least 10 acres (Bradstock 74). In other words, an alternative community founded on egalitarian, non-ownership based principles in the post-revolutionary context of Civil War England (in which Charles I had been publicly beheaded [1649] as a symbol of the commonwealth's supremacy over the monarchy) was found to be too revolutionary and was efficaciously suppressed by an empowered middle class seeking to maintain its hegemony.

Andrew Bradstock notes that analysis of the extent to which the Diggers presented a real threat to local communities in their planting of the commons should 'guard against exaggerating the impact that the St. George's Hill Digger colony might have had on the local community. It is worth remembering that the Diggers only ever occupied a small part of Walton Heath, and even if their numbers had swelled as much as they hoped and their opponents feared, it is unlikely that their activities would have completely prevented Walton's inhabitants from enjoying the rights they claimed over their commons' (75). Again the relational contingencies out of which contradiction and paradox erupt in community are in evidence. What happens when competing visions of the commons are at stake, one traditionalist and based on a context that associates the management of the commons with propertied classes, and the other radical because it associates the commons with egalitarian principles in which private property is an aberration of a basic right to the land that grounds community?

Winstanley evolved a theory of community that linked the earth's community with freedom, which was only achievable as a function of true 'community of spirit.' His pamphlet *The Law of Freedom in a Platform* (1652) is, as observed by Bradstock, 'a contribution to the [post-civil-war] debate on the economic nature of the commonwealth ... At its heart was the definition of what a community was ... the vision in *The Law of Freedom* [was] of a community made up of individual households, governed locally by magistrates, but with no private property, and with the intense accountability of political representatives' (55). In the *True Levellers Standard Advanced,* Winstanley argues to

> Make the Earth a Common Treasury, without grumbling ... And hereby thou wilt *Honour thy Father, and thy Mother*: Thy Father, which is the Spirit of Community, that made all, and that dwels in all. Thy Mother, which is the Earth, that brought us all forth: That as a true Mother, loves all her Children. Therefore do not thou hinder the Mother Earth, from giving all her Children suck, by thy Inclosing it into particular hands, and hooding up that cursed Bondage of Inclosure by thy Power. (cited in Bradstock 68-69)

Remarkable in this passage is how Winstanley interconnects Biblical tropes with anti-enclosure, anti-property arguments that link community to earth, family to community, and that appeal to an underlying natural law that seeks equitable access to the commons as a function of these interconnections. The rights implications of such an appeal are enormous and not without their contradictions, especially in light of the role played by Christianity in the colonial accumulation of property and assimilation of cultural difference as a function of state hegemony. Radical expressions of Christian doctrine were too radical for Christians whose sense of religious purpose only extended as far as the property-line of their enclosure.

Winstanley's views were an entirely logical extension of post-civil war anti-monarchic sentiment reacting to the anti-egalitarian aspects of sovereign rule. These anti-monarchic, egalitarian sentiments arose from a notion of freedom defined by a core relationship between the commons and the common people, the community of rights that was unthinkable without the commons that made community possible. Winstanley understood that 'the freedom which the common people have got, by casting out the Kingly power' lies in having the 'land of their nativity for their livelihood, freed from intanglement of Lords, Lords of Mannours, and Landlords, which are our task-masters' (Hopton 39). In the same address *To the Lord Fairfax, Generall of the English Forces, and his*

Councell of War, Winstanley locates the real nature of the battle being fought over how to constitute community:

> ... in this work of Community in the earth, and in the fruits of the earth, is seen plainly a pitched battaile between the Lamb and the Dragon, between the Spirit of love, humility and righteousnesse, which is the Lamb appearing in flesh; and the power of envy, pride, and unrighteousnesse, which is the Dragon appearing in flesh, the latter power striving to hold the Creation under slavery, and to lock and hide the glory thereof from man: the former power labouring to deliver the Creation from slavery, to unfold the secrets of it to the sons of Men, and so to manifest himselfe to be the great restorer of all things. (ibid. 34)

The ethical import of these words is significant insofar as they envisage an earth-based notion of community, with the logical result of private property being enslavement. Even though heavily inflected by the Biblical rhetoric and tone found throughout Winstanley's work, the ideas are largely concurrent with rights ideals based on equitable access to a creative, embodied commons with inalienable links to the earth as a spiritual principle. How truly radical these ideas were may perhaps be measured by the efficacy with which they were attacked and ridiculed.

In his *A Declaration from the Oppressed People*, Winstanley takes these ideas even further in depicting property as the basis of inequality and thus an affront to the earthly community he seeks to establish.

> For after our work of the Earthly community is advanced, we must make use of Gold and silver, as we do of other mettals, but not to buy and sell withal; for buying and selling is the great cheat, that robs and steals the Earth one from another: It is that which makes some Lords, others Beggers, some rulers, others to be ruled; and makes great Murderers and Theeves to be imprisoners, and hangers of little ones, or of sincere-hearted men ... We say, while we are made to hinder no man of his Priviledges given him in his Creation, equal to one, as to another: what Law then can you make, to take hold upon us, but Laws of Oppression and Tyranny, that shall enslave or spill the blood of the Innocent? And so your Selves, your Judges, Lawyers, and Justices, shall be found to be the greatest Transgressors, in, and over Mankinde. (Corns 33-34)

Use-value is not equivalent to property value in Winstanley's vision of community – a radical imagining of the commons as a non-commodifiable space. Property necessitates class and class generates inequality and injustice. Tyranny and oppression are the logical outcome of property, predicated on principles of restrictive accumulation and taking-from as opposed to dissemination and giving-to. How was it possible to have fought a civil war over principles of freedom and egalitarianism and yet deny the veracity of what Winstanley was arguing? Winstanley's insights were doubly threatening. Not only did they expose an overweening systemic weakness in how class structure operated as a function of property enclosure, which was always necessarily an undermining of equality. But his analysis also exposed the inherent failure and hypocrisy behind the revolutionary principles ostensibly behind the English civil war.

How possible is it to imagine, in these terms and in these conflicted contexts, a public sphere untainted by property as the dominant mode for ordering community? This radical challenge to community is, in a post-modern world structured almost entirely on the principle of capital accumulation, perhaps Winstanley's most enduring, perplexing legacy. The truth of his observations is counter-poised against the extreme logic of capital wholly based on principles of enclosure and ownership as made manifest in neoliberal worldviews. Echoes of this troubling legacy abound in contemporary discourses. As Kitty van Vuuren points out in a discussion of public broadcasting, 'a fundamental paradox inherent in the public sphere [is that] access, participation and the quality of discourse in the public sphere are connected to its enclosure, which limits membership and participation through a system of rules and norms that govern the conduct of a group. By accepting the view that a public sphere is governed by property rights, it follows that an open and universally accessible public sphere is neither possible nor desirable' (Van Vuuren). What can community mean if its underlying connection to the commons that is the unpropertied, unenclosed earth has been corrupted (seemingly) beyond repair by structures that limit who has access to the commons as a function of class, wealth, and power?

The strange (perhaps not so strange) case of Gerrard Winstanley tells of a widespread pattern involved when oppositional communities confront hegemony: revolutionary notions of community enacted through direct action (who knew that digging and planting corn could be revolutionary?) are violently suppressed using community self-interest as the very justification for the suppression. What might this dynamic reveal about the capacity for dominant communities to address legitimate calls for change and diversity that challenge their own self-interest?

FEEDING THE PEOPLE / PEOPLE FEEDING THEMSELVES

'For a colonized people the most essential value, because the most concrete, is first and foremost the land: the land which will bring them bread and, above all, dignity.' –(Fanon 44)

Johnny Mack, Toquaht scholar of Indigenous and democratic constitutionalism, defines liberalism as 'a mode of governance that places value on the person and protects the person's individual liberty and private property' (298). In his essay 'Hoquotist: Reorienting through Storied Practice,' he situates the problematic relationship between community and state in a contemporary Canadian context. He then identifies how and why communities are conceived of not as natural groupings linking families within the state but as competing with state self-interest:

> Ultimate authority rests in the sovereign, which receives its authority directly from the people. Its primary obligation is thus to individuals, and it is committed to protecting those individuals from the molestations of social groupings and the presumptively insular ontologies that groups are thought to perpetuate. As it relates to indigenous people, liberalism has sought first to thin political allegiances to the tribe and thicken their connection to the democratic state. Indigeneity in this context would survive insofar as it was consistent with underlying principles of the liberal state. The degree to which such consistency exists is a contested subject that is fought out within liberal society's deliberative institutions. In the case of Canada, these deliberative institutions include legislative procedure, court judgment, and treaty agreement. (298)

In contrast to the state's suspicion of communities, Mack explains that the Nuu-chah-nulth word *ha'houlthee* refers to everything within the boundaries of a Nation's territory, the object of colonial plunder being 'both ourselves and the land we belong to' (292). Again the community is said to belong to the land, not the land to the community. Nonetheless, in their inevitable dealings with the colonizers First Nations had to modify this principle somewhat, to adapt the language to the colonizers' intransigent position on land as titled property, an object whose sole telos is ownership.

While Mack works in legal studies, his conception of the individual's relationship to community, governance, leadership, ownership or stewardship of land and water diverges in significant ways from non-Native views and settler concepts of law. At first his discussion of *hoquotist*, a word encapsulating a metaphor and an entire story about the Nuu-chah-nulth's state of disorientation as a result of colonialism, is told as a sad and angry story of loss. But through the teachings and storied lessons of his elder Wickaninnish ('English' name, Cliff Atleo Sr.) Mack comes to understand that what is lost is not an essence or a thing but the habit and knowledge of practices that can be re-learned. The issue then becomes how his community will reorient itself in a process that also parallels and enacts decolonization. Governance in this community is associated with the leader's commitment to feeding the people, again a leadership concept that necessitates a long-term vision of stewardship, conservation, and sustainability:

> One thing I have noticed, and I have told this to many chiefs, is that when you stand up and say you want to feed the people, others, without understanding why, will help you. People will come from all over the place ... If you start doing this, people will start to have pride, without preaching to people that you have to have pride. All this plays itself out in the support they give to the chief. Along with their support comes the preparation. The practice. People will have to go out and get the fish, and hunt. They will practice their songs and dances. All the chief has to say is 'I want to feed the people.' (303)

As we have seen in other instances, the land is the source that nourishes not only hungry mouths, but cultural practices of song and dance, language, and community engagement unified in the former practices.

In the case of chiefs who neglect or relinquish this responsibility of feeding the people, Wickaninnish advises that the community should host the feast *for* him, *even* in his absence. This advice lifts the community out of inertia and any sense of hopelessness due to the leader's inactivity, and discourages useless blame of, and dependency on, leaders who do not practice the communal ways. The outcome is deeply participatory and communal in that the community teaches or inspires the leader through example and practice, thereby assuming collective leadership. Community practice necessitates productive reconciliation with sources of community conflict and failure. The irony is that such initiatives come from individuals (like Wickaninnish) connecting with other individuals. The communitarian web requires these nodes of contact that are an aspect of conjoined beings, neither wholly singular nor wholly plural. Individual and community do not form a binary opposition in everyday, lived practice.

Ethnographer Ruth Benedict, student and colleague of the German-American anthropologist Franz Boas,[3] describes how communal practices originate with individuals:

> There is no more communal authorship in folklore than there is a communal designer in ironwork or a communal priest in religious rites. The whole problem is unreal. There is no conceivable source for any cultural trait other than the behaviour of some man, woman or child. What is communal about the process is the social acceptance by which the trait becomes a part of the teaching handed down to the next generation. (cited in Bringhurst 136)

In other words, individuals who have been formed in the community and who sustain a relationship to it (even a negative one) produce new knowledges and practices that only become such, as they are integrated (socially accepted) into cross-generational ways of being. This rich dynamic necessitates both sides of the binary, with neither dominating, an ethical relationship that has vast implications for rights practices that (wrongly) privilege either the individual or the aggregate.

While it is always problematic to make comparative leaps between cultures, Mack's story about communal feasts remains a telling (indirect) indictment of government at all levels: can we imagine a politician making it his or her mission to feed the people? Yet countless community organizers in the diffused urban sense of 'community' do just that. Food banks, NGOs, religiously affiliated organizations, socially conscious farmers who donate to food banks rather than ploughing their unprofitable crops back into the ground, and anti-poverty groups often take up the enormous slack of neoliberal governments who have all but absolved themselves of such a basic responsibility in the name of profiteering and privatization.

The issue of poverty emerges in another recent urban story about immigrants for whom it is a struggle to buy nutritious food. While very different from Mack's story of traditional community leadership, the case of a doctor who took it upon himself to improve the diets of poor patients resonates with a similar insight linking basic rights, dignity, and community spirit. This story of what can happen when an individual decides to feed the people has led to the investigation of a medical doctor in danger of losing his license over allegations he improperly signed off on forms that allowed some people on social assistance to claim an extra allowance to buy special food items. Dr. Roland Wong 'held a special clinic where he signed 100 special diet allowance forms for a group comprised mostly of women from Toronto's Somalian Canadian community' ('Doctor probed' 2). When questioned about his motives, Dr. Wong explained that he felt social assistance rates are too low: 'Right now people are living on meagre amounts. The main thing right now is to raise the rates ... They're looking for means to increase their means to survive' (ibid. 1). The news report makes no mention of what 'special' food consists of, and focuses instead on how the cost of the province's special dietary allowance program has jumped fivefold in 7 years presumably due to this kind of 'fraud' by doctors.

The Ontario Coalition Against Poverty (OCAP) believes that people must work together to demand the social assistance to which they are entitled. In cities like Toronto, where reasonable rent for decent or even sub-standard housing is non-existent, where buildings that could be converted into social housing are routinely sold to developers to turn into more high-end condos, more and more people end up homeless. The government's tactic is to make these people invisible by driving them out of the core, and especially away from the parks closest to government buildings. An OCAP campaign headline demands social housing instead of social cleansing, and they encourage people to obtain the special diet allowance since welfare rates are so low that recipients often are forced to make the impossible decision between paying the rent and feeding their families.

Madeleine Meilleur, the then Minister of Community and Social Services for the province of Ontario is reported to have referred 2,300 cases of what the Ministry considers fraudulent special diet claims to the police for investigation. Though the Ministry claims to provide income and employment supports to Ontarians in need so they can move toward self-sufficiency in their communities, the mandate is carefully scripted to make no mention of support to people living in poverty who are perhaps chronically unemployed: 'Ontario Works provides financial and employment assistance to eligible people in temporary financial need' ("Ontario Ministry" 2). One might ask how a government ministry can even be called *Community* and Social Services (our emphasis) when its mandate is to identify those few who are eligible for help to eat a healthy diet, while screening out most poor people.

Visionary individuals who work together for the collective good advance communities that address basic needs in an equitable way and move on from there as needs and inequities arise: these individuals are visionary not because they belong to a plutocracy, not because they have more money, not because they have celebrity. They are visionary in their relative anonymity and in their understanding of their own agency in relation to a greater common good. That individual-centred discourses of rights have pre-empted the notion of a common good is one of the major challenges facing discourses that re-conceive rights as a more nuanced intersection between individual self-interest and that common good. What is often forgotten in this debate is the extent to which key aspects of the common good invariably overlap with individual self-interest, through access to nutritious food, clean water, a sustainable environment, healthy work conditions, and the like.

Blessed with a climate that allows year-round farming, the traditional knowledge of organic farming, and the vision to feed themselves, a primarily Latino community in Los Angeles turned 14 acres of urban wasteland into a thriving community garden with over 100 plant species. But people who decide to feed themselves through such initiatives also run into problems with government. The well-documented case of South Central Farm in Los Angeles, California is a frustrating story of government ineptitude and corruption, developers' greed, and community defeat, as well as the promising story of new community trends in self-sufficiency and sustainable agriculture. These, the largest community gardens in the U.S., originated from the biggest riot in its history in 1992, after the acquittal of the police officers responsible for beating Rodney King in a widely publicized act of police brutality that involved a violent beating and tasering: 'By the time the police, the U.S. Army, the Marines, and the National Guard restored order, the casualties included 53 deaths, 2,383 injuries, more than 7,000 fires, damages to 3,100 businesses, and nearly $1 billion in financial losses. Smaller riots [also] occurred in other cities such as Las Vegas and Atlanta' ('Rodney King'). Since the riot expressed not only the minoritized (aggrieved) Black community's outrage at the legal system's blatant racism, but also its general sense of historic disenfranchisement, the municipal government responded by securing unused land through eminent domain seizure (compulsory purchase, acquisition, or expropriation). This legal practice is based on the state's power to buy private property with due compensation to the owner but without the owner's consent, and, in this case, to delegate the property to a third party who will devote it to public or civic use. At first, the state's sovereign control over all land with the right of expropriation seemed to actually benefit the poor. At the end of Scott Hamilton Kennedy's award-winning 2008 documentary film *The Garden*, one of the women farmers who is an indigenous Chicana expresses her sense of belonging, and then her sense of being lost upon eviction: 'without the land, we are nothing' (Kennedy, S. H. n.p.).

The farmers who became that third party in this eminent domain seizure case numbered approximately 350 families organized into a self-governing, elected body, primarily filled by women. The farm and its families prospered from 1994 to 2006 when after years of legal wrangling, dirty backroom deals among the municipal government, the owner-developer, city councilors, and an organization called 'Concerned Citizens of South-Central Los Angeles' (who were more interested in acquiring dirt soccer fields than in the poor feeding themselves), the government sold the farm back to the owner Ralph Horowitz, who then proceeded to evict the farmers and bulldoze the land. In a twisted turn of events, the Annenberg Foundation's announcement that they would buy the farm for the community came a few weeks later than the deadline Horowitz had set for the farmers to come up with $16.3 million (though the 1986 eminent domain valuation had been only $4.8 million, a clear case of profiteering on Horowitz's part). The families evicted from South Central Farm got an offer from the city of Los Angeles to provide them with about half the acreage of the original farm, but the mere 3 acres made available to the community in 2009 were situated under high voltage power lines, posing health risks from electromagnetic radiation.

What the Academy Award nominated film *The Garden,* together with most of the critical writing about the South Central Farm or of the aftermath of the 1992 L.A. riots all fail to explain is why compensation primarily for African Americans resulted in Mexican Americans temporarily cultivating the land. It is clear that the Latinos have an advantage in that they retain strong connections to the land and to farming even when their access to land is tenuous and controlled by government and corporations. African Americans have a more troubled relationship to the land given that they were forcibly brought in chains to the Americas and made to work on plantations as slaves. English colonizers were careful to separate Africans of shared cultural descent to ensure that they would not be able to communicate with each other in their native languages, thereby promoting cultural genocide and community erasure more effectively. Though Native Americans were also enslaved they still had the communal belief that they belonged to the land the Europeans invaded and exploited, together with the prophecies that the land would one day reclaim itself. The history of abolition promoted by abolitionists is self-congratulatory and glosses over the fact that releasing people into a racist society to fend for themselves in a capitalist economy is not freedom at all. Imagine if, instead of this combination of abandonment and discrimination by the state, African Americans had been compensated with former plantation lands to ensure their sustainable self-sufficiency. This compensation, of course, never happened and is as remarkable a failure of the ethics of encounter as was the corrupt deal that forced Haiti after it gained its independence in 1804 to repay French slave owners for their losses, a situation that effectively bankrupted the country for generations.

In *Freedom Dreams*, African American scholar Robin Kelley examines several such radical imaginings including those of The Republic of New Africa, an organization that advocated reparations to the descendants of slaves and the building of a new nation within the U.S. that would part ways with capitalism to embrace cooperative economics. This vision shares – with indigenous thinking about co-existence – the concept of the multination-state, where different worldviews are not suppressed into a false unity under the dominant Eurocentric paradigm. As in indigenous thinking, the African also stresses the communitarian model of society rooted in the land. According to Kelley 'land is wealth, pure and simple. Historically, it has been fundamental for economic independence and sustainability, not to mention a central source of heritable wealth in the United States' (125). But Kelley outlines how systemic racism has prevented African Americans from acquiring land and how even those who became homeowners 'suffered discriminatory policies and practices from lending institutions, real estate firms, and the Federal Housing Administration' (125). Kelley goes on to connect community formation with land: 'land is space, territory on which people can begin to reconstruct their lives. The dream, after all, is to create a new society free of the overseer's watchful eye. How can any group of people govern itself without land?' (125).

As in Wright's novel *Carpentaria* the notion of community becomes fraught when invoked by paternalistic abolitionists in this case in the antebellum period, whose idea of freedom was to set up 'Negro villages' with a focus on 'enterprise, thrift, and individual accumulation – in short, their goal was to instill ex-slaves with middle-class capitalist values in order to prepare them to be productive members of the mainstream' (Kelley 6). How different were the maroon settlements and Brazilian *quilombos* of fugitive slaves! Rather than being experiments conceived and controlled by the colonizers, these self-formed communities were religiously and politically syncretic, and in that sense, inherently experimental. Syncretic communities are the hallmark of survival when adapting to hybridized new circumstances beyond the original community's control. They are in evidence throughout the Caribbean and South and Central American diasporic slave communities that survive to this day. Palmares, the most famous of these syncretic *quilombo* communities, located in the northeastern state of Alagoas in Brazil, was established in the early 1600s and survived most of the 17th century. It was home to an estimated 12,000-30,000 people who took back their freedom and formed their community without state permission, and who resisted several military campaigns by Dutch and Portuguese colonists to annihilate them. Palmares was a multiethnic confederacy with a strong Native American presence, and also accepted whites and other immigrants who embraced its radical communitarian ideals of freedom.

Unfortunately, in the U.S. no such autonomous Black communities evolved during the colonial period and any advances for freed slaves and their descendents were dictated by the state. Shortly after the American Civil War there was talk of land reform and the proverbial '40 acres and a mule' for each freed black. But this minimal restitution never materialized. African Americans have a spotty history of agricultural opportunities because plots of land were granted and retracted at the whim of governments. In 1845 some 40,000 freed slaves were settled on 'Sherman's Land,' 400,000 acres [along the Atlantic coast] in Georgia and South Carolina, but in 1865 President [Andrew] Johnson reversed Sherman's Field Order 15 by ordering that virtually all plantation lands given to freed slaves be returned to the original plantation owners ('Federation of Southern Cooperatives' 1-2).[4] At the peak of black land ownership in 1910, 218,000 black farmers were full or part owners of 15 million acres of land, but by 1992 only 18,000 black farmers were left owning 2.3 million acres (ibid. 3-4).

The dominant trend in agriculture is the concentration of land ownership by huge agribusiness corporations that reduce farmers to contractees with little decision-making power or independence. Tim Pigford, a black farmer who lost his farm and home in North Carolina in a foreclosure after the USDA (U.S. Deptartment of Agriculture) denied him a loan, succinctly puts the black farmers' plight into historical perspective: 'The government never wanted Afro-Americans as land owners' (Singer 3). During the late nineteenth century, Jim Crow laws deprived black people of their civil rights thereby supporting a command-and-control system of farm contracting, and the New Deal farm programs displaced many black and white tenants and sharecroppers, and even disfavoured black farmers owning land adjacent to or near white farms that had better access to subsidies and inducements to expand (Reynolds 9). The history of marginalized and racialized people pitted against each other in constant competition for the crumbs from the masters' tables further complicates how the compensation deal after the 1992 race riots played out as depicted in *The Garden*.

Instead of focusing on the details of the dispute over South Central Farm, we would highlight the widespread plight of poor people who due to under- or unemployment, or to low wages and high prices, cannot feed themselves and their families adequately. The South Central Farmers website states that shockingly 27 million Americans are without access to fresh, affordable food, a crisis that led to a bi-partisan group in the U.S. House of Representatives creating a National Fresh Food Financing Initiative. The actual Resolution links the obesity epidemic to a lack of fresh fruits and vegetables for at least 23 million low-income Americans, and resolves to provide 'communities across the United States with critical one-time loan and grant financing to help fresh food retailers overcome initial barriers to entry into underserved, low-income communities, and [to] support renovation and expansion of existing stores so they can provide the healthy foods that communities want and need' ('National Fresh Food').

The resolution clearly favours retailers, and ignores the fact that they are not social service providers, but profit makers who have already shown themselves less interested in establishing stores in neighborhoods where people spend less and sometimes cannot even afford to buy fresh produce. Grocery chains that receive such a loan are under no obligation to stay in the community – they can pocket the money (presumably the taxpayers'), and pick up and leave as soon as they decide that selling to the poor is not as profitable as selling to the rich, a situation that is clearly foreseeable before accepting the loan/grant. The unjust practice of *redlining* is always already at work in most business plans designed only to maximize profits for owners and shareholders. Redlining refers to identifying poor or racially diverse regions on a map to either avoid providing services there, or to charge more for fewer and poorer quality services and products than the normal going rates in more affluent, white neighborhoods. According to supply and demand economics, price functions to equalize the quantity demanded by consumers and the quantity supplied by producers, resulting in an economic equilibrium of price and quantity. This theory is clearly disproved in social reality where class division, grave financial inequalities, and reverse redlining (charging poor and racialized or otherwise minoritized people more) destroy any possibility of equilibrium.

African-American comedian Chris Rock offers up a biting satirical comparison of affluence and redlined marginalization: 'I hate the black mall. There is nothing in the black mall but sneakers and baby clothes. I guess that's all they think we're doing: running and fucking. Fifteen sneaker stores: Footlocker, Athlete's Foot, Foot in Your Ass. In the white mall they have big-ass stores. Valet Parking. Personal shoppers' (24). In the routine entitled 'Supermarket Sweepstakes,' he takes on the food desert issue, and challenges the desire to 'buy black' in a self-deprecating way that makes it clear that supporting your disadvantaged community is a near impossibility in a country where resources are so unequally distributed: 'It's easy to shop black if all you want is a pack of potato chips … When I was kid my mother used to drive an hour to get food and I never knew why, until I grew up …' (24); 'There's nothing fresh in a black supermarket, unless you count "fresh from the can." There's no red meat. The meat is brown. And if you do get some red meat, you better cook it *that* day because it's gonna be spoiled tomorrow. You'll wake up and locusts will be having a convention on the meat – and all because you wanted to shop black' (25).

Demographic studies clearly show that poor and racialized neighborhoods have a disproportionate number of liquor stores and *only* poorly stocked 'convenience' stores with little nutritious food. The motivation behind providing poor, racialized people with liquor and guns instead of food and education is transparent, and needs no economic theoretical analysis. In his non-fiction novel *Black Like Me,* John Howard Griffin relates the concerns and plans of black communities during the height of the Civil Rights Movement: 'Black thinkers spoke of turning the ghettos into gardens, taking over their own schools, building a "nation within a nation"' (190). These thinkers and the people in black communities saw the injustices perpetrated by the old exploitative system, in which all the businesses including the big chain grocery stores were owned by white men. Even when black people spent money in those stores, their dollars went into white banks that routinely refused black people small-business or housing loans. In response to this systemic injustice, the community organized and sent spokespeople to stores to demand that they hire black personnel at all levels including the managerial: 'and furthermore, they had to bank the proceeds of that particular ghetto operation in black banks which would not discriminate against black people in loans. The stores had to comply, and this was so successful in Chicago that the techniques spread across the country' (191).

Institutions, in a state plagued by systemic racism, tend to discriminate against non-white citizens. Black farmers were given the '"opportunity" to buy land in the flood plain of the Roanoke River, while whites had land made available to them out of the river's reach' in the 1940s; to this day black farmers routinely wait a year for USDA loan approvals while their white counterparts receive the same approval in two or three months; only 56% of black applicants receive loans compared to 84% of white applicants (Singer 2-3). This situation can be radically changed, through community-based cooperative models in farming and in other business ventures. ShoreBank is a mission-based American community development and green bank that has acquired other banks in danger of relocation forced by white flight from redlined neighborhoods. Its mandate is to support neighborhoods that have been disadvantaged by redlining through providing mortgage and renovation loans to low and middle income families, as well as engaging in international development projects in about 30 countries. Similarly, a Rural Business Report (Reynolds) advises further development of cooperative farming as a way of sustaining black farmers and encouraging young people to join forces in providing higher quality products than large agribusiness.

Returning to our thoughts on culturally incommensurable conceptions of land, and conflicts between state governments and communities, it becomes clear that land as private property does not provide the life-support it is meant to for the majority of the world's population, and not for an increasing number of inhabitants of even the wealthiest countries. Despite United Nations conventions and World Health Organization recommendations, governments do not consider themselves responsible for feeding the people, and do not even provide communities with support to feed themselves. They cover up this abdication of their responsibility by promoting self-help and voluntary effort: 'Health promotion can be addressed in terms of individual consumers' responsibilities as well as in terms of their rights – their responsibilities to give up smoking, eat healthier foods and take more exercise, for example, abstaining from drug and alcohol abuse and refraining from indulging in un-safe sex' (Mayo 158). While Marjorie Mayo of the Centre for Urban and Community Research (CUCR) situates this market-dominated approach predominantly in the UK during the eighties and early nineties, and welcomes a more holistic approach in current community development models, the reality on the ground is not keeping up with these new theories. Mayo's discussion of community media focuses on interactive methods to get people to voice problems and envision solutions, but what much research on community development ignores is the harsh political reality of governments and corporations actively seeking to disempower and disenfranchise communities.

A large proportion of the world's population should be engaged in farming, one of the most fundamental activities that millions of people, indigenous and settlers alike, see as their heritage and vocation. There are no convincing arguments to support taking this practice away from individuals, families, and communities to turn it over to a handful of chemical and agribusiness corporations that make righteous claims about the need for genetically modified and engineered crops and animals to feed the world's poor. The Trade-Related Intellectual Property Rights (TRIPS) agreement was drafted by a coalition of corporations behind closed doors, and then imposed on 125 countries through the World Trade Organization (WTO). African countries, India, and Central America demanded a stop to patenting life and to bio-piracy but were blocked by Europe and the U.S., making it clear that there is no democratic process in this business, and that patented organisms are not designed to help poor countries develop but rather to rob them of their rights to self-determination, their time-tested traditional crops, and community farming.

A case study of Brazil shows that huge tracts of arable and privately owned land lie fallow, while Brazil's poor are unemployed and starving. Roughly half of Brazil (some 980 million acres) is considered suitable for agricultural use, but only 150 million acres are regularly used to grow grain. So while agribusiness claims that GM crops (including so-called terminator seeds) are required to feed the world, lack of productivity is a political problem that will never be solved by science and technology. The monstrous, anti-life and monocultural concept of terminator technology, which assures that second-generation genetically modified plants are sterile, overturns the most basic tenets of community, namely, renewability and sustainability as part of a shared commons of knowledges and practices that actually work. Terminator technology, itself developed cooperatively by the United States Department of Agriculture (USDA) and the Delta and Pine Land Company, now owned by Monsanto, was touted as the future even when the technology itself was founded on a perverse form of anti-productivity wholly based on profit and creating global dependency on corporate monocultures. Despite having been stopped in its tracks for the moment, largely by Brazil and India, the two largest democracies in the developing, majoritarian world, the concept and technology do exist as an exemplary form of unethical thinking about the way in which the ancient, shared culture of farming can be remade in neoliberal terms. Privatization, economic dependency in the name of profiteering, monocultures, concentration of ownership, all point to the breakdown of community. In Brazil, some landowners have such enormous amounts of land that even by farming a small portion of it they can make millions a year, and can personally afford to ignore the rest. But can any society afford to ignore the injustice created by the inequitable access to land? Or by the unethical application of technologies that pervert the legacy of millennia of shared knowledge and community making?

The Brazilian photojournalist Sebastião Salgado published a book of photos entitled *Terra: Struggle of the Landless* inspired in part as a reaction to the massacre of a group of farm labourers in the Brazilian state of Pará in April of 1996. These photos commemorate the courage of landless peasants who risk their lives by squatting, and farming land that is privately owned. In his mordantly honest introduction, Portuguese writer José Saramago insists that there is nothing easier to understand than the history of the world that plays itself out in Brazil, and wherever else a few people have robbed the majority of their means to a decent living.

> Peopling in dramatic fashion this landscape and this social and economic reality, drifting between dreams and despair, are four and a half million rural homeless families. The land is there, before their eyes and their arms, the immense half of an immense country, but these people (how many all told – fifteen million? twenty million? even more?) cannot enter it to work, to live with the simple dignity that only work can confer due to the voracious descendants of the men who first said 'This land is mine' and found others like them ingenuous enough to believe that saying it was enough. They surrounded the land with laws to protect them, with police to guard them, with governments to represent and defend them, with gunmen paid to kill. The nineteen dead at Eldorado dos Carajás were merely the latest drop of blood in the long martyrdom that has marked the persecution that cost 1,636 lives between 1964 and

> 1995, causing misery for the peasants of every state in Brazil and particularly for those in Bahia, Maranhão, Mato Grosso, Pará and Pernambuco, where more than a thousand have been murdered. (12)

The same martyrdom kills indigenous and other marginalized people in all colonized countries even where governments, paramilitaries, and private gunmen can no longer get away with massacring people with complete impunity. A recent article about the Guaraní of Brazil outlines how suicide, especially by youth, results from loss of land and the subsequent breakdown of culture. Amilton Lopes, local indigenous leader, describes the effects of encroachment on her people: 'The estate owners bought land and brought in cattle and soy and turned our land into monoculture plantations ... now we have nowhere to live, to gather native medicines, or to find food for our children, and there are no houses for us' (Frayssinet 2). People who were capable of living self-sufficiently on the land are now exiled, and forced to work as labourers on plantations and sugar mills under conditions that replicate colonial slavery. Suicide is the reaction to what many indigenous youth worldwide see as a complete lack of options: 'One young indigenous person commits suicide every 10 days on average in the centre-west Brazilian state of Mato Grosso do Sul' (ibid. 1). Among the Inuit people, suicide rates are 11 times the national average for Canada with 83% of those committed by people under the age of 30 ('Inuit Health Topics').

Instead of generalizing about the high rates of suicide among indigenous peoples it is important to identify what factors in those communities either foster or prevent wellbeing. While Canada would seem not to have much in common with a poor country like Brazil, indigenous people in both countries suffer similar problems resulting from colonization and cultural genocide. Communities that are able to sustain cultural continuity through practicing traditional means of survival, the circulation of cultural knowledge through storytelling and counseling by elders, and through an abiding, lived connection to the land have no suicides or dramatically lower rates than those communities where these practices have been extinguished. In Canada 'There are two important exceptions to the tragic suicide statistics in First Nations communities: Native Elders have a significantly lower suicide rate than non-Aboriginal senior citizens and *reserves where traditional culture has been preserved or rebuilt have lower rates* than those without tradition. Culture then is a protective factor against suicide' ('What Are the Contributing Factors'; our emphasis). Culture is sustained and transmitted by communities and the two concepts of culture and community are not dissociable.

In India, an estimated 200,000 farmers committed suicide in the last 13 years when their GM crops failed or they were bankrupted by the contracts they had with 'life science' corporations. These contracts disallow saving seeds from one season to the next, and force farmers to use corporate products or face trumped-up charges of patent infringement.

> The new hybrid seeds, being vulnerable to pests, required more pesticides. Extremely poor farmers bought both seeds and chemicals on credit from the same company. When the crops failed due to heavy pest incidence or large-scale seed failure, many peasants committed suicide by consuming the same pesticides that had gotten them into debt in the first place. In the district of Warangal, nearly 400 cotton farmers committed suicide due to crop failure in 1997, and dozens more committed suicide in 1998. (Shiva 2000 10)

Suicide rates plummet wherever farmers take control of their crops by freeing themselves from these unjust contractual agreements and perverse notions of corporatized agriculture. As Shiva reports, 'in small villages across the length and breadth of India now you see little placards, placards that the WTO negotiators will never see, which say "This village is a GE-free, patent-free, chemical-free zone." And in fact those are the *kinds* of villages where [people] aren't committing suicide' (Shiva 1999 5).

Despite numerous scientific studies proving these important social factors to community wellbeing, policy studies departments, right-wing think-tanks, and government consultants fight a bitter ideological battle against Native peoples' cultural rights. A leading Canadian university press published *Disrobing the Aboriginal Industry: The Deception Behind Indigenous Cultural Preservation* by Frances Widdowson and Albert Howard, even though it manifests all the features of hate literature. This is not to suggest that hate literature should be censured – differential dialogue is part of any healthy community's birthright and legacy. What is troubling is that any press would publish a work without scholarly merit by authors who clearly have made no effort to learn anything about aboriginal culture. The text presents a systematic attempt to discredit all aspects of aboriginal life, knowledge, and beliefs. The authors confuse self-government with reliance on white government, and advocate for 'human integration' as opposed to Native sovereignty, which they equate with, in a remarkably offensive stretch of the imagination, racial segregation and even Nazism.

John Richards, another university professor identified as one of Canada's foremost political intellectuals on Wikipedia, also works for an influential think-tank that advises Canadian prime ministers on Aboriginal policies. His advice is that government should 'rethink the premises of Canada's Aboriginal policy independently of the premises of the tribal chiefs and their organizations such as the Assembly of First Nations' (*Turtle Island* 2). These approaches are a profound betrayal of communitarian thinking and the ethics of encounter we advocate in this book. While these cases seem to be particularly virulent and irrational reactions against sharing power and respecting the differences among communities, they belong to a long tradition of assimilationist politics, as Patricia McCormack reminds us:

> In Canada, the *place* where the opposing nature of indigenous narratives about Canada and their place within it was first clearly articulated, was the reaction in 1969–1970 by a number of Canadian native organizations to the federal government's proposed white paper. Foremost among these was the Indian Chiefs of Alberta, who published their 'Red Paper' in 1970. The government's policy paper argued that the cause of Indian problems was their special legal status, which prevented full equality of Indians and integration into Canadian society. The Indian chiefs wanted their special treaty and aboriginal rights acknowledged and recognized, historical grievances addressed fairly, and meaningful participation in any policies that affected them. While this alternate analysis was not new, it represented a unified statement of century-old concerns and issues. (114)

The assimilationist agendas of governments, bolstered by misguided consultants who disregard the needs and knowledges of marginalized communities, only alienate and further disadvantage those who have already been pushed to the margins by centuries of colonialist policies. Those who genuinely seek to empower marginalized communities must see their role as cooperative and not paternalistically top-down. In fact, regardless of the degree of education community workers and teachers have, they must be open to learn more and different knowledges from those communities. What marginalized people have in common is the knowledge that they need meaningful development in order to live with dignity. The inhabitants of contemporary *quilombos* in Brazil, slum dwellers living on the edges of urban centres of the third world (and let us remember that there are pockets of third world poverty in the wealthiest countries), and Native peoples on reservations or separated from their communities and struggling to survive in the mainstream, all know that they need education to secure a better life. But their views on what is relevant to learn often differ from state curricula.

In the domain of education, too, community interests can clash and even be ideologically and philosophically incommensurate with Western values and epistemology, and approaches to pedagogy. Guillermo Gómez Peña, Mexican (now Chicano) performance artist's revision of definitions for first world/third world and beyond are useful for rethinking competing perspectives instead of unthinkingly accepting purely capitalistic economic indicators:

> First World: a tiny and ever shrinking conceptual archipelago from which 80% of the resources of our planet are still administered and controlled.
> ...
> Third World: the ex-underdeveloped countries, and the communities of color within the ex-First World.
> ...
> *Fourth World: a conceptual place where the indigenous inhabitants of the Americas meet with the deterritorialized peoples, the immigrants, and the exiles; it occupies portions of all the previous worlds.* (245; our emphasis)

Founder of Aide à Toute Détresse (ATD) / Fourth World Movement, Father Joseph Wresinski started his radical anti-poverty work in one of the poorest suburbs of Paris. His most influential insight is that even the poorest of the poor understand their oppression, and have the most informed ideas about how to improve their situation. Above all Wresinski 'knew that what was most humiliating was for no one ever to ask poor people for their opinion, not to recognize their values, their experiences, and much less to permit them to express their hopes' (Van Genugten and Perez-Bustillo 53). To remedy this, he founded a world organization to give these people a name and a sense of belonging to a wide spread community that worked through solidarity for social change.

A Peruvian member of the Fourth World families of Cusco (Cuzco) who participated in the organization's second congress in New York and

Washington in 1994, brought international stories home to his community. He told them that he had seen poor people begging, homeless people sleeping in the streets of these wealthy cities: 'I also let them know that we, the poorest of the poor, can be found on all five continents, and that despite differences of race or language, we are one people, and that we have important things in common such as our stories, and our commitments to solidarity with each other which is being lost among the richer societies because of individualism' (ibid. 57). Such a planetary imagining of community expresses faith in poor people's capacity to help themselves and each other through communitarian ethics and practice. This approach is diametrically opposed to the cynical developmentalism promoted by international financial institutions and aid programs based on charity (instead of dignity), or on forcing neoliberal ideology and economics on poor countries in exchange for loans.

Within this reconceptualized Fourth World, the educational needs and desires of what Gómez Peña refers to as the deterritorialized would clearly differ from the dominant society's perspective. Once assimilation is rejected, the need to recuperate cultural identity and knowledges demands a revisionary look at histories that were silenced by colonial powers. The tensions between mainstream public education and the deterritorialized – whether African Americans, First Nations, Latinos, and other racialized immigrants – manifests in all colonized and hybridized territories. Why are the dropout rates so much higher for minoritized students? Could it be that the education designed by the state and its experts does not seem relevant or meaningful to those whose histories are systematically ignored and whose cultures are debased?

In her seminal essay on 'Language and Literature from a Pueblo Indian Perspective,' Leslie Marmon Silko remembers that Pueblo children were taught to read with Dick and Jane books, which perpetuated culturally, even geographically, alien and hence alienating details. For instance, robins were said to fly south, which did not make sense to the Pueblo students since *their* robins do not exhibit this behavior, but publishers in the north fail to take these location-specific details of the story into account. In an ironic twist of fate, Silko suggests that since Pueblo students were denied the more sophisticated and engaging education that could have come with the teaching of canonical Western texts, the education received in the Bureau of Indian Affairs schools did less damage since it was too irrelevant to displace the Pueblos' own stories: 'Whatever literature we were exposed to at school (which was damn little), at home the storytelling, the special regard for telling and bringing together through the telling, was going on constantly' (Silko 57-58). Duane Champagne also notes that the unified nation-state model promotes strong programs of assimilation through education, but that this tends to backfire: 'Such programs are coercive, since native peoples are often insistent on preserving their own cultures, although during periods of forced acculturation such views may go underground and be hidden from state officials and members of the national community' (Champagne 15).

In an extensive 'Survey of Post-Secondary Education Programs in Canada for Aboriginal Peoples' written for UNESCO by Cathy Richardson and Natasha Blanchet-Cohen, the authors note that many Native students seem unable to decide on a program of study even when they have the opportunity and funding to attend a post-secondary institution. The authors hypothesize that these students lack any role models in their communities as part of the legacy of the residential school system that deracinated people without giving them the skills or knowledge to achieve career goals. Add to this the inferior Kindergarten-Grade 12 education provided to marginalized students or communities, and it is no wonder that even those who graduate lack vision, passion, or a concrete sense of empowerment and direction.

Educators and curriculum developers may notice that certain groups of students tend not to engage with the books, ideas, and research projects prevalent in a homogenous/homogenizing dominant school system, then concluding that these students do not have the intelligence or cultural (read: *racial*) aptitude to follow the academic curriculum. Instead of considering epistemological differences and diverse approaches to teaching and learning styles based on community-based knowledge, administrators stream these students into programs that are less challenging but do not necessarily teach the practical skills that might make them successful in either the job market or in negotiating the yawning gap that exists between their own community formation and the world into which they are supposedly being trained to integrate.

The pointed questions posed by Richardson and Blanchet-Cohen make it clear that education reflects and imposes ideology and a specific epistemology:

> What are the criteria for evaluating post-secondary education? How can post-secondary education be both about increasing the number of people with degrees, and about providing higher education that is culturally-grounded, and provides students with the

> tools to transmit their culture? How can the latter be achieved when formal education is fundamentally at odds with First Nations' worldviews and traditional educational methods? (5)

We turn, yet again, to Silko, this time to *Ceremony* because this short novel is a profound comparative study of clashing epistemologies and how they translate to agricultural and healing practices. These competing knowledges drive a wedge between the protagonist Tayo, and his cousin Rocky who sees education as his passport to the white world. Though Tayo is the cultural and racial hybrid, he values the old ways and understands that science does not have all the answers to community practices in specific environmental-based circumstances. Once Tayo decides to raise Mexican cattle in the arid region of New Mexico, he realizes that local knowledge and improvisation will produce better results than the generalizations and impositions of government policies and science:

> 'See, I'm not going to make the mistake other guys made, buying those Hereford, white-face cattle. If it's going to be a drought these next few years, then we need some special breed of cattle' ... The problem was the books were written by white people who did not think about drought or winter blizzards or dry thistles, which the cattle had to live with ... 'I guess we will have to get along without these books,' he said. 'We'll have to do things our own way. Maybe we'll even write our own book, Cattle Raising on Indian Land, or how to raise cattle that don't eat grass or drink water.' (75)

Cousin Rocky, on the other hand, has internalized the racism of white education and interprets Tayo and his uncle's practical approach as stubborn backwardness and ignorance:

> 'Those books are written by scientists. They know everything there is to know about beef cattle. That's the trouble with the way the people around here have always done things – they never knew what they were doing.' He went back to reading his book. He did not hesitate to speak like that, to his father and his uncle, because the subject was books and scientific knowledge – those things that Rocky had learned to believe in. (76)

Rocky's attitude is symptomatic of how, according to Brian Calliou, 'modernization theory reflects this assimilationist attitude by arguing that industrialization and technological progress [were] inevitable and that traditional economies and traditional values would perpetuate underdevelopment. Unless aboriginals dropped their old ways, they would not succeed and would only have themselves to blame' (47).

In a world divided by the abyssal line, knowledge in the singular and the legality that enacts that knowledge are seen as belonging to the First World, which constructs its identity in opposition to the imagined ignorance and chaos on the other side of the line. In such an oppositional imagining of the world's peoples, no real credit can be given to those on the 'underdeveloped' side regardless of their cultural strength and advances. It is ironic – but nevertheless in full accordance with this supremacist logic – that indigenous knowledge about the healing properties of plants, for example, is not valued and disseminated as such, but is instead stolen and patented by corporations:

> Largely preserved in oral traditions, the knowledge and wisdom of indigenous peoples – in this case, the healing power of plants – is transmitted across generations within family and apprenticeship relations. Presently, pharmaceutical companies, often the very constituencies who devalue this knowledge, are making enormous profits, while indigenous peoples remain unrewarded. Many consider the patenting of indigenous knowledge or 'bio-piracy' a double threat, first of creativity and innovation, and second, of stolen knowledge and economic profit. (Champagne ix)

There are numerous examples of Monsanto and other corporations patenting seeds worldwide that have been cultivated for millennia. A type of corn grown in Mesoamerica for thousands of years, for instance, is now a 'product' for which indigenous Mexicans will have to pay for the 'right' to continue planting (Champagne x). In Karnal, India, Monsanto secretly planted GM rice knowing that it would contaminate this oldest variety of rice (the best quality of basmati rice is to be found in the old Karnal district, also known as the rice bowl of India). When the local farmers discovered this crime they burnt the crop, but farmers cannot keep up with or contain these covert corporate operations ('Monsanto ...' 4).

Bio-piracy, an extension of the original theft of communal land, must be examined in the context of colonization as a continuum into present neocolonialist practices that indigenous and other deterritorialized people continue to fight. Territorial fascism is one of the forms of social fascism identified by de Sousa Santos relating to this ongoing and expanding colonization, almost always in new colonial territories inside states that were once subjected to European colonialism (19). In a lesson on decolonization, Silko identifies the first step for non-Natives as simply acknowledging that 'our' home is built on stolen land. She doesn't demand an apology or guilt trip non-Natives, for apologies are often only public relations gestures, and feeling guilty is another form of self-indulgence. Like most indigenous people, Taiaiake Alfred does not envision a settler pack-up policy with non-Natives heading back to lands they've never even seen: 'When we say "Give it back," we're talking about Settlers demonstrating respect for what we share – the land and its resources' (153). Like Silko, Alfred rejects guilt suggesting that it is a monotheistic concept foreign to Onkewhonwe cultures and that it only leads to moral paralysis. Instead, restitution should be an 'acknowledgement and acceptance of one's harmful actions and a genuine demonstration of sorrow and regret, constituted in reality by putting forward a promise to never again do harm and by redirecting one's actions to benefit the one who has been wronged' (153). Might this form of restitution be the foundation for an embodied ethics of encounter that respects the relational contingencies binding the community inexorably to the land?

Earth As the Basis of Democracy / Democracy in Support of the Earth

> The reason the world needs Roundup-Ready crops is because herbicide tolerance prevents the weeds from stealing the sunshine.
> –(Monsanto cited by Shiva 1999)

> These Indians are foolish. They don't understand. We are preventing the bees from usurping the pollen. –(Cargill cited by Shiva 1999)

> The majority of diverse cultures do not see other species and plants as 'property' but as kin. –(Shiva 2000 123)

Viewing the world's food supply as a repertoire of patentable genes to profit corporations at the expense of communities worldwide is possibly the greatest threat to our collective future, much more widespread and of more devastating consequences than the Al-Qaeda terrorism dominating the agendas of governments and mass media. The environmental disasters we discuss earlier in this book, Bhopal, the Deepwater Horizon catastrophe, the Exxon Valdez, to which we might add the Chernobyl nuclear meltdown, and the ecological carnage wrought by sustained military interventions throughout the twentieth century – these all point to a sustained attack on the very basis of what makes community possible. Like the Gulf of Mexico Dead Zone – an area of some 6000-7000 square miles of hypoxic waters in which life is virtually impossible as a result of the nitrogen and phosphorus rich effluent caused by agricultural fertilizer that accrues in the Mississippi River watershed – and like the Great Pacific Garbage Patch (or Pacific Trash Vortex), in which marine litter, largely plastic has gathered into an area (known as the North Pacific Gyre) that conflicting estimates put between the size of the state of Texas and the entire U.S. land mass – the BP disaster is part of a concerted failure by the sources of the pollution to respect the integrity of the water commons that is vital to the life of the planet.[5] These catastrophes in the making far exceed in their devastation and threat to all humans the effects of so-called global terrorism, and they are a direct consequence of the failure of elites that have placed themselves in opposition to a commons-based understanding of shared resources.

Wendell Berry, in his book *What Matters? Economics for a Renewed Commonwealth*, outlines how a

> victory over community or nature can be won only at everybody's cost. For example, we now have in the United States many landscapes that have been defeated – temporarily or permanently – by strip mining, by clear-cutting, by poisoning, by bad farming, or by various styles of 'development' that have subjected their sites entirely to human purposes. These landscapes have been defeated for the benefit of what are assumed to be victorious landscapes: the suburban housing developments and the places of amusement (the park systems, the recreational wildernesses) of the winners – so far – in the economy. But these victorious landscapes and their human inhabitants are already paying the costs of their defeat of other landscapes: in air and water pollution, overcrowding, inflated prices, and various diseases of body and mind. Eventually, the cost will be paid in scarcity or want of necessary goods. (97)

Scarred landscapes the world over are symptoms of failed community in the most perverse sense of the term, as meaning state and corporate conglomerate communities acting without regard for local environments. But these landscapes are also a call to action on the part of local community organizers everywhere. This abuse of the land largely results from how local community empowerment has been undermined by failed models of collective action based on the environmental neglect and self-interest that allow them to occur.

Water, to take but one aspect of the environmental commons, is vital to plant and animal life everywhere, and yet the marshalling of resources to address these issues is far outweighed by military spending. The politics of ignorance, ambiguation, and misdirection that permit this situation to exist are a profound mark of the concerted attack on communities globally enacted in the name of corporate and state agendas whose policies have been usurped by powerful lobbies of corporate pitchmen, arms dealers, and ethically compromised technocrats. In this section we examine notions of earth democracy, which are directly opposed in theory and practice to the death-dealers and polluters whose concept of the public commons is non-existent or limited to their immediate self-interest. Activist-scientist Vandana Shiva coined the term *earth democracy*, (also the title of one of her books 2005) to express a set of principles based on inclusion, non-violence, reclaiming the commons, and freely sharing the earth's resources: 'Earth Democracy is both an ancient worldview and an emergent political movement for peace, justice, and sustainability. Earth Democracy connects the particular to the universal, the diverse to the common, and the local to the global. It incorporates what in India we refer to as *vasudhaiva kutumbkam* (the earth family) – the community of all beings supported by the earth' (2005 1).

Again, we begin with a relationship to the land. Plants, like water, are part of the biosphere or the living world and connected to the land in more ways than just their immediate root systems. Jeremy Rifkin, the American critic of the biotech industry who also founded The Foundation on Economic Trends, warns that there is a second generation of GM plants about to be released that are designed to code for proteins to produce vaccines, chemicals, drugs, and vitamins. Treating a plot of land as if it were an isolated laboratory shows a profound level of ignorance about the living world, or complete disinterest beyond profit-making at any cost, as Rifkin argues:

> When we seed millions of acres with these plants, what happens to foraging birds, to insects, to microbes, to the other animals, when they come in contact and digest plants that are producing materi-

> als ranging from plastics to vaccines to pharmaceutical products? There hasn't been as much as a single parliamentary debate anywhere in the world on introducing this second generation of pharmaceutical and chemical-producing plants. (6)

Ten companies own the proprietary seeds to approximately two-thirds of the world's major crops, and with Monsanto's monopolizing expansion into this area, it has now become the largest supplier of vegetable seeds and the largest biotech company in the world. In response to this kind of growth, Monsanto faces at least 20 antitrust lawsuits, which are laws to control the creation of monopolies that would reduce competition, supposedly the basis for capitalism's self-correcting equilibrium and wide-spread business opportunities ('Monsanto ...' 9).

Beyond the legal issues with this monopoly are profound ethical and rights issues having to do with stewardship of plant culture that is the result of millennia of development. The shift to corporate ownership of community-produced and community-managed food commons is a radical break from a form of farming and knowledge sharing that has made the current state of seed biodiversity possible. The attempt to restrict this biodiversity via corporate monocultures is a significant, misguided attack on communitarian ways of negotiating and stewarding centuries-old adaptations of farming practices that have largely been successful. Shiva notes that the World Trade Organization's claim of promoting competitiveness 'seems to be a strange kind of competition in which the biggest corporations of the world want to compete-out the smallest peasant, every butterfly and every bee and every element of biodiversity' (Shiva 1999 2).

Antitrust laws, however, focus primarily on specific disputes over patents and not on the overall monopolization in any given area whether biotechnology or information technology. For example, under the Obama administration, the U.S. Justice Department expresses 'interest in pursuing any misuse of patents as part of an aggressive probe into agriculture' ('Update 1 – US pledges to probe, bust agribusiness monopolies' 2). Note that the problem is identified as *misuse of patents*, ignoring that any patent is already a misuse of ownership law over the earth's creations that should be collectively tended to for the common good. Most of the ethical debates also stick to one conceptual category such as 'intellectual.' So, for instance, the proponents of *intellectual* property are challenged by the proponents of the *intellectual* commons. But the leap from seed to intellect is barely questioned since the precedent-setting U.S. Supreme Court ruling that a genetically engineered organism can be patented.

Subsequent court cases continue to split hairs on whether the patentable entity qualifies as an invention or a discovery – on whether the discovered microorganism exists in nature or has been sufficiently modified to qualify as 'man-made.' This individualistic and corporate-driven concept of legally owned knowledge contrasts to the point of being incommensurate with an indigenous or collective perspective on humans' organically-based hybridization of plants occurring over thousands of years and involving sustained collective knowledge sharing. The absurdity of crediting any one individual or company with ownership rights to an organism – a concept that has enormous political implications for communities – does not even enter the picture in current legal cases. This shows how compromised are the legal contexts and foundations for even beginning to establish an effective understanding of what the true stakes are in assigning the patent of complex life organisms, whose existence has only been made possible by generations of largely anonymous farmers and communities who are never even part of the equation when it comes to assigning corporate ownership of this form of so called intellectual property.

There are other ways of imagining the relationship of mind (or intellect) to other organisms, without erecting the intellect as a disembodied legal power that subjugates organisms and bodies to its will. The neem tree of India, whose name *azak darakt* means 'free tree,' has a long list of medical properties (anti-fungal, anti-inflammatory, anti-arthritic, anti-bacterial, contraceptive, anti-diabetic, sedative, and so on) and has been adopted as the symbol for a liberation movement to free knowledge systems and biodiversity from bio-piracy of the sort described above (Shiva 2001 5). The tree has a longstanding cultural significance, both symbolically and materially, in Hindu culture. Summer festivals celebrate it and a widespread understanding of its medicinal properties has existed for centuries. This linking of knowledge and cultural systems (in the plural) with biodiversity reveals a perspective from which mind is considered to work in solidarity with other organisms. In 1995,

> the European Patent Office (EPO) granted a patent on an anti-fungal product, derived from neem, to the US Department of Agriculture and multinational W.R. Grace and Company [a company that makes chemical catalysts and silica-based products that in turn let other companies make products from refined crude oil]. The Indi-

> an government challenged the patent when it was granted, claiming that the process for which the patent had been granted had actually been in use in India for over 2,000 years. In 2000, the EPO ruled in India's favour but the US multinational mounted an appeal claiming that prior [work] about the product had never been published in a scientific journal. On 8 March 2005, that appeal was lost and the EPO revoked the Neem patent rights keeping the tree free of these patent restrictions. ('Neem')

The kind of thinking that reduces public commons knowledge to singular, predatory ownership via a corporation is symptomatic of what Shiva calls *monocultures of the mind*, a limited and limiting mindset that cannot grasp diversity as one of the foundational aspects of civilization and one of the most important expressions of global community.

Bio-piracy has a long history closely linked to European colonization. In a seventeenth-century story from Kerala, India, the Portuguese are caught 'uprooting pepper vines and carrying them away to the ships' without any prior negotiation or agreement with the people or their political leaders. When the Zamorin (monarch) is advised of this theft, he calmly answers: 'Ah, don't worry too much. They may take the vines but how can they take our monsoons,' showing an ecologically sophisticated and holistic worldview ('Abduction of Turmeric' 1). The Zamorin could not have anticipated how biotechnology might actually take away monsoons, create them where they would not naturally occur, or alter rain patterns in any other way. Rifkin explains how scientists have extracted the gene out of a bacteria that allows ice crystals to form: 'The idea was to seed our agricultural regions with the ice-minus bacteria,[6] which would edge out the traditional bacteria that makes frost,' begging a question of cosmic proportions: 'What if ice-minus were introduced, as they planned, across entire agricultural regions of the world, and it edged out the traditional ice-forming bacteria, which we think plays a role in rain patterns?' (Rifkin 1-2).

The story from Kerala prefaces an article that examines how India's sanguine magnanimity in the face of bio-piracy was to end: 'Abduction of turmeric provokes India's wrath: the war to rescue neem, turmeric and other goddesses of India's bio-diversity from knowledge pirates' fast-forwards us to 1995 and the U.S. patenting of turmeric in wound healing, a cure that has been known in India for centuries. Traditional knowledge develops over long periods of time involving collective experimentation that is often more spiritual than rationalistic. Following a long list of turmeric's health benefits, its social and spiritual powers are also significant, as with the neem tree: 'Roots are exchanged between people as a formal symbol of goodwill. Indians place freshly uprooted plants at the altar during Pongal [a January festival dedicated to the sun god Surya] and offer worship' ('Abduction of Turmeric' 2). Spiritual health and physical health are intertwined with what the land produces: 'For Indians turmeric is a benevolent goddess. For sound reasons, it transpires. Indian physicians had always packed their kits with turmeric' (ibid. 2-3). The turmeric root is connected to the land in the broadest understanding and cannot be reduced to anyone's ownership of a singular intellectual property. To do so is to betray the social, historical, and material interactions that this particular root has had with the communities that have nurtured it and built up systems of knowledge based on its properties, symbolic and otherwise. In this communitarian worldview, the intellect is not a disembodied and de-spirited inventing and discovering machine separate from the organisms with which it interacts.

The injustices that arise from the warped Eurocentric view of humans owning the rights to organisms have individual and global ramifications: 'consider the implication of "turmeric patent" number 5,401,504. If an expatriate Indian in America sprinkles turmeric powder – just as her ancestors in India have done for centuries – on her child's scrape, she would in fact be infringing US patent laws and was open to prosecution' (ibid. 3). Ridiculous as it sounds, there have been cases in which precisely this so-called legal principle has been invoked successfully by biotech firms like Monsanto. When Monsanto's genetically modified 'Roundup Ready Canola' was found in Saskatchewan canola farmer Percy Schmeiser's fields in 1997, Monsanto sued him for patent infringement. A Canadian Supreme Court ruling (5-4) in favour of Monsanto stated that Monsanto's patent was valid and that infringement had occurred: 'The patent infringement finding was based solely on the determination that Schmeiser had recognized the cross-contamination, and knowingly went on to collect the crossbred seed, then replant and harvest it the next year. No punitive damages or the costs of the technology use fee were awarded to Monsanto, as the Supreme Court also ruled 9-0 in Schmeiser's favor that his profits were exactly the same with or without the presence of the Roundup Ready Canola' ('Percy Schmeiser').

Schmeiser, in a David-and-Goliath struggle, has gone on to sue Monsanto for contaminating his fields, in cases that have been settled out of court where Monsanto has effectively agreed to pay the clean-up costs of the contamination. Schmeiser has stated 'I have always campaigned on the right of a farmer to save and re-use his own seed. This is what I have been doing for the last 50 years. I will continue to support any efforts to strengthen the rights of a farmer to save and re-use his own seed' (ibid.). His case is exemplary of the dangers to traditional farming methods and communities posed by corporate monoculture.

On the global plane, bio-piracy and the patenting of the healing property of plants divest communities of their own commons and steal traditional knowledge for economic profit, thereby legally prohibiting the sharing of that knowledge for the common good. It is likely that patents of this sort will even curtail research because, in this legalistic scenario, independent researchers will worry more about possible liability, than about intellectual freedom and freedom of expression. In the case of the article 'Abduction of Turmeric,' the success story of two Indian scientists who discovered the commercial potential of an herb called *arogya pachcha* is touted. Strangely enough, the authors of this article buy into the same Western logic of patenting organisms, in this case, because the Kanis tribe became co-holder of the patent, given their centuries-long use of this herb to supplement sparse diets. Here, a blind eye is turned both to collective traditional knowledge as a grounding value *in itself* and to the spiritual powers associated with this herb, thus favouring a Western commerce-based mode of legality and ownership. It is ingenuous to credit specific tribes with such ancient knowledges given the complex history of inter-tribal trade and sharing that pre-dates contemporary notions of globalization. The very notion of isolated, specific tribes with their own exclusive knowledge and customs is a Eurocentric form of classification that exists only in museum showcases.

An additional danger to recognizing traditional knowledge in this commercializing way is the possible depletion of plants through overharvesting. The commercialization of everything – from goji berries one year to acai berries the next – shows that the First World has an insatiable appetite for traditional knowledge packaged as a quick fix to any number of ailments, from obesity to impotence. In a similar impulse to follow Eurocentric taxonomy – in this case, as preemptive self-defense against bio-piracy – the Council of Scientific and Industrial Research of India is compiling a 'massive data base that will record all practical ideas proposed in Indian knowledge systems. [Once created, this record] will deny bio-pirates – on the basis of prior knowledge of their use having existed – the patents they seek to profit by' (ibid. 6). Here again, the citizens of the South compromise their own worldview and life practices in adopting the invaders' logic to protect themselves from the injustices wrought by that very logic. What will happen to those practical ideas that escape the data gatherers? Will they not automatically be seen as fair game by their exclusion from the database?

The WTO has pushed to globalize the TRIPS (Trade-Related Intellectual Property Rights) agreement that came to be included in the General Agreement for Trade and Tariffs (GATT) during the Uruguay Round of GATT, and to ensure that these trade agreements trump the U.N. Convention on Biological Diversity. As Shiva notes: 'this confirms the environmental movement's fears that the WTO sacrifices the environment for trade. Through the WTO, the rich North is committed to protecting corporate monopoly rights, even if this means undermining protections for nature and people guaranteed by international agreements and national constitutions' (Shiva 2001 4). In response to this biocolonialism exercised through trade agreements drafted by corporations of rich countries, The African Group and India demanded a stop to patenting organisms, and to make the WTO subordinate to the Convention on Biological Diversity.

Concerned citizens of all countries are joining voices to support biodiversity, instead of accepting the unjustly dominant role played by corporations and powerful governments in global relations. According to de Sousa Santos's definition of the precautionary principle in the context of the ecology of knowledges, 'preference must be given to the form of knowledge that guarantees the greatest level of participation to the social groups involved in its design, execution, and control and in the benefits of the intervention' (36). The organic farming movement is international and includes Americans and members of rich countries working alongside Majority World members.

The increasing presence of women in positions of power is strengthening a community-oriented agenda to defend biodiversity. Shiva tells how she filed a patent challenge as Director of the Research Foundation for Science, Technology and Ecology together with Linda Bullard, former President of the International Federation of Organic Agriculture Movements (replaced in 2008 by another woman president: Katherine DiMatteo [IFOAM]), and Magda Alvoet, former Health and Environment Minister of Belgium (Shiva 2001 4). While in global economic and political terms the First World's supremacist tactics to impose corporate dictatorship divides the world, international alliances cross that divide to reclaim earth democracy as a necessary corrective to attacks on community-based models of social organization.

> These broad-based alliances [are formed] between public-interest scientists and the people, between producers and consumers, between North and South ... Since most people in the South are farmers, and only 2 percent of the world's farmers survive in the North, movements for food democracy will take the shape of consumer movements in the North and both farmers' and consumer movements in the South. (Shiva 2000 122)

In establishing these cross-cultural, global alliances to preserve the principles of local and regional community-based practices, the earth democracy movement works out of a fundamental premise that links all aspects of community to the material and spiritual relations it sustains with the land on which it lives, and from which it draws its sustenance. The ethics of encounter with the earth and its by-products is not defined by commercial exploitation but by principles of renewal that are co-creatively generated as an aspect of the commons. This is possible only when community and earth are understood to be in a profoundly contingent relation to each other.

The Italian political philosopher, Antonio Negri, in his book *Reflections On Empire*, argues that exploitation is 'command over and within the expropriation of co-operation, in other words within the possibility of blocking the activity of the multitude' (165). Negri continues,

> Exploitation, thus, inserts itself precisely within the richness of the common and into the productivity of the multitude, and attempts to block its expression, to render it dumb, to strip the flesh from it, to distance it, and to disappropriate it. By now we have to concede a powerful materiality, which affects all aspects of the body – it is an expropriation, an un-fleshing which moves against the singularity, against the 'common,' and which obviously comes into conflict with the practice bubbling up from the expression of the 'common' and from the processes of its construction. (ibid.)

However problematic are Negri's reductive notions of 'multitude' and 'singularity,' his insight on the exploitation of the commons and how it impacts not only the productivity but also the embodied autonomy of the commons is acute. The earth democracy movement seeks to restore co-operation at a local level within ethical structures that respect the full implications of the land as the material and spiritual source of all human community and culture.

Education and Development in An Ecology of Knowledges

Brazilian *quilombos* or *mocambos* (maroon settlements),[7] mentioned earlier in this section, are historically the polar opposites of the North American Indian reservation system, since the *quilombos* are self-founded and governed. Anne Kogan's review of the documentary film *Quilombo Country* (2008) looks at the positive and negative aspects of life in these autonomous settlements with an eye to understanding that idealizing any form of community in and of itself can be misleading: 'Today, many residents view themselves as carrying on the fight against injustice by continuing to live in the *quilombos*, maintaining their traditions and fighting for their land rights ... Struggles over land ownership have led to a host of other problems. *Quilombo* residents want their children to get an education, but cannot afford to send them to cities and refuse to leave their homes for fear of losing their land' (1). Clearly, while the benefits of this kind of community include a degree of self-government and cultural survival it is unfair that the inhabitants are deprived of education and opportunities for diversifying their work and economies.

The same can also be said for First Nations reservations where poverty and equitable access to resources are major challenges. Ultimately, the best education would come from community members themselves, since education is not ideologically neutral, and state school systems impose the dominant, largely inflexible model:

> Although there is a plethora of non-governmental organizations (NGOs), unilateral and multilateral organizations involved in 'development' work, it is the World Bank (WB) that leads them in the conceptualization and practice of 'development.' This construct's profound power and broad enveloping reach is such that even the severest criticism never goes beyond its grand scheme, but stays there, trapped as a variant, a reform or even as radical change – but always falling within the all-encompassing ideological and political net of capitalist 'development.' (Flores 2)

What forms of knowledge and skills could people bring back to their communities to improve life by adding in a complementary way to their own cultural knowledge? The power of hybrid pedagogies that respect both local community need and global imperatives has largely gone by the wayside in thinking through meaningful pedagogical reforms at all levels of education, but especially for the youngest citizens of the planet. Moreover, given that environmental devastation is the outcome of industry as invented and exported by European countries from the core to the periphery, how must Western epistemology change radically before it finishes off the planet irrevocably? Too often the core sets itself up as the all-knowing benefactor whose mission is to develop the periphery, yet it is undeniable that in the grand scheme of the biosphere, the land and water base of all life, Western knowledge has done more harm than good as it has been practiced until now. It is therefore arrogant and ignorant to pursue education and development according to the same colonialist scheme that assumes knowledge is produced in the north and altruistically disseminated in the south (or among the colonized Natives of the north).

'Global social injustice,' says de Sousa Santos, 'is intimately linked to global cognitive injustice' (11). Returning to his mapping out of the abyssal lines that supremacist thinking draws in order to aggrandize itself against what it imagines as the savage and lawless other situated on the other side of the line, de Sousa Santos defines the consequences of Northern abyssal epistemologies policing the boundaries of relevant knowledge as 'a massive epistemicide [that] has been under way for the past five centuries, whereby an immense wealth of cognitive experiences has been wasted' (37). The question for those who see ourselves as global citizens – connected to each other and all life – now becomes how to change our thinking to a post-abyssal and pluralistic thinking in order to recuperate some of those silenced experiences.

De Sousa Santos predicts that intercultural translation will be the biggest and most important challenge of the 21st century in order to turn monoculture, mono-knowledge into inter- and intra-knowledges: 'Post-abyssal thinking can thus be summarized as learning from the South through an epistemology of the South. It confronts the monoculture of modern science with the *ecology of knowledges*' (27; our emphasis). We would clarify that north/south distinctions of this sort are largely accurate but not enough to recognize the various indigenous cultures situated in northern regions that were colonized by Europeans, and to also recognize the Africans forcibly brought to the north as slaves. All binary oppositions confound themselves: north/south, east/west are crude generalizations that place regions in relation to European colonialism. To de Sousa Santos's observation on the abyssal line we would add that colonized spaces exist in all regions of the world, as Gomez Peña illustrates in his new cartography of the Fourth World consisting of the deterritorialized, the indigenous, the immigrants, exiles, and those who find community across and in spite of borders.

We are now facing up to the fact that Western power is disproportionately inflated in relation to Western understanding of the world. Our very survival depends on a massive epistemological shift toward an ecology of knowledges that is open to learning from other systems of thought and to hybridization. Knowledge in this pluralistic transcultural sense is infinite and according to de Sousa Santos will lead us to post-abyssal thinking, even if at present the epistemological diversity of the world still lacks conceptual form or adequate language. This shift implies moving from science as a monopolistic knowledge to science as just one aspect of a more complex and culturally diverse ecology of knowledges that includes 'popular, lay, plebeian, peasant, or indigenous knowledges' (4). It would also mean a turning of worlds to right the upside-down world associated with colonialism and its hegemonic epistemology that renders all other knowledges non-existent while promoting monoculture (and death) under the guise of science.

Scientific discourse in the West is highly compromised by its relation to military technology and the perverse application of scientific theory to killing in the name of imperial culture. DARPA, the Defense Advanced Research Projects Agency that gave us the Internet (itself a triple whammy cocktail of the ad industry, the porn industry, and the paranoia of the military-industrial complex) was created in 1958 (as ARPA) in response to the Soviet launching of Sputnik, the first earth-orbiting unmanned satellite in October 1957. DARPA's mission, from the start, has been to keep U.S. military technology ahead of the nation's potential enemies' technology. Its annual budget, as one aspect of the vast network of American scientific research devoted to military applications, is 3.2 billion dollars, about the foreign debt of Mozambique as of April 2010. A roster of its active projects includes: high productivity computing systems; HULC battery-powered human exoskeletons; protein design processes; remote-controlled insects; DARPA Silent Talk, a planned program attempting to identify EEG patterns for words and transmit these for covert communications; and the 'Combat Zones That See initiative, whose objective is to "track everything that moves" in a city by linking up a massive network of surveillance cameras' ('DARPA'). The massive resourcing of this sort of knowledge system, which is state (imperial)- and corporate (profit)-directed as opposed to life-centered and community-based at the expense of other forms of knowledge, is a major ethical issue facing global communities of all sorts. The complicity of science as an episteme with these destructive military forces is one of the great failures of Western knowledge, as well as being one of the great challenges for global ecologies of knowledge based on alternative community practices.

De Sousa Santos prophesies the liberatory dimension of this shift in thinking away from colonial, hegemonic, militarized models:

> Through these knowledges it is possible to nurture an enhanced value or concept of commitment that is incomprehensible to the positivistic and functionalist mechanisms of modern science. From such a nurturing will develop a new capacity for wonder and indignation, capable of grounding a new, non-conformist, destabilizing, and indeed rebellious theory and practice. (39-40)

It is not enough to generate alternatives within the same hegemonic and colonial power structures – de Sousa Santos insists that the critical task ahead of us to attain global cognitive justice requires an alternative thinking of alternatives. In other words, thinking about alternative social practices within the same limited epistemology tied to the same oppressive socio-economic system only amounts to tinkering and band-aid solutions. How do we shift gears to open our thinking toward other knowledges that can produce meaningful, sustainable change?

Such transcultural and hybrid forms are starting to emerge in various forms. Initiatives like the Indigenous Education Institute based in Santa Fe, New Mexico, promote an ecological or transcultural approach to Indigenous and Western forms of knowledge. According to its own statement, the Indigenous Education Institute (IEI) was created for the preservation and contemporary application of ancient Indigenous ways of knowing. The goals of the IEI include:

> initiating and maintaining collaborative research involving traditional knowledge holders; organizing, articulating, and developing strategic and realistic application of the research to Indigenous education in order to provide cultural enrichment and empowerment to succeeding generations; preserving and maintaining the diversity of Indigenous languages and cultures; enhancing recognition of Indigenous science, in juxtaposition with Western science, through processes that respect the honor and integrity of both ways of knowing; researching and developing relevant systems of Indigenous strategic planning and evaluation, to enhance organizational

> effectiveness; supporting Indigenous communities in the research of their own knowledge and needs, enabling responsible capacity building to effect transformational and sustainable change; promoting global networking among Indigenous communities to enhance the awareness and inter-relationships of Indigenous ways of knowing; supporting responsible stewardship for Mother Earth and the Cosmic Order. ('Indigenous Education Institute')

These goals offer up a useful imagining of what alternative worldviews and epistemologies might look like: at once codified in Western discourses of organizational effectiveness, responsible capacity building, and research but respectful of traditional epistemic systems that begin with stewardship and the integrity of alternative epistemic forms. A concrete example of transcultural research results is *Sharing the Skies*, a book published by the Indigenous Education Institute in which constellations are interpreted through Navajo and Greek worldviews researched in accordance with indigenous protocol but also in conjunction with National Aeronautics and Space Administration (NASA) imaging.

Such hybrid initiatives need to be fostered, developed, and implemented in conjunction with other national colleges and universities (and other alternative pedagogies and institutions). International and interdisciplinary work in indigenous and community studies requires informed engagement with the ethics of encounter as a foundational principle for creating hybrid knowledges. Education about different worldviews and epistemologies is the key to living (and surviving) in multi-national states and in a negatively globalized world run by the economics of piracy and exploitation.

Developmentalism or mal-development forced on poor countries will change to true development for all only when all people are educated out of a worldview based on supremacy and greed. By 'developmentalism' we mean top-down development as imposed by institutions that invest money in a poor country to benefit the elites, or the transnational corporations who then get the contracts for lucrative projects such as the building of big dams. This is also called 'mal-development' by Shiva, and other proponents of communitarian, grassroots development, which is true cultural and economic advancement. Education, by contrast, involves not only accumulating knowledge, but also unlearning harmful stories to which developmentalism and exploitative science belong as a kind of narrative. Science as practiced and taught in the Western tradition is seen as gravely unethical to many people of the world, because it disconnects living things from each other.

Mixed-blood Chickasaw writer Linda Hogan imagines all the connections she sees in a photograph taken by Dorothea Lange who documented the Great Depression:

> White, seemingly abandoned, the horse races in fear over a world just plowed, a torn land, no vegetation left, no water, and no place to go in order to live. It runs over the turned soil that just a short while ago, only moments before, had been long grasses and prairie abundance. In this picture is a geography of hopelessness and torn earth. The horse knows and reveals the truth of broken land, the unbearable histories and geographies that are far from invisible. (194-95)

Hogan relates the horse's panic to that of indigenous peoples, and clearly her use of 'geographies' and 'histories' in the plural are not the disciplines we learn about as objective archives of facts and information alone. She also meditates on why indigenous people's attachment to the land, through stories, ensures their survival in the face of devastation. She tells of the European propensity to pass fiction as fact, in the way that explorer-exploiters did when drawing maps of uncharted places and illustrating them with sea monsters and cannibals. Colonial fear of the unknown is so often fear of nature, and fear of the racialized other. The mind disconnected from the land imagines nature as a dark void inhabited by terrifying spectres instead of as a mother. The ensuing fear and paranoia drives much of the scientific urge to dissect, classify, and dominate. Hogan differentiates Native conceptions of existence by suggesting that they are based on stories primarily about being connected: 'Unlike phantom islands and malingering worlds, our stories and myths remain because skin isn't where a person ends. We live not only inside a body but within a story as well, and our story resides in the land as sure as the vision of Dorothea Lange's desperate, running horse' (204).

In a hilariously subversive account of challenging grade school science, Chickasaw mixed-blood writer Gerald Vizenor remembers:

> The science teacher demonstrated how electrical shocks stimulated the leg muscles of a dead frog. The common green frogs, captured over the weekend near the creek and held in a glass case, seemed to leap much higher dead than alive. The frogs were to be dissected once the teacher had desensitized the students with the scientific method. Some of the fifth grade girls were sick, their noses wrinkled like permanent cultural scars. The sick girls were allowed to

leave the room, the first level of elimination in the scientific colonization of nature. (48)

The scientific method is shown to be shocking to girls and to the Native boy Griever, who identifies with the frogs and challenges the teacher as their spokesperson: '"Do frogs have science teachers?" Griever pressed his nose and one cheek hard against the glass case and watched the teacher move between the frogs inside. The teacher ignored the question ... "Do frogs know who they are?" Griever threw his question from a distance, over the case of live frogs' (48, 49). While this kind of pan-being imagination is common in children, the teachers in this story attribute it to the superstitions of an inferior race. One of them opines: 'The cause of his behavior, without a doubt, is racial. Indians never had it easier than now, the evil fires of settlement are out, but this troubled mixedblood child is given to the racial confusion of two identities, neither of which can be secured in one culture' (49).

The teacher's purely racialized interpretation of what the African American writer and civil rights activist W.E.B. Du Bois had termed 'double-consciousness' (4) is doubly funny given that Griever seems not to be torn between white and Native culture, but to understand the situation from both human and frog perspectives. The boy later liberates the live frogs, and when interrogated by his teacher, reveals that he is more concerned with the frogs' judgment than that of authority:

> 'Griever de Hocus,' the science teacher summoned in a firm tone of voice. 'Little man, where have you hidden our frogs?'
> 'No place,' he promised.
> 'We must have the frogs to finish our experiment,' she demanded with thumbs held high, blood-red fingernails extended.
> 'The frogs are alive,' he pleaded.
> 'Griever, give me the frogs this instant.'
> 'The frogs all jumped over the fern,' he explained ...
> 'Mark my words, little man, you will be punished for this,' said the teacher. She snapped her fingers and ground her teeth
> 'Not by the frogs.'
> 'This is a scientific experiment.'
> 'Not by the frogs.' (50-51)

Seemingly the story of a boy's childish identification with frogs, it is also a parable about our being answerable first and foremost to the earth.

Griever's defiance of bad science and the arbitrary authority that upholds it comes from a deeply informed rebellion rooted in a cultural practice that sees community as extending beyond the human. De Sousa Santos envisions this sort of resistant, empathic knowing as the emergent theory and praxis of subaltern, oppositional cosmopolitanism.

Griever's knowledge is eccentric and troubles Western modernity. Like de Sousa Santos's description of acting with *clinamen* (a small unanticipated swerve away from the norm or the expected), a small boy's defiance does not effect a dramatic break – even if the 'squeamish' girls in the class seem to share his insight. Rather, Griever's reaction provokes 'a slight swerve or deviation whose cumulative effects render possible the complex and creative combinations among atoms, hence also among living beings and social groups' (41).[8] Griever's defense of the frogs is not a purely subjective impulse but comes from his Aboriginal cultural knowledge. Silko also tells about how Pueblo children were terrified of having to conduct experiments on frogs in science class because their elders had taught them that affronting these creatures would result in severe droughts, an idea that is contemptuously dismissed by their white teachers as primitive superstition. But frogs drink through their skin and are an important part of the ecological chain having been around for over 360 million years – their decline and that of other amphibians is the sign of a significant threat to biodiversity globally, and an indicator of global environmental degradation. Griever the frog-saver and the Pueblo children terrified at the ramifications of killing a frog in the name of science have knowledge that is important and accurate.

In both the Vizenor and the Silko examples, the two conflicting knowledge systems seem irreconcilable and we may well wonder how transcultural translating could bridge the gulf between thinking of all life forms as interconnected and sacred, and at the same time advancing science through experimentation. Should the objectives of science become informed by indigenous insights to make it less anthropocentric and more holistic? How can educators and researchers radically rethink the very reasons for which they pursue science?

This process of rethinking pedagogies via integrative principles that address different ecologies of knowledge simultaneously seems to be emerging in the past few years with interesting examples occurring, for instance, in the study of botany and zoology. Recent research in those fields is slowly starting to deviate from the Western assumptions of human superiority to other life forms, and the philosophical tradition of distinguishing human intelligence by contrasting humans with animals to conclude that animals have little or no intelligence or emotional life. While proposing special rights for dolphins is still anthropocentric in that they are coming to be viewed as deserving of rights based on their similarities with humans (and thus their need for special consideration), others (perhaps mostly non-scientists) are starting to recognize that there is a great diversity of knowledges and forms of intelligence, and that these might be infinite once they start to be combined. Thomas I. White discusses anthropomorphic assumptions and how to challenge them via interspecies ethics in his book *In Defense of Dolphins*: '[Diana] Reiss's idea that dolphins represent an *alien* intelligence, then, helps us avoid anthropocentrism by suggesting a new and important set of questions. How do we make sure that our evaluation of the intellectual and emotional abilities of dolphins doesn't assume that "different" means "inferior"? Are traits like *intelligence* best defined in a way that is specific to different species? Is *person* the best concept to use in such an investigation? Is there another concept we can use ... to ensure that our characterization of dolphins is free from unintentional species bias?' (12). These questions get at the heart of the epistemological shift that occurs when reductive categories of being (inferior/superior; intelligent/unintelligent, feeling/unfeeling, sentient/insentient, and so forth) are supplanted with an all-encompassing respect for the diversity of knowledges and ways of being within a complex and interconnected ecology. Integrated, relational, land-based manifestations of community as a diverse ecology of practices, knowledges, and intuitions (feelings and spirit) move us in this direction in which not only are individual needs (the traditional framework for rights discourses) understood within this larger framework, but also community needs (the non-traditional aspect of rights discourses).

It seems incredible that over the centuries, science has discovered so little about plants and animals. Only in the past few decades have researchers entertained the possibility that trees can send signals of impending danger to other trees and even to other life forms. Biologist Ian Baldwin sums up the discovery of his 20 years of research on the communication among plants and insects and how he thinks chemical signaling developed: 'You're wounded. You emit something. An insect responds. A mutualism evolves' (cited in Russel 2). Baldwin and co-researcher and writer Joseph Schultz published their findings in a book that became a bestseller, *The Secret Life of Plants*. But other less imaginative scientists were dismissive, and their negative responses made it difficult to get funding for Baldwin and Schultz, and potentially other botanists attracted to their approach. The intransigent narrow mindedness and orthodoxy of the mainstream scientists speaks volumes of the challenges facing anyone who dares to imagine how reality works outside of their disciplinary, and even epistemological box.

Recent research proves the hypothesis that plants communicate with each other and with different species of insects:

> For example, when caterpillars feed on corn, tobacco, and cotton, the beleaguered plants produce airborne chemicals that attract parasitic wasps. The chemical cries for help are quite specific, attracting only the wasps that lay their eggs in the type of caterpillar infesting the plant. 'Plants are not just saying, "Yes, I am damaged," they are also saying specifically who is damaging them. It is such an intricate and fabulous system,' says Consuelo De Moraes, an assistant professor of entomology ... (Russel 2)

Why has this kind of research only recently emerged? One reason relates to a shift in the stories we tell (in and out of science) and the questions we ask of those stories, with the Western story of human and white scientific supremacy being displaced by non-Western stories that allow us to imagine other ways of understanding the world. In a telling slip between epistemologies scientist Marcel Dicke speculates 'if plants talk to their bodyguards, then why would their neighbors not take advantage of that and eavesdrop on the message?' (ibid. 3). Such a question conceives of the tree as an individual engaged in a private conversation with its allies, and one might wonder why the neighboring trees would have to eavesdrop instead of being included in the conversation for the survival of the community.

Eduardo Galeano gathers stories from around the world, and retells them in vignette form, like snapshots that expand beyond the narrative frame through the reader's imagination. While this brief story is based on the scientific facts we have been considering, Galeano stresses the communal significance of tree language:

Diálogo verde

Parecen inmóviles, pero respiran y andan, buscando luz.
Y hablan. Poco se sabe; pero está probado, al menos, que cuando un árbol sufre golpes o lastimaduras, se defiende transpirando veneno y lanza una señal de alerta a los árboles cercanos. Por el aire

viajan palabras que en idioma árboles dicen: peligro, y dicen: cuidado. Y entonces también los árboles cercanos se defienden transpirando veneno.
Quizás ha sido así desde que los primeros árboles se irguieron sobre la tierra, y se multiplicaron, y tan inmensos fueron los bosques que, según dice la tradición, una ardilla podía recorrer el mundo de rama en rama.
Ahora, entre desierto y desierto, los árboles sobrevivientes mantienen viva esta antigua costumbre de buenos vecinos.
(2005 106)

[Green Dialogue

They seem immobile, but they breathe and wander, seeking light. And they talk. Little is known, but it is proven, at least that when a tree suffers blows or wounds, it defends itself by sweating poison and sends a warning signal to neighbouring trees. Words travel through the air, which in tree language mean: *danger*, and *be careful*. And then the neighbouring trees also defend themselves by sweating poison.
Maybe it's been this way ever since the first trees stood tall on the land, and they multiplied, and so immense were the forests that, they say, a squirrel could circle the world from branch to branch.
Now, from desert to desert, the surviving trees keep this ancient neighbourly custom alive. (our translation)]

This reading of biotic communication disrupts notions of disconnectedness, and points forward to a thinking that understands biotic contingencies that emerge from such connections. There is, in short, an ethics of encounter required to address this otherness that speaks in ways we do not always understand. Scientist and author Diana Beresford-Kroeger offers unique insights into the complex relations that inalienably link the life of forests with human community: 'A functioning forest is a complex form of life. It is interconnected by its own flora and driven by the mammals, the amphibians and insects in it. It is kept in place by fungi, algae, lichens, bacteria, viruses, and bacteriophages. The primogenitors of the forests are trees. They communicate by carbon-coded calls and mass-market themselves by infrasound. The atmosphere links the forests into the heavens and the great oceans. The human family is both caught and held in that web of life' (48-49). Observations such as these, arising out of a conjoined scientific and poetic sensibility, radically challenge use-value notions of biotic systems as things inherently defined by their quantitative exploitability for human profit. This is one of the reasons why the emergence of this kind of botany has been slow and why it rightly threatens the business interests of monoculture:

> Information from the wild, where few researchers have ventured, could lead to truly revolutionary changes in agriculture. Farmers now rely on heavy pesticide use because domestic plants, which have been bred for high yield, have often lost their native chemical defenses and cannot call out for help. A wild cotton plant, for example, can emit up to 10 times more airborne emissions that summon parasitic wasps to attack infesting caterpillars than a hybrid can. (Russel 4)

Even if biotechnology claims that the aim of genetic modification is to reduce the use of pesticides, how can scientists, given their relative ignorance about 'the secret live of plants,' predict how modifying them will effect their native defence systems, their cultures and languages as embodied in and among complex biotic systems? The most innovative approaches to applying the holistic research of plants' inherent capabilities is happening in the Majority World, while the countries with the most access to research funding continue under the ideological and financial yoke of monoculture science.

The 'Universal Declaration of the Rights of Mother Earth' coming out of the World People's Conference on Climate Change held in Cochabamba, Bolivia in 2010 affirms in its preamble that 'to guarantee human rights it is necessary to recognize and defend the rights of Mother Earth and all beings in her and that *there are existing cultures, practices and laws that do so*' (1; our emphasis). This affirmation of already existing knowledge recuperates those knowledges that have been ignored, disdained, and plundered. It also means that we do not have to reinvent the wheel or try to imagine practices or laws without precedent. Being open to other knowledges does not imply the kind of struggle involved in becoming specialized in a narrow discipline, and so should not be dismissed as beyond anyone's reach. Mother Earth is defined in the Declaration as 'a living being,' who is a unique, indivisible, self-regulating community of interrelated beings that sustains, contains, and reproduces all being' (2). This understanding of the world can be communicated to young children through stories to form the basis of holistic education that increases in complexity as all knowledge systems do, but the kernel is a simple story of earth democracy accessible to all. The complexity arises in how we fulfill our various obligations, one of them being to 'establish precautionary and restrictive measures to prevent human activities from causing species extinction, the destruction of ecosystems or the disruption of ecological cycles' (ibid. Article 3.i). Living in diverse communities, we have the required knowledge to fulfill such obligations as long as the ethical outlook is in place to guide practical interventions that make a real difference in the lived experiences of people.

The 'Universal Declaration of the Rights of Mother Earth' directly addresses the ethical dimensions of how all things are aspects of a diverse, interdependent ecology (of biotic forms, of knowledges, of practices). The integration of environmental rights into such articulations is a growing movement predicated on the ecological diversity that is a fundamental aspect of planetary interdependencies. No community is thinkable without the nested and complex interrelations that arise from the plural forms of ecological being that make life possible. These plural forms are part of a public commons whose protection and sustenance devolve upon communities of interest everywhere. 'Charter 08,' the December 2008 manifesto by Chinese intellectuals and rights activists (marking the 60th anniversary of the Universal Declaration of Human Rights) while written out of a private property conceptual framework that mimics the ethical premises of the UDHR at the expense of thinking the public commons related to community rights, nonetheless, in its seventeenth recommendation, argues for the 'Protection of the Environment. We need to protect the natural environment and to promote development in a way that is sustainable and responsible to our descendants and to the rest of humanity. This means insisting that the state and its officials at all levels not only do what they must do to achieve these goals, but also accept the supervision and participation of nongovernmental organizations' ('Charter 08').

Notable in this articulation is the compromised language of protection of the environment offset by the right to economic development as well as the dependence on (always already failed) state mechanisms to achieve these goals via the intervention of NGOs. Nowhere is the language of alternative forms of social organization, that is, the language of the rights of community as the key player in achieving such a balance, evident. 'Development' may well come to mean in the future, should the destructive over-exploitation of global resources not be addressed, finding ways to survive in a resource-depleted, ecologically compromised world where the means to sustain life are tenuous and eroding. Communities, precisely because they are proximate social expressions of biotic, material, and ecological realities and diversities, are crucial to thinking rights in these global, environmental terms precisely because they are the first line of contact with their localized environments. While a remarkably progressive and courageous document within Chinese, and indeed, global contexts, 'Charter 08' only reinforces the need for even more radical and critical revisionary thinking about the means to safeguard and sustain the biotic realities without which life would be impossible. Community rights and responsibilities are one aspect of this radical re-imagining of a form of distributive justice informed by more than narrow human self-interest driven by state or corporate agendas predicated on hegemony and profiteering. Understanding these rights and responsibilities within a larger networked community of rights is a key precondition to addressing the rights of community as an expression of fundamental environmental and biotic rights writ large. This community of rights' most important feature is the right of community to protect the glocal, interconnected forms of ecology that allow life in its most basic material realities to flourish sustainably.

Education and pedagogy play a key role in the struggle to voice new forms of imagining rights more holistically. Alistair McIntosh invites us to imagine how the groundwork for radical change may be organized on the basis of education that is grounded in the recognition of the interconnection of all biotic forms. As the title of his book *Soil and Soul* suggests, he starts imagining such an education as rooted in the land, by studying the soil in transcultural ways that approach the land respectfully as Mother Earth. Western scientific knowledge then becomes a gift instead of a means to exploit and degrade the land: 'it might start with soil structure and why the biochemistry of organic farming sustains biodiversity, and go on to look at how biodiversity equates with an optimal balance of crops and animal stock, and that with animal welfare and human health' (117). McIntosh's book couples different areas of knowledge that have been disconnected from each other to generate wealth for a few, death and adversity for most. Limiting disciplinarity gives way to such areas of inquiry and creative intervention as energy alternatives, co-operative business structures, the economics of Fair Trade, ecological architecture and public transport systems, healing skills, participatory politics empowerment, resolution of conflict and nonviolent civic-defence strategies. All are interconnected with the diversity of knowing through 'artistic creativity and inspiration ... with poetics and story' but also with less rational but essential forms of life affirming energy that melds 'cherishing human life from cradle to grave ... with the discovery of beauty as the touchstone of what is good' (117).

McIntosh's thoughts on such a holistic education offer yet another interpretation of the vital significance of community as a process of coming into enlightened being: 'with the building of community as right relationship between soil, soul and society, powered up by the passion of the heart, steered by the reason of the head, and then applied by the skilled technique of the hand' (117). Similarly to the Declaration of the Rights of Mother Earth, McIntosh also affirms that 'humankind is already well on the way towards understanding most of these principles. It's just a matter of linking them up and applying them' (117). We would emphasize the diversity of all biotic communities, not just the human. A pressing need exists to deploy transcultural thinking rooted in an inclusively heterogeneous approach to the knowledges that make us diversely human, but also diversely dependent on the ecologies that give us our humanity. Saying as much is no idealized imagining of ethical engagement with the complex life systems of which we are only a part. It is a vital, lived necessity for renewing all forms of community as a function of our profound biotic dependence on the othernesses that give us meaning. This meaning, rooted in biotic difference and co-dependence, is where the rights of community and the community of rights find their overlapped ethical imperatives.

NOTES

1 Gandhi, as told by his grandson Arun, had a very elaborated notion of community associated with the concept of *ashram,* which in Hindu philosophy stands for the four stages of life through which a twice-born must pass: the student, the householder, the hermit, and the mendicant. All stages are aspects of community, even when they involve solitary practice or nomadism, both challenges to the community's capacity to generate self-critique (through asceticism) and generosity (through how it deals with poverty). Arun Gandhi's account of his introduction into communitarian practice via his grandfather's philosophies is revealing for what it teaches about inclusion, toleration as an aspect of selfishness, and generosity as perhaps *the* defining quality of a meaningful community, because none can survive unless all survive:

As a budding teenager in the 1940s I was intrigued by my grandfather's version of 'family,' where the head was Mohandas Karamchand Gandhi and his family was the entire human race. In 1946 my father, Manilal, Gandhi's second son, decided it was time to visit the family in India. I was 12 years old then and we needed relief from the hate and prejudice of apartheid in South Africa. While I had visited India earlier, this was the first time I was old enough to experience the difference between a conventional family and a 'Gandhi family.'

At that time there were close to 150 families living in Sevagram Ashram in Wardha, central India. This was, in a microcosm, Gandhi's vision of the future of family. Inclusiveness, he was certain, was the only way to save humanity from self-destruction. Teaching tolerance was anathema to Gandhi. People, he felt, should not tolerate each other and their differences, but learn to respect, understand, accept and appreciate each other. What we have today is a collection of people living in an area for convenience because circumstances have thrown them together.

Unless we stand to gain something, we prefer not to have anything to do with our neighbours. One day Gandhi's wife, Kasturba, was cooking in the ashram. This was unusual, so Gandhi stopped to ask: 'What are you cooking?' 'Ramdas,' she explained, referring to their married son, 'is going home to his family this afternoon and I thought I would make some sweets.' 'Do you make sweets for all those who visit the ashram and then leave?' Gandhi asked.

Surprised and bewildered by the question, Kasturba turned to face Gandhi and said: 'No.' 'Why not?' Gandhi asked. 'Are they not, like Ramdas, your children?' Kasturba knew why Gandhi had created the ashram but this was a dimension she had not considered. She quickly saw the wisdom in what he said and decided to make amends by not giving Ramdas the sweets, but making more and distributing them to all the children in the ashram. (Gandhi)

2 Martin Luther King is another example of a fighter for freedom and decolonization even though he was a pastor of a Baptist church and therefore associated with an institutionalized religion. Similarly, while Liberation Theology started in the Roman Catholic Church, it is now inter-denominational and international, thereby challenging and perhaps changing the dominant dualistic worldview that separates religion from politics, spiritual life from the material world.

3 Boas advocated an integrated understanding of anthropological realities. He states, 'In the course of time I became convinced that a materialistic point of view, for a physicist a very real one, was untenable. This gave me a new point of view and *I recognized the importance of studying the interaction between the organic and inorganic, above all the relation between the life of a people and their physical environment*' ('Franz Boas'; our emphasis).

4 'The orders were issued following Sherman's March to the Sea [and] were

intended to address the immediate problem of dealing with the tens of thousands of black refugees who had joined Sherman's march in search of protection and sustenance, and "to assure the harmony of action in the area of operations." General Sherman issued his orders after meeting in Savannah, Georgia with twenty ministers of the black community and with U.S. Secretary of War Edwin M. Stanton. Brig. Gen. Rufus Saxton, an abolitionist from Massachusetts who had previously organized the recruitment of black soldiers for the Union Army, was put in charge of implementing the orders. The orders had little concrete effect, as they were revoked in the fall of that same year by President Andrew Johnson, who succeeded Abraham Lincoln after his assassination' ('Sherman's Special Field Orders').

5 For a more complete analysis of the crisis facing ocean waters globally, see journalist Alanna Mitchell's *Sea Sick*, where she notes that the 'Gulf of Mexico's dead zone is one of about 407 in the world, a figure that has doubled each decade since 1960' (42). Mitchell notes that this spread is a combination of both chemical pollution by industry and agriculture but also is 'directly related to global climate change' (ibid.).

6 The ice-minus bacteria 'is a nickname given to a variant of the common bacterium *Pseudomonas syringae* (*P. syringae*). This strain of *P. syringae* lacks the ability to produce a certain surface protein, usually found on wild-type *P. syringae*. The "ice-plus" protein (Ina protein, "Ice nucleation-active" protein) found on the outer bacterial cell wall acts as the nucleating centers for ice crystals. This facilitates ice formation, hence the designation "ice-plus." The ice-minus variant of *P. syringae* is a mutant, lacking the gene responsible for ice-nucleating surface protein production. This lack of surface protein provides a less favorable environment for ice formation. Both strains of *P. syringae* occur naturally, but recombinant DNA technology has allowed for the synthetic removal or alteration of specific genes, enabling the creation of the ice-minus strain' ('Ice-minus bacteria').

7 The two terms are not always used consistently, but generally *quilombo* (from an Angolan word meaning encampment) refers to a large-scale runaway slave community that might encompass several *mocambos*, smaller units within the *quilombo* (also called *ladeiras* and *magotes*). Maroon, a modification of the American Spanish word *cimarrón* refers to fugitive black slaves, usually from the West Indies or Guiana.

8 The term '*clinamen*' is borrowed by de Sousa Santos from Epicurus and Lucretius and refers to the 'inexplicable "quiddam" that upsets the relations of cause and effect ... the swerving capacity attributed by Epicurus to Democritus's atoms' (de Sousa Santos 40). *Clinamen* is a creative power, a power of spontaneous movement. De Sousa Santos notes that Harold Bloom made

the concept current in literary theory to account for how 'a poet swerves away from his precursor, by so reading his precursor's poem as to execute a *clinamen* in relation to it' (14). Bloom's use of the term defines the individual's impulse to differentiate self from a percursor's influence, while we use the term to mean what de Sousa Santos sees as a shared creative and spontaneous movement.

SECTION 3

'Freedom to ... rise above a cruel planet'

The Paradox of Global Community – Neo-colonialism Versus Evolving Ecologies

Story and Imagination: Some Contexts For Thinking Global Community

Once upon a time there was a voracious spider whose web encircled the globe. His web smothered the furthest reaches of the planet, ravenous for insects to feed on, but starved to death because none were left – they had all been trapped and he had so gorged on them that he was incapable of the vast travel required to eat the decaying bodies caught in the vast barely perceptible filaments he had spun. Globalization and global community, are overused terms for the ever-spreading gyre of human contact facilitated by technology and capital flow, the permeability of the planet to every possible form of exploitation as the industrial net spreads wider and wider. They are overused but they are also current, and in this section we address the paradoxes embedded in notions of global community. For globalization is not only the story of the spider who smothered himself: it is also the story of the insects who saw the spider's designs and found ways to organize their communities to evade and challenge his reach. Somewhere between these two versions of the story lies the meaning of global community. Between the poles of the infinite growth-based model of human community and the localized resistances to that unsustainable model is a necessary rethinking of access to common-pool resources in a profit-driven economy, and what this will mean to the climate, the water, the land, and the diverse ecosystems that sustain all life on the planet.

The stories we consider in the opening sections of this portion of the book tell of specific migrants searching for ways to support their families, as well as those who end up in the squatters' communities proliferating in poor and rich countries alike. The brief and tragic stories ending in the death of individuals like Liu Chunlan and Robert Dziekanski, together with the squatters' stories from the borderlands, stand in for the multitudes who are forced to migrate to places they see as promising core sites for community, and those who are forced to the most peripheral sites to survive in make-shift camps that sometimes become viable communities. Individuals decide to leave their homes for many personal reasons: dreams, fears, hopes that we cannot fully know, as well as for economic reasons that somehow make their stories coalesce in the era of globalization.

The term 'globalization' is increasingly related to an interpretive context for seemingly disparate realities that mass media tend to represent as random. To say that the stories we look at in this section result from globalization would be a simplistic reduction, yet certain conditions have emerged during this period of so-called globalization that allow the material realities of this global logic to proliferate. Individuals separated from their communities and faced by oppressive state policing seem most vulnerable, while globalization disempowers communities from making decisions that best serve their immediate and long-term needs. This is because global models of economic organization that suit vast corporate networks of profit-driven ventures have superceded the even more vast network of local communities with their specific needs and relations to localized commons, histories, and environmental imperatives. How the individual, community, and nation-state intersect under the corporate pressures of globalization reveals that in rich countries, elites have divested government of power and sovereignty in order to better empower corporations, and that rich and powerful elites in poor countries follow the same trend, in the well-established colonial tradition of poor countries serving as client states to rich ones.

In *Planet of Slums*, a comparative study of urban slums in the Third World, American urban theorist Mike Davis notes that those with money and connections are often the ones to benefit from subsidized housing meant for the poor, and that the elites and the middle class (which in the Third World means being relatively well off) are 'extraordinarily successful in evading municipal taxation' (67). Furthermore,

> the urban rich in Africa, south Asia, and much of Latin America are rampantly, even criminally undertaxed by the local governments. Moreover, as financially hardpressed cities have come to rely on regressive sales taxes and user charges – these generate 40 percent of revenue in Mexico City, for example – the tax burden has shifted even more one-sidedly from the rich to the poor. Part of the blame must be assigned to the IMF [International Monetary Fund] which, in its role as the Third World's financial watchdog, everywhere advocates regressive user fees and charges for public services but never proposes counter-part efforts to tax wealth, conspicuous consumption, or real estate. Likewise, the World Bank crusades for 'good governance' in the cities of the Third World but undermines its likelihood by seldom supporting progressive taxation. (68)

Davis's observations about undertaxation, which is a form of tax evasion, in the developing world may also be applied to developed world nations: the 2010 fiscal crisis in Greece was brought on in part by a widespread abuse of the tax system. As Jeevan Deol notes in a comparative report on Greek and Indian tax issues,

> Economists estimate that Greece loses up to 15 billion euros a year through tax avoidance by individuals and small businesses, with over a quarter of Greek economic activity taking place in an unaccounted 'shadow economy.' More than half of Greeks declare an incredibly low income of less than 12,000 euros per year on their tax returns and many small businesses don't use cash registers or issue receipts. The usual way of solving a serious tax dispute in Greece is to apply the 'rule of thirds:' one-third of the tax bill to the government, one-third in the tax inspector's pocket and one-third saved by the taxpayer. None of these practices is unknown in India. Of course, it is not only Greece and India that have problems with tax collection. Between 10-15% of activity in most western European countries takes place in the shadow economy and the UK alone loses up to £4 billion per year in excise tax. Corporate tax evasion is equally widespread. (Deol)

This Monopoly game of tax evasion – in which elites, corporations, and international financial institutions almost always win – causes huge losses for the vast majority of individuals and communities. Security, health, environment, standard of living, equitable labour conditions, and direct control over one's life in a community are all impacted by tax evasion. Even more insidious are maneuvers to naturalize poverty and remit responsibility for dealing with global issues of poverty to the poor themselves. An example of this was the 'supremely odd' intellectual marriage in the 1970s between World Bank President Robert McNamara (formerly the chief planner of the war in Vietnam) and John Turner (anarchist architect). Davis examines how the two agreed on a cynically pragmatic and cost-effective approach to the urban crisis: 'Amidst great ballyhoo about "helping the poor help themselves," little notice was taken publicly of the momentous downsizing of entitlement implicit in the World Bank's canonization of slum housing. Praising the praxis of the poor became a smokescreen for reneging upon historic state commitments to relieve poverty and homelessness' (Mike Davis 72). The failure to address the connections between corporate responsibility to the public commons and the problem of poverty is characteristic of the globalist logic that privileges capital over people. Since corporations are only accountable to their shareholders, and since their prime motivation is profit, giving corporations more power, subsidies, fewer restrictions, self-regulation, and low taxes greatly diminishes democratic governance and equitable gains for the common good.

Canadian cultural critic and writer John Ralston Saul rejects the question: 'What is globalization?' yet situates this phenomenon in a specific time, emerging from a specific source:

> Globalization emerged in the 1970s as if from nowhere, fully grown, enrobed in an aura of inclusivity. Advocates and believers argued with audacity that, through the prism of a particular school of economics, societies around the world would be taken in new, interwoven and positive directions. This mission was converted into policy and law over twenty years – the 1980s and '90s – with the force of declared inevitability. (3)

The term 'globalization' is ambiguous in its double meaning: a process of dissemination from above as in its corporate manifestations, or from below through grassroots movements. Therefore we use the term *globalism* to identify a narrow, very specific ideology with its attendant propaganda. Ralston Saul's definition of globalization is more clearly served by *globalism*: the 'assertion that all civilizations from now on were going to be led by commerce ... the other constitutive parts of human activity – from politics to social policy to culture – were going to be perceived principally through the prism of economics, which, once released from most government interference, would find its own natural balances' (17-18). It is this more specific form of globalism that serves as our reference point in this section for discussing community, though the wider context is necessarily a long history of colonialism and Eurocentrism, with its symptomatic forms of othering: racism, classism, sexism, especially as these relate to the exploitation of resources and labour.

In a sly reversal of the usual Western belittling of the other, Ralston Saul calls globalization a regional belief system, and invites us to consider it through the eyes of the Majority World: 'globalization, looked at from a Chinese or Indian perspective, was always about Western-centred regionalism' (208). Furthermore, according to Ralston Saul, globalization is dead even if its former advocates can only admit this behind closed doors and never to the public. One of the by-products of globalism has been the lack of accountability by global corporate structures to non-experts – especially when it comes to such specialized topics as economics, which in globalist terms rules all aspects of culture and overrides all other concerns.

The macro policy of globalism is in radical opposition to local knowledges and to the local economics of the community marketplace. The paradox created by this abstraction is that it reduces so-called global culture to economic determinism while associating this model with tropes of freedom. However, when capital is free and corporate personhood's rights supercede local community rights, exploitation and injustice prevail. The stories we consider here are caught up in this paradox of economic determinism masked as global freedom: we cannot but interpret them as being representative of globalization, while adamantly arguing against globalism's self-rationalization as a form of radically anti-communitarian practice that even more paradoxically has brought into being communities of resistance. The double-edged sword of globalization, like the parable of the spider and the insects, pits entrapment in globalized and reductive discourses and exploitative situations, against oppositional, liberatory practices and stories generated by local communities that also spread globally.

Why look at only a few stories that circulate in stark journalistic outline? Our proposal is to imagine these stories' other dimensions, and from there, to imagine how we are implicated in creating the conditions that generate such harrowing experiences, and also to imagine how we might change those conditions. The suffering in these stories is underrepresented in the media and is especially alien to the affluent. In spite of this, imagination can form a bridge with the other that is maintained by solidarity: this is a key element of the community commons, the capacity to affiliate in ways that escape easy quantification and in ways that produce immeasurable solidarities. Like many others currently reflecting on the paradoxes of globalization, Michael Hardt and Antonio Negri also see globalized discourses as having two contradictory sides:

> On one face, Empire spreads globally its network of hierarchies and divisions that maintain order through new mechanisms of control and constant conflict. Globalization, however, is also the creation of new circuits of cooperation and collaboration that stretch across nations and continents and allow an unlimited number of encounters. This second face of globalization is not a matter of everyone in the world becoming the same; rather it provides the possibility that, while remaining different, we discover the commonality that

> enables us to communicate and act together. The multitude too might thus be conceived as a network: an open and expansive network in which all differences can be expressed freely and equally, a network that provides the means of encounter so that we can work and live in common. (2004 xiii-xiv)

If the imaginary of the nation-state is fading, a new planetary imaginary is emerging based on ecologically conceived relationships, in which the other's reality is recognized as meaningful and relevant. This is the imaginative dimension of human solidarity and it is a key construct in enabling community agency based on diversity rather than on deterministic monoculture. Paradoxically, this planetary imaginary is rooted in communitarian thinking that simultaneously locates local and specific experiences within a larger commons that has global meaning.

Diasporic and Fractured Communities: The Global Story of Liu Chunlan

> ***Paris, France. September 9, 2007.*** *When the police knocked on her door, Liu Chunlan threw herself out of the tenement-building window and died. She didn't have legal papers, and even though the police had come looking for someone else, the 51-year old Chinese woman panicked. As her son later described her plight, she died of fear. Her only hope of scraping together enough money for her son to marry and have a decent place to live with his wife drove Liu Chunlan to seek work in France. After the incident (which apparently was not the first of its kind) news reports stated that from now on, such police searches would be accompanied by fire trucks with ladders and nets, in preparation for catching people who throw themselves out of windows.*

Liu Chunlan's story contrasts starkly with the glowing reports on China, as one of globalization's top economic success stories. The details of her personal life experienced by millions of other Chinese reveal that workers make only a subsistence living; that as a result life is reduced to a daily struggle for mere survival; that there is no health care for those who can't pay for it, a major failure for any country that calls itself socialist, or has democratic pretensions. But commitment to providing health care for all regardless of financial means requires belief in and support of communities. When politically sanctioned entities are reduced to individual, family, and state, the one unit based on shared collective concerns and concerted action – community – is erased in order to draw the line between affluent families that have political power, and poor families who become dominated. In *Community On Land: Community, Ecology, and the Public Interest*, Janel M. Curry and Steven McGuire trace the history of this contested space between ruler and commoners back to the Third Century A.D. when Rome was occupied by 'corporate' families, and to later in the 11th to 13th centuries when corporate bodies like guilds and religious orders dominated (3-4). This contested space of domination is also material place, the land-base of the commons, thereby establishing a centuries-old struggle between the self-interest of corporate power and the community-interest of the commons.

In the contemporary context of globalized corporate fascism, governments of affluent countries limit and control trade to goods and money, but the economic devastation in poor countries drives millions of migrant workers like Liu Chunlan to seek employment in the centres of power and wealth, instead of in the transnational corporations operating in their own countries, for several good reasons. The massive flow of workers both legal and clandestine is obvious proof that either globalization is not providing sufficient employment in developing countries or that jobs alone are not enough to satisfy people. Migrant workers, for instance, also hope to benefit from basic rights denied them at home, enhanced labour protections, better working conditions, better access to recourse before the law. Globalization theory – and 'theory' perhaps implies more complexity than is merited by simplistic propaganda – claims that opening borders to the logic and laws of the market actually democratizes countries, yet there is mounting historical and contemporary evidence to the contrary. While this argument has been made repeatedly in support of the massive commercial penetration of China, other countries like Cuba are denied this benevolent democratization from above, and are punished instead with trade embargoes. Is this because Cuba is openly critical about how and why the U.S. is undemocratic both within its own borders and in its foreign relations?

The relationship between First and Third World countries must be considered in the historical context dating back through all the phases of colonization. We use the terms First and Third World here not to suggest that there is any inherent superiority or inferiority among countries, but simply as a an indicator of wealth and hegemonic power in the North/West in relation to colonized regions, which continue to struggle with a legacy of injustice and privation. All terms to differentiate among countries are problematic because the terms themselves cannot express historical processes and are open to different ideological interpretations. While we inevitably fall into using binaries like 'developing,' (usually still meaning 'underdeveloped') and 'developed,' it is also important to consider the ways in which rich countries are overdeveloped in their excessive environmental footprints, but also deformed or *mal-developed* in their human development as a result of over-consumption and the narrowing cultural choices created by, among others, media monopolies.

Increasingly militarized borders and alarmist reports of uncontrollable masses of migrants (often represented as criminals and terrorists) illegally crossing into affluent countries obscure the fact that those countries implement 'guest worker' programs whenever it suits their economies' needs. While these programs are ostentatiously promoted as aid to needy neighbors, in fact the need is equally pressing in Anglo-North America and in rich European countries. The various phases of the 'Bracero' program between Mexico and the U.S., and the guest workers programs that brought Turkish, Moroccan, and other North African workers into European countries were implemented to compensate for a severe lack of labourers in developed countries, or at least a lack of non-unionized labourers who would accept much lower wages, job insecurity, and restricted access to civil rights.

Ralston Saul identifies these programs as growing out of 'a radical reworking of late-nineteenth-century Taylorism' (96), with its confusion of men *as* machines. Frederick Winslow Taylor (1856–1915) was an American mechanical engineer who developed techniques for improving industrial efficiency, largely by exploiting workers. He is considered to be the father of so-called scientific management and was one of the leaders of the Efficiency Movement (1890–1932), which sought to eliminate waste and inefficiency from all forms of society. The key problem with Taylorism is how it commodifies human activity in purely quantitative terms while ignoring wider dimensions of human experience thus undermining the social benefits and values that are supposedly unrelated to productivity. Gantt charts that are visual aids for displaying tasks and managing workflow were one of the by-products of Taylorist principles as were concepts of human work as the standardized, mechanized repetition of tasks, managed by consultants who extracted every possible ounce of efficiency from their workers via 'enforced cooperation.' Management enforcing cooperation became a model for productivity taken on by many corporate structures and was at profound odds with forms of community organization predicated on a wider understanding of what human work means, and how it is best carried out. Ralston Saul notes how the theory was that *guest workers* would arrive in First World countries, along with their wives to look after them, and therefore their children. They would work, receive access to the social services offered citizens, but not become citizens – a combination guaranteed to provoke alienation and humiliation – and of course be prepared to be sent home whenever the host wished' (96-97). Clearly such unstable living conditions are not conducive to migrants being integrated into diverse communities. Their marginalized status often leads migrants to lead solitary lives or to become ghettoized as was the case with African American slave communities that came into being throughout the Americas as a result of colonial and industrial exploitation.

These days, guest workers' families are not usually welcome in the host country, creating serious problems in their countries of origin, with parental contact limited to remittances sent home from abroad. The resulting disintegration of families also spells the disintegration of communities. Increasingly, for example, able-bodied men and women abandon Mexican towns, leaving only children and the elderly to fend for themselves. Local economic activity disappears as a result, and these broken communities are left dependent on wages earned in the north. Those who stay and make their living in the drug trade, which is frequently the only game in town, further devastate communities. Understandably, when legal trade and business are monopolized by huge corporations droves of disenfranchised people must resort to the black market for their livelihood. Broken families and communities are replaced by gangs as the only viable social unit for many youth. Instead of learning life-affirming values, they learn to survive by violence. The long-term effects of this negative cycle of socialization on vast numbers of abandoned children will have an inestimable impact on the future of communities. Globally, the widespread instability resulting from this situation is a much greater threat to security everywhere than is terrorism.

Ironically, as soon as a country's GNP increases with tangible social improvements, guest workers are almost immediately brought in to fill agricultural and other labour-intensive jobs. Before joining the EU, Spain supplied agricultural migrant workers to more affluent countries, while now that entry into the EU has strengthened Spain's economy, workers are recruited from countries like Morocco and Romania. It is not clear whether greater prosperity means Spanish people are no longer willing to accept menial jobs, or whether companies choose migrants instead because these programs allow them to pay less than the national minimum wage. When asked why they are employing migrants, managers and owners make vague claims that their own countries' workers tire out more easily, while guest workers come with the sole objective of working and never complain. The message that emerges clearly here is that companies are supported by government programs to increase their private profits, while labour conditions and wages can be brushed aside as irrelevant as long as there are enough desperate foreigners to do the job.

These labour practices based on exploiting inequality also undermine communities. Equitable economics are rooted in community, the very foundation of human interconnectedness. Alastair McIntosh, whose work we discuss earlier in the book, traces his memories of how the Hebridean village where he lived 'evolved' from the practice of mutuality to a cash economy and how this process weakened communitarian ethics. He remembers that before the advent of refrigerators, these fisher folk would have to share their catch since fish must be eaten fresh. Mutuality was the very foundation of co-existence, but quickly eroded once as basic a technological advance as refrigeration allowed individuals to hoard instead of sharing.

> Mutual dependency was the glue that facilitated social cohesion. Now, because money (unlike fish and eggs) does not rot, it can be invested, yielding interest, a dividend or capital gains. Money thereby takes on second-order characteristics over and above its primary accounting role: it makes money out of itself. This has the effect of shifting benefit away from community and towards individuals. It assists the concentration of wealth, and that leads to an increasing rigidity in access to resources for the majority. (30)

This is not to say that we should all become Luddites in order to regress to pre-industrial community life-ways. But such stories help in understanding how economic behaviours evolved at odds with local community practices, and help to avoid simplistically equating egotism with human nature to justify injustice. Globalism attempts to hide the fact that power and wealth are becoming concentrated in fewer hands, leaving an increasing majority destitute and robbed of any control over their destiny. Its propaganda machine, most widely disseminated through mass media, employs narrow and skewed indicators to celebrate economic success without revealing that success is enjoyed by a shrinking minority. There is little or no dribble-down effect given that working people in rich countries lose their jobs when corporations move their plants to poor countries to better exploit workers there. In this way, all working people lose out. 'Such is the essence of neoliberal globalisation: competition subsumes the co-operative relationship. Government is forced out of the economy, but money then takes its place as king and it cares little for community or environment. Plutocracy – government by the rich – yields inevitably to oligarchy – government by the few' (McIntosh 31). The resulting global dynamics displace more people than ever before, and migrants become both pawns of the global system and its wild cards, since they refuse to stay put to be exploited to maximum corporate benefit in the Majority World.

Migrant workers are increasingly women in the service sector, while also being trafficked as slaves in international sex-trade operations. Despite the conspicuous concerns of rich countries to limit the flow of migrants, it is clear that those considered illegal especially benefit the countries where they work. These workers are the most vulnerable and therefore the most compliant: they must accept any terms of employment and have no recourse to secure decent wages, safe working conditions, or any benefits. In this sense, undocumented migrant workers are often worse off than those recognized and hosted as guest workers, since both kinds of workers live on a continuum of global exploitation.

The Taylorist theory that confuses humans and machines holds true for both kinds of workers as well as for those employed by transnational corporations operating in poor countries. Ralston Saul points out that the assumption is that people won't mind being treated like machines – being moved around like pieces of equipment, having to work inhumanely long shifts, performing dangerous and/or tedious and repetitious tasks that often result in physical injuries and long term disabilities – as long as their wages are marginally increased. In developing countries, this slight improvement in wages, say from starvation wages or complete unemployment to $2 U.S. a day still keeps the majority of workers below the poverty line. Yet according to the proponents of globalism, these workers should be satisfied with the improvement in their wages and have faith in ever-increasing progress through corporate globalization.

History shows that capitalism has always been intertwined with colonialism and the exploitation of labour. The fact that conditions for workers improved within affluent countries for a time does not disprove capitalism's dependence on cheap resources and labour exploited in the Third World. Colonialism in its earliest as well as contemporary manifestations has always provided the basis for making profits, and has increasingly widened the gap between rich and poor, accumulating wealth into ever fewer hands and vastly expanding poverty. The solution to these problems can no longer be found solely within nation-states. Our sense of global citizenship or planetary interconnectedness demands forms of governance and legal institutions to mediate the abyssal line separating rich from poor. McIntosh characterizes *metaculture* as 'a connection at a level of soul that goes deeper than superficial cultural differences; a connection simply by virtue of our underlying humanity. Such a bedrock of commonality is desperately needed in today's fragmented world. It arises not from "globalisation" as a business concept, but from the fact of being "one world"' (20). In short, alternative forms of global community that arise in the face of exploitation and capital accumulation reserved for the few are an appropriate response to globalized myths of community that co-opt the term while deforming it to suit their profit-driven self-interest.

There must be international efforts to move from unenforceable recommendations like those in The United Nations Global Compact and the International Labour Office's 'Working Party on the Social Dimension of Globalization' toward global legislation on wages, employment conditions, worker security, and environmental protection. Furthermore, the language of these documents is so heavily influenced by business interests that many of their recommendations ring hollow. The Global Compact ignores the fact that transnational corporations operate in poor countries precisely to take advantage of the lax laws regarding minimum wages, safety standards, freedom of association, collective bargaining, and environmental protections. In this context what can it possibly mean to recommend to businesses that '[E]stablishing genuine dialogue with freely chosen workers' representatives enables both workers and employers to understand each other's problems better and find ways to resolve them' (Principle Three)? Is the problem *really* one of understanding? Experience shows that corporations only respond to the threat of lawsuits, but even those costs are factored into the price of doing business. Laws have also been erected to defend corporations against public criticism. Liability laws relate to them as if they were persons whose reputations must be protected regardless of actual wrongdoing. Powerful interests have turned the tables against the common good and democratic free speech by potentially criminalizing well-founded criticism of corporations.

Our advocacy of international labour and environmental laws and courts supports resolving conflicts via global structures of mediation that can have profound glocal effects. These structures are necessary because conflicting interests can only sometimes be negotiated among shareholders at the community level, especially when a transnational corporation's self-interest is at stake. Curry and McGuire tell a number of encouraging stories about innovative, local, community-based resource management of rangelands, fisheries, and forests in the U.S. and Canada. One of the stories is about the Willapa Bay Alliance started in 1992 (on the southwest Pacific coast of Washington state in the U.S.) that includes as one of its founding members the Weyerhaeuser Company, scientists, and local multidisciplinary members working together to restore and preserve the ecosystem by responsibly managing salmon fishing, oyster growing, cranberry farming, and small-scale logging (217). 'The strategy is to procure as much agreement as possible while avoiding absolutes ... so, while the laws like the Endangered Species Act could be applied here to save the salmon, environmentalists are not using it and are choosing to build consensus instead' (218). In this case as in many others, community involvement in generating relationships of equality, together with the company's commitment to remain in one place for the long haul creates a new dynamics in which cooperation and collaboration clearly benefit all. It is unclear how this model might be applied outside of countries with enforceable environmental laws, and communities that have some leverage to create a level playing field among all members of the community (including the companies). While in this case, the environmentalists chose to avoid lawsuits and confrontation, it is vitally important to acknowledge that they had a choice and that the Endangered Species Act exists. Such a scenario differs radically from transnational corporations operating in poor countries precisely to avoid laws or consensual decision-making with local communities. The kind of alliance formation examined by Curry and McGuire does not preclude the need for international laws and courts. Perhaps if such a legal system made it unviable for corporations to continue exploiting vulnerable communities around the world, more of them would adopt forming alliances with them instead – but this is an enormous leap of faith that would require a major paradigm shift for corporations more than it would for the communities they exploit.

The dominant globalist practice is diametrically opposed to cooperation and equity. Most transnational corporations and the elites that own them pay little to no federal income tax, thereby putting the tax burden on middle-income earners. The lack of a sufficient tax base, as we have discussed earlier, has forced even the most affluent countries to slash social infrastructure much like the structural adjustment programs imposed on developing countries by the World Bank and International Monetary Fund. One of the greatest damages wreaked by globalization has been this free-loading of corporations together with the mobility that frees them from any long-term commitment to local communities. Fearful of losing more jobs to other countries, national governments make corporations exempt from social and environmental responsibilities, and even subsidize them. The only way to reverse this trend is through international cooperation among countries to legislate labour and environmental standards, and to set corporate taxes regardless of operation location. The Global Compact appeals to a company's reputation (read: *image*) and outlines practices for avoiding loss of profits and stock value (Principle Six). These appeals are clearly aimed at self-interest, and contrast with how international governmental bodies would have to base lawmaking and enforcement on justice with a view to protecting the human and environmental rights that are in the overarching interest of all communities everywhere.

International bodies already exist both for trade negotiation and criminal investigation and prosecution. There is, as we discuss elsewhere, the International Criminal Court – based on a treaty and joined by over 100 countries the ICC complements existing national judicial systems and steps in only if national courts are unwilling or unable to investigate or prosecute crimes against humanity, genocide, and war crimes; the International Court of Justice which is the principal judicial organ of the UN; the Inter-American Court of Human Rights; the European Court of Human Rights; and the African Court on Human and Peoples' Rights. A major problem characterizing international bodies is that historical power dynamics are replicated. The most powerful nations set themselves up as the judges or exempt themselves from being subject to the global rights reach of the organization, thereby making it unthinkable to have one of their own members put on trial. What is paradoxical here is the degree to which globalist discourses can be promoted in one's own national or economic self-interest whereas other structures of global organization that provide recourse for abuses and violations are deemed unacceptable and warrant exceptionalist behaviour. The time is long overdue to combine the negotiation of trade with a wider mandate of international criminal investigation and prosecution of corporations and governments involved in significant rights abuses and violations. The only way of avoiding domination by the First World in such international bodies would be for the greatest possible inclusion of other countries, whose interests would clearly be better served by *fair* trade than free trade. Internationalizing more legal instruments would benefit the majority, and though elites in some countries are more interested in accumulating personal wealth than ensuring justice for their own citizens, the struggle for social justice must be constant at all levels, and is made especially effective through community action.

Once citizens understand that politicians and lawmakers working to promote corporate interests too-often hijack laws, it becomes clear that they can no longer count on the judicial system to defend even individual rights, let alone community rights. One of the most promising movements in community education in the U.S. is the Daniel Pennock Democracy School, which was created by the Community Environmental Legal Defense Fund (CELDF) and Richard Grossman, co-founder of the Program on Corporations, Law, and Democracy (POCLAD), and first launched as a series of seminars at Wilson College in Chambersburg, Pennsylvania in 2003. By 2006 Democracy School had mushroomed to over a dozen locations and welcomes people of all ages, interests, and occupations to learn about taking control of their community and environmental rights, even in states where natural resources like water can be privately owned and depleted. Returning to McIntosh's hopeful insight that 'no place is more sacred, and no peoples more worthy of honour, than those that have made beauty blossom anew out of desecration' (93), Democracy School is clearly inspired and guided by this kind of faith in community renewal and justice in response to legal injustice. The school is named after Daniel Pennock, a teenaged boy who died as a result of being exposed to land-applied sewage sludge in 1995, after which his parents devoted themselves to ending this massive profit-making and life-threatening practice, thereby inspiring others to join forces to protect their environment. The Democracy School provides education for citizens and activists on 'how to reframe exhausting and often discouraging single issue work (such as opposing toxic dumps, quarries, factory farms, [and so forth]) in a way that we confront corporate control on a powerful single front: people's constitutional rights' ('What is Democracy School?'). The restorative power of community in such a context relies on pedagogy and the interlinked solidarity that establishes the rights of community via democratic and constitutional means, but is only one aspect of addressing the community of rights within traditional structures of collective empowerment.

What might it have meant to Liu Chunlan's life had she had access to such community-based structures of collective empowerment?

State Surveillance and Policing Versus Community-based Conflict Resolution: The Global Story of Robert Dziekanski

Vancouver International Airport, Canada. October 14, 2007. *A Polish man panicked after ten hours of waiting for his mother and not getting any help from airport officials. He had been sponsored by his mother to start a new life in Canada, where he could also help look after her as she aged. Four Royal Canadian Mounted Police arrived and immediately tasered Robert Dziekanski at least twice according to fellow traveler Paul Pritchard (but later confirmed as five times by an independent judicial inquiry) who videotaped the shooting and the man's final moments, footage posted on the Internet for all to see. Shortly after,* RCMP *Cpl. Dale Carr said he'd been getting angry calls from people, but that they're coming to conclusions based on one piece of evidence and not waiting for all the evidence to come out. He said that wouldn't happen until an inquest is held. Well, the inquest has now been held and that one piece of evidence obtained by an independent citizen has proved invaluable, and raises important questions about surveillance, police conduct, and citizens' rights to gather and disseminate information about state abuses.*

The story of Polish immigrant Robert Dziekanski ends abruptly without his even making it alive out of the Canadian airport. Even as a legal immigrant he received no assistance from the Canada Border Services Agency though he was at times visibly distraught according to eyewitnesses. Canada, which represents itself as a bastion of multiculturalism and tolerance, apparently lacks translation services at its international airports. When the obvious approach of communicating – even through gestures and sign-language, what we have earlier in the book referred to as *irrevocable hospitality* – was not forthcoming from officials or airport personnel, Dziekanski expressed his frustration by throwing a computer and then a piece of furniture, and banging on a glass door to try to get back into the secured area. The police who brutally killed him with repeated taser shots had not actually witnessed these outbursts, which had been picked up on security cameras. Who interprets these images, and according to what criteria, emerges as the crux of this story, though the reason for Dziekanski's decision to come to Canada relates to the previous story about migrant workers generally and the myths of global mobility for the poor. While capital and equity move freely and with remarkably few strictures, the story for workers and the poor who are struggling to deal with the consequences of global market shifts is quite different.

In more specific terms, this Polish man left his home country, like thousands of his compatriots whose former Warsaw Pact countries were subjected to what Ralston Saul describes as the most brutal application of globalization theory, namely, *crucifixion economics* (113). In Russia and other Eastern Bloc countries, this process involved massive privatization carried out almost overnight without any safeguards against monopolization and corruption, with the result that organized crime becomes a built-in feature of the savage capitalism in which power often never changed hands, just political hats. Former Communist Party Officials and Secret Service Police doled out amongst themselves the industries and other components of the vast, centralized public system from which they could now reap fully private profits. In obedience to globalization theory and policies dictated by rich countries and international financial organizations that would never tolerate such levels of insecurity and lawlessness within in their own borders, the countries that became case studies for crucifixion economics also did away with their social infrastructures, creating unprecedented unemployment and eliminating social services such as health care. Corporate globalists touted the ensuing bonanza for elites and middlemen as the road to democracy, freedom, and even human rights. But most people continue to experience it as poverty, insecurity, and hopelessness, with migration into the unknown seeming more promising than the newly liberalized Second World.

None of the possible backdrops to Dziekanski's story could be captured by the security cameras even though they are now equipped with computer programs that can supposedly distinguish much subtler gestures than his anger and despair: '*This aberrant-pattern recognition system* is already in use outside some banks, particularly in Britain, which is the leader in the field. Bank robbers apparently have patterns of behaviour just before they strike. Security experts say that terrorists do, too. And so the millions of cameras on streets throughout most of the Western democracies could rapidly be adapted to this idea of aberrant-pattern recognition' (Ralston Saul 242). As Ralston Saul observes, 'the idea that we all act normally unless we are bank robbers or terrorists is a profoundly controlling idea of individualism and society' (242). This belief that technology can identify and interpret human behaviours coupled with an immediate violent reaction on the part of officials instead of inquiry is increasingly blurring the boundaries between security and corporatized state terror. While the by-standers at Vancouver International Airport may have been disturbed and worried by Dziekanski's outburst, reports and witness accounts suggest that they were shocked and disgusted by the police response. One distraught or even violent individual's behaviour does not carry with it the dangerous implications of systematized police brutality. And this is especially so within a community context where *how* one responds to encounter ethically or not is the distinguishing mark of one's place in the community *and* the community's place within a larger network of communities.

Officials, both those working at the airport and the officers who responded to their call, lose their common sense for communicating when community values are replaced by institutional rules and regulations. People in positions of authority relinquish the true tools for conflict resolution, in favour of knee-jerk reactions involving excessive force. Speaking in more general terms about core values that should inform all interactions, the authors of *Peacemaking Circles* observe how even at the community level, we are conditioned to react defensively instead of responding openly when faced with a conflict:

> We find ourselves deviating from our core values, though, not because we want to but because we don't know how to bring our best values to conflicts. Instead, following the models we've observed in others and in our institutions, we make an automatic, unconscious switch from the values we aspire to flowing to those we believe are necessary to hold our own in conflict. Switching to a combative set, we become people we don't recognize or want to be. (Pranis et. al. 48)

A disturbing aspect of Dziekanski's story is the RCMP's combative response toward an unarmed and distraught individual, a response that was shown in the final report on the incident released in June 2010 to have been marked by the deliberate misrepresentation of their actions. A more reasoned response informed by core community values would have involved implementing the precautionary principle, or even the principle of basic hospitable encounter predicated on compassion and an attempt to understand the contexts for distraught behaviours. At the very least, taser use as a substitute for basic principles of encounter showed the commons to have been defined by the RCMP as a space for cowardice and Taylorist violence. The most efficient solution as demonstrated in the four officers' actions was violence and death.

What is truly shocking in the incident is the symbolic power of state-violence being exerted in this way, and reducing the richness of community responses that any country might be capable of producing when faced with a similar situation, to a sick parody of a Rambo-esque solution to conflict. Several reviews of tasers have since been conducted in Canada including one ordered by the then Public Safety Minister, Stockwell Day who nevertheless resisted calls by critics for a moratorium on the weapon. A further development in the taser story implicates James Cairns, Ontario's deputy chief coroner, who publicly advocates the use of tasers as an expert on the subject, while having his travel to their conferences paid for by Taser International and associated manufacturers of the weapon. Since Dziekanski's death 'Taser has repeatedly urged journalists to contact Dr. Cairns for his pro-taser views' (Alphonso).

In a typical attempt to take advantage of the perverse laws protecting the corporation's personhood, Taser International filed an application arguing that the first phase of the inquest harmed its reputation. The application was thrown out, and the British Columbia commission decided to have the RCMP participate in independent research on Tasers ('RCMP apologize to Dziekanski's mother'). The inquiry also recommended that severe limits be put on taser use in B.C., but the Police Association of Ontario seemed uninfluenced by this story, wanting to equip even more officers with tasers, and arguing that 'when used appropriately, these weapons remain an effective option for police services in carrying out their responsibilities and protecting communities' ('Ontario to standardize Taser Training').

Communities are not, however, consulted as to whether they agree with this view, since decisions are entrusted to only those individuals considered 'experts.' Ironically, the company that makes the weapon has more 'expert' (read: *self-interested/biased*] input as to its use than do community members. The defining of communities in the above police statement, draws a problematic differentiation between those needing protection and those whose lives can be put at risk because they are reduced to their offending acts (or how their inoffensive but troubled acts, as in the case of Dziekanski, can be misinterpreted by state functionaries). A holistic definition of community would include those who commit crimes, as well as the police – this is how the peacemaking circle approach conceives of working towards solutions for everyone involved in a conflict, especially since the community aspects of violence or conflict implicate more than just the perpetrator.

Amnesty International reported in June 2007 that in the span of fifteen months, six Canadian men had died after being shocked with tasers, and that in the U.S. coroners have listed the taser in autopsy reports as a contributory factor in more than 30 deaths in recent years ('Canada: Inappropriate and Excessive Use of Tasers'). The weapon's increased abuse paves the way for normalizing its use in other ways, and for naturalizing state violent response to perceived security threats against protestors and other people whose actions, while perhaps agitated and seemingly erratic to authorities, do *not* constitute criminal actions. In one case reported by Amnesty, police tried to rouse an unconscious man with taser shocks ('Canada: Inappropriate and Excessive Use of Tasers'). Imagine watching the security camera images (or watch the video on the Internet) of the RCMP repeatedly hitting Dziekanski with the 50,000 volt taser while yelling 'Hit him again, hit him again,' as just one in a series of similar incidents. Would the security cameras identity police behaviour as aberrant and especially so with regard to community standards of acceptable and just behaviour?

If such an incident were brought to a peacemaking circle, the behaviour of all members involved in the conflict would be considered. As it currently stands, the disciplinary process for so-called 'rogue' officers takes a long time, and they are often reinstated without having the opportunity to reflect upon their actions with the help of other perspectives from outside the force. Internal police follow-up simply recommends taking more careful aim to avoid the heart area and genitals, and avoiding the use of tasers on elderly people. A community approach would take a much deeper look at how the person pulling the taser trigger feels; how the myth that this weapon is non-lethal alters the user's reaction, judgment, and sense of responsibility; how there are consequences for misuse of the weapon in irresponsible ways that effect, and reflect on, the entire community.

The sense of power, similar to that inspired by violent video games, helps produce wildly excessive police behaviour encouraged by a weapon whose trigger can be repeatedly pulled to cause pain and shocked panic in the victim with only a marginal chance of fatality. How does such behaviour relate to globalization? War, terrorism, the perceived and/or pretended threat of terrorism, and subsequent expansion of militarization, surveillance, and security supported by the military-industrial complex have developed parallel to and in mutual support of corporate globalism. The narrow economic motivations behind violent world domination are constantly obscured by an equally narrow ideological discourse that promotes militarized responses to any perceived threat against the status quo. Violent response is naturalized even as it betrays stated convictions about rights and ethics, and this is entirely congruent with global patterns of egregious response to conflict. Within nations, even ones with traditions of civil liberty, this deeply antagonistic and combative worldview translates into police actions against their own citizens that are eroding democratic rights.

Dziekanski's story encapsulates contradictory uses of technology and the struggle of the state to control media, while community members struggle to tell their perspectives through media. How were the competing narratives of the RCMP and eyewitnesses shown to be radically at odds by the images captured by security cameras and the video taken by Dziekanski's fellow passenger Paul Pritchard, later posted on the Internet? Police confiscated Pritchard's camera thereby making him realize that the footage he had taken was worth retrieving and publicizing ('Taser video shows RCMP ...'). State surveillance is undermined by the witness's power to record and disseminate authoritarian abuses. While like most innovative communications technology, the Internet was largely a military invention, it can be equally useful to those who oppose authoritarianism and spread dissent. Pritchard's reflective action to turn from passive bystander to active witness is one that must be widely encouraged. That said, communities must not take for granted the democratic potential of the Internet, given that communications technology is not widely available worldwide, and that multinational companies are developing software to limit access and to aid authoritarian governments to persecute dissidents. Companies like Yahoo!, Microsoft's MSN, and Google all act as ICPs [Internet Content Providers] in China, and some like Yahoo have routinely blocked words, phrases, and web addresses censored by Chinese authorities, and even over-blocked content without being asked to by authorities, to ensure the continuity of their lucrative licenses. Some of these companies obey and even anticipate what the Chinese government expects from them, while they seemingly have nothing to fear from their own Western governments. 'Yahoo was criticized by the U.S. Congress when it released to Chinese authorities information relating to the email account of Shi Tao, a Chinese journalist who was arrested in 2004,' but criticism did not prevent what happened to the dissident: Shi Tao was sentenced to 10 years in jail for revealing state secrets ('Yahoo settles case...'). Yahoo!'s collaborative response to information requests from the Chinese government has made it complicit in the criminal conviction of at least four Chinese government critics. Once again recommendations for corporations to self-regulate in such matters are futile. This situation could be changed if companies were brought before an international court and held accountable by international standards for their complicity in the abuse of human rights – or if these corporations were forced to be responsive to the community standards in place where their employees actually live and work.

The UN Special Rapporteur stresses that online expression should be guided by international standards and be guaranteed the same protection as is awarded to other forms of expression ('Race to the Bottom'). In this case, both the Chinese government (acting in the name of state security) and Internet Companies (acting in the name of profits) are guilty of violating rights. Canada, the U.S., and other rich countries have little moral grounds for challenging the abuses of the Chinese government, given that they rely heavily on goods and capital from this major trading partner. It is imperative that people continually expose and oppose corporate and government complicity in human rights violations everywhere. While totalitarianism must be fought primarily by a country's own localized populations, support from international solidarity movements communicates to governments that they cannot act with impunity indefinitely.

Despite its obviously simplistic and reductive lens, corporate globalism has deployed one of the most cynical and insidious propaganda machines of all times. The biggest deception of globalism is the false democratization that it claims to promote through economic development, while rendering invisible the roots of economic disparity and rejecting any reflection on class difference within nations, and differences among nations based on historic exploitation through colonization and imperialism. Propagandistic discourse about why the West must defend itself through pre-emptive attacks on so-called rogue states or anyone who opposes Western privilege (represented as love of freedom) on whatever grounds has filled corporate media to such an extent, that little space has been left for considering the much greater and more urgent threat of environmental collapse.

Argentine cultural theorist Walter Mignolo identifies one of the most fundamental distortions of Western thinking as the denial of coevalness among the planet's inhabitants, and examines how relocating people from geographical places into a chronological hierarchy served the racist colonial project. Hence, so-called underdeveloped people were – and are still, according to developmentalism – viewed as being in the childhood phase of development while Europeans and Euramericans imagine themselves in the adult stage. Mignolo theorizes that 'the current stage of globalization, driven by transnational corporations, is nonintentionally contributing to the restitution of space and location and to the multiplication of local histories' (36). While Mignolo overstates this outcome given the spatial indeterminacy of global capital markets and the unfettered mobility of corporations, his observation suggests a productive way to view Majority World countries as prophetic of our shared planetary future.

The main contention against globalization is that it has not delivered on the promise of economic growth for all, but the language of this school of economics skirts the issues by reducing them to the illusive concept of economic growth measured as Gross National Product, foreign investment, and exports – indicators that are usually disconnected from the material realities and standard of living of the majority of the population, especially in poor countries.[1] Noam Chomsky doesn't mince words but is more specific about who benefits and who is kept subjected:

> The main goal of NAFTA, we can now concede, was not to achieve the highly touted wonders of 'trade' and jobs, always illusion, but to ensure that Mexico would be 'locked in' to the reforms that had made it an 'economic miracle' (for U.S. investors and Mexican elites), deflecting the danger detected by a Latin America Strategy Development Workshop at the Pentagon in September 1990: that a 'democracy opening' in Mexico could test the special relationship by bringing into office a government more interested in challenging the U.S. on economic and nationalist grounds. (Jameson and Miyoshi 366)

One can argue that according to globalism's own simplistic theory, special relationships should not exist. On what grounds is there a special (read: *political*) relationship between two countries when their borders are supposed to be open for 'free' trade and all trade subject only to the laws of the market?

To give just one concrete example of the countless contradictions between globalist theory and practice, the terms of Mexico-U.S. trade are clearly manipulated and imposed by the more powerful partner. Mexican oil sold at a cheap price to the U.S. in exchange for cheap American corn is a win-win situation for the U.S., while spelling economic, environmental, and cultural losses for Mexico. Given that oil is a nonrenewable and nearly depleted resource, there is no reason for it to be cheap, while cheap corn sold to a country where corn is sacred while also being a food staple can only be seen as dumping. Furthermore, the import of cheap American corn destroyed the local cultivation of this crop and introduced GMO corn in regions where peasant farmers were deeply opposed to genetically modified technology for ethical and environmental reasons. To complicate matters further, arbitration bodies like the World Trade Organization fight tooth-and-nail any trade restrictions based on ethical, environmental, or health concerns, thereby robbing people of their democratic right to make localized, community-based choices, and in the process robbing countries and communities of their sovereignty. As Wole Soyinka, Nigerian author and Nobel winner (1986) argues in the preface to the Reith Lectures, 'Lapses in governance must be objectively examined, flawed and cruel policies of state identified and changed – in short, all remote causes, especially the political, subjected to a remedial process' (xiv). Remedial process requires dissident community. State security apparatuses that exhibit increasing fear of legitimate criticism and transfer that fear to other forms of security paranoia present a sustained threat to peaceful and equitable community relations.

We can imagine how differently Robert Dziekanski's arrival in Canada would have been handled by a localized community response, as opposed to the punitive, state-sanctioned paranoia that ended his life.

'Thieving'/Labouring Community: Scapegoating Untouchables

The recent liberation movements in South Asia have replaced the enigmatic (to non-Indians) term for 'untouchables' with the self designation Dalit, meaning in the Marathi language 'ground,' 'suppressed,' 'crushed,' or 'broken to pieces.' This mixed population spread out over India, Nepal, Pakistan, Sri Lanka, and Bangladesh, has origins that are just starting to be excavated from under centuries-thick layers of religions – Hinduism, Buddhism, Islam, Christianity, and Sikhism – both imposed on and embraced by these people – and always syncretized. It is said that regardless of the dominant religion Dalits had converted to over the centuries, they always dedicated an altar to an unknown (foreign) god, signaling a kind of radical openness to difference. Dalits make up more than a sixth of India's population – approximately 160 million people – according to some accounts, while others say it is impossible to calculate their population given its diversity and diffuse nature. They are the ultimate subaltern in South Asian studies but more recently are also referred to as the 'cosmopolitan subaltern,' indicating that they are the most dominated and silenced and yet diversified and open to difference.

Dalits occupy the bottom rung of the Indian caste system and have traditionally been forced to perform the most menial and foul of tasks: cleaning up excrement and the remains of dead animals. In the paradoxical inversion typical of power, those who force Dalits to deal with the most infectious matters, also charge them with being unclean and contagious, hence untouchable. This physical-metaphysical double bind has worked to subject Dalits, especially women and children, to all kinds of rights abuses and violations, from public insults to torture and killing. Some Dalits have nonetheless managed to run the gauntlet of systemic obstacles to complete postsecondary education, and to work as lawyers and politicians in support of their people.

Given the Dalits' historical exclusion from, and their ongoing ill treatment in schools, their stories are only now beginning to move from a long oral tradition to circulate in print. Liberation theologian, James Elisha Taneti scoured the accounts of missionaries with a critical eye to their biases, and the accounts of other observers of cultic practices like festivals and rituals, in search of the 'Liberative motifs in the Dalit Religion' (Elisha). His article, intent on gathering observations, is more descriptive than interpretive: some of the practices observed are opaquely symbolic and invite transcultural speculation. We are indebted to his compilation and eagerly accept the invitation to ponder the Dalits' acts of subversive defiance as an alternative expression of community.

It is sometimes difficult to discern the Dalits' habits from their oppressors' superstitions and vicious slanders: they are rumoured, for instance, to eat carrion regardless of how the animal died, as noted by the Anglican missionary F. Colyer Sackett. Other accusations belong to the genre of slanderous superstition. Dalits are said to spread pollution in a radius of seventy-four feet (exact measurement no less); their shadows can pollute all the water in a well; the sound waves from their mouths are considered so adulterated that they had to cover their mouths with a little pot when speaking to a Hindu (until they started being used as messengers, when this aspect of their contagion mysteriously disappeared); the smoke from their funeral pyre was feared to contaminate the village and so they had to bury their dead, instead of cremating them as was the general practice. Elisha says of the Dalits of Andhra Pradhesh that they 'were the original inhabitants of the lands but later pushed to the fringes of village settlement' and were 'barred from entering the village lest they spread an atmosphere of pollution around them' (Elisha). While in rights documents and networks Dalits are often distinguished from indigenous tribes, this might be due to the specific caste imposed on them, blurring and even erasing their ethnic identities and origins. The Charter of Dalit Human Rights assertively rejects these impositions and identifies Dalits as 'the people of Mother Earth, people from a labouring community, people who believe [in] and live a sustainable life and people who belong to and are rooted in the community' (Shinde 26).

Deviating from, and openly criticizing the Universal Declaration of Human Rights for limiting rights to individuals, Dalits 'consider [that] the UDHR as well as other Human Rights treaties have developed a human rights discourse based on individual liberty. For those of us whose life is an eternal struggle for survival it is the security of communities that is paramount ... We demand [that the] discourse of individual security ... be taken to its next logical step in the context of the Dalits ... the security of the community of people' (27, 28). Another article, asserting the Dalits' identity, might sound solipsistic at first glance, but on deeper consideration the poetic logic glimmers with radical mutualism. The Article asserts the 'Dalits as people, claiming that it is our Earth, an earth that is Dalit in character' (26). Why is 'our Earth' capitalized and then immediately referred to as 'an earth'? How can this earth be Dalit in character? Is this a radical subversion of what the elites consider filth? Do excrement, the dead, the soil combine to make up the suppressed 'ground' to which Dalits radically claim to belong – belonging so completely that Dalit community and earth become one?

The Dalit Rights Charter is characterized by language that is more emotional than we are accustomed to seeing in rights instruments: 'We are anguished,' 'We are ashamed,' We are enraged,' 'We recall,' together with the more conventional 'We consider' and 'We demand.' Reading the Charter against the observations collected by James Elisha provides much food for thought about why Dalits have been demonized and scapegoated. Speaking like indigenous people who have been colonized anywhere in the world, accentuated by insights that also evoke Marxism and Liberation Ethics, one of the Articles in the Dalit Declaration reads: 'We are anguished: That Dalits have been denied access to resources like land, water and other means of production ... By taking away land from people who have worshipped the land, Dalits have been deprived of a long cherished relationship with the earth. Both culturally and economically they have suffered deprivation' (Shinde 30). Similarly, their criticism of discriminatory Hindu theocracy ['one of the worst and barbaric forms of the Varnashrama Dharma is 'untouchability,' which no sensible human can think of. That this is a religion, is an insult to the whole of humanity' (28)], together with their insistence that 'the needs of Dalits are in the material realm and not in the metaphysical' (28) also resonate with materialist criticism of rights instruments that get lost in abstractions not grounded in a lived social practice.

What could be the basis of this centuries-long demonization of Dalits? Elisha's research reveals that in Dalit religion deity is manifested in feminine form and that while both 'priests' and 'priestesses' mediated with the Deity and officiated at sacrifices, women led the cult with the male priests assisting them in a secondary role. 'The priests' according to Elisha (and we wonder if 'shamans' wouldn't be a more accurate term for both 'priest' and 'priestess' in this deeply earth-based worldview) 'were also experts in the art of "black magic"' (Elisha). What starts to emerge from these details is a matriarchal culture and feminine-centred religion that explains the many taboos against Dalits and their persecution by patriarchal Hindu culture.

Another important finding by Elisha is that Dalit spirituality is protest, which he asserts is also implicit in their very lifestyle. In one perplexing ceremony the usually scapegoated Dalits radically reverse the social order of things by abusing their dominators in carnivalesque style: 'As she [a Madiga priestess] rushes about spitting on those who under ordinary circumstances would almost choose death rather than to suffer such pollution from a Madiga, she breaks into wild, exulting songs, telling of the humiliation to which she is subjecting the proud caste people. She also abuses them all thoroughly' (Wilber Theodore Elmore quoted by Elisha). Elisha then asserts that 'this ritual has been well integrated into the religious life of Hindus. Though she humiliates them by spitting, it was said, the caste people would eagerly wait for their turn and would not be satisfied "without a full measure of her invective"' (Elisha).

This dynamic between scapegoat and authority suggests that Hindu caste members forged their identity in relation to the Dalits as other, in an early version of Orientalism as discussed by Palestinian-American cultural critic Edward Said. According to Said, imperialist Europeans shaped their identity through a process of othering and exoticizing the Orient that they continued to replicate in relation to all other people they colonized. The scapegoat is an imaginary construct: the community lays the blame for its sins upon an individual, who thereby comes to embody those sins, and is then expelled from the community, symbolically cleansing those who remain on the inside. We must carefully note that the community in the case we discuss here is the dominant, patriarchal Hindu community, and that the scapegoat is not one of their own, but an entire community of people who embody opposing values.

While the Dalits clearly fulfill this expiatory role for their dominators, these seem to depend even further on the Dalits to punish their sins in a variety of highly dramatized rituals. This inversion recalls Hegel's interpretation of the master-slave dialectic, yet European philosophy seems inadequate to describe a situation in which the slave is not solitary, but sees herself as first and foremost a community member. After the harvesting of grains, two Dalits from different social groups – Mala and Madiga – normally considered rivals, pair up and are permitted not only to enter the village, but to beg in a remarkable way: 'Mala would go to each doorstep abusing the family with the filthiest language known to him. The rhythm of the drum heightens the Mala's fury to abuse them more. And caste people were to reciprocate this gesture politely by giving a winnowful of grain' (Elisha). Reciprocity and carnivalesque role reversal suggest a form of community that is potentially invertible, even momentarily. What might this mean for communities in which the scapegoat can embody values and symbolic powers that overturn hegemonic relations, however symbolically?

In another ritualized act carried out as part of the harvest festival, Dalit men were permitted by the landlords to 'loot' the grain stores, in what Elisha calls 'a token reclaiming of the produce for which Dalits labored' (Elisha). This practice – both symbolic ritual and material restitution – is reminiscent of Russian literary theorist Mikhail Bakhtin's discussion of the significance of carnival in Rabelais's writing. Throughout the world, carnival traditionally celebrates the inversion of roles: the rich and powerful are demoted and humiliated by the poor and marginalized, who are thereby temporarily promoted to dominance. Bakhtin and later cultural theorists interpret this ritual as a kind of escape valve allowing the disenfranchised to let off some steam for a few days or weeks, and then to go back to servitude instead of arming a revolution. The Dalits' practice of looting the grain stores of their landlords also brings up an interesting challenge to Western thinking about representation, as it confounds symbolic or ritual act, drama, and actual theft seen from the authorities' perspective. This last aspect, which missionaries seem to have appreciated most, led them to report that Dalits were 'thieving communities' (ibid.). In thieving, even symbolically, the Dalits reveal the structures of inequality imposed on them, a radical break from the oppression of being untouchables. The latter term, in its evocation of no imaginable contact with the other, strikes at the very meaning of community, which is constituted by multiple acts of proximity that require such contact. Thievery in such a context merely exposes the emptiness of a structure of community predicated on the unthinkability of something actually being untouchable.

One wonders if the traveling Romas of Europe have any ancestral or cultural connection with Dalits, and if they perhaps fulfill similar functions camping on the peripheries of cities and towns that they can now enter, but where they tend to be seen as transgressors. We recall a conflict in a French village where one of the 'Gitains' who was accused of stealing asparagus from a garden ended up being killed in a struggle with the French villager, who insisted on defending his produce with a gun that was reported to have gone off accidentally. Indian activist and solidarity networker Pardeep Attri is trying to unravel the connections between Hungarian 'gypsies' – a term of identity he says is used as an insult to indicate a cheat – and Dalits in India. After exchanging emails with Derdák Tibor from Hungary, who responded to an article posted on the Internet by Attri, many connections were discovered in the material and social circumstances linking the Dalits and the Roma and in the possible migration of Dalits to Hungary at least a thousand years ago. Activists denounce the representation of Roma as thieving communities and attribute allegations of theft strictly to negative stereotyping and systemic violence against these people of colour. The danger in the flat-out denial of theft is that there are abundant records of Roma even claiming theft and trickery as legitimate means of survival, thereby discrediting the categorical position of their own defenders. Would it not make more sense to examine the alternate hidden significance of such practices, perhaps dating back to the rituals of retribution described above? Can thieving be interpreted in more complex ways than the narrow legalistic one based on the rights of the individual to private property? Does thieving challenge the dominant view of the individual's right to private property whose provenance through thievery against communities is often obscured by official history? Do thieving and trickery reject the very terms of engagement dictated by the dominant?

The marginalization and persecution of people who are driven off their land, and reduced to bonded labour and other forms of servitude, begs all kinds of larger questions about who the real thieving communities are. In their Charter, the Dalits accuse not just religion or government, but civil society for their oppression, thereby further problematizing how 'civil society' is often used interchangeably in other contexts with the positive term 'community.' Claiming to be a distinctive culture in a multicultural country, Dalits hold the dominant society accountable and demand that each member of civil society change their own thinking and behaviour to respect Dalit community:

> We recall: That the history of denial of opportunities to the Dalits and intended exclusion of the Dalits from all social, political and economic institutions is much more ancient than the establishment of the National State in its present form. That it is the civil society that is actively guilty of the caste system and untouchability ... Now the responsibility for reversing such a situation lies with them. (Shinde 31)

The many humiliating reversals – some actual like the original usurpation of the Dalits' land and livelihoods, others more symbolic, ritualistic, and even subversively humorous like the Dalits' enactments of retribution against Caste members – all revert back to those who are unjust because they dominate and refuse to recognize the rights and values of earth-bound communities. Thieving communities reclaim their rights to what has been stolen from them by exposing structures of power as symbiotically dependent on their having been scapegoated, 'touched' by the oppressor who is responsible for having produced an aberrant form of community predicated on untouchability. The rights of community here entail the right to self-definition in the face of hegemonic intransigence to recognize historic inequalities, precisely the trajectory that the Dalits' fight for rights has taken.

The wider community rights principle in the Dalits' struggle is the right of marginalized communities to steal back their identity, to make themselves as they see themselves. American philosopher Martha Nussbaum's discussion of African American communities dealing with the problem of gangs concludes:

> local communities ought to play a role in deciding what rights their members do and do not have [in this case an ordinance related to gang-loitering]. When a community is politically effective, and when it is prepared to shoulder within itself the burden that its proposals impose, such a community should be entitled to redefine rights ... Judges are paternalistic if they insist on this older conception of rights when the communities themselves want rights to look different. (Nussbaum 274)

Marginalized communities struggle to voice their own histories and cultural realities as the basis of exercising their rights. This process of empowerment through telling local stories is a crucial aspect of any attempt to formulate what the rights of community might come to mean within the community of rights.

Communitarian Values and the Politics of Self-Sameness: Community at/beyond the Borders

Community is too often used to name some version of a gated collectivity, a monoculture, or hierarchical, exclusionary structure based on economic self-interest. One of the more obvious examples of predatory individualism calling itself community is 'the transgenic crop science community,' but even 'the university community' is a misnomer given that there is limited transdisciplinary discussion in any university, especially of issues critical to our planetary wellbeing. The term has become emptied of its richly insurgent, potential meanings through the misuse and abuse of corp-speak. Corporatized institutions hold so-called 'town-hall' meetings in farcical mimicry of communities that practice consensual decision-making in non-hierarchical diversity, a structure alien to institutions but useful for producing the illusion of democratic process. To recuperate this most fundamental value of co-existing peacefully in diversity, we can think transculturally by listening to and enacting multiple stories about community practice. The word that has lost its meaning either through cynical or romanticizing cooptation, can recuperate its significance through transcultural translation(s) in which embodied presence and enacted agency, across all forms of social practice, point toward the becoming possible that is the limit-horizon of community. The right to access this agency in communitarian dialogue is a fundamental premise to thinking about all other forms of rights. These rights rest on complex relations of purpose and exchange between humans, but also other forms of sentience and biotic, ecological, and environmental relations rooted, as we argue in section two, in the very land that makes humanity possible.

Earlier we considered how narrow identification of self-sameness in a community actually creates an entropic effect that is counter-productive to self-renewal and sustainability. Throughout the world, there exist entrenched communities determined to expel, subjugate, or destroy difference.

We looked briefly at such examples as the stoning to death of women accused of transgressions decided by a male elite. Such examples of murderous unity abound, and are justified by fundamentalist and dogmatic religious and political ideologies. Cults, even those aligning themselves with well-founded religions, have been in the public eye when coercion takes the form of seriously abusing or killing members. But most instances of intolerance are not so dramatic and easily seen for what they are.

Here we consider the geo-political border, its imaginary manifestations, and the hybrid, contestatory, and improvising practices associated with border thinking as an expression of the ecology of knowledges and the ethics of encounter. As discussed earlier, the line dividing Mexico and the U.S. is fertile ground for thinking about culture clash, legal and humanitarian issues, and the effects of human migration and militarization on fragile desert land. Much has already been written on the crisis involving thousands of undocumented border-crossers. But *how* that crisis is represented remains ideologically contentious. Space does not allow us to tell the history of Mexico, from the root causes of the Mexican Revolution, to the devastating effects of the North American Free Trade Agreement (NAFTA) on the majority of that country's people, the collapse of its economy in 1994, and all the other factors that leave impoverished Mexicans little choice but to pack a plastic bag and head for the border – a nightmare journey Charles Bowden calls the new version of the Middle Passage (2008 89): 'They are no longer migratory workers. They are the refugees from a collapsing economy and a barbarous government and their journey is biblical and we should call it Exodus' (90).

While the border leads Americans to think that the main threat to the U.S. economy, stability, and self-sameness comes from Mexicans, Bowden reminds us of the global extent of desperation, and the U.S.'s need to hold back the human flood: 'Open the U.S.-Mexican border? Mexicans would be trampled to death by Asians storming up the open route and also by other Latin Americans, you know those folks the U.S. government calls OTMs, Other Than Mexican' (91). Such is the state of the Majority World under neoliberal globalization, which is a delusional dream of self-sameness that is also an attack on community diversity: the dogma of the 'free' market and how it self-regulates to anoint with prosperity all those who believe and sacrifice. When the dream turns out to be a lie, people leave their beloved communities and migrate into the hostile unknown rather than being left behind to die.

Few would argue with Bowden's assertion that the migration is of biblical proportions and that, though it cannot be stopped, it also cannot be granted free passage. The irresolvable nature of this situation expresses all the meanings of cataclysm: a violent social or political upheaval or disaster, a great change, a great (human) flood or deluge. In terms of being a crisis, 'cataclysm' also means a decisive moment and a turning-point. The border remains permeable even through the extensive barrier walls already constructed, forcing migrants to cross at places where the danger of dying in the desert is greatly increased. The existing portion of wall had been breached 3,363 times between 2005–2009 with the average repair costing $1,300 (Wood). Nevertheless, the U.S. administration proposes to spend billions of dollars more to construct and maintain a new fence that would extend over 600 miles along the U.S./ Mexico border.

Immigration researchers like Wayne Cornelius, Director Emeritus of the Center for Comparative Immigration Studies at the University of California, are skeptical about whether additional investments in the fence would discourage desperate people from finding new ways to breach it. After 4,000 interviews with undocumented and potential migrants, Cornelius can say with some degree of certainty that even those who get caught and turned back will continue trying with the success rates upwards of 95% by the second or third attempt (Wood). Chicano writer Luis Alberto Urrea tells the story of how 'a group of German delegates attending a multinational conference on immigration in San Diego was taken to view the new stretch of fence along the border' (14):

> They peered through the fence at the Mexicans peering back at them. The hosts, various well-meaning Saviors of the American Way, thought the practical Germans would be impressed with the brilliant engineering of the fence. Imagine their alarm when the TV cameras went on and the German spokesman, visibly distressed, turned away from the border and said into the mike, 'We tore down our wall?' And walked away. (Urrea 14)

Of course the difference here is that the Germans were reunited, while the American fence is meant to keep out people of another nation. But to what extent can humanity be divided along old bio-political lines in an age of such economic and social upheaval and in an age where cultural hybridization is an inevitable (if unintended) consequence of colonization?

What do globalization and NAFTA mean to most people when freedom of movement is prohibited? What happens when only capital and goods are permitted to flow, while unemployed people are condemned to struggling in an economy collapsed by the very doctrine and application of globalization? The walls both deny and prove our interdependence. 'I wonder if the Border Patrol ever feels betrayed,' Urrea asks, along with a host of other survey sounding questions that bring into sharp focus that interdependence:

> Do you like lettuce? How about tomatoes? Onions, Garlic. Peaches. Avocados. Cotton.
> Sugar.
> Oranges. Apples. Cherries. Cabbage. Cauliflower. Asparagus. Grapes. Pecans. Walnuts. Pumpkins.
> And you don't want to spend $15.00 for a quart of strawberries or $5.30 for a can of peas. How abut $20.98 for a pair of Jockey shorts?
> It's called agribusiness, multinational free enterprise, and if for no other reason that that, the border will never be closed. Unless, of course, U.S. citizens suddenly develop strong backs again, and a ferocious work ethic, and brave, very brave, hearts. (15)

Other difficult questions would immediately arise if the U.S. actually managed to seal the border. What would happen within Mexico and, south of its border, to countries whose economies cannot sustain their populations, and how would the even greater catastrophe of starvation there impact on the U.S.? Again, realistic responses that take interdependence into account show international relations to be more intricately interwoven than globalism would like to admit:

> Imagine a closed border. Instant Mexican revolution! What then? What would happen to the American Way of Life with a burning two-thousand-mile-long back porch? How many untold millions of refugees would then cross the border? How long before outside assistance would be sought by one side or the other? How long before we were forced into battle? ... Below Mexico, Central America is as dry as San Diego's chaparral, and people there are eager for a good-sized match to fly down and ignite them. Smoke from Hollywood to Medellín. (16)

Though thousands of migrants cross the border illegally every day, some of the most destitute Mexicans stay and work the garbage dumps to scavenge everything they use to survive. These squatters' communities, perched on the edges of huge dumps, some of which are the final destination for imported American garbage, tell us much about how people organize to co-exist, and make the best of the worst imaginable living conditions. Urrea calls the set of rules by which the dump workers live 'extraordinarily humane and sane':

> Rule #1: Watch for heavy machinery. Those who do not become mulch.
> Rule #2: No children in the trash.
> Rule #3: Women are equal to men in the trash.
> Rule #4: Old-timers and kids are allowed to work the outer edges of the trash, where the tractors push things down the slopes and the slopes themselves act as sifters, rolling the best things out across the face of the new King Kong pyramid.
> Rule #5: A special safe area is set up by the healthy workers. This area is set apart, avoided by trucks and the tractors. It has inviolate boundaries, could almost be roped off. And everybody honors it. The occasional truckload is directed over there, or young men carry a few bags there and toss them in. In this special section, the disabled and the old are allowed to do their share. They can work all day, safely, aside, not competed with or jostled or in harm's way. But working hard, nevertheless.
> There is no welfare in the dump, but there is work, care, sweat, and dignity. (42)

It might strike us as surprising that the dump would *not* be ruled by the doctrine of the survival of the fittest. Its social organization also contrasts with the indignity suffered by many of the maquiladora workers who make slave wages in these 'Free Trade Zone' factories, and are also subjected to pregnancy tests, denied bathroom breaks, and other indignities. The dump scavengers do the fine-tuned recycling that the rest of us do not:

> The workers pick out recyclables – aluminum cans, glass bottles, metal scraps and cardboard boxes – and sell them for cash. If they find a piece of furniture or a mattress, they use it. If they find semi-

> edible food, they eat it. And if they find a toy with just a few broken parts, they bring it home for their kids. Everything a person needs to survive can be found in a dump. Poverty-stricken people across the world have known this for decades. Thousands, maybe more, live at landfills worldwide, but there aren't any exact statistics – these are the untouchables, the invisibles, the forgotten and the ignored. (Morlan)

It is important to acknowledge that the trash sorters work hard, and that their work even at the local level of a specific dump benefits the planet. At the same time, we must also recognize that these workers toil in a dangerously toxic stew where methane fumes cause spontaneous explosions and fires, and people are exposed to all kinds of germs, bacteria, parasites, and hazardous industrial waste. While the dump workers must be recognized for contributing enormously to reducing waste by recycling in dumps in the Majority World (entry into such sites is strictly controlled and illegal in affluent countries), we must also recognize that they should not be living and working in such inhumane conditions, and that we should all assume responsibility for reducing and recycling garbage.

Teresa Jaramillo, a Catholic nun with 'Medical Missions' works at a neighbourhood called 'Fausto Gonzales' that grew out of the dump and freely shares her thoughts on charity and community building. She is opposed to handouts, not because they make people lazy as the greedy assert, but because it makes beggars out of those who are not. Furthermore, she makes it clear that helping others isn't as easy as throwing a little money at them or donating stuff: 'if people want to help, they have to get their hands dirty' (Morlan). The problem with charity, as she sees it, is that there is no relationship between the giver and the receiver, whereas getting your hands dirty means working together with people. Community is built of this embodied, proximity to others who toil alongside you.

During an interview, Jaramillo welcomes a group of Boston kids who have come to work on weatherizing and improving the houses. It is clear that working together benefits both the community members and the volunteers. Everyone learns practical skills as they apply them to the task at hand, but more importantly they learn about each other in a process of transcultural understanding, cooperation, and community building. The process of community building also involves creating pedagogical spaces as a free aspect of the community commons. A visiting New Yorker who decided to teach the basics with the help of a former student and a few members of the neighbourhood started precisely this sort of community-oriented pedagogy. Jaramillo explains that a sense of community has to be built together with a sense of ownership, by which she means not private property but taking ownership of one's life and having some control over one's destiny. Education and cultural literacy are key aspects of this aspect of community formation, and the free access to information and pedagogy is one of the most important elements in creating renewable, achieved community.

Jaramillo comments that at first the settlement didn't feel like a community, a lack she attributed to people having come from all over Mexico and essentially being strangers to each other. This situation soon changes once mutualism kicks in. People watch out for each other, and the give and take of shared living and shared concerns, shared challenges and triumphs, create a diverse and functioning community. People have to watch out for each other, because a real community is never a utopia: there are, as community members comment, 'some bad apples' involved in drugs and other criminal and potentially dangerous activities. The inclusive conceptualization of this community – with the 'bad apples' seen as part of the bushel – contrasts with what Zygmunt Bauman sees as the paranoid understanding of 'community' increasingly taking hold in urban centres, where the affluent inhabit gated 'communities' associated with comfort in contrast to the dangerous ghettoes and trespassers lurking beyond those gates:

> Safe neighbourhood visualized as armed gatekeepers controlling the entry; stalker and prowler, who have come to replace the early modern bugbear of *mobile vulgus* [the fickle mob], jointly promoted to the rank of new public enemies number one; a paring down of public areas to 'defensible' enclaves with selective access; separation in lieu of the negotiation of life in common; the criminalization of residual difference – these are the principal dimensions of the current evolution of urban life. And it is in the cognitive frame of this evolution that the new notion of 'community' is formed. (115)

The Mexican community growing out of the dump is wholly populated by this dreaded *mobile vulgus,* a term meaning mobile or transient commoners. The community cannot divide itself along these absolutist lines between deserving and demonized, and accepts that there is difference and even danger within. The term *mobile vulgus* which used to mean 'fickle mob' is even less accurate as a descriptor for complex communities like those colonizing dumps. This situation is clearly not characterized by ochlocracy or mob rule, especially when mob rule is defined as the intimidation of constitutional authority. To the contrary, the community of the dump emerges as a response to institutional neglect and the abuse of constitutional imperatives that guarantee equality and dignity in the exercise of one's relation to the state. Community formation in this case, is not the chimera that Bauman considers from an exclusively Western perspective, as if it were the only possible one:

> 'Community' feels good because of the meanings the word 'community' conveys – all of them promising pleasures, and more often than not the kinds of pleasures we would like to experience but seem to miss. To start with, community is a 'warm' place, a cosy and comfortable place. It is like a roof under which we shelter in heavy rain, like a fireplace at which we warm our hands on a frosty day. Out there, in the street, all sorts of dangers lie in ambush; we have to be alert when we go out, watch whom we are talking to and who talks to us, be on the look-out every minute. In here, in the community, we can relax – we are safe, there are no dangers looming in dark corners (to be sure, hardly any 'corner' here is dark'). (1-2)

Clearly, the Mexican community of Fausto Gonzales is not such an imaginary community, nor is it a wholly comfortable place by any affluent standards. And it doesn't have any reason to imagine dangers lying outside of its boundaries, because there are plenty in plain view. Interestingly, this aspect of diversity also contributes to making it a community. Considering such a settlement a community is far from an idealization, or a static view of achievement turned object. Belonging to a community does not mean that the inhabitants of places like Fausto Gonzales are home-free.

The tentacles of corporate development are penetrating to privatize the most peripheral and precarious sites, thereby divesting slum dwellers of the little freedom they had previously enjoyed in their improvised communities:

> Many options previously available to low-income people, such as unused public land, are disappearing rapidly even as access to peripheral land is becoming increasingly restricted. Indeed, vacant

> land on the urban fringes and elsewhere is being assembled and developed by corporate developers, legally and illegally ... the problem was just as acute where most of the land was in the public domain (Karachi and Delhi) as where the periphery was mostly private property (Manila, Seoul, Bangkok). (Ellen Brennan cited in Mike Davis 90)

According to the United Nations, more than one billion people now live in the slums of the cities of the South, and slum populations, according to UN-HABITAT, are currently growing by a staggering 25 million per year (Mike Davis 201). In Majority World countries where most of the population is still traditionally made up of small-scale farmers, people are forced to leave the land due to lack of adequate agrarian reform and irrigation, or because of rich countries dumping products with the help of unjust trade agreements. Once their small plots are no longer viable even to just feed the family, people migrate toward the cities in hope of finding employment. Many others are driven from the countryside by war and seek some kind of refuge on the edges of cities. Massive unemployment means that most end up peddling trifles like gum and kleenex, giving of themselves whatever they have to offer in exchange for a few pennies: performing acrobatics, juggling, fire-breathing kerosene, singing during red lights at busy intersections, all family members right down to the youngest children, working – yet unable to earn enough to secure the basic rights of food and shelter. Displaced and destitute people have built slums for over two centuries but they now encircle every major city in the Majority World. Homeless people also squat in more precarious and temporary settlements in the most affluent countries, where wealth does not contribute to social welfare. Judging by the stories coming out of such settlements, most do not turn into 'communities like any other' as Jaramillo says about Fausto Gonzales.

The tent cities popping up in Anglo North America are reminiscent of Depression-era U.S. when they were dubbed Hoovervilles after the president of the time Herbert Hoover, so they are not an entirely new phenomena even in the richest country in the Western hemisphere. These makeshift communities are the signs of the collapse of capitalism and the failure of governments and the so-called free market to provide a decent living for those who are willing and able to work. Those who cannot work because of injuries (many of them war-related as is the case with substantial numbers of U.S. veterans), psychological problems, and addictions have been failed as well, since they should be cared for by community structures within the larger state. Massive closures of mental health institutions have forced people, who are unable to fend for themselves, into the street. We may well wonder why anyone would want to belong to a nation-state and to recognize its government as one's elected representatives, when the most vulnerable citizens receive such inadequate support within that social structure.

The disconnect between state and citizens is most acutely felt in these situations that clearly constitute a social crisis, yet are downplayed by politicians and mass media. While governments pay lip service to community, rights-centred community governance would recognize the marginalized as community members like any other. Instead, police and media often refer to them as 'campers' who are represented as simply breaking city bylaws by pitching their tents in parks. In a news report on homeless squatters in Vancouver, the caption under a photo depicting police physically forcing people to move reads: 'police arrested five campers after they refused to take down the tents they set up at downtown's Beacon Hill Park ('Victoria Police Clear Tent City, Arrest 5.'). The article reports that 'the tents were set up at Beacon Hill Park following a B.C. Supreme Court ruling that struck down a city bylaw, calling it a deprivation of homeless people's liberty and security under the [Canadian] Charter of Rights and Freedoms' (ibid). In response to this ruling, the city of Vancouver passed a new bylaw limiting sleeping hours to between 9 pm and 7 am, showing that lawmaking is as makeshift and lacking in long-term planning as is the squatting.

In self-serving language that cynically used the term 'our homeless community' represented as 'vulnerable,' RCMP and Toronto Police explained the need to evict homeless people from the boundaries of the site of the G20 summit meeting held in June 2010 in Toronto:

> The ISU (Integrated Security Unit) is concerned about the safety and security of our most vulnerable communities. We have been working with the City's Shelter, Support & Housing Administration to try and address the needs of our homeless community in [advance] of the Summit. For safety reasons, members of the homeless community will not be permitted access into the security perimeter once it has been secured. (Mullins)

The people in question had been threatened with arrest and not so benevolently warned about having to move away from the 'red zone.' The language used by the police in representing their motives to the press is cynical for several reasons. Firstly, for anyone to distinguish the homeless as a threat to a billion dollar security apparatus is simply fatuous. But for the security apparatus to appropriate the language of possession ('our homeless community') while then subjecting them to the exigencies of state security is another example of the 'gated-community' use of the term even if attached to the most disenfranchised. To suddenly take an interest in the vulnerability of said communities also smacks of cynicism, since their vulnerability is due to the state's lack of concern – lack of adequate affordable housing, lack of rent control, lack of adequate social services, lack of jobs – and is an ongoing and growing crisis, and not only a 3-day concern for G20 security. This is especially the case since the Canadian government was able to conjure up over a billion dollars to pay for putative security (and other) costs during the Summit while continuing to devote virtually no commensurate resources to resolving issues of homelessness.

Some Police officials, like Patrick O'Bryan head of the Reno police department, seem to discern the root causes of the problem and warn that there is a growing crisis: 'Unless some type of miracle happens and we, as Americans, start investing in humans first and other things second, I wouldn't be surprised to be facing this again next spring the way things are going' (Harper). Solutions, though, rarely come via miracles and we have to be more specific about how to invest in humans. A good start would be to listen to the stories of the destitute and homeless. A reporter for BBC notes how in a tent city 40 miles east of Los Angeles 'what is striking is the range of people here: whites, African-Americans, Hispanics, the old and young including some with babies. And they tell a variety of stories too' ('Tent City Highlights U.S. Homes Crisis'). These include such ironic stories as the one told by Vietnam vet Benson Vivier who, thanks to a leg operation, can walk again after spending years in a wheelchair. But this health improvement cost him his disability payments, so not being able to find a job, he can no longer pay the rent and is, as a result, homeless. The ubiquitous bumper stickers about support for 'our troops' that we discuss earlier in the book are in such a circumstance ludicrous. What support do our veteran troops get once they have returned? Other stories tell of family disputes, houses burning down, deaths of family members who had shared money or housing, addictions, being fresh out of prison, and some say they are the victims of America's recent foreclosure crisis brought about by the rapacious practices of the investment 'community' (ibid).

The reaction of governments to tent cities has spanned short term tolerance, removal, relocation to areas where they become less visible (out of sight, out of mind) or attempts to reintegrate individuals into regular housing, with the government funding the difference between high rents and what individuals on welfare or low salaries can afford to pay (devised by Toronto's Emergency Homelessness Pilot Project [EHPP]). This last option proves, rather unbelievably, to be more cost-effective than building shelters that many homeless people avoid, and most cities governed in accordance with neoliberal policies will no longer even consider rent control.

The EHPP also provides an interesting contrast with the community formation of places like Fausto Gonzales, where poor people work together and with others to build and maintain a long-term community, where decision-making becomes collective and consensual. In interviews with the EHPP some of the people evicted from 'tent city' say they are happy to be separated from certain fellow squatters whose continued presence would make drug or alcohol rehabilitation difficult. But others express a sense of loss: they miss friends and sitting around the bonfire. In affluent societies, the poor are seen as social outcasts and have a hard time forming communities that are politically self-aware, given that inequality and class war are taboo subjects in the neoliberal state. While in economic terms, Mexican communities that grew out of garbage dumps are impoverished their members have a sense of belonging to a community in ways that their counterparts in affluent countries can never experience for the long-term. Living in a shelter, an institutionalized state of exception, or having the government pay for your inflated rent certainly provides immediate relief from the dangers of living on the street, but it cannot provide the dignity that comes with people understanding their situation as marginalized and responding to the problems that come with marginalization as a community.

We can speculate that the adversity of the Mexican situation, the collapse of the Mexican economy, the overwhelming numbers of people living off the garbage (because they have been forced off the land), the Mexican government's corruption and callous disregard for its most marginalized citizens, have all somehow contributed to those same citizens forming communities. In countries where the numbers of homeless people are steadily growing (and who are too often mythologized as suffering from addictions and other mental health problems) there is less empathy for them among the general public, thereby directly supporting the government's lack of effective action. Comparing the stories of marginalized people from vastly different regions of the world raises some interesting transcultural questions. Can the community building encountered by storytellers like Urrea and Morlan in Mexico happen in less desperate geopolitical contexts? Can the governance of a city become more democratized precisely because of the diverse challenges posed by poor people? What lessons can be learned from radical experiments involving civil society and empowering communities in the Majority World?

Viewed through our planetary interconnectedness, the mushrooming of slums cannot be blamed simplistically on any country's governance. International trade agreements and financial institutions, together with all historically vested interests and the abuses of class privilege have all contributed to further impoverishing the poor. Once our interconnectedness is recognized, these unjust structures can be dismantled at local community and planetary levels. One of the many examples of networking worldwide in support of local changes is a recent victory aided by a massive online campaign by the Avaaz community in Brazil. This organization describes itself as 'a 5.5 million-person global campaign network that works to ensure that the views and values of the world's people shape global decision-making. ("Avaaz" means "voice" or "song" in many languages.) Avaaz members live in every nation of the world; our team is spread across 13 countries on 4 continents and operates in 14 languages' (*Avaaz.org* 'About Us'). The victory in this case is the passing of the 'clean record' law, banning any politician convicted of crimes like corruption and money laundering from running for office. Nearly 25% of Brazil's Congress is under investigation with 330 candidates for office already facing disqualification shortly after the passing of this law.

This kind of international and inclusively democratic process of challenging anti-communitarian state practices could also conceivably inform and work in conjunction with international courts of law to finally bring participatory decision-making and change-making into the legal system. Such a worldwide support base would also reduce First World domination of international courts. At the municipal level, Porto Alegre is another example of place-based legal culture in which the city's budget is allocated through a participatory process. 'The city is divided into sixteen regions, and groups topics for discussion into five themes: i) transportation, ii) education, leisure and culture, iii) health and social welfare, iv) economic development and taxation, v) city organization and urban development' ('Case Study 2'). Themes four and five show that development is not defined exclusively by business but is balanced by taxation and organization. The concrete results of these researchers reported to the World Bank include the following improvements:[2]

> Between 1989 and 1996, the number of households with access to water services rose from 80% to 98%; percentage of the population served by the municipal sewage system rose from 46% to 85%; number of children enrolled in public schools doubled; in poorer neighborhoods, 30 kilometers of roads were paved annually since 1989; and because of transparency affecting motivation to pay taxes, revenue increased by nearly 50%. (3)

In their study *The Porto Alegre Experiment*, French researchers Marion Gret and Yves Sintomer state that 'in Porto Alegre, popular participation is not merely a generous idea; it is embodied in concrete mechanisms [that] drive it ... the principle of the participatory budget combines four different spheres: the executive, the legislature, civil society and the specific organisms of the participatory structure' (26). This last sphere of participatory structure is worth examining in some detail, especially to understand how its outcomes differ radically from the ways in which development is often decided by developers in most cities around the world. Urban development typically occurs with little meaningful input from municipal governments whose very members often have vested interests in the companies that benefit from the contracts, and little or no input from civil society, which usually only responds reactively once ill-conceived development is already underway and cannot be stopped by unorganized public outcry.

The participatory pyramid sphere of the Porto Alegre budget is a convergence of territorial and thematic dynamics, further broken down into different levels:

> The first is micro-local. The second comprises the districts into which the city is divided: concrete proposals (such as building a school, providing water, installing street lighting), put forward by residents on the micro-local level, are enumerated and classified to determine the priorities at the district level. The third level is represented by the Participatory Budget Council that brings together the priorities of the different districts of the city in order to divide up municipal investments. The thematic dynamic is similar, but discussions centre on precise issues (such as health, assistance for teenagers, environmental issues) at the municipal level. (31)

The governance of Porto Alegre and especially the participation of civil society and poor people in that governance has radically changed the way politics usually gets done to benefit the elite. While such inclusive participation poses special challenges in sustaining effectiveness, institutionalization, and scale (matters that Gret and Sintomer address in detail), the overall improvements have significantly counterbalanced the most negative aspects of corporate capitalism. No doubt the system will constantly need to be adjusted to meet challenges and to become ever more inclusive, but the ideological and ethical foundations for foregrounding the common good have been laid, and those democratic principles will guide democratic praxis. All cities globally can look to Porto Alegre for guidance and inspiration, one of the reasons it has hosted the first three sessions of the World Social Forum.

While it is vital to democratize municipal governance, especially since urban centres are becoming home to most countries' populations, some think that the revitalization of democratic principles will more likely happen in rural areas. Creative writer, farmer, and wise man Wendell Berry sees it this way:

> My feeling is that if improvement is going to begin anywhere, it will have to begin out in the country and in the country towns. This is not because of any intrinsic virtue that can be ascribed to rural people, but because of their circumstances. Rural people are living, and have lived for a long time, at the site of the trouble. They see all around them, every day, the marks and scars of an exploitive national economy. They have much reason, by now, to know how little real help is to be expected from somewhere else. They still have, moreover, the remnants of local memory and local community. And in local communities there are still farms and small businesses that can be changed according to the will and the desire of individual people. (155)

Berry invests hope in the *individual's* ability to make change (as opposed to invoking collective change) on the basis of his compelling argument about why we are all implicated in the 'total economy' (what we have been calling corporate fascism). His affirmation of *existing* communities is an important antidote to the wholesale denial of community that confuses jaded utopian language with the possible realities beyond the gates of the European city. Berry locates communities in the here and now. Though he fully acknowledges the erosion of communal practices due to the loss of freedom caused by corporate domination, he affirms that the seeds of rebirth are still in the land.

Speaking for Americans, but in terms relevant to most inhabitants of post-industrial countries, Berry contends that as individuals we abdicate our responsibilities and get others to do *our* work and to provide services by proxy, thereby relinquishing our freedom but also exploiting others. Once we have abdicated our responsibilities, by allowing, for instance, corporations to manufacture all our goods in Third World countries, we also lose the freedom to make ethical choices to benefit our communities and the exploited communities who do our work for us: 'Our major economic practice, in short, is to delegate the practice to others' (178) and 'The trouble with this is that a proper concern for nature and our use of nature must be practiced, not by our proxy-holders, but by ourselves' (179). Far from coming to defeatist conclusions, Berry believes that 'if people begin the effort of taking back into their own power a significant portion of their economic responsibility, then their inevitable first discovery is that the "environmental crisis" is no such thing; it is not a crisis of our environs or surroundings; it is a crisis of our lives as individuals, as family members, as community members, and as citizens' (179). But declaring a crisis is not the same as negating the existence of community, and as we noted previously, a crisis is a turning point – a decisive moment to take action.

The diversity of communities like Fausto Gonzales in Mexico, squatters' settlements in all the Fourth World places (where the indigenous meet with the deterritorialized, the immigrants, and the exiles), cities like Porto Alegre, virtual support networks for democratization, and the anonymous country towns and farms that contribute to global community diversity all contradict the monoculture imposed by globalized corporate totalitarianism. These are wildly different places. Some, like the rural country towns of the U.S., are nearly abandoned and quietly waiting to bloom again. Others are chaotic and populated mostly by children and youth demanding a future. The neighborhood gardens blooming across northern cities to feed people local foods, for at least a few months of the year, are one of the many initiatives to take ownership of the lives and destinies of communities back into collective terms congruent with public commons and public trust principles.

Such achievements conjure up scenarios of the serene greening of concrete jungles, but must not lull us into focusing exclusively on our own emerging empowerment. Mike Davis reminds us of the Pentagon's plans for total war, a concept we discuss elsewhere in this book, to support the total economy:

> With cold lucidity, they now assert that the 'feral, failed cities' of the Third World – especially their slum outskirts – will be the distinctive battlespace of the twenty-first century. Pentagon doctrine is being reshaped accordingly to support a low-intensity world war of unlimited duration against criminalized segments of the urban poor. This is the true 'clash of civilizations.' (205)

This too is our shared reality and nightmare – our shared project of community resistance to such a death-dealing and fundamentally evil view of global relations. Davis counters this curse of globalized state terror imposed by merchants of death with the following: 'If the empire can deploy Orwellian technologies of repression, its outcasts have the gods of chaos on their side' (206). Community in its relational contingencies – its chance-based proximate inter-dependencies – is the great fount of chaotic, co-creative renewal and resistance.

Concerted Community: Sun Ra's Improvised/ Improvising Communities and the Creative Commons

Musical improvisation is perhaps the most widely practiced form of musical activity and the least understood, and certainly the most marginalized (Bailey ix). Yet, improvisation is, by its very nature community-oriented. It mimics community dialogues (concordant, discordant) and community histories in a creative commons. Improvisation calls on both the individual and the collective to create the terms of the dialogue as a dynamic embodied spectacle of exploration. Improvising communities like those associated with the African American diasporic jazz community are also, in this sense, very much improvised communities. They present, as we show in this brief interlude dealing with Sun Ra (1914–1993) a remarkable form of resilient community practice that has made exceptional contributions to the creative commons locally – and globally. Whatever the names one associates with African American musicking – blues, jazz, free jazz, Dixieland, gospel, ragtime, R&B, bebop, hip hop, and even turntabling – perhaps no other attempt to suppress a culture through enslavement has yielded as rich a history of creative practices of resistance founded in community improvisations and adaptations.

As globalized forms of music making have become enabled via various dissemination technologies and the increased mobility of musical memes, the collision of multiple forms of musical difference in improvised contexts has become more ubiquitous. Diasporic improvised and improvising communities are a result of this globalization effect: their stories of displaced, aggrieved, enslaved, exploited, and segregated community and the astonishing capacity for resistance to these conditions that culminated in the Civil Rights Movement are important and have been given voice by many key figures in that movement, from W. E. B. Du Bois through to Malcolm X and Martin Luther King Jr. In this section we examine briefly the remarkable and controversial life of Afrofuturist Sun Ra: community-builder, prolific contributor to the creative commons, and visionary rights activist. Sun Ra is emblematic (via his diffuse and prolific aesthetic practices) of imagining what community may mean in the context of diasporic realities that produce both oppression and liberatory discourses.

American scholar Giles Gunn's *Beyond Solidarity* notes how

> many diasporan peoples have developed senses of community around experiences of discrimination, loss, marginalization, exploitation, exclusion, and exile or, more positively, around shared experiences of larger historical, cultural, political, or religious forces – but that such senses of community often resist being defined in absolutist terms even when such terms are routinely invoked. Such diasporan worlds, whether in Southeast Asia or northwest Africa – being products of intercultural and cross-cultural contact and association that are endlessly in motion, richly hybridized, constantly redefined, and inevitably shadowy – are far less likely to share a common identity than a common set of identifications. (44)

Sun Ra's displacement of identity to cosmic spaces via his claim to not be of this earth makes explicit this logic of resistance to either tropes of oppression or of liberation, an ambiguous reconfiguring of identity as a community of practices that refuse easy inscription into positivist or negativist discourses. Instead, Sun Ra proposes a mobile re-invention of self rooted in creative improvisatory practices that arise from a community of people who share aesthetic goals, who do so in close embodied spaces via practices of daily living together, and who undertake the discipline of making community present as a form of performative enactment.

Sun Ra's musical practices were inseparable from his practices of community-building – ironically so because of his insistence that he came from the cosmic elsewhere of Saturn, an allegory for his refusal to accept the terms imposed by racist white America on Black communities: 'Sun Ra's insistence on interplanetary citizenship and traveling the spaceways via ancient Egypt, identifies an important and crucial motif in his approach to making music that was not of the Earth, that was not bounded by geography, history nor the particular social context of the day' (Saunders-Arratia). The here and now were not sufficient to what he called the 'white world,' a place of which he could only have a 'vague knowledge' due to segregation (Abraham xxix). Even stranger is how Sun Ra's status within the black community was as an outsider, largely a function of his esoteric intellectualism: 'Sun Ra was one of jazz history's great outsiders. Although he single-mindedly led variously named Arkestras continuously from the mid-1950s until his bodily form passed on in 1993, his more than 200 recordings and scores of singles were never widely distributed during his career. Ignored by the dominant commercial interests that shaped the careers of many of his peers, Sun Ra and his Arkestra nevertheless focused on a quest to find new musical idioms, new sounds and new ways of playing and performing, which for him were new and unique ways of communicating' (Saunders-Arratia).

An outside insider making outside music based on his inside experience of the community from which he came, Sun Ra's contradictions are the stuff of black community reality, where being both inside and outside culturally was a fundamental side-effect of segregation and ghettoization. Key in Sun Ra's aesthetics, regardless of his being an 'inside outsider,' was the enactment of self-reliance that exemplified localized social practices and their capacity to be revolutionary and ideologically challenging. Ra exemplified what Charles Seeger – the father of protest singer Pete Seeger and also a noted musicologist and participant in the President Franklin Delano Roosevelt's Works Projects Administration (WPA) – had imagined as one of the purposes of music: 'The point of departure for any worker new to a community ... should be more toward the development of local leadership than toward dependence upon outside help' (Wilkinson 124). Ra's insistently localized practices drew upon community resources while also challenging and expanding them. These practices reflected a commitment to the self-empowering practices and discourses that played such a crucial role in civil rights undertakings associated with African American diasporic communities' struggles for equality.

A 'constant striving for conceptual liberation and re-inscription' inflects Ra's music (Abraham xiv-xv) for, as James Wolfe notes, liberatory discourses require re-inscription in order to allow these discourses to proliferate within a wider range of the cultural bandwidth. Community-building for Sun Ra entailed addressing the black community via collective music given form by those who joined him in his vision. He 'sought to make his musicians ... his community, a community he would recruit and train, who would live together and devote themselves entirely to his music and teaching, musician-scholars who he would tear free from outside interests and worldly distractions to be on twenty-four hour musical and spiritual call ... The Arkestra would be family, with all the African-American resonance of the word for unity and survival and resistance ... They would be an example of what a group of black men could achieve together' (Szwed 97). In doing so Ra came to practice both a localized vision of community and a cosmic, planetary vision: liberation came out of aesthetic discipline, which was only possible within a community of like-minded practitioners.

Similar community formations predicated on racial and ethnic unity in the face of discrimination are to be found across a wide range of social practices associated with jazz and improvised musicking: jazz collectives, as they have been called by Charley Gerard, include the Jazz Composers Guild associated with the late multi-instrumentalist Bill Dixon and pianist and poet Cecil Taylor, which morphed into the Jazz Composers Orchestra Association under the direction of Carla Bley; the Chicago-based Association for the Advancement of Creative Musicians (AACM) founded in 1965 by Muhal Richard Abrams, Jodie Christian, Steve McCall, and Phil Cohran; the St. Louis-based Black Artists Group (BAG) founded in 1968; the Jazz and People's Movement founded in the 1970s as a protest group aimed at breaking up the exclusion of black jazz musicians from the lucrative television market; and the Collective Black Artists formed in 1969 and founded on the core principle that 'black artists were the spokesmen for the black community and, as such, must be supported by it' (Gerard 95). All these groups sought a form of expressive liberation within a context of sustained discrimination based on ethnicity and class.

Self-generating communities, like those surrounding Sun Ra's aesthetic and political practices are frequently aligned with larger cultural movements. Indeed, all of the organizations we mention above enact a striking relationship between the artistic and social practice of community, with important caveats about reducing these varied practices to the same practice. Musician and social historian George Lewis's account of Sun Ra in relation to the AACM concludes with a description of how Sun Ra and the AACM had 'crucial differences' arising from notions of collectivity. AACM member Joseph Jarman recounts how 'I also went to audition for Sun Ra's band, and I could have been accepted, but I just got a feeling I probably shouldn't. [Sun Ra and the Experimental Band] were similar in many ways, except the philosophical approach and concept was different. In Sun Ra's organization he had everything to say and do. In Muhal's [Richard Abrams] organization [the AACM] everybody could say and do. That was the big difference' (Lewis 162). Community dominated by a singular vision was, in Jarman's reading, not as desirable as community constituted by multiple empowered voices. His comments reflect on the danger of idealizing any one form of making community, however resistant or prolifically generative. The tensions between different visions of what collective means, always necessarily an aspect of dynamic, living communities is but one of the challenges Sun Ra, the AACM, and others in the movement to assert Black culture had to confront.

American cultural critic George Lipsitz cites Néstor García Canclini's argument that 'commercial marketers and private foundations now serve as the primary patrons and generators of artistic activity, usurping a role formerly filled by social movements and the state. Like so many of the revolutionary transformations of our time, this change has gone largely unanalyzed, even though it has enormous consequences. The imperatives of commercial culture, and of what Canclini calls tax evasion masquerading as philanthropy, are poor substitutes for the kinds of support previously given to artistic endeavors by social movements and the state. The new forms do not erase the oppositional potential of art by any means, but they do function to suppress systematically the kinds of self-expression and self-activity characteristic of the "community-based art making" and art-based community making that did so much to create new artistic and social spaces in the past by linking artistic practices to social conditions' (123). Lipsitz, in his astute analysis of the Black Artist Group, notes how it was exemplary of

> how the state and social movements during the 1960s combined to fashion a space for dynamic cultural activity. At the same time, this history shows how charitable foundations and commercial culture quickly reach their limits when they have to confront the kinds of creativity that emerged from the Black Arts movement in general and from BAG in particular. The destruction of antipoverty programs, cutbacks in state spending on the arts, and the defeats suffered by the social movements of the 1960s leave young people in St.

> Louis and other cities today with fewer options and opportunities for the kinds of self-expression that BAG nurtured and sustained. (123-24)

Self-expression is a key precondition and measure of community ethics and the commitment to civil rights. And, in a very substantive way, it is a crucial marker of liberation and autonomy within structures of community practice. U.S.-based models of community organization aligned with civil rights outcomes have analogues elsewhere in the Americas.

The Afro-Brazilian movements' declaration of November 20th as a Dia da Consciência Negra [Black Awareness Day] is one recent example of yet another diasporic community addressing issues of racial marginalization and oppression via creative strategies of self-empowerment and cultural resistance. Based on the date when Zumbi dos Palmares, one of the last leaders of the Palmares *quilombo*, died in 1695, the Dia da Consciência Negra is meant to generate both local and national reflection in Brazil on slavery, discrimination, and a cultural history associated with racism. These forms of local community resistance that are part of a wider global battle to end discrimination are exemplified in the samba schools of Rio de Janeiro and São Paulo that recuperate and disseminate cultural forms specific to diasporic communities. Brazil is the second largest Black state in the world after Nigeria with a population of 70 million Afro-Brazilians and also the fifth largest country in the world and one of the top ten economic powers globally. Yet, as João Jorge, the president of the Afro-Brazilian cultural movement Olodum states, in discussing the plight of Afro-Brazilians, the struggle for identity and access to equitable resources in Brazil is ongoing and fraught by incorrect perceptions of the global community about the nature of Brazilian democracy as being truly interracial: '*Nous sommes l'unique communauté victime de discrimination sur la planète qui n'arrive pas à dire, ni en dehors du Brésil ni même ici, qu'elle est en pleine lutte!*' ['We are the only community on the planet victimized by discrimination that does not say, neither in nor out of Brazil, that we are in the middle of a struggle'; (our translation; Hazard and Kali 53)]. Articulations such as these echo the civil rights struggles against discrimination to which Sun Ra contributed his creatively resistant aesthetic practices. So global community in this context references widespread liberation struggles that cross national lines but are nonetheless localized in specific national sites where specific battles need to be fought.

For Sun Ra, liberation was personal but also deeply connected to a wider vision of global relatedness: '*Freedom to me means freedom to rise above a cruel planet* ... Under terrific opposition, I have tried to show ... my goodwill to the world, simply because I know this can be a better world for every person, people or peoples' (Abraham xxx, xxxv; our emphasis). One of the ironies of Ra's own personal history is that his parents, Cary and Ida Blount, had moved (before Ra was born) to Birmingham, Alabama from Demopolis, which had once been a French utopian community, but was also a 'trading center in the large plantation area of west-central Alabama, near the Mississippi line' (Szwed 7). Even more bizarre is that the white French expatriates who founded Demopolis (The City of the People) came to the U.S. to escape a slave rebellion on the sugar plantations of Haiti in the early nineteenth century. Birmingham, where Ra grew up, became in 1963 the flashpoint of the civil rights movement, with the Southern Christian Leadership Conference (SCLC) leading the charge to overturn the city's discrimination laws via nonviolent direct action. Additionally Birmingham was the city in which Martin Luther King, Jr., whose leadership contributed to the successful outcome of the protest, was arrested for the thirteenth time, an event commemorated in the Birmingham Civil Rights Institute in the so-called Civil Rights District that includes both the 16th Street Baptist Church and the Alabama Jazz Hall of Fame located in the Carver Theatre.

Ra grew up in a space of historical contradictions rife with racist hypocrisy (white escapees from a black slave rebellion founding a 'utopian' community), delusional community making (a city of the 'people' founded in a land of slaves by former slaveholders), and the unavoidable resistance that was to arise and make itself manifest in the civil rights movement. Such strange collisions are at the core of America's racist history. What could freedom and democracy mean if they were so easily co-opted by dominant culture while slavery, segregation, and racism continued to exist?

Sun Ra's musical vision, and his poetic vision expressed in numerous writings, imagined

> constituting a community [that] mirrors the universe, an artist's vision of the black sacred cosmos. It is a music ... made collectively ... As a teacher [Sun Ra] worked to awaken his followers. Like Nietzsche, he unflinchingly assaulted received Christianity ... as he did history's proudest achievements, freedom and democracy. He questioned the polarities of good and evil, transvalued many of the basic terms of Western culture, putting them in question, mocking

> their pomposity. 'Truth' was not to be seen as good, or even neutral: it was always the consequences of language and the result of some exercise of power – and both of the latter were in a state of babble. (Szwed 383-84)

The recognition that truth is relative and dependent on where one is located within a structure of power is not trivial, especially from within the context of the civil rights movement, which sought to undermine racist and so-called truths about African Americans' disposition to be slaves and oppressed. Ra's music, like the music of another great American outsider, Frank Zappa, is the equivalent of what biographer and jazz critic John Szwed calls an *ontological shock* in that it attacks the embedded premises of a profoundly anti-rights ideology based on racial superiority and static relations of power between the oppressed and the oppressor.

One cannot underestimate the degree to which conjuring up such a shock took enormous resources of tenacity, courage, and imagination. As Charles Mingus, another revolutionary improviser in the same tradition notes in his autobiography *Beneath the Underdog*, the black community (in Mingus's case, Watts, a Los Angeles neighbourhood) 'had its own pecking order like any average American community of working Negroes still too busy slaving as free men to evaluate themselves and their true position in society' (65). Sun Ra had a similar understanding of the historical contingencies related to enslavement that he expressed in his early polemical broadsheets: 'The negro is too busy trying to be like someone elses [sic] idea of life to stop and be what is right that he should be' (Corbett 116).

Ra's combination of improvisation and aleatoric adaptation to immediate circumstances, spiritual esotericism, and his deeply rooted practice of communitarian life based in creation and discipline offered a lifeline out of nihilism, oppression, and precarity. It did so while sustaining itself as an autonomous localized expression of the rights of an outside community within larger oppressive entities based on race. Improvising community, then, meant also *being* an improvised community that by moving away from an imposed ('someone else's idea of life') notion of community identity challenged the hegemonies at work in racist America.

In a late poem titled 'Calling Planet Earth (January 1990)' Ra says 'There is something in the / cosmos / called Fellowship. Reach for it ... If you pay dues for something / worth / infinite value you will get / what is due you on an / infinite eternal plane of being / compensation: so valuable / there is no / place to measure its worth' (Abraham 5). By improvising community in localized circumstances Ra was also stepping outside the constraints of the local into comprehensive, interconnected notions of cosmos and fellowship, the liberatory value of which was (in his philosophical and musical worldview) without or beyond measure.

Might Ra's musico-poetic vision be an exemplary model for thinking beyond atrophied structures of collective relations that undermine the creative power of the commons in their failure to accept improvisation and adaptation as at the very core of the generative, rights-affirming powers that sustain the concerted community?

Revisionary Histories and Healing Stories

Returning to Ralston Saul's contention that globalization suddenly appeared out of nowhere in the 1970s, it is true that as a narrow and very specific ideology masquerading as scientific theory, proselytized as religious faith in the immutable economic laws of the market, globalization manifested itself in a specific way. Ralston Saul's detailed overview of world history and economics suggests that the roots of this ideology reach back to European imperialism, but his commitment to competitive capitalism controlled by democracies grounded in nation-states whose governments' purpose is to promote the public good, disallows his critique from delving too deeply into the darker workings of capitalism. To understand capitalism's dependence on colonialism and slavery as legacies that necessarily reproduce themselves in new guises – neocolonialism and new forms of slavery and servitude – requires a comparative study of international economics and politics. Ralston Saul's linking of the nineteenth century Opium Wars (also known as the Anglo-Chinese Wars), in which England forced China to accept payment in opium from India instead of silver for goods traded, and the global machinations of contemporary pharmaceutical corporations reveals just such a continuum. Yet Ralston Saul seems to think that these forms of exploitation are deviant and not inherent to capitalism. Majority World thinkers tend to be more aware of how abuses are repeated as a function of the system – the capitalist system, the globalized, modernized world-system – because the dominated have a better understanding of injustices inherent in a system via their experience of them in the flesh, as opposed to those whose material comforts are supplied by that same system. Ralston Saul intuits this in his hopeful conclusion that the end of the globalist period might also mark the end of the Western rationalist period, and 'the beginnings of a major rebalancing in which other cultures, with more complex ideas of what makes up a society, are coming to the fore. And those of us in the West will just have to learn to keep up and to understand what makes such a major change positive for us' (278).

Despite the growing awareness in the West of other histories auguring other ways of being, Eurocentric theories are making a comeback in the European Union. Renowned intellectual, musician, and administrator for French President Nicolas Sarkozy's program of neoliberal reforms, Jacques Attali traces the history of democracy (rooted in individual liberty) linked to ever freer markets located in specific city-states where power, money, and freedom seemingly spring from internal creativity and local resources. The historical list comprises the nine market-democracies: Bruges, Venice, Antwerp, Genoa, Amsterdam, London, Boston, New York, and currently Los Angeles. There is no discussion of indigenous cultures in the Americas or anywhere else despite those cultures' history of extensive trading networks. Attali is interested only in hegemonic, imperialist expansion that he idealizes as a democracy-generating free market. His work also completely ignores democratic practices in rural communities since this case too fails the criterion of world domination fetishized by this kind of political ideology.

The over 400-page tome is entitled *Une brève histoire de l'avenir* [*A Brief History of the Future*] and brief it is given that only the last chapter is dedicated to what Attali terms *hyperdemocracy* – for all intents and purposes, the social democratic version of Francis Fukuyama's end of history. Attali envisions the source of this hyperdemocracy in Europe, growing out of the United Nations, the Security Council, and the G8, which he anticipates will accept some of the G11 nations like India, Brazil, and Indonesia to form a planetary government. What allows Attali to circumscribe the world in such a Eurocentric power structure is his invented history of market-democracy that excludes all forms of ethics, justice, community history and diversity, and human intercourse including trade that is peripheral to the nine hearts of commerce he identifies. Attali envisions a radical departure from injustice, a realizable utopia free of poverty where the wonders of technology will suddenly be equitably accessible, where merchant imagination will resist its own worst excesses and protect the environment for future generations. Nowhere does he find the source for such a massive paradigm shift, and he even predicts that the preceding decades will be characterized by extreme egotism and solipsism. How then will the Western imagination embrace community as the basis for peace without any reference to other cultural influences or even the possibility that Western culture would have to be eclipsed before such a radical transformation could take place?

Attali's vision of a planetary government and its security system to defend total economy reads like an hallucinatory blend of Hollywood adventure and chilling technological totalitarianism:

> *Ce gouvernement planétaire se donnera les moyens militaires de lutter contre les mafias, le trafic de drogue, l'exploitation sexuelle, l'esclavage, le dérèglement climatique, le déversement des déchets et les attaques (accidentelles, terroristes ou militaires) par des nanorobots et autres pathogènes autorépliquants, qui pourraient détruire la biomasse: une gelée bleue (arme nanotechnologique absolue) entre les seules mains du gouvernement planétaire pour combattre la gelée grise. Une force planétaire d'assistance et de sécurité, dotée des meilleurs équipments ... protégera l'environnement et luttera contre les pirates ...* (379)
>
> [This planetary government will give itself the military means to fight against mafias, drug-trafficking, sexual exploitation, slavery, climate change, garbage disposal, and attacks (accidental, terrorist, or military) by nanorobots and other self-replicating pathogens that could destroy the biomass: a blue gel (absolute nanotechnological weapon) in the sole hands of the planetary government to combat the grey gel. A planetary aid and security force, outfitted with the best equipment ... will protect the environment and will fight against pirates ...] (Our translation)

Attali links these planetary institutions and instruments to Western militarized hegemony and technologies. But he overlooks the rather obvious conflicts of interest between the G8's economic domination and the struggle for peace and social justice by those who are disenfranchised by and within the world-system.

Josephine Grey, founder of the Toronto community-based anti-poverty group Low Income Families Together (LIFT), reminds us of the importance to 'advocate for the creation of alternative international trade and investment agreements and processes to ensure that these regimes are bound by commitments made and obligations undertaken by governments to human rights, environmental protection, human security and sustainable social and economic development' (Grey 4). Grey proposes the caveat – entirely overlooked by Attali – to 'increase participation of those most affected, often those exposed to the worst environmental conditions, and the landless in the process of claiming human rights and remedies and defend[ing] them from retribution' (4). Moreover, Grey calls on 'all who want to work towards the enforcement of the human rights framework ... to engage communities and organizations in participatory research and evaluation ... to involve communities and local governments in human rights and ecological education and advocacy and in building capacity to fulfill rights to housing, health, education and public services such as clean drinking water' (4).

This foregrounding of community as primary source of knowledge inverts the top-down hierarchy promoted by neoliberal ideologues like Attali, and shifts the focus from paranoid security and total war scenarios to achieving human, community, and environmental rights through the massive participation of civil society. Instead of conceiving of government's role as paternalistically informing and dictating to the masses through its experts and its enforcement apparatuses, this participatory community-based model assumes ownership of information through experience and direct observation in order to inform government and to hold it accountable to act on that information in accordance with international human rights conventions.

Argentine scholar Enrique Dussel (who himself was attacked and nearly killed by state paramilitaries in 1973) interprets globalization as the culmination of Eurocentric modernity that demands a complete rethinking of how political philosophy must become critical through what he calls analectic thinking: *the opening of the self to the other as other*. For Dussel the most prominent and persistent characteristic of Eurocentric rationality – now primarily manifest as U.S. imperialistic rationality due to that country's current economic and military domination – is the systematic obliteration of the other. This violent rationality has taken many forms, from Heidegger's solipsistic appropriation of the other seen as a mere shadow of the self, to the subjection of the other as slave labourer or even underpaid worker. The context of Dussel's study, his point of departure, is the material fact that 85% of the planet's population is poor, marginalized, and underdeveloped. Specific historical events and processes, driven by those whose worldview has always been based on an ontology that denies the other's worth and very reality, created these material circumstances. Such a worldview generates and feeds off stories that are harmful because they promote domination and violence against the other, whether that other is human, another species, or an inanimate aspect of the biosphere. The history of Western knowledge – from a religious vision that violently splits the self into the mind/body dualism and projects a better world beyond the earth (habitat of beasts and barbarians), to the gradual scientification of politics, economics, sociology – reveals a process of abstraction that strips knowledge of its ethical and practical roots: in the body and in the land. When did this world-view of not belonging to the earth, and so being obsessed with dominating the earth, become a world-system? Dussel traces the concept of 'World History' back to 1492, the 'discovery' of the Americas, and the Eurocentric sense of world domination, as European power expanded westward and eastward into empires and systems that had previously co-existed (2001 351).

What we currently call postcolonial thinking (for lack of a better term), converges on the idea that solutions to world poverty cannot possibly originate in the West precisely where injustice has been systemized through economic domination. Majority World thinkers, including indigenous peoples living in rich countries, question the 'post' in 'postcolonial' and 'postmodern' pointing out that these terms still predicate the present on European culture. Post-modernity is still entangled with modernity, and is therefore unable to recognize fully the workings of neocolonialism from the perspective of the colonized. Dussel proposes that positive change can only come from transmodernism inclusive of 'moments that were never incorporated into European modernity, which will subsume the best of European and North American globalized modernity, and affirm from outside of that modernity the essential components of their own excluded cultures, to develop the new future civilization of the twenty-first century' (2001 390; our translation). These multifarious accounts of reality, previously silenced by the narrow and skewed discourse of 'World History,' provide us with an extensive repertoire of healing stories. They are healing in that they liberate the silenced word and offer multiple transcultural perspectives, thereby revising and expanding history, which in the process turns from being an object to a process of intercultural dialogue shared across and among communities.

Exchanges among scholars, activists, artists, and entire communities from the north and south, east and west, are finally starting to redefine the terms of engagement, and to encourage two-way border-crossing of the abyssal line that totalitarian monoculture constantly attempts to draw in order to exclude. In Dussel's terms, analectic thinking can move us from the will to impose Western models and values toward a radical acceptance of difference, not just in theoretical discourse but in the praxis of human exchange, a way of encountering the other driven by the ethics implicit in our collective relational interconnectedness.

A praxis of human exchange is proposed by Ralston Saul and many others who think that the misery of the current era could be wiped out almost overnight by simply canceling the developing world's debt. To do so would be an ethical recognition that the initial terms of the loans were unjust in the first place, and that this and other injustices can be acknowledged and corrected. This would be the international expression of restitution that we have previously discussed in relation to Alfred's and Silko's responses to colonialism: that settlers acknowledge that their home is built on stolen land, and that they resolve to change the terms of encounter to base them on respect. Such a decision would auger a new era in planetary relations because cancellation of the debt would allow poor countries to develop their social infrastructures, instead of being bled dry in interest payments to international banks. Too often even those Western proposals that seem in solidarity with Majority World peoples overlook that poverty was created by outsiders (often in collusion with governing elites), and that what is needed is not *more* help from the West, but freedom from Western intervention.

In 1969 Lester Pearson, the Canadian Prime Minister who won the Nobel Peace Prize (1957), advocated a 0.7% pledge of a country's resources from its Gross National Product to aid developing nations. Forty years later not a single G8 country has met this target that has been ratified and endorsed at multiple international and national meetings, but never acted on in allocating actual substantive resources. The Engineers Without Borders (University of Waterloo) site ('What is the 0.7% Pledge?') gives a short historic timeline of the 0.7% pledge, itself a supposed expression of international cooperation and community in which the community of the world's richest nations have failed abysmally. The timeline below follows the 0.7% pledge from inception of the idea to its current reality:

> 1969 – The president of the World Bank asks Canadian Prime Minister Lester B. Pearson to form the Commission on International Development. The Commission's report, 'Partners in Development,' makes the recommendation that developed countries commit 0.7% of their GNP to official development assistance (ODA).

1970 – The UN General Assembly makes this target a commitment by passing Resolution 2626. The Canadian Parliament also commits to reaching the 0.7% pledge by the mid 1970s. A key paragraph from Resolution 2626 states:

'In recognition of the special importance of the role which can be fulfilled only by official development assistance, a major part of financial resource transfers to the developing countries should be provided in the form of official development assistance. Each economically advanced country will progressively increase its official development assistance to the developing countries and will exert its best efforts to reach a minimum net amount of 0.7 per cent of its gross national product at market prices by the middle of the Decade.'

– International Development Strategy for the Second United Nations Development Decade, UN General Assembly Resolution 2626 (XXV), October 24, 1970, para. 43

1975 – The Canadian government discusses their failure to reach the 0.7% pledge, and re-adjusts their goals to achieve the commitment by 1985.

1985 – The Canadian government cannot fulfill the 0.7% pledge because there is not enough money in the bank.

2002 – Attendees at the International Conference on Financing for Development in Monterrey, Mexico reaffirm their commitment to the 0.7% pledge in Paragraph 42 of the Monterrey Consensus, stating that 'we urge developed countries that have not done so to make concrete efforts towards the target of 0.7% of gross national product (GNP) as ODA to developing countries.' This commitment is repeated again at the World Summit on Sustainable Development in Johannesburg later in the year.

2005 – At the G8 Summit in Gleneagles, Scotland, all G8 members from the European Union commit to reaching the 0.7% target by 2015.' ('What is the 0.7% Pledge?')

The most recent G8/G20 meeting in Toronto, Canada (June 2010) again failed to honour Pearson's pledge made more than 40 years ago. A report in the *Asian Tribune*, published by the *World Institute For Asian Studies* (Vol. 10 No. 82) describes unequivocally, in its assessment of the group communiqué that emerged from this summit, the magnitude of the failure:

> In 1970 the UN General Assembly committed to providing 0.7% of Gross national product in aid. This was recommitted to by rich countries attending the 2002 Monterrey Consensus on Financing for Development, and at the G8 meeting in Gleneagles in 2005 where European members of the G8 also recommitted to reaching the 0.7% target, by 2015. The aid commitment of the G8 countries is still below the 0.7% of GDP commitment they have given more than 40 years ago.
>
> - Aid levels from G8 member countries Canada and Japan have dropped, by 10.2 per cent and 9.5 per cent respectively.
> - Aid from the United States registered a small increase from 0.19 to 0.20 per cent of GDP.
> - The United Kingdom remains on target for its aid commitments, reporting a jump from 0.43 per cent of GDP in 2008 to 0.52 per cent in 2009.
> - France has increased its aid from 0.39 per cent to 0.46 per cent of GDP.
>
> Together the eight countries making up the G8 represent about 14% of the world population, but they represent about 60% of the Gross World Product. The majority of global military power is with seven in the top 8 nations for military expenditure, and almost all of the world's active nuclear weapons. In 2007, the combined G8 military spending was US$850 billion. This is 72% of the world's total military expenditures. Four of the G8 members, the United Kingdom, United States of America, France and Russia, together account for 96–99% of the world's nuclear weapons.
>
> When it comes to global poverty, the situation is obscene. More than half the world's population lives on less than $2 a day. That's nearly 3 billion people, and includes 97 per cent of the population in Uganda, 80 per cent in Nicaragua, 66 per cent in Pakistan, and

> 47 per cent in China, according to the World Bank. At the same time, the top fifth of countries account for 86 per cent of world GDP, and the 225 richest people have a combined wealth of more than $US1 trillion, which is equal to the annual income of the poorest 47 per cent of the world's population. GCAP [Global Call to Action Against Poverty],[3] the world's largest anti-poverty alliance with coalitions in more than 100 countries, has expressed their extreme disappointment with the communiqué from the G8 Summit. (Gonsalkorale)

The dismal picture of international community presented in these sorts of global observations only gets worse when specific examples of international community aid efforts are examined. The 12 January 2010 earthquake in Haiti produced a $1.8 billion aid response but months after the quake Paul Farmer, a respected doctor and founder of Boston-based Partners in Health (and a deputy special envoy for the United Nations to Haiti) told Congress that only 3% of that amount had made its way into the hands of the Haitian government, itself decimated by the quake but also notoriously inefficient and corrupt. At the writing of this book, more than 96% of the debris from the disaster remains to be cleared and some 1.6 million people are living in atrocious conditions in tent camps in the middle of hurricane season (Sacchetti). The summer 2010 monsoon flooding in Pakistan, which affected some 20 million people with 8 million of those needing urgent assistance according to a UN report, produced a shamefully slow and ineffectual response from the international community. With some 20% of the country flooded, extensive crop damage in a country where 70% of the people are employed in agriculture, severe and varied health challenges to large populations, and large numbers of refugees displaced from homes that have been destroyed, the slowness of the international response (combined with the Pakistani governments' own muddled and highly ineffective reaction to the catastrophe) points to the problematic nature of global community configurations (Shah, Traynor, Tran).

The greater the size of the corporate entity invoked in the name of community, in other words, the more problematic is its ability to respond effectively to the local conditions that require empowered embodiment in order to be addressed effectively. This is one of the reasons why the rights of community need to be instated as a function of localized responses to situations that larger corporate entities cannot address except as a by-product of their own self-interest, a fact addressed in some detail by case studies found in Rebecca Solnit's work, discussed earlier, on community responses to disaster: 'Disaster reveals what else the world could be like – reveals the strength of that hope, that generosity, and that solidarity. It reveals mutual aid as a default operating principle and civil society as something waiting in the wings when it's absent from the stage' (313).

While the above timeline and the facts associated with the failures round the 0.7% pledge point to a shameful indication of the lack of will on the part of affluent countries to develop international community, it can also be argued that the pledge itself is problematic both in pragmatic and ethical terms. It side-steps the issue of corporate greed aided by international financial institutions like the World Bank and International Monetary Fund that dictate devastating development projects to poor countries, together with the structural adjustment plans to qualify them for the loans. If massive debt is caused by such loans and, if poor countries are exploited by transnational corporations, then why should governments take on the restitution – especially when such a small percentage of the tax-base is corporate? Furthermore, the money to finance the 0.7% pledge would presumably come from citizens' taxes. Those citizens may very well ask why that money is going elsewhere, when their own countries' poor face long-term endemic problems related to access to resources as is the case with so many Aboriginal communities who lack basic support. Another problem arises in how to distribute the money from the pledge: would it go directly to the governments of poor countries when so many of these are dictatorships, oligarchies, or just so corrupt that development monies are certain to line the pockets of the ruling elite without ever benefiting the poor? How would effective tracking mechanisms be put into place to measure efficacious delivery of resources to those most in need? Who would judge which governments are deserving of the aid? Would not such judgments inevitably reflect rich countries' biases against states seen as politically subversive, simply because they do not obey the orthodox tenets of neoliberal capitalism? Wouldn't many of the countries most in need of aid be on the 'rogue' list decided by powerful countries giving the money? How would the money reach those communities that are most marginalized by the national government in multiethnic states that persecute minorities? If other methods were devised to finance communities directly instead of national governments, who could tell if the NGOs in charge of leading 'development projects' weren't working to benefit themselves and transnational corporations, as they have often been shown to do?

These are only some of the most obvious pragmatic questions around how money from the pledge would be allocated and distributed. The ethical questions lead us back to Sister Jaramillo's straightforward critique of charity as making beggars of people who aren't. In ethical terms, wouldn't it be important to differentiate aid from restitution? In this sense, canceling the debt would address the unfair loan arrangements and usurious interest rates, and at least partially penalize the institutions that set unfair terms of engagement. As liberation theologians assert, people are poor because they have been robbed, and those repeated acts of thievery are not acknowledged through giving aid or charity.

Given that globalization was just emerging as a total economy at the time of Pearson's proposal to pledge 0.7% and was not yet so obviously supported by total war, it is understandable that such an initiative would have been conceived in good faith. At this point in history, the public has lost trust in governments to perform such altruistic deeds. Current supremacist globalism dictates the most complete enactment of destructive intervention, and illustrates how development theory generally tends to serve elite interests. Many observe that our growing awareness of the negative conditions created by corporate globalism recasts the nation-state as a site of opposition. The collusion between national governments and corporations is equally disillusioning and offers important insights into the workings of power as we have discussed at length in this book.

The realization that emerges from these betrayals is that civil society, led by those who are marginalized and exploited, must reevaluate the meaning of democracy, and other Western concepts based on exclusionary politics. Through social movements, people worldwide are empowering their communities to make choices: buying or reclaiming land and communally building homes for themselves, securing their food by dealing directly with farmers who practice sustainable agriculture, and by creating cooperative purchasing networks based on the principles of fair trade, educating themselves and their children through free schools and other alternative and holistic pedagogical approaches motivated by liberation ethics and the will to heal the planet through decolonization and democratization.

These community-based practices emerge from a vision of social justice that is ecological in its plurality and its local rootedness. Natural, diverse communities (as opposed to large NGOs or other organizations that pay themselves and spend considerable portions of their budgets on advertising and fundraising) can best advance each other's true development. By networking through technological means and face-to-face encounters, community members are increasingly benefiting from sharing knowledge across different cultures. This kind of horizontal interconnecting of distant communities is a paradoxical effect of globalization and perhaps the greatest challenge to monoculture as it monetizes the ecological wealth of differences and possibilities that make up *our* world, *our* commons.

NOTES

1 The policies and ideology associated with globalism are referred to as both neoliberal and neo-conservative, because while the general thrust of opening borders to trade and lifting tariffs and doing away with other protectionist measures are considered to be liberalizing strategies, the thinking behind these strategies was supported by massive funding from neo-conservative organizations, foundations, and think-tanks to schools of economics, yet another instance of the corporate take-over of universities that ultimately inhibits academic freedom (Ralston Saul 33-34).

2 Interestingly, while the study (called a 'note' and published as part of the Social Development Notes) was done by Swarnim Wagle and Parmesh Shah of the Participation and Civic Engagement Group *in* The World Bank, a disclaimer appears at the bottom stating that 'the views expressed in this note are those of the author(s) and do not necessarily reflect the official policies of the World Bank' (1).

3 The GCAP can be accessed at <http://www.whiteband.org/>.

SECTION 4

'Choice words set a seed in the child'

Event Horizons of the Possible and Kiviuq's Story

Community Beyond Measure: 'Everything is one'

All rights discourses are predicated on encounter and contingent relationship. Unavoidable, chance encounters with the other of family, of territory and land, of species otherness, of differences both within and without how one defines belonging to community – these encounters with the flesh, with the soil, with the intimacy of being in another's presence, and being called upon to respond to that presence, mark whatever community may mean as a ceaseless state of relational becoming.

This book has posed more questions than answers about what community may mean, what it is continuously struggling to become. There are answers to what community *may* mean in the fully diverse forms it has taken globally: and they are unstable and need to be understood through the crucibles of ethical forms of encounter and renewability, adaptation and improvisation in response to changing circumstances, respect for difference as one of the means by which community renews itself, and ongoing self-critique. The answers are here and in the moment and they have enormous bearing on rights issues locally, globally, and glocally: what qualities will define how you encounter otherness and difference? Do you choose violence over non-violence? Compassion over loathing and fear? Integrity of purpose and respect for the interconnection of all biotic form or environmental apocalypse and self destruction? Narcissism over altruism? Equitable being over injustice?

If it is a truism to suggest that an interconnected skein of simple and complex relations horizontally organized and inter-dependent are at the core of community, then we need to understand what we mean by contingency. As the basis for thinking about relational becoming, contingency points to the play of uncertainty and chance that determine and even over-determine relations. At its etymological roots, 'contingency' has links with the word *contact*: 'from L. contactus 'a touching,' from pp. of contingere 'to touch, seize,' from com- 'together' ...+ tangere 'to touch' ('Contact'). Remarkable here is the connection in the original sense of the word in Latin between chance relations and 'touching together.' Community embodies contingency in both the chance interdependencies that arise out of it and in the contact, the coming into proximity with the other that allows for contact, touching, intimacy. The extent to which these sorts of relational agencies generate community is beyond quantitative discourse. And in discussing community, we advocate shifting the ground from the dominant forms of discourse that prioritize the quantitative over the qualitative: the supplements that escape measure, externality, and hence the logic of property and ownership.

When Friedrich Wilhelm Nietzsche, following on nineteenth-century German philosopher Arthur Schopenhauer, posited the question of attaining an ideal form of human being 'on the basis of a regulated, self-initiated activity' (Nietzsche 148), that is, on the basis of a disciplined individualism, he found it to be an insufficient way toward achieving this goal. Instead, Nietzsche, who in *Beyond Good and Evil* had vigorously critiqued herd mentalities and an overweening approach to rights based on the eradication of difference, suggests the duty of human achievement is not the duty of the 'solitary individual' (ibid.): 'on the contrary, through them [solitary individuals] one is integrated into a powerful community, one that, to be sure, is not held together by external forms and laws, but by a fundamental idea. This is the fundamental idea of *culture*, insofar as it is capable of charging each of us with one single task: *to foster the production of philosophers, artists, and saints within us and around us, and thereby to work toward the perfection of nature*' (ibid.). In other words, community, as defined outside of external form and law, is the crucible that allows for achievement of a state of being that is the highest expression of the co-creative relations that exist between the natural and the human.

Community is, in some very important senses, defined by the things it produces that are beyond measure: feeling, affiliation, nested interconnections, improvised responses, and ephemeral adaptations to in-the-moment challenges. This aspect of the community commons that is beyond measure is where we locate rights discourses predicated on an ethics of encounter. In such a community space difference, contradiction, and opposition are mediated in co-generative, co-creative, equitable ways. Communities highly skilled in these mediations are achieved, diverse communities. A vital aspect of this achievement depends on recognizing the social practice of community as constitutive of an important sphere of rights: the community of rights *and* the rights of community. Communities that embody these rights practices immeasurably enrich the global commons. Moreover, these communities provide remarkable models within the global commons of successful adjudications of competing legitimacies, self-interests, and priorities across a wide range of social practices, resource realities, and rights contexts.

Communities that rely on a myth of the individual as the standard of rights achievement are in contradiction with themselves. Neither the individual nor the community can be said to exist as an essentialized, hypostasized entity. They both *do* and *do not* exist as useful metaphors for imagining relational contingencies. Inter-relations, collective inter-dependencies constitute the social sphere, and there are vast variations in the degree to which singular and collective entities within that sphere shape and re-shape themselves through their inter-connectedness. A basic rights principle in this context is that of *equality in difference*: corporate entities that do not observe this principle, whether they be lobbies, governments, ethnic groups, political partisans, and other forms of collective structuring where self-interest is imposed at any cost, are in profound opposition to a defining aspect of the rights of community.

The larger the corporate form that defines itself as a community the more suspect it is in its commitment to diversity and the community of interests on which it is built: again Nietzsche deconstructs antiquarian notions of corporate community as dangerously blind because they have lost sight of the very diverse specificities that make local, intimate community viable:

> The antiquarian sensibility of a human being, of a civic community, of an entire people always has an extremely limited field of vision; most things it does not perceive at all, and the few things it does see, it views too closely and in isolation; it is unable to gauge anything, and as a result it regards everything to be equally important, and consequently the individual thing to be too important. There is no criterion for value and no sense of proportion for the things of the past that would truly do them justice when viewed in relation to each other; instead, their measure and proportions are always taken only in relation to the antiquarian individual or people that looks back on them. (137)

Excess of scale breeds blindness. Stale antiquarian notions of the individual and the people become the false mark that assigns value to relations that are infinitely more diverse and rich in their power to shift meaning, create new ecologies of knowledge. How is it possible, in other words, to imagine the event-horizon of the possible if the basis for this vision is tied to limiting notions of relation that blind large corporate entities? One aspect of this vision pertains directly to the localized relations of biotic life forms and the contingencies that allow for sustainability or not. Corporate entities that self-define as communities for strategic political reasons based on nationalist or jingoist state sentiment have those values as a way of directing their self-interest to suit those outcomes. But when those outcomes put at risk vast and complex interwoven biotic relations that need to be seen and understood from the perspective of diverse and localized communities, there is a problem relating to how scale deforms understanding.

Rights undertakings are a vital expression of community. Often these undertakings are embedded in a cultural commons, a field of production that may not be considered a material resource to the community but is nonetheless a crucial aspect of community identity, history, and agency. Stories, myth, theatre, music, visual representations are in this way defining aspects of the community's commons. These are the places where, in the face of relentless pressures to subordinate community to corporate interests, the commons is restored to community. Communities in which the principle of equality in difference is evident can be more diverse and open to difference than larger entities like the State. Their potential role in designing rights legislation and embodying it through their local agency is a crucial aspect of their potential. Such communities beyond measure are the event-horizon of the possible and set an important standard for rethinking how to generate diverse, co-creative, empowered agents for change.

An ongoing trap for community theory lies in definitions of community based not only on tradition (Nietzsche's antiquarianism) but also on self-sameness. Community in this sense is a measure of self-sameness at the expense of difference. Rights discourses that focus on community as an expression of diverse ways of being in relation to others present an important alternative to this dominant narrative. Jean-Luc Nancy, whose work we reference earlier in the book, subtly gets at the struggling *in* to community even as community can be seen as something that we are absent from or even that we refuse in a globalized context:

> An exigency appears here that will have constantly ... inhabited our thoughts and always accompanies in various ways a concern that in the end is common to our absence of community, perhaps to our refusal of community and of a communitarian destination: how to do justice, not only to the whole of existence, but to all existences, taken together but distinctly and in a discontinuous way, not as the

> totality of their differences, and differends ... but as these differences together, co-existing or co-appearing, held together as multiple – and thus together in a multiple way, if one can put it this way, or as multiple together, if we can state it even less adequately ... To do justice to the multiplicity and to the coexistence of singularities, to multiply thus, and infinitely singularize the ends, such is one of the concerns left to us ... Justice rendered to the singular plural is not simply a demultiplied or diffracted justice. It is not a unique justice interpreted according to perspectives or subjectivities – and nonetheless it remains the same justice, equal for all although irreducible and insubstitutable from one to the other. (61)

Justice in Nancy's terms arises from specificity and irreducibility, the recognition that diversity of relatedness is a key aspect of all social relations and thus must be embedded in any attempt to get at what rights mean. The community of rights seen in this light thrives in the diversity of the challenges it must address as a function of co-existent, co-creative multiple and singular beings. Rights discourses understood in this light are both multiple and singular, both driven by specificity and by a universality predicated on equality in difference. The problem is how to move from this perception to embodied, meaningful outcomes that respect the specific rights of community within the diversity of the community of rights.

Another problem facing community rights theory is the way in which community is co-opted as a trope for mainstream, dominant culture and dominant hegemonies. How to evolve a rights discourse focused on community rights that go beyond reductive notions of the human as the subject of thinking about rights? In other words, how to get to a definition of community that recognizes all the component parts that make it (community) possible, which in turn requires broader notions of an ecology of rights in which individual rights are an aspect of a much more complicated whole. To what extent can notions of progressive rights discourse(s) be defined by how they deal with multiple forms of difference that extend to all life in the fullness of the relational contingencies that is the biotic community (conjoined twins, interspecies relations, extreme forms of disability that are nonetheless productive of tremendous creativity, catastrophic poverty, and all forms of environment that make life possible)? The more human communities define themselves in ways that are incommensurate with a deep understanding of the degree to which the biotic community as a whole allows for human existence, the more rights-compromised are those communities. The Aldo Leopold epigraph to this book is a clear expression of this idea: 'A thing is right when it tends to preserve the integrity, stability and beauty of the biotic community. It is wrong when it tends otherwise' (262). Rights structures that do not address the reality of the biotic community as a whole are failed structures in desperate need of revision.

The inter-relatedness of different forms of being is the base condition of community and is the ground upon which rights discourses stand – and the narratives of how these forms of being are in ethical relation to each other (or not) becomes a defining characteristic of particular communities. If community is defined in relation to ownership that allows for exploitation (as per the community of capitalists) there is a master-narrative at work that has rights dimensions. The problem, then, is how to morph dominant narratives of community into lived, progressive alternatives in which pathological master narratives are subverted, overturned, and displaced with more informed and diverse visions. How to shift dominant discourses, then, that reduce the nature of being human to the binary of individual/community? What social practices provide alternatives to this form of reductive thinking about social relations? What forms of cultural literacy, what epistemes need to be created in order to move in the direction of actualizing relational contingencies via the ethics of encounter? Again, community in the sense we use it becomes an allegory of the event-horizon of the possible: an uncertain, dynamic, adaptive, self-critical form of engaging with diversity and encounter in co-generative ways predicated on renewal, sustainability, and respect for the interconnections that govern all forms of being.

Story is a crucial way that we create, critique, and renew community and plays a crucial role in thinking community agency and identity. Not only stories that preserve values, characters, histories, affiliations, and collective knowledge but also stories that critique, imagine differently, and describe utopian alternatives. We have deliberately avoided addressing utopian community formations, like the 'universal city' of Auroville in south-India 'where men and women of all countries are able to live in peace and progressive harmony above all creeds, all politics and all nationalities. The purpose of Auroville is to realise human unity' (*Auroville*). These deserve a full-length account in and of themselves and this book has not been the place to provide such an account.

If anything, there is a remarkable doubleness to utopian writing. On the one hand utopias tend to invoke and reflect on dystopian conditions, either by comparison with the reality they are critiquing or by the satirical ways in which they undermine their own premises. Some utopian writing, like *Woman on the Edge of Time* (1976) by Marge Piercy, which tells the story of a middle-aged Hispanic woman who has visions of two possible futures, one utopian and the other dystopian, do both simultaneously. Utopia is always a response to its dystopian other, the shadow that haunts the possibility of a better world. But there is also a remarkably consistent strain in utopian writing in English that addresses pragmatic rights principles related to egalitarianism, democracy, common ownership (as in *News from Nowhere* by William Morris (1892)], the respect for gender equality (as in *Gloriana, or the Revolution of 1900* [1890] by Lady Florence Dixie), the respect for scholar-artisans (as in *Christianopolis* [1619] by Johann Valentin Andreæ), environmental or ecological principles based on sustainability (as in *Ecotopia: The Notebooks and Reports of William Weston* [1975] by Ernest Callenbach), and the danger of self-sameness (as in *The Giver* [1993], by Lois Lowry, which is about a future community where everything is the same and choice does not exist). Through all of these brief examples it is clear that the key aspects of thinking community in relation to rights are clearly aligned with writings that struggle to imagine alternatives to clear and present dystopias.

In a remarkably cogent way, then, the community of rights and the rights of community mirror the utopian struggle to imagine the event horizon of the possible struggling to address a here-and-now marked by the lack of egalitarianism, by property greed, by the troubled state of democracy, and by the sustained attacks on the environment waged by modernity. In this latter sense, greed, violence, systemic disempowerment, ecological devastation are at the root of the challenges facing community and rights discourses generally. Both rights and communitarian discourses address these issues as a processual, dynamic response to human potential: an event horizon of the possible embedded in all communities, all individuals. They do so, in their most achieved form, not by recourse to a herd mentality approach but by respect of the principle of equality in difference, a respect for the necessary, generative power of difference.

We remind readers that the word *utopia*, in the sense in which Sir Thomas More used it in his 1516 book of the same name, has a double-edged meaning as both a non-place and as a good place: at once non-existent yet an event-horizon of a potentially worthy ideal. More used the book as a way of putting into relief the extreme contrasts between his own, far-from-perfect, early modern European culture and the putatively exceptional practices of the Utopians, which include slavery, euthanasia, internal passports that permit travel on the island, and an injunction against premarital sex.

Even Utopia is anything but a palatable alternative to the absolute monarchic practices of European states. Numerous pre-twentieth and twentieth-century writings that imagine some form of utopian alternative as a way of describing or critiquing current realities tell us that story. Community is neither the idealized space of the utopian 'nowhere,' nor is it the co-opted space of hegemonic self-realization: though it can contain elements of both these forms of relation. What community is, is the necessary, the unavoidable, space of encounter with oneself through the other, with the other through oneself, and with the infinite shades of what it means to be 'in-relation-to' being in all its unknowability, in all the variations of meaning it generates.

Idealized communities are deceptions, as More's allegory shows but also as plentiful examples from the world of the real show. In the pristine inlets, valleys, and rainforests of Clayoquot Sound that covers over 2,600 square kilometres (1,000 square miles) on the west coast of Vancouver Island, a fierce battle has raged among environmentalists, logging companies, and indigenous peoples: 'Debate over the future of the region led to the largest civil disobedience protests in Canada's history with over 10,000 people standing on logging blockades and more than 800 people arrested. A 1999 agreement signed by environmental groups, First Nations and the logging company McMillan Bloedel to voluntarily put the pristine valleys off limits to logging signaled the end of intense campaigns' ('Clayoquot Sound not saved'). First Nations argue that they need the money from such resource-based ventures to deal with grinding poverty on the reserves, poverty brought on by unequal access to resources on their territory. Environmentalists argue that such a unique ecosystem must be preserved as a communal resource for all, natives and non-natives.

Clayoquot Sound was made into a UNESCO Biosphere Reserve in 2000. This designation has proved, in the view of the First Nations Environmental Network, 'to be a disaster to the area.' Local communities have been 'inundated by fish farming, logging and other industrial interests, and the [Clayoquot Biosphere Reserve] Board is run by many people from outside Clayoquot Sound, many in the forestry sector. Attempts to protect the wild salmon and ancient forests have been ignored for economic strategies where industrial influences are socialized into the regional communities framework' and 'Ecotrust and the Clayoquot

Biosphere Reserve Board have teamed up to jointly share in millions of dollars of Federal Government money and are currently planning further forestry programs in the area' ('Clayoquot Sound: What's Really Going On?').

The Clayoquot Biosphere Trust locally represents UNESCO's Clayoquot Sound World Biosphere Reserve. The reserve was established to mediate the competing interests of different stakeholders including residents, locally elected councils, local First Nations band councils, ENGOS (environmental non-governmental agencies), industry, and Canadian provincial and federal governments. Iisaak Forest Resources began logging Clayoquot Sound in the same year (2000) as the Biosphere Reserve was established. Iisaak is a joint venture between MacMillan-Bloedel (now Weyerhaeuser, one of the largest pulp and paper companies in the world) transnational forestry company and the Nuu-chah-nulth First Nations. The designation of the area as a UNESCO World Biosphere Reserve has not, in other words, been what it seems – an attempt to preserve a unique biosphere, as opposed to a way of making the extraction of key resources from the Reserve more palatable (we note the distinction between the terms 'reserve' and 'preserve'). In spite of the UNESCO designation,

> At the end of July 2006, a new set of Watershed plans was approved, opening the door for logging in a further 90,000 hectares of forest in Clayoquot Sound, including the pristine old-growth valleys. As of 2007, both logging tenures within Clayoquot Sound are now controlled by first nation logging companies. Iisaak Forest Resources controls Timber Forest License (TFL) 57 in Clayoquot Sound. MaMook Natural Resources Ltd, in conjunction with Coulson Forest Products, manages TFL54 in Clayoquot Sound.' ('Clayoquot Sound' *Wikipedia*)

In the case of Iisaak Forest Resources, which began logging the Sound in 2000, their public site claims in a press release that,

> The falling of the first tree signifies a new beginning for the communities in Clayoquot Sound. An environmentally responsible forest services company, Iisaak is supported by five major environmental groups. On June 16, 1999, a landmark agreement was signed between Iisaak Forest Resources and Greenpeace Canada, Greenpeace International, Natural Resources Defense Council, Sierra Club of British Columbia, and Western Canada Wilderness Committee.

> 'Iisaak can be a model of locally controlled, value driven forestry that respects and protects the full range of forest values. As such it will be the cornerstone of a prosperous, diverse and innovative economy for all the communities in the Sound,' said Vicky Husband, Conservation Chair, Sierra Club of BC. 'We are very hopeful that Iisaak will benefit both the environment and the local people of Clayoquot.' ('Vancouver Island First Nations')

The conflict over logging in Clayoquot Sound points to the danger in idealizing any form of community being as unconflicted, or as an idealized space of mythical purity. Communities embody these conflicts and are measured by how they negotiate and mediate solutions to conflict in ways that are equitable. So the contested space of Clayoquot Sound embodies this inherent tension that is an important aspect of the commons. It embodies the struggle to reconcile competing interests. The historic inequities that have generated poverty for First Nations in Canada are a major factor in the corporatization of Native culture in order to address legitimate community needs but also, as pointed out above, as an expression of how 'industrial influences are socialized into the regional communities framework' ('Clayoquot Sound: What's Really Going On?'). And this all happens within the context of 'The original inhabitants of Clayoquot Sound, the Nuu-chah-nulth people (mentioned earlier in our discussion of Johnny Mack's work), [who had] a guiding philosophy of *Hishuk-ish ts'awalk*. This means *everything is one,* which recognises that communities, cultures, economies, and environments are interwoven and impact one another' ('Clayoquot Sound' *VancouverIsland.org*).

This brief overview of the ongoing challenge that is Clayoquot Sound points to key issues we have addressed throughout this book. One of these is the rights perspective that integrates the community of rights and the rights of community as a basis for developing realizable, pragmatic, equitable outcomes to challenges such as these. From within such a context the rights of the local community may well supercede the rights of the larger (more illusory because less proximate) community, represented by state and corporate interests. In such a scenario a full contextual understanding of the balanced relationship between the local community and its needs would have to be implemented for larger entities seeking to exploit that community and its resources. The truth here is that a rights of community approach, implemented with this perspective, would understand that endemic poverty and lack of equitable sharing of resources have for too long been a condition of the Nuu-chah-nulth people, especially when you have a culture that is inseparable from the land on which it lives.

The Nuu-chah-nulth are well-known for their potlatch ceremonies, in which the host honours guests with the giving of gifts. Even the word 'potlatch' is a word of Nuu-chah-nulth origin and the culture is predicated on this important symbolic and material ceremony, which redistributes wealth, creates and reinforces alliances, and commemorates historical events. A rights of community approach to Clayoquot Sound's resource struggles would need to understand the cultural context of the Nuu-chah-nulth people and their deep understanding and respect for sharing. A rights of community approach would also need to understand that from first contact with European culture in the eighteenth century the challenges to the Nuu-chah-nulth people have included decimation by smallpox, malaria, and sexually transmitted diseases that killed almost 90% of the population ('Nuu-chah-nulth people'), and pressure on their traditional ways of life that include the fisheries and the forests of their territory, and of course the need to adapt to modern contingencies wrought by settler culture. Only then could an equitable determination of how to share those resources arising from the needs and cultural sensibilities of that culture be thinkable in relation to other communities of interest.

Home cultures based in local communities anchored to specific territorial sites by history, by local knowledge, and by precedent conventions deservedly gain first rights to their own resources. Such a view threatens corporate personhood and state hegemony. These latter entities have benefited from the focus on individual rights in several ways. The massive imbalance in power and economic resources between large state entities and individuals (especially when access to legal resources to enforce rights requires extremely deep pockets), for instance, makes it impossible for an individual to access rights on an equal footing with a state or a corporation. Moreover, the threat of whole communities mobilizing against injustice because their right to do so is enshrined as a legal, constitutional, or ethical principle is a distant one (to states and corporations) because such rights really do not exist under the general rubric of the rights of community. Further, it is corporate entities like the state and transnationals that have usurped to themselves the definition of community and community personhood in ways that real, localized, proximate communities have not. Yet the reality is that a proper, ethical approach to imagining the event horizon of the possible that is our collective rights future must address the rights of community – and this is a profound threat to the status quo for state and corporate entities.

This threat is one of the reasons, we think, that the rights of community within the community of rights have been largely set aside and ignored. What might it have meant for the Nuu-chah-nulth people to have had a clause in the UDHR they could turn to in support of their right to sustainable use of their own resources in ways that allowed for sharing within a wider economic bandwidth but that began by benefiting their own local communities? Article 27, which we've discussed earlier, stipulates that *persons* belonging to ethnic, religious or linguistic minorities 'shall not be denied the right, *in community* with the other members of their group, to enjoy their own culture, to profess and practise their own religion, or to use their own language' (our emphasis). But the same Article lacks any reference to the community's own land and resources, thereby showing again the Eurocentric and self-interested denial of land as the basis of community, and in turn as the basis for individual life.

In fairness, there have been a number of charters, conventions, and covenants drafted over the decades serving as amendments to the UDHR, like the International Covenant on Economic, Social and Cultural Rights whose first Article stipulates that '1) *All peoples* have the right of self-determination. By virtue of that right they freely determine their political status and freely pursue their economic, social and cultural development. 2) *All peoples* may, for their own ends, freely dispose of their natural wealth and resources without prejudice to any obligations arising out of international economic cooperation, based upon the principle of mutual benefit, and international law. In no case may a people be deprived of its own means of subsistence' ('International Covenant'; our emphasis). Clearly the two points of this article are in tension, especially since the definition of prejudice is vague enough to override the community's self-determined status and development – all the more so when that community has been colonized and marginalized. What can such an affirmation of freedom mean to communities who have been denied treaties during colonization? Or to those who are still in litigation to have their treaty rights recognized and enacted? Or to those who see themselves as invoked in the phrase 'all peoples' but who have been left out of equitable resource sharing in the nation-state paradigm? How do such stipulations benefit specific communities, when neoliberal policies have erected trade agreement laws to trump all others?

Remarkably, June 2011 marked the historic move to include First Nations peoples under the Canadian Human Rights Act thus closing a thirty-year legislative gap in which First Nations peoples did not have the same rights protections as other Canadians. Until this date, it was assumed that the Indian Act afforded sufficient protection and might be difficult to mesh with the Human Rights Act whose purpose, according to a CBC report, is 'to ensure equality of opportunity and freedom from discrimination for all people in Canada' ('First Nations people' 1). Strangely, the wording 'all people of Canada' meant for thirty years the exclusion of First Nations peoples. In typical media fashion, the subtitle of the news report announcing that First Nations are now covered under the rights act, subordinates ethical imperatives to financial details: 'But who will pay for cost to comply with act?' The article mentions the deplorable conditions on Native reserves characterized as 'Third World' by former Canadian Prime Minister Paul Martin, but given the dominant paradigm governing human rights discourse, the issue becomes whether First Nations governments or the federal government will now have to make buildings wheelchair accessible.

A local community based approach to this discussion would have to get at the root of the enormous disparity between First Nations and settler communities. Is it fair to shift the focus from continuing colonial domination to the specifics of discrimination contained in the act? What if poor communities cannot afford material upgrades to avoid discrimination against people with disabilities, for example? While the inclusion of First Nations in legal rights protections and instruments is long overdue, the Commission sets the terms by defining discrimination from the dominant, privileged perspective. Understandably, communities lacking clean drinking water and other basic services, worry about how they can comply with codes imposed by those who take such services for granted. The Canadian Human Rights Act (1985) clearly states in Section 2 ('Purpose') that it is based on

> the principle that all individuals should have an opportunity equal with other individuals to make for themselves the lives that they are able and wish to have and to have their needs accommodated, consistent with their duties and obligations as members of society, without being hindered in or prevented from doing so by discriminatory practices based on race, national or ethnic origin, colour, religion, age, sex, sexual orientation, marital status, family status,

> disability or conviction for an offence for which a pardon has been granted.

Yet for thirty years Canada's First Nations peoples were not covered by the very act that sought to prevent discriminatory practices on the basis of a number of factors including ethnic origin. The systematic way in which First Nations peoples and communities had for years suffered discrimination and lack of equal opportunity was embedded in the way in which they were invisibly excluded from the very legislative act meant to make such discrimination illegal. The painful contradiction points to how carefully any form of legislative rights instrument must be critically understood and contextualized in relation to how people actually live their day-to-day material lives. Local community understanding in such a situation trumps high-flown legislative rhetoric that has no necessary material consequences for the most marginalized and disenfranchised.

The lack of inclusive directive principles that address differential access to material privilege and equality (itself a hazy loophole-ridden concept) and the lack of a deeper understanding of how community rights that operate at the local level are also ways of empowering individual rights (for they too are a component of the community of rights) are major problems that need remedying. The reality is that such rights are highly controversial because they challenge corporate and state hegemonies and they also present, in their own local iterations, the potential for abuse and violation. The rights of community, then, require redress from their having been set-aside by the so-called rights revolution. This is especially so because so many non-Western views of rights, like the potlatches of Nuu-chah-nulth people, always already include a concept of community deeply at odds with Western rights structures that privilege individual rights over community rights. The community precedes, literally and figuratively, the individual and is the relational contingency that the individual must always negotiate. Surely, aspects of that relationship embodied in what we mean by community need clear articulation within the remarkable skein of rights instruments and discourses that the last sixty years have produced?

Coda: The Parable of Kiviuq

We end by returning to the story of Kiviuq, the hero of the Inuit oral storytelling epic we briefly mention earlier in the book.[1] Shared story is the basis of community and, like the utopian narratives we discuss briefly earlier on, have many things to teach. We realize this is not our story to tell or retell. And yet, like all ancient stories that persist, Kiviuq's narrative carries its meanings forward to those who listen carefully to the story and the rich meanings it holds. What can we learn from it?

Kiviuq is a survival story and a prophecy at once: both a parable of intergenerational justice and a marker of the ways in which community narratives articulate intangible cultural resources associated with collective memory, the community commons that exists beyond economy and reductive quantification, and recurrent ethical challenges that communities must face as the deepest expression of their values and beliefs. Inuit elder, Bernadette Patterk says of Kiviuq: 'I learned the story by listening many times to my grandfather. If we listen carefully we'll pick up what we need, *but many will not learn*' ('Comments from Nunavut Elders'; our emphasis). Elder Mariano Aupilardjuk adds: 'All Inuit feel the story is real and that it has usefulness in life. If we were raised in only happy times we wouldn't learn. We have both good and bad in life. To survive is to do our best even in hard times, and grow mature, strong and respected' (ibid.). Eli Kimaliardjuk an elder of Chesterfield Inlet avers, 'Because I heard storytelling from my grandmother I received the strength to live and survive. If there were no stories to go by, to survive or to learn to hunt and live, there would be nothing to learn from. My grandmother also gave me the gift of storytelling. As I understood it Kiviuq could have lived 4,000 or even four million years ago, it doesn't matter' (ibid.). All these insights point to the living relationship story has to daily, meaningful actions – the actions that sustain survival (or not); the actions that address the inevitable good and the bad; the affiliations with elders that teach a continuity of being in the world sustaining values even as that world changes around us; the timelessness of the struggle to survive, to be in relation to the world that births us.

Kiviuq's story changes depending on who tells it: not all details of the story are the same. It is also closely rooted to actual geographies: the exact rock on which Kiviuq's mother stood awaiting his return is known to Inuit elders (and is visited). The location seems to be unknown to outsiders and is intriguingly ambiguous given that versions of the story span the northern regions of at lease two vast continents. As a shamanic principle of renewal, continuity, and prophecy, Kiviuq's birthdate is not known, and he is, by most elders' accounts, still alive today, if threatened by how the world has failed to listen to what he has to teach. In some tellings Kiviuq's story begins with an orphan and his grandmother.

The community taunts the orphan, abusing and ridiculing him. His grandmother turns him into a seal (the first of many such inter-species transformations in the story), who lures the hunters of the village out to the water where they drown. In real community there are consequences to unethical conduct: impunity is unthinkable.

Community persecution of the orphan and his grandmother turns into retribution: the evil in the village community is attacked. Kiviuq appears in the story as the only survivor of the hunters who die chasing the seal-boy. He survives because he has never ridiculed or abused the orphan in any way. But he is lost in the ocean, as if to say that he still had responsibility for how his community treated the orphan. A penance must be paid and that penance will give him the knowledge he needs to survive. This knowledge is the necessary restitution to the failed community he has been forced to abandon. So begins the story that releases Kiviuq to his transformational odyssey – in scapegoating, outcasts, marginalized yet empowered affiliations between the elder and the orphan that call out for respect. Kiviuq embodies the fractured community and is both the prophecy of right action and the reminder of wrongs committed by the community that is destroyed.

Another version of the story told by Niviuvak Marqniq begins with Kiviuq's father being murdered by members of his own community. His grandmother takes Kiviuq in and cares for him, clothing him in *qiviuq*, a particular kind of sealskin prized by hunters. Kiviuq becomes a seal after being trained by his grandmother and lures the men who killed his father into the open water where they die. Again, an orphan is mistreated. Evil in the community is excised. Or is it?

Another version of the story begins with Kiviuq's father, who is half-man, half seal and a great hunter. He shows the hunters in his community how to hunt seals by finding their breathing holes during a brutal winter. He descends into a hole to call out a seal and a hunter kills him with his spear. The incident haunts the child Kiviuq because of the conflicts it causes. How does an orphan deal with loss – especially if the loss has been caused by the community in which he lives?

The story ends, if it has an ending, and if its multiple beginnings even point to there being a singular end, with Kiviuq married to goose woman. They create four eggs together and Kiviuq eats two of them and raises the other two as his children. As what happens throughout the story, Kiviuq's knowledge grows in direct relation to his ability to cross boundaries between his humanity and the land that engulfs him, between his human identity and its co-dependence on his animal relations. When his bird offspring leave him, Kiviuq yearns after them and follows them South to the land of the birds. He can only get there by passing through a riverkeeper who tells him to jump on a fish to take him to his children.

The riverkeeper has the knowledge to travel through what Inuit elders call *silaup puntunga*, meaning variously a hole in the environment or the universe, an opening in the physical world that allows great distances to be traveled quickly. In some stories this hole is associated with the penis of the riverkeeper (sometimes called the fishmaker), one aspect of the co-creative principle of renewal and procreation. Kiviuq's journey is fraught with obstacles that test his will and his capacity to act to survive: his survival stands in for the survival of an aspect of the community that has been destroyed by its cruelty, its incapacity for right action. But Kiviuq, according to some, has to face the obstacles he encounters because he has abandoned his mother: she sets the obstacles that give him knowledge because she has been left alone. Again abandonment and affiliation need redress: the community mourns its loss and demands restitution.

Using his shamanic powers Kiviuq sings his way across the landscape, marrying and mating with (and sometimes escaping) what he encounters. He is literally and figuratively transported by the shamanic power of words and song that take him through the *silaup puntunga,* the hole in the world to the southern lands. The songs he sings carry the mapping knowledge he needs to survive the journey. Kiviuq follows the riverkeeper's advice and is reunited with his goose-wife and children, who cannot believe that he has come from the other side of the land to be with them. There Kiviuq's cheeks turn to stone as he ages. He may still be alive in the South: 'Those who saw him most recently (in the 1940s, according to Samson Quinangnaq,) say that his face was getting covered with lichens and that he had a very hard time moving around, especially in winter. When he dies there will be no more air to breathe and life on earth will end' ('The Goose Wife').

Elder Bernadette Uttaq affirms that 'Choice words set a seed in the child' meaning that stories of value set lifelong intentions. She continues, 'Kiviuq and other important story characters are in our lives today. Kiviuq was a good person, and like him we can be great. Their acts set a value, a way of living, of seeing consequences. Life has already been set out by Kiviuq for people and animals. I'm using analogy to simplify what will always be. It is set out but not written. It is very powerful'

('Comments from Nunavut Elders'). And elder Annie Peterloosie affirms, 'We learn right and wrong [Kiviuq] ... All stories guide us to do right by others and thus live a long life' (ibid.).

Right action and sustainable life (long-life) are interlinked in the power of story to inform and shape community. Through its stories community teaches that one can *never* listen closely enough. One can *never* examine the values and meanings that community embodies closely enough. This truth is what will always be. Oral storytelling that conveys the myriad teachings embedded in a story like Kiviuq necessitates proximity to elders, to each other. Out of the troubled intimacy of that encounter, which asks that we interpret, give meaning, assign value, learn by confronting obstacles, arises the shared meanings of community. Like Kiviuq, its end signifies the end of all living things on earth. Like Kiviuq, its story remains to be retold as a yearning for the affiliations we have lost with our environment, with our identity born out of the multiplicity of encounters we cannot avoid, the multiple histories we embody.

In these not so simple truths lies the challenge of becoming and facing into the event-horizon of the possible, how we tell the stories of what might come to be. The rights of community reside in stories like these, which have the power to influence judgment and right action. *Choice words* – the right choice of words, the choice of right words – do indeed set a seed in the child who embodies the community of possibility, the possibility of community.

What might it mean to understand these stories within a larger frame of the community of rights, defined by the community of stories that continue to ask that we listen to each other more diligently, more intensely, more compassionately as we learn together to do right by others, and in so doing do right for ourselves?

NOTES

1 All references in this section derive from the 'Kiviuq's Journey' site (co-created by storyteller Kira Van Deusen, Robert MacNevin, and the Kitikmeot Heritage Society), and the John Houston film *Kiviuq* (2007).

Works Cited

'Abduction of Turmeric provokes India's wrath.' *GoodNewsIndia*. D V Sridharan, 2007. 19 May 2010. http://www.goodnewsindia.com/Pages/content/traditions/turmeric.html.

'About Us.' *AVAAZ.ORG*. 4 Aug 2010. http://www.avaaz.org/en/about.php. Web.

Abraham, Adam, Ed. *Sun Ra Collected Works Vol. I: Immeasurable Equation*. Phaelos Books & Mediawerks, Chandler, AZ: 2005. Print.

AFP. 'Facebook membership hits 500 million mark.' 21 July 2010. *The Vancouver Sun*. 3 August 2010. http://www.vancouversun.com/technology/Facebook+membership+hits+million+mark/3306031/story.html. Web.

Agamben, Giorgio. *The Coming Community*. Trans. Michael Hardt. Minneapolis: University of Minnesota Press, 1993. Print.

Alfred, Taiaiake. *Wasáse: Indigenous Pathways of Action and Freedom*. Peterborough: Broadview Press Ltd., 2005. Print.

Alphonso, Caroline. 'Supreme Court upholds compensation for breach of charter rights.' 23 July 2010. *The Globe and Mail*. 5 August 2010. http://www.theglobeandmail.com/news/national/british-columbia/supreme-court-upholds-damages-claim-in-charter-rights-breach-case/article1649475/. Web.

Alphonso, Caroline, et. al. 'Taser firms picked up coroner's tab to give lectures.' *The Globe and Mail*. 30 Nov 2007. A1. 30 Nov 2007. www.ppao.gov.on.ca/pdfs/sys-tas-gam8.pdf. Web.

Amos, Jonathan. 'Gulf oil spill volume estimated from video.' *BBC News* 23 September 2010. http://www.bbc.co.uk/news/science-environment-11400394. Web.

Aptheker, Herbert, Ed. *The Correspondence of W.E.B. Du Bois Vol. 3*. Amherst: Amherst University of Massachusetts Press, 1978. Print.

'The Aristocracy of Our Monied Corporations.' *The Community Environment Legal Defense Fund: Corporate Rights*. 4 August 2010. http://www.celdf.org/article.php?list=type&type=41. Web.

ATD Fourth World. ATD, 2010. 27 July 2010. http://www.atd-fourth-world.org/en.html. Web.

Attali, Jacques. *Une brève histoire de l'avenir*. Paris: Arthème Fayard, 2006. Print.

Auroville. Auroville Universal Township, 2010. www.auroville.org. Web.

Bailey, Derek. *Improvisation: Its Nature and Practice in Music*. New York: Da Capo Press, 1993. Print.

Bauman, Zygmunt. *Community: Seeking Safety in an Insecure World*. Cambridge: Polity Press, 2003. Print.

Baxi, Upendra. 'Writing about impunity and environment: the "silver jubilee" of the Bhopal catastrophe.' *Journal of Human Rights and the Environment* 1.1 January 2010: 23-44. Print.

Begay, David and Nancy C. Maryboy. *Sharing the Skies: Navajo Astronomy*. Tucson: Rio Nuevo Publishers, 2010. Print.

Benjamin, Walter. *The Arcades Project*. Ed. Rolf Tiedemann. Cambridge: President and Fellows of Harvard College, 1999. Print.

Bennett, Alan. *Getting On*. London: Faber and Faber Ltd, 1972. Print.

Beresford-Kroeger, Diana. *The Global Forest*. New York: Viking Penguin, 2010. Print.

Berry, Wendell. *The Long-Legged House*. Washington, DC: Shoemaker & Hoard, 2004. Print.

– *What Matters? Economics for a Renewed Commonwealth*. Berkeley: Counterpoint, 2010. Print.

– *Sex, Economy, Freedom & Community*. New York: Pantheon Books, 1992. Print.

Biehl, Jody. 'The Death of a Muslim Woman: "The Whore Lived Like a German."' 3 February 2005. *Der Spiegel*. 5 August 2010. http://www.spiegel.de/international/0,1518,344374,00.html. Web.

Bindman, Geoffery. 'Bringing International Criminals to Justice.' *Human Rights, Human Wrongs: The Oxford Amnesty Lectures*. Ed. Nicolas J. Owen. Oxford: Oxford University Press, 2003: 138-163. Print.

Blanchot, Maurice. *La Communauté inavouable*. Paris: Éditions de Minuit, 1983. Print.

Block, Peter. *Community: The Structure of Belonging*. San Francisco: Berrett-Koehler Publishers, 2008. Print.

Bloom, Harold. *The Anxiety of Influence: A Theory of Poetry*. Oxford: Oxford University Press, 1997. Print.

Bollier, David. 'They Still Enclose the Commons, Don't They?' 30 April 2010. *On The Commons*. 4 August 2010. http://onthecommons.org/they-still-enclose-commons-don8217t-they. Web.

Bowden, Charles. *Blue Desert*. Tucson: University of Arizona Press, 1988. Print.
– *Some of the Dead Are Still Breathing*. Orlando: Houghton Mifflin Harcourt, 2009. Print.
Bowden, Charles and Julián Cardona. *Exodus/Éxodo*. Austin: University of Texas Press, 2008. Print.
Bowen, John Richard. *Islam, Law, and Equality in Indonesia: An Anthropology of Public Reasoning*. Cambridge: Cambridge University Press, 2003. Print.
'BP's Oil Spill: The Effect on Communities and Public Health.' *Sox First*. 26 August 2010. http://www.soxfirst.com/50226711/bps_oil_spill_the_effect_on_communities_and_public_health.php. Web.
Bradstock, Andrew, Ed. *Winstanley and the Diggers 1649-1999*. New York: Frank Cass, 2000. Print.
Brewin, Bob. 'Defense Unable to Track Deployed Troops Psychiatric Drugs.' 8 June 2010. *Nextgov*. 4 August 2010. http://www.nextgov.com/nextgov/ng_20100608_2900.php. Web.
Bringhurst, Robert. *A Story as Sharp as a Knife*: *Vol. 1 The Classical Haida Mythtellers and Their World*. Vancouver and Toronto: Douglas & McIntyre, 1999. Print.
Bruyea, Sean. 'Federal treatment of disabled veterans disgraceful.' Rpt. from *The Edmonton Journal* 27 January 2010 on Veterans UN/NATO Canada. http://vetsunnatocanadaen.multiply.com/journal/item/854/Federal_treatment_of_disabled_veterans_disgraceful. Web.
Butler, Judith. *Giving An Account of Oneself*. New York: Fordham University Press, 2005. Print.

Caillou, Brian. 'The Culture of Leadership: North American Indigenous Leadership in a Changing Economy.' *Indigenous People and the Modern State*. Eds. Duane Champagne, Karen Jo Torjensen and Susan Steiner. Oxford: Rowan & Littlefield Publishers Inc., 2005. Print.
'Canada: Inappropriate and Excessive Use of Tasers.' *Amnesty International*. May 2007. Amnesty News. 4 Aug 2010. http://www.amnesty.ca/amnestynews/upload/AMR2000207.pdf. Web.
Canadian Human Rights Act (1985). 7 July 2011. http://laws-lois.justice.gc.ca/eng/acts/h-6/page-1.html. Web.
Carroll, Rory. 'US chose to ignore Rwanda genocide.' 31 March 2004. *The Guardian* UK. 5 August 2010. http://www.guardian.co.uk/world/2004/mar/31/usa.rwanda. Web.
'Case Study 2 – Porto Alegre, Brazil: Participatory Approaches in Budgeting and Public Expenditure Management.' March 2003. *Social Development*

Notes. 4 Aug 2010. http://siteresources.worldbank.org/INTPCENG/1143372-1116506093229/20511036/sdn71.pdf Web.

'Casualties of the Iraq War.' *Wikipedia*. Wikimedia Foundation Inc., 2010. http://en.wikipedia.org/wiki/Casualties_of_the_Iraq_War. Web.

CBC News. 'Doctor probed for alleged welfare abuse.' 9 December 2009. *CBC News*. 16 December 2009. http://license.icopyright.net/user/viewFreeUse.act?fluid+NjIy. Web.

CBC News. 'NYT: BP's Oil Spill Fines Could Hit $63 Billion.' 17 June 2010. *CBC News*. 17 July 2010. http://www.cbsnews.com/stories/2010/06/17/business/main6590719.shm. Web.

Champagne, Duane. 'Rethinking Native Relations with Contemporary Nation-States.' *Indigenous People and the Modern State*. Eds. Duane Champagne, Karen Jo Torjensen and Susan Steiner. Oxford: Rowan & Littlefield Publishers, 2005. Print.

'Charter 08, a plea for human rights in China.' Trans. Perry Link. 26 January 2009. *AsiaNews.it*. http://www.asianews.it/index.php?l=en&art=14313. Web.

Cheney, John. 'Land Conflict Resolution Within Autonomous Space.' *SIT Graduate Institute/SIT Study Abroad* (Spring 2004): 1-36. http://digitalcollections.sit.edu/cgi/viewcontent.cgi?article=1533&context=isp_collection. Web.

Chomsky, Noam. Interviewed by Amy Goodman. 'Noam Chomsky: "The Center Cannot Hold: Rekindling Radical Imagination."' 31 May 2010. *Democracy Now!* 4 August 2010. http://www.democracynow.org/2010/5/31/noam_chomsky_the_center_cannot_hold. Web.

– 'Free Trade and Free Market: Pretense and Practice.' *The Cultures of Globalization*. Eds. Fredric Jameson and Masao Miyoshi. Durham and London: Duke UP, 1998.

'CIA worked in tandem with Pakistan to create Taliban.' 7 March 2001. *The Times of India*. 5 August 2010. http://www.hartford-hwp.com/archives/51/099.html. Web.

Cissé, Youssouf, Jean-Louis Sagot-Duvauroux, and Aboubaker Fofana. Eds. *La Charte du Mandé et autres traditions de Mali*. Paris: Albin Michel, 2003. Print.

Clarke, D. B. 'The Concept of Community: A Re-Examination.' *Readings in Community Work*. Eds. Paul Henderson and David N. Thomas. London: William Clowes, 1981: 32-37. Print.

'Clayoquot Sound.' *VancouverIsland.com*. 5 August 2010. http://www.vancouverisland.com/regions/towns/?townid=3935. Web.

'Clayoquot Sound.' *Wikipedia*. Wikimedia Foundation Inc., 2010. http://en.wikipedia.org/wiki/Clayoquot_Sound. Web.

'Clayoquot Sound not saved.' 31 July 2006. *Greenpeace Canada*. 5 August 2010. http://www.greenpeace.org/canada/en/press-centre/press-releases/clayoquot-not-saved/. Web.

'Clayoquot Sound: What's Really Going On?' *First Nations Environmental Network*. 5 August 2010. http://www.fnen.org/?q=node/37. Web.

Clifton, Eli. 'Suicide Rate Surged among Veterans.' *Inter Press Service* (IPS). 13 January 2010. http://ipsnews.net/news.asp?idnews=49971. Web.

'Coltan.' *Wikipedia*. Wikimedia Foundation Inc., 2010. 29 July 2010. http://en.wikipedia.org/wiki/Coltan. Web.

'Comments from Nunavut Elders on Storytelling.' *Kiviuq's Journey*. 5 August 2010. http://www.unipka.ca/Quotes.html. Web.

'Communes of France.' *Wikipedia*. Wikimedia Foundation Inc., 2010. http://en.wikipedia.org/wiki/Communes_of_France. Web.

'Community.' *Life Positive*. 5 August 2010. http://www.lifepositive.com/mind/community/community.asp. Web.

'Community Organizing.' *The Community Environmental Legal Defense Fund*. 4 August 2010. http://www.celdf.org/section.php?id=27. Web.

'Connecting to Everything You Care About.' 19 April 2010. *The Facebook Blog*. 3 August 2010. http://blog.facebook.com/blog.php?post=382978412130. Web.

'Contact.' *Online Etymology Dictionary*. 5 August 2010. http://www.etymonline.com/index.php?term=contact. Web.

Corbett, John, Ed. *The Wisdom of Sun-Ra: Sun Ra's Polemical Broadsheets and Streetcorner Leaflets*. Chicago: Whitewalls, 2006. Print.

Corns, Thomas N., Ann Hughes and David Loewenstein, Eds. *The Complete Works of Gerrard Winstanley*. Oxford: Oxford University Press, 2009. Print.

'Corporate Personhood.' *Reclaim Democracy*. 5 August 2010. http://reclaimdemocracy.org/personhood/. Web.

Crawford, Neta C., Catherine Lutz, Robert Jay Lifton, Judith L. Herman and Howard Zinn. 'The Real "Surge": Non-Combatant Death in Iraq and Afghanistan.' 22 January 2008. *Carnegie Council*. 4 August 2010. http://www.cceia.org/resources/articles_papers_reports/0003.html. Web.

'Criticism of Facebook.' *Wikipedia*. Wikimedia Foundation Inc., 2010. 3 August 2010. http://en.wikipedia.org/wiki/Criticism_of_Facebook. Web.

Curry, Janel M. and Steven McGuire. *Community On Land: Community, Ecology, and the Public Interest*. Oxford and Maryland: Rowman &

Littlefield, 2002. Print.

'DARPA.' *Wikipedia*. Wikimedia Foundation Inc., 2010. 3 August 2010. http://en.wikipedia.org/wiki/DARPA. Web.

'Dartmouth College v. Woodward.' *Wikipedia*. Wikimedia Foundation Inc., 2010. 4 August 2010. http://en.wikipedia.org/wiki/Dartmouth_College_v._Woodward. Web.

Darwin, Charles. *The Origin of Species*. Madison, WI: Cricket House Books, 2010. Print.

Davis, Mike. *Planet of Slums*. London and New York: Verso, 2006. Print.

Davis, Wade. *The Wayfinders: Why Ancient Wisdom Matters in the Modern World*. CBC Massey Lectures. Toronto: Anansi, 2009. Print.

De Montaigne, Michel. 'On Habit: and on never easily changing a traditional law.' *The Complete Essays*. Ed. Michael Andrew Screech. New York: Penguin Group, 1991: 122-139. Print.

'Deepwater Horizon oil spill.' *Wikipedia*. Wikimedia Foundation Inc., 2010. 29 July 2010. http://en.wikipedia.org/wiki/Deepwater_Horizon_spill#cite_note-plumsundergulf-15. Web.

Delanty, Gerard. *Community*. London: Routledge, 2003. Print.

Deol, Jeevan. 'Column: Tax evasion and the crisis in Greece.' 15 May 2010. *The Financial Express*. 4 Aug 2010. http://www.financialexpress.com/news/column-tax-evasion-and-the-crisis-in-greece/618950/. Web.

Dickinson, Tim. 'BP's Next Disaster.' 22 June 2010. *Rolling Stone*. 5 August 2010. http://www.rollingstone.com/politics/news/17390/120130. Web.

Dozier, Kimberly. 'Leaked tales from the front lines paint a dark portrait of Afghanistan.' 25 July 2010. *The Globe and Mail*. 4 August 2010. http://www.theglobeandmail.com/news/world/leaked-tales-from-the-front-lines-paint-dark-portrait-of-afghanistan/article1651348/. Web.

'Draft: Universal Declaration of the Rights of Mother Nature.' 27 April 2010. *Indigenous News*. 5 August 2010. http://indigenews.kisikew.org/forum/viewtopic.php?f=2&t=2601&start=0. Web.

Du Bois, W. E. B. 'Of Our Spiritual Striving.' *The Souls of Black Folk*. Charleston: Forgotten Books, 2008: 3-10. Print.

Dunning, Jenni. 'U.S. bill would make it illegal to take a picture of a farm.' 15 March 2011. *thestar.com*. http:www.thestar.com/printarticle/954181. Web.

Dussel, Enrique. *Ethics and Community*. Trans. Robert R. Barr. New York: Orbis Books, 1988. Print.

– *Hacia una filosofía política crítica*. Bilbao: Desclée de Brouwer, 2001. Print.

Dyck, Arthur J. *Rethinking Rights and Responsibilities: The Moral Bonds of Community*. Washington, DC: Georgetown University Press, 2005. Print.

El-Tablawy, Tarek and Sinan Salaheddin. 'Audit: U.S. can't account for $8.7b in Iraqi funds.' 27 July 2010. *The Globe and Mail.* 5 August 2010. http://www.theglobeandmail.com/news/world/audit-us-cant-account-for-87b-in-iraqi-funds/article1652933. Web.

Elisha, James 'Liberative Motifs in Dalit Religion.' *Bangalore Theological Forum* 24.2 (2002): n .pag. 2 August 2010. http://www.religion-online.org/showarticle.asp?title=2451. Web.

Erasmus, Georges. 'Georges Erasmus: The LaFontaine-Baldwin Lecture 2002.' *The LaFontaine Baldwin Lectures Volume One*. Ed. Rudyard Griffiths. Toronto: Penguin Canada, 2002. Print.

Esguerra, Richard. 'Facebook's Broken Promises: Facebook Apps Leaking Private Data to Advertisers and Trackers.' *Electronic Frontier Foundation*. 18 October 2010. http://www.eff.org/deeplinks/2010/10/facebooks-broken-promises-facebook-apps-leaking. Web.

Evans, Michael. BP Oil News/Independent Reporting on the BP Deepwater Horizon Gulf Oil Spill. 'Oil Spill Pictures' 9 June 2010. http://bpoilnews.com/oil-spill-pictures/oil-spill-pictures-bp-coverup-first-amendment/. 17 July 2010. Web.

'Extinction.' *Wikipedia*. Wikimedia Foundation, Inc., 2010. 5 August 2010. http://en.wikipedia.org/wiki/Extinction. Web.

'Facts and Figures' *Amnesty International Report 2010*. 4 August 2010. http://thereport.amnesty.org/facts-and-figures. Web.

Fanon, Franz. *The Wretched of the Earth*. New York: Grove Press, 2004. Print.

Federation of Southern Cooperatives Land Assistance Fund. N.p., 2010. Web. 29 July 2010. http://www.federationsoutherncoop.com/. Web.

Filewod, Alan. 'Coalitions of Resistance: Ground Zero's Community Mobilization.' *Performing Democracy*. Eds. Susan C. Haedicke and Tobin Nellhaus. Michigan: University of Michigan, 2004: 89-103. Print.

– 'The Spectre of Communi**.' *Canadian Theatre Review* (Spring 1995): 3. Print.

Fillion, Kate. 'Gender expert Leonard Sax on the empty world of girls.' 3 May 2010. *Maclean's*. 10 May 2010. http://www2.macleans.ca/2010/05/03/gender-expert-leonard-sax-on-the-empty-world-of-girls-impressing-each-other-with-sex-booze-and-facebook%E2%80%94while-parents-opt-out/. Web.

'First Nations people now covered under rights act.' 17 June 2011.

CBC *News*. 8 July 2011.
http:www.cbc.ca/news/canada/story/2011/06/17/human-rights.html. Web.

Fischlin, Daniel and Martha Nandorfy. *The Concise Guide to Global Human Rights*. Prologue by Vandana Shiva. Montreal: Black Rose Books, 2007.

– *Eduardo Galeano: Through the Looking Glass*. Montreal: Black Rose Books, 2002.

Fisk, Robert. 'US troops say goodbye to Iraq.' *The Independent*. 20 August 2010. http://www.independent.co.uk/opinion/commentators/fisk/robert-fisk-us-troops-say-goodbye-to-iraq-2057387.html. Web.

Flores, Roberto. 'From Disillusionment and Abandonment to Autonomy: Zapatista Bilingual Indigenous Education in Chiapas, Mexico.' 23 June 2003. *In Motion Magazine*. 7 May 10.
http:www.inmotionmagazine.com/auto/zbiel.html. Web.

Foster, Cecil. *Where Race Does Not Matter: The New Spirit of Modernity*. Toronto: Penguin Canada, 2005. Print.

'Franz Boas.' *Wikipedia*. Wikimedia Foundation Inc., 2010. 2 Aug 2010. http://en.wikipedia.org/wiki/Franz_Boas. Web.

Frayssinet, Fabiana. 'Guaraní of Brazil suffering breakdown of culture, suicides.' *InfoSud Human Rights Tribune*. 5 January 2010.
http://www.humanrights-geneva.info/spip.php?article4443. Web.

Galeano, Eduardo. *Bocas del Tiempo*. Santiago: Pehuén Editores, 2005. Print.

– 'Message to the Mother Earth Summit: The Rights of Human Beings and the Rights of Nature Are Two Names of the Same Dignity.' *MRZine*. Monthly Review Foundation, 2010. 7 June 2010.
http://mrzine.monthlyreview.org/2010/galeano210410p.html. Web.

Gandhi, Arun. 'Community Weaving – A Universal Thread.' *Life Positive*. 2 August 2010. http://www.lifepositive.com/spirit/masters/mahatma-gandhi/community.asp. Web.

Gearans, Anne and Robert Burns. 'WikiLeaks details thousands of unreported Iraqi civilian deaths.' 23 October 2010. *The Toronto Star*.
http://www.thestar.com/news/world/article/880198 – wikileaks-details-thousands-of-unreported-iraqi-civilian-deaths?bn=1.Web.

Gerard, Charley. *Jazz in Black and White: Race, Culture, and Identity in the Jazz Community*. Westport: Praeger, 1998. Print.

Gewirth, Alan. *The Community of Rights*. Chicago: The University of Chicago Press, 1996. Print.

Gillam, Carey. 'Update 1-US Pledges to probe, bust agribusiness monopolies.' 12 March 2010. *Reuters*. 19 May 2010.
http://www.reuters.com/assets/print?aid=USN1215754320100312. Web.

Gillingham, John. 'The Beginnings of English Imperialism'. *Journal of Historical Sociology* 5.4 (December 1992): 393-409. Print.

Goodale, Mark. *Surrendering to Utopia: An Anthropology of Human Rights.* Stanford: Stanford University Press, 2009. Print.

Goodell, Jeff. 'The Poisoning.' *Rolling Stone.* 5 August 2010: 59-65. Print.

Gómez-Peña, Guillermo. *The New World Border.* San Francisco: City Lights, 1996. Print.

Gonsalkorale, Raj. 'G8 Muskoka Summit; Rich country donors still well off-track on their aid commitments.' 28 Jun 2010. *Asia Tribune.* 4 Aug 2010. http://www.asiantribune.com/news/2010/06/28/g8-muskoka-summit-rich-country-donors-still-well-track-their-aid-commitments. Web.

'The Goose Wife.' As told by Samson Quinangnaq. *Kiviuq's Journey.* 5 August 2010. http://www.unipka.ca/Stories/Goose_Wife.html. Web.

'Governing the Commons: The Evolution of Institutions for Collective Action.' *The Cooperation Commons.* 4 August 2010. http://www.cooperationcommons.com/node/361. Web.

Gret, Marion and Yves Sintomer. *The Porto Alegre Experiment: Learning Lessons for Better Democracy.* London and New York: Zed Books, 2005. Print.

Grey, Josephine. 'How can we use the human rights framework and international law to protect the future of the planet?' (unpublished). For contact information and other publications see website for LIFT (Low Income Families Together) http://www.lift.to/lift/home.htm. Web.

Grothhaus, Michael. 'Foxconn: Apple supplier in China roughs up reporter.' 19 Feb 2010. *TUAW.* 3 August 2010. http://www.tuaw.com/2010/02/19/foxconn-apple-supplier-in-china-roughs-up-reporter/. Web.

Groussot, Xavier. *General Principles of Community Law.* Groningen: Europa Law Publishing, 2006. Print.

Griffin, John Howard. *Black Like Me.* (with Robert Bonazzi Afterword) New York: Signet, 1996. Print.

'Gun Control Lawsuit News.' 21 October 2005. *Online Lawyer Source.* 4 August 2010. http://www.onlinelawyersource.com/news/lawsuit_ban.html. Web.

'Gun Deaths – United States Tops The List.' 4 May 2002. *MedicineNet.* 5 August 2010. http://www.medicinenet.com/script/main/art.asp?articlekey=6166. Web.

'Gun violence in the United States.' *Wikipedia.* Wikimedia Foundation Inc., 2010. http://en.wikipedia.org/wiki/Gun_violence_in_the_United_States. Web.

Gunn, Giles. *Beyond Solidarity: Pragmatism and Difference in a Globalized World.* Chicago: University of Chicago Press, 2001. Print.

Habermas, Jürgen. *The Structural Transformation of the Public Sphere: An Inquiry into a Category of Bourgeois Society*. Tans. Thomas Burger and Frederick Lawrence. Cambridge: MIT Press, 1991. Print.

Haneke, Michael. 'Les racines du mal.' *La Presse, Arts et Spectacles* 22 (May 2009): 3. Print.

– dir. *The White Ribbon*. X-Filme Creative Pool et al., 2009. DVD.

Hardt, Michael and Antonio Negri. *Commonwealth*. Cambridge: Harvard University Press, 2009. Print.

– *Multitude*. Cambridge: Harvard University Press, 2004. Print.

Harper, Tim. 'Nevada Tent Cities Rise in Shadow of Casinos.' 17 Oct 2008. *The Toronto Star.* 4 Aug 2010. http://www.thestar.com/printarticle/519057. Web.

Hazard, Damien and Pascal Alain Kali. 'Irruption des mouvements noirs.' *Manière de voir: Le Monde diplomatique*. Special Issue: 'Là où le Brésil va ...' 113 (Octobre-Novembre 2010): 53-56. Print.

Herman, A. L. *Community, Violence, and Peace: Aldo Leopold, Mohandas K. Gandhi, Martin Luther King Jr., and Guatama the Buddha in the Twenty-First Century*. Albany: State University of New York Press, 1999. Print.

Hess, Charlotte and Elinor Ostrom, Eds. *Understanding Knowledge as Commons: From Theory to Practice*. Cambridge: MIT Press, 2007. Print.

'The High Cost of Cheap Oil.' *World Rainforest Movement*. 4 August 2010. http://www.wrm.org.uy/publications/oil1.html#viewpoint. Web.

Hoffman, Michael. 'UAV Pilot Career Field Could Save $1.5 Billion.' 2 March 2010. *Air Force Times*. 4 August 2010. http://www.airforcetimes.com/news/2009/03/airforce_uav_audit_030109/. Web.

Hogan, Linda. *The Woman Who Watches Over the World: A Native Memoir*. New York: W. W. Norton & Company Inc., 2001. Print.

Hopton, Andrew, Ed. *Gerrard Winstanley Selected Writings*. London: Aporia Press, 1989. Print.

Howard, Rhoda. *Human Rights and the Search for Community*. Oxford: Westview Press, 1995. Print.

Hurst, Timothy B. 'Spam Wasted 33 Billion Kilowatt-Hours of Electricity in 2008.' 20 April 2009. *Clean Technica*. 3 August 2010. http://cleantechnica.com/2009/04/20/spam-wasted-33-billion-kilowatt-hours-of-electricity-in-2008/. Web.

'Ice-minus bacteria.' *Wikipedia*. Wikimedia Foundation Inc., 2010. http://en.wikipedia.org/wiki/Ice-minus_bacteria. Web.

Indigenous Education Institute. Indigenous Education Institute, 2006. 2 August 2010. http://www.indigenouseducation.org/index.html. Web.

'International Covenant on Economic, Social and Cultural Rights.'

16 December 1966. *Charter of the United Nations*. 5 August 2010. www2.ohchr.org/english/law/pdf/cescr.pdf. Web.

International Federation of Organic Agriculture Movement. IFOAM, 2008. 27 July 2008. http://www.ifoam.org/index.html. Web.

Inuit Health Topics. NAHO, 2008. 3 August 2010. www.naho.ca/inuit/e/healthtopics/suicideprevention.php. Web.

'Israel: Failure to Probe Civilian Casualties Fuels Impunity.' 21 June 2005. *Human Rights Watch*. 4 August 2010. http://www.hrw.org/en/news/2005/06/21/israel-failure-probe-civilian-casualties-fuels-impunity. Web.

Jameson, Fredric and Masao Miyoshi, Eds. *The Cultures of Globalization*. Durham and London: Duke UP, 1998.

Jefferies, Stuart. 'A rare interview with Jürgen Habermas.' 30 April 2010. *Financial Times*. 5 August 2010. http://www.ft.com/cms/s/o/eda3bcd8-5327-11df-813e-00144feab49a.html. Web.

Jefferson, Thomas. *The Writings of Thomas Jefferson, Volume X*. Charleston: BiblioBazaar, LLC., 2008. Print.

Jepson, Kris. 'Secret files raise questions over civilian casualties.' 26 July 2010. *Channel 4 News*. 4 August 2010. http://www.channel4.com/news/articles/politics/international_politics/wikileaks+files+raise+questions+over+civilian+casualties/3723897. Web.

Johnson, Samuel. *Taxation No Tyranny* (1775). In *The Works of Samuel Johnson, LL.D. with an Essay on His Life and Genius by Arthur Murphy*. Vol. 2. New York: Alexander V. Blake, 1846: 426-38. Print.

'Kabul War Diary.' 26 July 2010. *Wikileaks*. 4 August 2010. http://wardiary.wikileaks.org/. Web.

Kaval, Allan. 'Tsigane, c'est aussi une culture ...' *Marianne*. 2-8 October, No. 702, 2010: 74-75. Print.

Kelley, Robin D. G. *Freedom Dreams: The Black Radical Imagination*. Boston: Beacon Press, 2002. Print.

Keltner, Dacher. *Born To Be Good: The Science of a Meaningful Life*. New York: W.W. Norton & Company, 2009. Print.

Kennedy, Alan. 'Camberwell Coal Mine. (in Australia).' 1 July 1991. *Mining Magazine*. 4 August 2010. http://www.allbusiness.com/energy-utilities/coal-industry-coal-mining/7327236-1.html. Web.

Kennedy, Scott Hamilton, dir. *The Garden* (documentary film). Oscilloscope Pictures, 2008. DVD.

King Jr., Martin Luther. 'Letter From Birmingham Prison.' 16 April 1963.

African Studies Center, University of Pennsylvania. 27 July 2010. http://www.africa.upenn.edu/Articles_Gen/Letter_Birmingham.html. Web.

King, Thomas. *One Good Story, That One.* Toronto: HarperCollins, 1995. Print.

– *The Truth About Stories.* Toronto: House of Anansi Press Inc., 2003. Print.

Kiviuq. Dir. John Houston. Drumsong Communications, 2007. DVD.

Kiviuq's Journey: An Inuit Hero's Epic Quest. Diavik Corporation, 2008. http://unipka.ca/Index.html. Web.

Kogan, Anne. 'Can Brazil's Quilombos Survive?' 25 September 2005. *In These Times.* 6 May 2010. http://inthesetimes.com/article/3321/can_brazils_quilombos_survive. Web.

Kollock, Peter. *Communities In Cyberspace.* London: Routledge, 1999. Print.

Lanier, Jaron. *You Are Not a Gadget: A Manifesto.* New York: Alfred A. Knopf, 2010. Print.

'Legal Definition of Community.' *The 'Lectric Law Library.* 4 August 2010. http://www.lectlaw.com/def/c260.htm. Web.

Leigh, David. 'Afghanistan war logs: Secret CIA paramilitaries' role in civilian deaths.' 25 July 2010. *The Guardian* UK. 4 August 2010. http://www.guardian.co.uk/world/2010/jul/25/afghanistan-civilian-deaths-rules-engagement. Web.

Leopold, Aldo. *A Sand County Almanac.* New York: Ballantine Books, 1970. Print.

Lévesque, Claude. 'Les États-Unis se retirent.' 20 August 2010. *Le Devoir.* A1, A10. Print.

Lévy, Elisabeth. 'Amartya Sen et la "Parabole de la flute."' 14 January 2010. *Le Point.* 4 August 2010. http://www.lepoint.fr/archives/article.php/413630. Web.

Lewis, George E. *A Power Stronger Than Itself: The* AACM *and American Experimental Music.* Chicago: University of Chicago Press, 2008. Print.

Lipsitz, George. *Footsteps in the Dark: The Hidden Histories of Popular Music.* Minneapolis: University of Minnesota Press, 2007. Print.

'List of Countries by Number of Troops.' *Wikipedia.* Wikimedia Foundation Inc., 2010. 4 August 2010. http://en.wikipedia.org/wiki/List_of_countries_by_number_of_troops. Web.

Lynch, Jennifer. 'Applying for Citizenship? U.S. Citizenship and Immigration Wants to Be Your "Friend."' *Electronic Frontier Foundation.* 12 October 2010. https://www.eff.org/deeplinks/2010/10/applying-citizenship-u-s-citizenship-and. Web.

Mack, Johnny. 'Hoquotist: Reorienting through Storied Practice.' *Storied Communities: Narratives of Contact and Arrival in Constituting Political Communities*. Eds. Hester Lessard, Rebecca Johnson, and Jeremy Webber. Vancouver: University of British Columbia Press, 2010: 287-307. Print.

Marshall, S. L. A. *Men Against Fire: The Problem of Battle Command*. Norman: University of Oklahoma Press, 2000. Print.

Masnick, Mike. 'Online Communities Patented; Lawsuit Against Facebook Moves Forward.' 5 April 2010. *Techdirt*. 3 August 2010. http://www.techdirt.com/articles/20100402/1625538855.shtml. Web.

McClelland, Mac. '"It's BP's Oil:" Running the Corporate Blockade at Louisiana's crude-covered beaches.' 24 May 2010. *Mother Jones*. 25 August 2010. http:motherjones.com/print/61012. Web.

McCormack, Patricia A. 'Competing Narratives: Barriers between Indigenous Peoples and the Canadian State'. *Indigenous People and the Modern State*. Eds. Duane Champagne, Karen Jo Torjensen and Susan Steiner. Oxford: Rowan & Littlefield Publishers Inc., 2005: 109-20. Print.

McIntosh, Alistair. *Soil and Soul: People Versus Corporate Power*. London: Aurum Press, 2004. Print.

MacKinnon, Mark. 'Inside China's gated communities for the poor.' 18 July 2010. *The Globe and Mail*. 5 August 2010. http://www.theglobeandmail.com/news/world/inside-chinas-gated-communities-for-the-poor/article1644361/. Web.

Marsh, Charles. *The Beloved Community: How Faith Shapes Social Justice, From the Civil Rights Movement To Today*. New York: Basic Books, 2005. Print.

Martens, Pam. 'Heralded by the Supreme Court as Fair, Vast Private Judicial System Exposed as Fraud.' 20 July 2009. *Counterpunch*. 17 July 2010. http://www.counterpunch.org/martens07202009.html. Web.

Masnick, Mike. 'Online Communities Patented; Lawsuit Against Facebook Moves Forward.' *Techdirt*. 5 April 2010. http://www.techdirt.com/articles/20100402/1655388855.shtml. Web.

Mason, Rowena. 'Pressure over "blood minerals."' *Financial Post*. 13 September 2010: FP1, FP3. Print.

Mayo, Marjorie. *Cultures, Communities, Identities: Cultural Strategies for Participation and Empowerment*. New York: Palgrave, 2000. Print.

Mignolo, Walter D. 'Globalization, Civilization Processes, and the Relocation of Languages and Cultures.' *The Cultures of Globalization*. Eds. Fredric Jameson and Masao Miyoshi. Durham, N.C.: Duke University Press, 1998: 32-53. Print.

Miller, Rich. 'Federated Consolidates, Cuts 290 Jobs.' 20 September 2006.

Data Center Knowledge. 5 August 2010. http://www.datacenterknowledge.com/archives/2009/10/13/facebook-now-has-30000-servers/. Web.

Mingus, Charles. *Beneath the Underdog: His World as Composed by Mingus*. Ed. Nel King. New York: Vintage Books, 1991. Print.

Mitchell, Alanna. *Sea Sick: The Global Ocean in Crisis*. Toronto: McClelland & Stewart, 2009. Print.

Morlan, Kinsee. 'Home sweet dump: Tijuana landfills are home to hundreds of people who depend on garbage for their livelihood.' 15 Jan 2008. *San Diego City Beat*. 4 Aug 2010. http://www.sdcitybeat.com/sandiego/print-article-5368-print.html. Web.

'Monsanto, Genetic Pollution and Monopolism.' *SourceWatch*. Center for Media and Democracy, 2010. 19 May 2010. http://www.sourcewatch.org/index.php?title=Monsanto,_Genetic_Pollution_and_Monopolism. Web.

Mullins, K.J. 'Are Toronto's homeless really being offered help?' 29 May 2010. *Digital Journal*. 4 Aug 2010. http://www.digitaljournal.com/print/article/292689. Web.

Murphy, Brenda L. and Richard G. Kunn. 'Community: Defining the Concept and its Implications.' *Canadian Nuclear Waste Management Organization* (June 2006): 1-44. Print.

Nancy, Jean-Luc. *Being Singular Plural*. Stanford: Stanford University Press, 2000. Print.

– *The Creation of the World or Globalization*. Albany: State University of New York Press, 2007. Print.

– *The Inoperative Community*. Minneapolis: University of Minnesota Press, 1991. Print.

– *La communauté affrontée*. Paris: Éditions Galilée, 2001. Print.

Nandorfy, Martha. 'Differentiating Liberating Stories from Oppressive Narratives: Memory, Land, and Justice." *Storied Communities: Narratives of Contact and Arrival in Constituting Political Community*. Eds. Hester Lessard, Rebecca Johnson, and Jeremy Webber. Vancouver: UBC Press, 2011: 333-350. Print.

National Coalition for Homeless Veterans. Facts & Media. 19 August 2010. http://www.nchv.org/background.cfm. Web.

'National Fresh Food Financing Initiative.' Resolution in the U.S. House of Representatives. 27 July 2010. http://www.policylink.org/atf/cf/%7B97C6D565-BB43-406D-A6D5-

ECA3BBF35AF0%7D/NFFFI%20resolution%20for%20introduction%2009.pdf. Web.

Navdanya. Navdanya Trust, 2009. 5 August 2010. Web.

'Neem.' *Wikipedia*. Wikimedia Foundation Inc., 2010. 29 July 2010. http://en.wikipedia.org/wiki/Neem#cite_note-N000123-3. Web.

Negri, Antonio. *Reflections on Empire*. Cambridge: Polity Press, 2008. Print.

'News Release: WHOI Scientists Map and Confirm Origin of Large, Underwater Hydrocarbon Plume in Gulf.' Woods Hole Oceanopgraphic Institute. 19 August 2010. http://www.whoi.edu/page.do?pid=7545&tid=282&cid=79926&ct=162. Web.

Nietzsche, Fredrich Wilhelm. *The Nietzsche Reader*. Eds. Keith Ansell-Pearson and Duncan Large. Malden: Blackwell Publishing, 2006. Print.

Nussbaum, Martha C. *Hiding From Humanity: Disgust, Shame, and the Law.* Princeton: Princeton University Press, 2004. Print.

'Nuu-chah-nulth people.' *Wikipedia*. Wikimedia Foundation, Inc., 2010. 5 August 2010. http://en.wikipedia.org/wiki/Nuu-chah-nulth_people. Web.

'NYT: BP's Oil Spill Fines Could Hit $63 Billion.' CBS News. 17 June 2010. http://www.cbsnews.com/stories/2010/06/17/business/main6590719.shtml. Web.

'Oilsands mining linked to Athabaska River toxins.' CBC News. 30 August 2010. http://www.cbc.ca/canada/story/2010/08/30/oil-sands-athabasca-river.html?ref=rss. Web.

Olive, David. 'Olive: Jobs is both a genius and a jerk.' 21 July 2010. *The Toronto Star.* 2 August 2010. http://www.thestar.com/business/companies/apple/article/838519 – olives-jobs-is-both-a-genius-and-a-jerk?bn=1. Web.

'Ontario Ministry of Community and Social Services.' *Government of Ontario, Canada*. Queen's Printer for Ontario, 2010. 16 December 2009. http://www.ontario.ca/en/your_government/009831>2. Web.

'Ontario to standardize Taser training.' 30 March 2010. *The National post*. 5 August 2010. http://www.nationalpost.com/story.html?id=2743891. Web.

Oreskovic, Alexei. 'Facebook '09 revenue neared $800 million.' 18 June 2010. *Reuters*. 3 August 2010. http://www.reuters.com/article/idUSTRE65H01W20100618. Web.

Orwell, George. *Essays*. Ed. John Carey. New York: Alfred A. Knopf, 2002. Print.

Ostrom, Elinor. *Governing the Commons: The Evolution of Institutions for Collective Action*. Cambridge: Cambridge University Press, 2003. Print.

O'Toole, Megan. '"Honour killing" cases spark debates over religion, racism.' 24 July 2009. *National Post*. 4 August 2010. http:www.nationalpost.com/news/canada/story.html?id=1822941. Web.

PBS Online. 'Harvest of Fear: Interviews: Jeremy Rifkin.' No Date. *PBS Online*. 19 May 2010. http://pbs.org/wgbh/harvest/interviews/Rifkin.html. Web.

Patel, Raj. *The Value of Nothing*. New York: Picador, 2010. Print.

Pearson, Prime Minister Lester B. 'The Four Faces of Peace: The Honourable Lester Bowles Pearson's Acceptance Speech Upon Presentation of the Nobel Peace Prize in 1957.' *United Nations Association in Canada*. 4 Aug 2010. http://www.unac.org/en/link_learn/canada/pearson/speechnobel.asp. Web.

'Percy Schmeiser.' *Wikipedia*. Wikimedia Foundation Inc., 2010. 29 July 2010. http://en.wikipedia.org/wiki/Percy_Schmeiser. Web.

Philips, Matthew. 'BP's Photo Blockade of the Gulf Oil Spill.' 26 May 2010. *Newsweek*. 25 August 2010. http://www.newsweek.com/2010/05/26/the-missing-oil-spill-photos.html. Web.

Pipher, Mary. *Reviving Ophelia*. New York: Riverhead Books, 2005. Print.

Pranis, Kay, et.al. *Peacemaking Circles: From Crime to Community*. Minnesota: Living Justice Press, 2003. Print.

'Principle Six.' *United Nations Global Compact*. 4 Aug 2010. http://www.sportexx.de/AboutTheGC/TheTenPrinciples/principle6.html. Web.

'Principle Three.' *United Nations Global Compact*. 4 Aug 2010. http://www.sportexx.de/AboutTheGC/TheTenPrinciples/principle3.html. Web.

Proudfoot, Shannon. '"Honour killings" of females on rise in Canada: Expert.' 23 July 2009 *National Post*. http://www.canada.com/news/Honour+killings+females+rise+Canada+Expert/1821831/story.html. Web.

'Race to the Bottom.' 9 Aug 2006. *Human Rights Watch*. 4 Aug 2010 http://www.hrw.org/en/reports/2006/08/09/race-bottom-0?print. Web.

'RCMP apologize to Dziekanski's mother." 3 April 2010. *The National Post*. 5 August 2010. http://www.nationalpost.com/news/canada/story.html?id=2758423. Web.

Reynolds, Bruce J. 'Black Farmers in America, 1865-2000: The Pursuit of Independent Farming and the Role of Cooperatives.' *United States Department of Agriculture* (1994): 1-24. 5 January 2010. http://www.rurdev.usda.gov/RBS/pub/RR194.pdf. Web.

Richardson, Cathy and Natasha Blanchet-Cohen. *Survey of Post-Secondary Education Programs in Canada for Aboriginal Peoples*. Victoria: University of Victoria Institute for Child Rights and Development and First Nations Partnership Programs, 2000. Print.

Rifkin, Jeremy. 'Harvest of Fear.' August 2000. *PBS*. http://www.pbs.org/wgbh/harvest/interviews/rifkin.html. Web.

'Rights of Nature.' *The Community Environmental Legal Defense Fund*. 4 August 2010. http://www.celdf.org/article.php?list=type&type=42. Web.

Risen, James. 'World's Mining Companies Covet Afghan Riches.' 17 June 2010 *New York Times*. 4 August 2010. http://www.nytimes.com/2010/06/18/world/asia/18mines.html. Web.

Rock, Chris. *Rock This!* New York: Hyperion, 1997. Print.

Rockwell, Paul. 'Partners in Crime: US Complicity in the War Crimes of Saddam Hussein.' 23 December 2010. *Common Dreams*. 5 August 2010. http://www.commondreams.org/views03/1223-11.htm. Web.

'Rodney King' *Wikipedia*. Wikimedia Foundation Inc., 2010. 3 Aug 2010. http://en.wikipedia.org/wiki/Rodney_King. Web.

Roman, Karina. 'The swelling anger at Veterans Affairs.' CBCNews. 19 August 2010. http://www.cbc.ca/canada/story/2010/08/19/f-veterans-anger.html. Web.

Russel, Sharman Apt. 'Talking Plants.' 1 April 2002. http://discovermagazine.com/2002/apr/featplants/article_print. Web.

Sacchetti, Maria. '7 months after quake, squalor unabated.' *The Boston Globe*. 9 August 2010. http://www.boston.com/news/world/latinamerica/articles/2010/08/09/despite_18b_in_aid_haitians_life_remains_grim/?page=1. Web.

Sachs, Susan. 'WikiLeak's purveyor of secrets is guarded about himself.' 26 July 2010. *The Globe and Mail*. 4 August 2010. http://www.theglobeandmail.com/news/technology/wikileaks-purveyor-of-secrets-is-guarded-about-himself/article1652290/. Web.

Salgado, Sebastião. *Terra: Struggle of the Landless*. Preface by José Saramago. London: Phaidon Press Limited, 1997. Print.

Santini, Jean-Louis. 'Un vaste nuage d'hydrocarbures est détecté dans les profondeurs du golfe du Mexique.' *Le Devoir*, 20 August 2010: A3. Print.

Santos, Boaventura de Sousa. 'Beyond Abyssal Thinking: From Global Lines to Ecologies.' *Review* 30.1 (2007): 1-66. Print.

Saul, John Ralston. *The Collapse of Globalism: And the Reinvention of the World*. Toronto: Penguin, 2009. Print.

Saunders-Arratia, Philip and Andrew Johnson. '"There Are Other Worlds ..." Sun Ra for the 21st Century and Beyond.' *PopMatters*. 3 August 2010. http://www.popmatters.com/music/reviews/r/rasun-reissues.shtml. Web.

Shah, Anup. 'World Military Spending.' 7 July 2010. *Global Issues*. 5 August 2010. http://www.globalissues.org/article/75/world-military-spending. Web.

Shah, Saeed, Ian Traynor, and Mark Tran. 'Pakistan floods: US announces extra $60m in aid.' *The Guardian*. 19 August 2010. http://www.guardian.co.uk/world/2010/aug/19/pakistan-floods-obama-aid-increase. Web.

'Sherman's Special Field Orders No. 15.' *Wikipedia*. Wikimedia Foundation Inc., 2010. 3 Aug 2010. http://en.wikipedia.org/wiki/Sherman%27s_Special_Field_Orders,_No._15. Web.

Shinde, Prem Kumar. *Dalits and Human Rights*. Delhi: Isha Books, 2005. Print.

Shiva, Vandana. *Earth Democracy: Justice, Sustainability, and Peace*. Cambridge MA: South End Press, 2005. Print.

– 'The Global Campaign Against Bio-piracy and Changing the Paradigm of Agriculture.' 26 November 1999. *1999 International Forum on Globalization*. 20 February 2010. http.www.ratical.com/co-globalize/idg112699VS.html. Web.

– 'North-South Conflicts in Intellectual Property Rights.' *Synthesis/Regeneration*. 25 (Summer 2001): N. Pag. 20 May 2010. http:web.greens.org/s-r/25/25-14.html. Web.

– *Stolen Harvest: The Hijacking of the Global Food Supply*. Cambridge MA: South End Press, 2000. Print.

Silko, Leslie Marmon. *Ceremony*. New York: Penguin Books, 1986. Print.

– *Gardens in the Dunes*. New York: Simon & Schuster, 2000. Print.

– 'Language and Literature from a Pueblo Indian Perspective' *Yellow Woman and a Beauty of the Spirit*. New York: Touchstone, 1996: 48-59. Print.

– 'Poetics and Politics.' Interview with Larry Evers. April 6, 1992: 1-43. 29 July 2010. poeticsandpolitics.arizona.edu/silko/silko.pdf. Web.

– *Yellow Woman*. New York: Simon & Schuster, 1997. Print.

Singer, Stu. 'Black Farmers Fight Gov't Discrimination.' *The Militant* 61. 3 (Jan 1997): n.p. 5 January 2010. http://www.hartford-hwp.com/archives/45a/206.html. Web.

Smith, Justin. 'December Data on Facebook's US Growth by Age and Gender: Beyond 100 Million.' 4 January 2010. *Inside Facebook*. 3 August 2010. http://www.insidefacebook.com/2010/01/04/december-data-on-facebook%E2%80%99s-us-growth-by-age-and-gender-beyond-100-million/. Web.

Smith, Kenneth L., Ira G. Zepp, Jr. 'Martin Luther King's Vision of Beloved Community.' *Religion Online*. 5 August 2010. http://www.religion-online.org/showarticle.asp?title=1603. Web.

Solnit, Rebecca. *A Paradise Built in Hell: The Extraordinary Communities That Arise in Disaster.* New York: Penguin Group, 2010. Print.

Soyinka, Wole. *Climate of Fear: The Quest for Dignity in a Dehumanized World.* New York: Random House, 2004. Print.

'Statistics.' *Facebook.* Facebook, 2010. 3 August 2010. http://www.facebook.com/press/info.php?statistics. Web.

Szwed, John F. *Space is the Place: The Lives and Times of Sun Ra.* New York: Pantheon Books, 1997. Print.

'Tarnak Farm Incident.' *Wikipedia.* Wikimedia Foundation Inc., 2010. 4 August 2010. http://en.wikipedia.org/wiki/Tarnak_Farm_incident. Web.

'Taser video shows RCMP shocked immigrant within 25 seconds of their arrival.' 15 November 2007. *CBC News.* 5 August 2010. http://www.cbc.ca/canada/british-columbia/story/2007/11/14/bc. Web.

'Tent City Highlights U.S. Homes Crisis.' *BBC News.* 14 Mar 2008. Americas. 4 Aug 2010. http://news.bbc.co.uk/2/hi/americas/7297093.stm. Web.

Thompson, Mark. 'America's Medicated Army.' 5 June 2008. *Time Magazine.* 4 August 2010. http://www.time.com/time/nation/article/0,8599,1811858,00.html. Web.

Thoreau, Henry David. *On the Duty of Civil Disobedience.* Radford, VA: Wilder Publications, 2008. Print.

Turtle Island Native Network. Tehaliwaskenhas Bob Kennedy, 2010. 29 July 2010. http://www.turtleisland.org. Web.

'Universal Declaration of Human Rights' *United Nations Human Rights.* OHCHR, 2010. 29 July 2010. 29 July 2010. http://www.ohchr.org/EN/UDHR/Pages/Language.aspx?LangID=eng. Web.

'Universal Declaration of the Rights of Mother Earth.' *World People's Conference on Climate Change and the Rights of Mother Earth.* 7 February 2010. http://pwccc.wordpress.com/2010/02/07/draft-universal-declaration-of-the-rights-of-mother-earth-2/. Web.

'Update 1 – Yahoo settles case over Chinese dissident e-mails.' 13 November 2007. *Reuters.* 5 August 2010. http://uk.reuters.com/assets/print?aid=UKN1361605822007111 3. Web.

'Update 1 – US pledges to probe, bust agribusiness monopolies.' 21 March 2010. *Reuters.* http://www.reuters.com/article/idUSN1215754320100312. Web.

Urrea, Luis Alberto. *By the Lake of Sleeping Children.* New York: Anchor Books, 1996. Print.

'U.S. intelligence apparatus so vast, doubts grow over cost and effectiveness:

report.' 19 July 2010. *The Globe and Mail.* 29 July 2010. http://www.theglobeandmail.com/news/world/americas/us-intelligence-apparatus-so-vast-doubts-grow-over-cost-and-effectiveness-report/article 1644503. Web.

Van Genugten, William and Camilo Perez-Bustillo, Eds. *The Poverty of Rights.* London & New York: Zed Books Ltd., 2001. Print.

Van Vuuren, Kitty. 'Community broadcasting and the enclosure of the public sphere.' *Media Culture & Society* 28.3 (May 2006): 279-392. http://mcs.sagepub.com/content/28/3/379.abstract. Web.

'Vancouver Island First Nations.' 'Company Launch Conservation-based Harvesting in Clayoquot Sound.' *Iisaak Forest Resources Ltd.* 5 August 2010. http://www.iisaak.com/PRFirstTree.html. Web.

Vanier, Jean. *Community and Growth.* Toronto: Griffin Press, 2003. Print.

'Victoria Police Clear Tent City, Arrest 5.' 17 Oct 2008. *CBC News.* 4 Aug 2010. http://www.cbc.ca/canada/british-columbia/story/2008/10/17/bc-victoria-tent-arrests.html. Web.

Vizenor, Gerald. *Griever: An American Monkey King in China.* Minneapolis: University of Minnesota Press, 1990. Print.

Weber, Bob. 'Deformed fish found in lake downstream from oilsands.' *Toronto Star.* 17 September 2010. http://www.thestar.com/news/canada/article/862603 – deformed-fish-found-in-lake-downstream-from-oilsands. Web.

'What are the Contributing Factors to Aboriginal Youth Suicide?' *Nan Youth.* Nishnawbe-Aski Nation, 2004. July 27 2010. http://nandecade.ca/article/residential-schools-77.asp. Web.

'What is Democracy School?' *The Community Environmental Legal Defense Fund.* 4 Aug 2010. http://celdf.org/section.php?id=149&printsafe=1. Web.

'What is La Via Campesina?'11 July 2007. *La Via Campesina.* 5 August 2010. http://viacampesina.org/en/index.php?option=com_content&view=category &layout=blog&id=27&Itemid=44. Web.

'What is section 13 of the *Canadian Human Rights Act*?' Canadian Human Rights Commission. 2010. July 27, 2010. http://www.chrc-ccdp.ca/proactive_initiatives/hoi_hsi/qa_qr/page1-en.asp. Web.

'What is the 0.7% Pledge?' *Engineers without Borders: University of Waterloo Chapter.* 4 Aug 2010. http://uwaterloo.ewb.ca/point7/what. Web.

White, Matthew. 'Source List and Detailed Death Tolls of Twentieth Century Hemoclysm.' *Twentieth Century Atlas.* 4 August 2010. http://users.erols.com/mwhite28/warstat1.htm. Web.

White, Thomas I. *In Defense of Dolphins: The New Moral Frontier*. Malden, MA: Blackwell Publishing, 2007. Print.

Widdowson, Frances and Albert Howard. *Disrobing the Aboriginal Industry: The Deception Behind Indigenous Cultural Preservation*. Montreal: McGill-Queen's University Press, 2008. Print.

Wilkinson, Alec. *The Protest Singer: An Intimate Portrait of Pete Seeger*. New York: Knopf, 2009. Print.

Williams, Lindsey. 'Two Whistleblowers Report Mistreatment of Veterans Remains.' 7 April 2009. *Whistleblowers Protection Blog*. http://www.whistleblowersblog.org/2009/04/articles/news-1/two-whistle-blowers-report-mistreatment-of-veterans-remains/. Web.

Williams, Raymond. *Keywords: A Vocabulary of Culture and Society*. London: Fontana Paperbacks, 1983. Print.

Wilson, James. 'The Individual, the State, and the Corporation.' *The Cambridge Companion to Chomsky*. Ed. James Alasdair McGilvary. Cambridge: Cambridge University Press, 2005: 240-259. Print.

Wood, Daniel B. 'Billions for a US-Mexico border fence, but is it doing any good?' 19 Sept 2009. *The Christian Science Monitor*. 4 Aug 2010. http://www.csmonitor.com/USA/2009/0919/p02s09-usgn.html. Web.

Woods, Clyde. *Development Arrested: The Blues and Plantation Power in Mississippi Delta*. New York: Versa, 1998. Print.

– 'Do You Know What it Means to Miss New Orleans? Katrina, Trap Economics, and the Rebirth of Blues.' *American Studies: An Anthology*. Ed. Janice A. Radway. Oxford: Blackwell Publishing Ltd., 2009: 506-514. Print.

Wright, Alexis. *Carpentaria: A Novel*. New York: Atria Books, 2009. Print.

Young, Abe Louise. 'BP Hires Prison Labor to Clean Up Spill While Coastal Residents Struggle.' 21 July 2010. *The Nation*. 27 August 2010. http:www.thenation.com/print/article/37828/bp-hires-prison-labor-as-residents-struggle.html. Web.

Young, Iris Marion. 'The Ideal of Community and the Politics of Difference.' *Feminism & Community*. Eds. Penny A. Weiss and Marilyn Freedman. Philadelphia: Temple University Press, 1995: 233-57. Print.

Index